The Bolshevik
Seizure of Power

The Bolshevik
Seizure of Power

S. P. MELGUNOV

edited and abridged by **SERGEI G. PUSHKAREV**

in collaboration with **BORIS S. PUSHKAREV**

translated by **JAMES S. BEAVER**

from the original Russian edition

Kak Bol'sheviki Zakhvatili Vlast'

Oktiabr'skii perevorot 1917 goda.

Santa Barbara, California
Oxford, England

Library of Congress Catalog Card No. 72-77828
ISBN Clothbound Edition 0-87436-084-6
Paperbound Edition 0-87436-085-4

American Bibliographical Center-Clio Press, Inc.
2040 Alameda Padre Serra
Santa Barbara, California

European Bibliographical Center-Clio Press
30 Cornmarket Street
Oxford OX1 3EY, England

CONTENTS

FOREWORD

This book of Melgunov's tells us much that we need to know about the Bolshevik Revolution of 1917. Its translation into English is an important service.

How is it that so big an event as that Revolution, taking place more than half a century ago, can still be so poorly understood? Our first inclination might be to blame the rulers of the Soviet Union, who have shown such ruthless ingenuity in the rewriting of history. But we outside the USSR are also to blame: the political explosiveness of the topic, the difficulty of treating it fairly, and perhaps most of all the overwhelming bulk of relevant published material — these have made it exceptionally hard for historians anywhere to produce good works of synthesis about the Bolshevik takeover.

Melgunov's is one of the very best to date. Many readers will already be familiar with Robert V. Daniels's *Red October,* in which special tribute is paid to Melgunov's work. The two books complement each other. Where Daniels covers a longer time span and strives above all to produce a clear basic narrative, Melgunov focuses on the days just before and after October 25 and tells much more about certain aspects of the story. He is especially valuable for the crucial fortnight of uncertainty right after the coup, when many participants on all sides thought the Bolshevik adventure would soon be reversed.

Along with the wealth of information he assembles, Melgunov puts forward his own interpretations. He challenges the view that the Bolshevik victory of October was the logical and necessary sequel to the February Revolution. Those who hold that view — including both some who have and some who have not regarded the collapse of tsarism as inescapable even apart from the war — owe it to themselves to weigh Melgunov's thoughtful arguments. Even if they do not revise their opinions, they are likely to find that Melgunov has raised the plane upon which that question must be debated henceforth.

This English edition, although an abridged version of the original, adds significant improvements which go a long way toward remedying some of the shortcomings of Melgunov's book. The editors have expanded Melgunov's bibliography. They have supplied identification for most of the numerous actors in the drama. Remarkably, they have even hunted up and added precise citations to the sources of many of the quotations included in the original work.

vii

Sergei Germanovich Pushkarev, who with the active help of his son Boris supervised the preparing of this English edition, is the sort of scholar Melgunov himself might well have asked to do the job. Like Melgunov, Mr. Pushkarev was born in the Russia of the 1880s. Like Melgunov, he was trained as a historian and became known for his careful scholarship and thorough knowledge of the Russian past. Like Melgunov, he opposed many features of the tsarist system and as a moderate socialist sought ways of reforming the government and improving the lot of the people. In the years 1917-1920 he, like Melgunov, struggled at great personal risk against the emerging dictatorship of the Bolsheviks. And like Melgunov he was forced into emigration, where he continued his scholarly research and, despite many obstacles, made noteworthy contributions to better understanding of the history of his native land. Fortunately for us Mr. Pushkarev in his eighties is an active scholar with additional projects under way.

Ralph T. Fisher Jr.

University of Illinois
Urbana-Champaign

ABOUT THE AUTHOR

The distinguished Russian historian Sergei Petrovich Melgunov was born into an old Moscow family in January 1880, the son of a historian and educator. Completing his secondary education in 1899, he entered the historical-philological department of Moscow University, where he finished his studies and passed his final examinations in 1904.

From 1900 to 1910 he worked for the influential Moscow liberal newspaper *Russkiia Vedomosti* (Russian Gazette). During that period Melgunov's attention was focused on the history of the relations between Church and State in Russia and of the Old Believers and other sectarian religious movements, not in their purely religious aspects but in regard to their social, political, and economic significance. In 1905-06 two collections of Melgunov's essays appeared under the title *Tserkov' i gosudarstvo v Rossii* (Church and State in Russia). Later, in 1919 and 1922, two more collections on these subjects were published, *Religiozno-obshchestvennyia dvizheniia XVII-XVIII vv. v Rossii* (Socio-Religious Movements in Russia in the Seventeenth and Eighteenth Centuries) and *Iz istorii religiozno-obshchestvennykh dvizhenii v Rossii XIX veka* (On the History of Socio-Religious Movements in Russia in the Nineteenth Century).

After the Revolution of 1905 Melgunov assumed an active role in Russian political life, becoming deputy chairman of the Central Committee of the People's Socialist party (*partiia narodnykh sotsialistov*), a moderate group of democratic intellectuals who rejected the extremism of the major parties of the Left. He combined his political interests with scholarship, and contributed as an author or editor to a number of important historical publications. Among these were the multi-volume, collectively written works *Velikaia Reforma. Russkoie obshchestvo i krest'ianskii vopros v proshlom i nastoiashchem* (The Great Reform: Russian Society and the Peasant Question, Past and Present), 1911-12; *Otechestvennaia voina (1812) i russkoie obshchesvo* (The Patriotic War of 1812 and Russian Society), 1912; *Kniga dlia chteniia po istorii novago vremeni* (A Reader in the History of Modern Times); and *Masonstvo v iego proshlom a nastoiashchem* (Free-masonry, Past and Present), 1914-22. From 1913 to 1919 Melgunov edited (together with Vasili I. Semevsky until 1916) a historical periodical *Golos Minuvshego* (Voice of the Past), which was dedicated mostly to the history of revolutionary movements. Some of these publications were printed by a cooperative publishing house *Zadruga,* which Melgunov organized in 1911.

Authors and typesetters alike had an equal voice in running the enterprise, regardless of the number of shares they held. Melgunov believed this type of cooperative to be a practical form of socialism. Despite the protests of its staff, *Zadruga* was closed by the Bolsheviks in 1923.

During the Revolution of 1917, Melgunov participated in the political and journalistic activities of his People's Socialist party, and after the Bolsheviks seized power he found himself in sharp opposition to the government. He became one of the founders of the underground *Soiuz Vozrozhdeniia* (Alliance for the Rebirth of Russia), formed to organize active resistance to the Bolshevik regime. Melgunov was arrested five times by the political police, tried in 1920 together with other "counterrevolutionaries," and condemned to death. The death sentence was commuted to ten years imprisonment, but after serving one year he was released as a result of the solicitations of the Academy of Sciences and of the aged anarchist Prince Peter A. Kropotkin.

In 1922 the new chief of the political police, Viacheslav R. Menzhinsky, offered Melgunov a choice: exile in northern Russia or exile abroad. Melgunov and his wife, following a large group of scholars and politicians expelled by the Bolshevik government earlier that year, left Russia and settled in Berlin. With other former members of *Zadruga* he established in Berlin the publishing house *Vataga,* and resumed publishing *Golos Minuvshego* under the name *"Na chuzhoi storone."* In 1923 *Vataga* published Melgunov's *Dela a liudi Aleksandrovskogo vremeni* (Events and Personalities of the Epoch of Alexander I), a collection of articles written by him in Russia. His book *Krasnyi terror v Rossii 1918-1923,* appeared in 1924. It was translated into English with the title *The Red Terror in Russia* (London and Toronto, 1925), as well as into French, German, Italian, Spanish, and Dutch. In 1924 Melgunov moved from Berlin to Paris, where he wrote several monographs on the Russian Revolution and after World War II edited a periodical *Vozrozhdenie* (Renaissance) and a magazine *Rossiiskii Demokrat.* He was prominent in the attempts to consolidate Russian émigré political activities in Europe in the early 1950s.

The most important and fruitful work of Melgunov's life in exile was a series of monographs on various aspects of the Revolution of 1917. The series includes *V gody grazhdanskoi voiny, (N.V. Chaikovsky)* (N.V. Chaikovsky in the Years of the Civil War); Paris, 1929. Nikolai V. Chaikovsky, a prominent member of the People's Socialist party, was one of the political leaders of the anti-Bolshevik struggle in the period 1918-20. *Tragediia Admirala Kolchaka; iz istorii grazhdanskoi voiny na Volge, Urale i v Sibiri* (The Tragedy of Admiral Kolchak: History of the Civil War in the Regions of the Volga River, the Urals, and Siberia); 3 vols. Belgrad, 1930-31. *Na putiakh k dvortsovomu perevorotu (Zagovor pered revoliutsiei 1917 goda)* (On the Way to a Palace Revolution: Conspiracy on the Eve of the February Revolution of 1917);

Paris, 1931. *"Zolotoi nemetskii kliuch"* k *bol'shevitskoi revoliutsii* (The German "Golden Key" to the Bolshevik Revolution); Paris, 1940. In this small book Melgunov developed the theory that during World War I the German government generously financed Bolshevik defeatist propaganda in Russia. Documentary evidence proving his assertions was found in the German archives after World War II. *Sud'ba Imperatora Nikolaia II posle otrecheniia* (The Fate of Emperor Nicholas II After His Abdication); Paris, 1951. *Kak bol'sheviki zakhvatili vlast'; oktiabr'skii perevorot 1917 goda* (How the Bolsheviks Seized Power: the Coup d'Etat of October 1917); Paris, 1953. Melgunov's books on the Revolution of 1917 are based on thorough and scrupulous studies of the literature of the period and of the sources available to him. They all include a critical evaluation of the sources, which often are partisan, evasive, and conflicting. The author's purpose was to find the truth in a labyrinth of contradictory material and to ascertain the facts while exposing the numerous legends that cloud them.

After Melgunov's death in Paris in May 1956 two more monographs were published from completed manuscripts: *Legenda o separatnom mire; kanun revoliutsii* (The Legend of a Separate Peace: the Eve of the Revolution); Paris, 1957; and *Martovskie dni 1917 goda* (The March Days of 1917); Paris, 1961. Finally, in 1964 Melgunov's memoirs and diaries were published in Paris by his widow, Paraskeva Evgenevna Melgunova, who edited them and added interesting excerpts from her diaries for the period prior to the departure of the Melgunovs from Russia in October 1922.*

*For biographical sketches of Melgunov, see N. Oulianoff "In Commemoration of S.P. Melgunov," *The Russian Review*, vol. 17, No. 3, July, 1958; S. Germanov [Pushkarev] "Istoricheskie Trudy S.P. Melgunova (K ego 75- letiiu)," *Mysl'*, No. 5, 1954, Posev, Frankfurt/Main.

ABOUT THE BOOK

Unfortunately, only one of Melgunov's books on the Russian Revolution, *The Red Terror,* has been translated into English. We have selected his volume on the Bolshevik seizure of power for translation because of the singular importance of the event and because very few detailed and critical analyses of it are available in English. As Robert V. Daniels states in his *Red October* (New York, 1967), "On the one hand there is an abundance of raw material [for a study of the October Revolution] — the newspapers, memoirs and published documents — so much so that it is almost impossible for one author to take account of the whole mass. On the other hand, there is a serious lack of detailed and objective historical studies . . . . On the October Revolution itself, one book stands out: S.P. Melgunov, *Kak bol'sheviki zakhvatili vlast.*" (p. 247)

Melgunov was thoroughly familiar with the basic Soviet collections of sources, such as *Krasnyi Arkhiv* (The Red Archives); *Proletarskaia Revoliutsia* (The Proletarian Revolution); *Krasnaia Letopis'* (The Red Chronicle); *Khronika Sobytii* (The Chronicle of Events for October 1917); and *Oktiabr'skii perevorot* (The October Upheaval), edited by N. Rozhkov, 1918. In addition, having started work on this book during the 1930s, he had the benefit of extensive personal contact with many participants in the events of 1917 and of the use of such depositories of unpublished materials as the Russian Historical Archive in Prague, which was turned over to the USSR after World War II. He made extensive use of the periodical press of the time and of émigré publications.

Basing his analysis on this wealth of data, Melgunov presents a sobering and unglorified account of the Bolshevik coup d'état. The author does not promote any grand historical theory and strives merely to "reconstruct" the facts, with meticulous attention to detail. But in his critical comparison of the sources he does make many personal comments and casts polemical barbs at those who have ideological axes to grind or past positions to justify.

It is precisely some of these qualities that have made the translation of Melgunov's work into foreign languages difficult. With little conceptual perspective to guide him, the uninitiated reader tends to be confused by the multitude of unfamiliar names and documentary details, and the significance of the personal asides is often lost to him. Therefore, it seemed advisable to abridge and edit the book for the English edition. Most of the polemical passages have been omitted, as have many sections (such as chapter three of the Russian text) that have no direct bearing on the main subject — how the Bolsheviks seized power in the capital, Petrograd.* Part three of the original Russian text, which is devoted to the Bolshevik uprising in Moscow and the struggle against it, has also been omitted. On the other hand, explanatory notes, many references to sources, a list of persons, a list of periodicals, a revised and expanded bibliography, and an editorial introduction have been added.

The editors express their deep appreciation to the author's widow, Mrs. P.E. Melgunov, for her help and encouragement. The editors are most grateful to Mr. James S. Beaver, who, undertaking the arduous task of translation chiefly because of his interest in the history of the period, accepted remuneration far below that which would be customary for such a service; to Miss Marilu Sanchez, who translated the first chapter; and to Miss Marina Sultan, who helped in editing and typing the translation. Final responsibility for the translation rests with the editors, who have revised the original draft in detail.

All dates in the introduction and the main body of the text are according to the Old Style, Julian, calendar, which was in use in Russia until February 1918. In the twentieth century the calendar ran thirteen days behind the Gregorian calendar used in the West.

S.G.P.
B.S.P.

*St. Petersburg was given the more Russian-sounding name Petrograd in 1914 after the outbreak of World War I, and was renamed Leningrad after Lenin's death in 1924.

INTRODUCTION

The Provisional Government, which appeared in Russia as a result of the February Revolution and formally assumed power after the abdication of Emperor Nicholas II, consisted mostly of members of the left-liberal Constitutional Democratic ("Kadet") party, also known as the People's Freedom party. The prime minister of the government was the benevolent and idealistic Prince Georgi Lvov, head of the Union of Zemstvos, elected provincial councils inherited from the pre-revolutionary period. Other colorful figures in the government were the minister of foreign affairs, Paul Miliukov, indisputable leader of the Kadets and a well-known historian; the minister of war, Alexander Guchkov, a Moscow industrialist and leader of the moderate-liberal "Union of October 17" ("Octobrists"); and Alexander Kerensky, the minister of justice, a young, temperamental, and eloquent lawyer, who was a member of the Socialist Revolutionary party and leader of the small faction of *Trudoviks* (Labor Group) in the fourth Duma, the last national House of Representatives summoned under the old regime. As the only socialist in the cabinet Kerensky considered himself "the spokesman of democracy" and enjoyed great popularity.

The political position of the Provisional Government was very precarious from the start. The revolution had completely and abruptly destroyed the administrative and judicial apparatus of the former empire, and the new government had no administrative bodies of its own at the local level. In provincial cities it appointed commissars to replace the former governors, but in fact they became figureheads without defined duties and with no real authority. The local militia, formed to replace the disbanded police, proved to be weak and ineffective.

Another source of weakness for the Provisional Government was its dependence on the support of the Petrograd Soviet of Workers' and Soldiers' Deputies, a council formed at the beginning of the revolution and which held the real political power in the capital.* The soviet was dominated by two

---

*A similar soviet — the word means council — sprang into existence in the capital during the revolution of 1905. The Petrograd Soviet of 1917 was organized by the radical parties, which summoned representatives of the Petrograd workers and mutinous regiments to the Tauride Palace on February 27, just after the outbreak of the revolution. When constituted, the soviet was composed of one elected representative for every thousand workers and one for each company.

parties belonging to the so-called revolutionary democracy (that is, the various socialist parties, except the Bolsheviks), the Social Democrats (Mensheviks)* and the Socialist Revolutionaries, and was presided over by the Menshevik Nikolai Chkheidze. The most influential leaders of the "revolutionary democracy" were the Menshevik Irakly Tseretelli and the Socialist Revolutionary Victor Chernov. Maintaining that it represented the "toiling masses" and that the Provisional Government represented the bourgeoisie, the soviet assumed "the right and duty" to control all activities of the government. For this purpose, a Contact Commission was appointed by the executive committee of the soviet to keep watch over the government's actions. The soviet promised its support to the government only "as far as" *(postol'ku polskol'ku)* its programs and activities met the needs and demands of the revolutionary democracy.

The powerful position of the soviet in Petrograd was assured by its ties to the large Petrograd garrison. "Order Number One" issued by the Petrograd Soviet on March 1 introduced "self-government" in all units of the Petrograd garrison, transferring real power in the barracks from the officers to elected soldiers' committees. The "Declaration of Soldiers' Rights," issued later, formulated the rules of the soldiers' "self-government," which, in effect, abolished the officers' disciplinary power over their men. Moreover, in accordance with the demands of the soviet, the government included in its program the fateful Article 7: "The troops that have taken part in the revolutionary movement shall not be disarmed or removed from Petrograd." Having received the enviable privilege of not being sent to the battlefront, and the honorable, as well as safe, assignment "to protect the achievements of the revolution" (which were not threatened by anyone), the Petrograd soldiers naturally regarded as their higher authority not the government, but the soviet, and therefore, the general whom the government appointed to command the garrison could be nothing more than a figurehead.

As a result, a strange duality of power prevailed in Petrograd. On one side, there was a legal government with formal responsibility but without real power; on the other was an institution possessing real power without responsibility.

A very serious conflict between the Provisional Government and the soviet soon arose over the most difficult and tragic question of the time, the war. While the government, and especially Foreign Minister Miliukov, declared

---

*The Mensheviks and the Bolsheviks were opposing factions of the Russian Social Democratic Labor party, and both retained the name until the Bolsheviks adopted the name Communist party in 1918. But during the revolution the Bolsheviks referred to themselves and were referred to as the Bolshevik party.

its intention of honoring Russia's commitments to its allies and to continue the war "to the victorious end," the socialist majority of the soviet favored the program of peace adopted in 1915 by the international socialist conference held at Zimmerwald, Switzerland, a program of peace "without victors and vanquished," "without annexations and indemnities, on the basis of the self-determination of nations." On March 14 the Petrograd Soviet issued a pathetic call to the peoples of the world and especially to "our brother-proletarians of the Austro-German coalition" to follow Russia, to "throw off the yoke of your semi-autocratic rule," to "refuse to serve as an instrument of conquest and violence in the hands of kings, landowners, and bankers," and to reestablish peace and the unity of the international proletariat. As an important practical step toward the achievement of a just and general peace, the Russian socialists planned the convocation of an international socialist conference in Stockholm, but all such appeals met with a lukewarm response from the Western socialists and no response from the majority of the German social-democracy. The conference in Stockholm never convened. Although the soviet recognized the duty of the Russian armed forces to defend the country when attacked, it became more and more difficult to maintain a combat spirit in the army when victory was declared unnecessary, even undesirable.

In its domestic policy the Provisional Government tried to realize the promises of its radical program. It ordered a reelection of zemstvos and municipal dumas on the basis of a general franchise, set up local committees to draw up plans for agrarian reform, and worked on an electoral law for a future Constituent Assembly. But it considered itself to be a temporary authority whose main task was to pave the way for the final settlement of all key questions by the Constituent Assembly. This legalistic position was not consonant with the mass psychology of a revolutionary time, with its exaggerated expectations, and it gave leftist demagogues a pretext for accusing the Provisional Government of betraying the needs and demands of the people, which supposedly had to be fulfilled immediately.

Neither the administrative structure nor the economic conditions of the country showed any improvement; in fact, they deteriorated. Along with the existing institutions of the zemstvos and the dumas, soviets of workers' and peasants' deputies were formed in provincial cities. The soviets had loud voices, but their duties were indefinite and variable. On the whole the populace in these cities looked more to the soviets than to the Provisional Government in Petrograd for authority. But the Mensheviks and Socialist Revolutionaries, who dominated the Petrograd and provincial soviets, spent most of their time in meetings and debates, while the economic conditions, especially in major cities, went from bad to worse because of the growing disorganization of transportation, the decline in labor productivity, and the depreciation of paper money.

The return from exile of the leader of the Bolshevik Party, Vladimir I. Lenin,* made the situation all the more difficult for the government. On April 4 Lenin announced his so-called April Theses, a list of policies and demands that he wanted the Bolsheviks to adopt as a program. He insisted that no support whatsoever be given to the Provisional Government, which he denounced as imperialistic, and demanded that all power be transferred to the soviets. He advocated the abolition of the police, the bureaucracy, and the standing army, the last to be replaced by a militia of the people, whose officers were to be elected; the immediate confiscation and nationalization of all privately owned land; and the control of industry and banking by the workers. The Bolshevik goal, he maintained, should not be the establishment of a parliamentary democracy "but a republic of soviets of workers', agricultural laborers', and peasants' deputies throughout the land, from top to bottom." In regard to the crucial question of the war, Lenin condemned what he called "revolutionary defensism," by which he meant the argument that the war must be continued in order to defend revolutionary Russia from the German and Austrian imperialists.

At first, even the Petrograd Bolshevik Committee voted thirteen to two to reject Lenin's program. But his iron will, persuasive power, and unlimited authority in the ranks of his party prevailed, and at the end of April the Bolshevik Party Conference approved Lenin's program. Now the Bolsheviks went to work.

They concentrated on two main points of the program. One was "land for the peasants." In reality the peasants already possessed four-fifths of the arable land, and the partition of landed estates which actually took place in 1918 increased their holdings by an average of only 16 per cent. But the land-hungry peasants had no idea of agrarian statistics, and cherished fantastically exaggerated hopes about what they would benefit from the seizure of the estates.

The other alluring promise was peace. As a means of achieving a "general and democratic" peace the Bolsheviks advised the Russian soldiers to fraternize with enemy troops at the front. Generously financed with German money (through secret connections in Copenhagen and Stockholm),** the Bolshevik peace campaign, conducted by hundreds of agitators and carried on

---

*The name *Lenin* was an alias adopted by him in his early days as a revolutionary in order to help prevent identification by the Russian police. His real name was Ulianov. Many other revolutionaries also adopted pseudonyms, by which they are known to history, as, for example, Stalin (Dzhugashvili), Trotsky (Bronstein), and Martov (Tsederbaum).

**See Z.A.B. Zeman, ed., *Germany and the Revolution in Russia 1915-1918: Documents from the Archives of the German Foreign Ministry.* London, 1958.

in newspapers and leaflets, met with considerable success among the war-weary and peace-craving soldiers. Fraternization actually began on the Russo-German and Russo-Austrian fronts. On the German and Austrian side, however, the fraternization was performed by specially trained propaganda and intelligence units, which were sent over to the Russian trenches. The naive Russian soldiers believed it to be genuine. The torrent of defeatist propaganda emanating from the Germans at the front and from the Bolsheviks in the rear gradually but steadily eroded the combat spirit and fighting ability of the Russian army.

The agonizing question of war and peace led to a sharp political conflict in Petrograd in April. To reassure the allied governments, which were disquieted by the turmoil in Russia and the passivity of Russian troops at the front, Foreign Minister Miliukov sent them a note declaring that Russia was determined "to carry the World War to a decisive victory" and that the Provisional Government "will, in every way, observe the obligations assumed toward our allies." The note caused stormy anti-war demonstrations in Petrograd. Placards carried by the demonstrators proclaimed Bolshevik slogans such as "Down with the war!" "Peace without annexation and indemnities!" "All power to the Soviets!" Anti-war demonstrators clashed with patriotic demonstrators, and blood was shed in the streets of Petrograd. On April 30 War Minister Guchkov resigned. The position of Miliukov became untenable, and he resigned from the government two days later.

Now the Provisional Government demanded from the leaders of the Petrograd Soviet that the socialists enter the government and share the responsibility. After fervent and protracted debates, the soviet decided to allow its representatives to enter the cabinet, and on May 5 the first coalition government of "bourgeois" and socialist ministers was formed. Prince Lvov remained premier and minister of the interior; Kerensky became the minister of war and the navy; Miliukov was replaced as foreign minister by the industrialist Mikhail Tereshchenko, who had no party allegiance; Victor Chernov, the leader of the Socialist Revolutionary party, became minister of agriculture; the Menshevik leader Irakly Tseretelli, who entered the cabinet reluctantly, chose for himself the modest job of minister of posts and telegraph. Out of a total of fifteen ministers only five were socialists, and the slogan of the Bolshevik crowds now became "Down with the ten capitalist ministers!"

Local soviets had by that time sprung up all over the country, and in June 1917 the first All-Russian Congress of Soviets of Workers' and Soldiers' Deputies convened in Petrograd. It was dominated by the Socialist Revolutionary and Menshevik parties. Out of 882 deputies with full voting rights there were 285 Socialist Revolutionaries, 298 Mensheviks, and 105 Bolsheviks, the rest representing small socialist groups. By a vote of 543 to

126 (with 52 not voting), the congress approved the participation of socialists in the coalition government, and in its political resolution stressed the government's duty "to strive persistently for the earliest conclusion of a general peace without annexation [or] indemnity and on the basis of self-determination"; the next point of the resolution requested the government "to further the democratization of the army and to increase its fighting power" — a rather difficult and contradictory task. The Congress elected an All-Russian Central Executive Committee of the Soviets (VTsIK), with the Menshevik Chkheidze presiding. In the same month the All-Russian Congress of Soviets of Peasants' Deputies created a similar executive committee headed by the Socialist Revolutionary Nikolai Avksentiev.

The new war minister, Kerensky, set himself the gigantic task of increasing the fighting ability of the Russian army, which was disoriented and confused because of conflicts between the military commanders, the government commissars appointed to supervise the officers and insure their loyalty to the new government, the elected soldiers' committees, and the Bolshevik agitators. In May and June Kerensky, ironically called by the officers "persuader-in-chief," made numerous trips to the front in order to explain the political situation to the soldiers and urge them to preserve military discipline and be ready to take the offensive against the enemy if ordered to do so by the high command. Impressed by Kerensky's eloquence, the soldiers usually applauded. But ordinarily after Kerensky's departure a Bolshevik agitator would take the floor and convince the men that it would be stupid to die for the profits of English, American, and French capitalists.

The patriotic elements within the army formed "shock companies" and "shock battalions" ready to fight and to die, and when an offensive was launched in Galicia on June 18, it had some initial success. However, after the German counteroffensive began on July 6 the demoralized soldiers fled in a wild and disgraceful retreat.

Meanwhile, two crises, one in the government and the other in the streets of Petrograd, further shook the unstable Russian Republic. On July 1 representatives of the Provisional Government concluded an agreement with the Ukranian Central Council *(Rada)*, which had been established by Ukrainian nationalists after the collapse of the old regime to govern the Ukraine as a semi-autonomous state. Under the agreement a large measure of autonomy was conceded to the region. Four cabinet ministers belonging to the Kadet party — A.A. Manuilov, Andrei Shingarev, Prince Dmitri Shakhovskoi, and Vasily Stepanov — announced that in their opinion the Provisional Government was not in a legal position to create an autonomous Ukrainian state and resigned from the cabinet.

The cabinet crisis led to the crisis of what became known as the "July Days." Bolshevik soldiers of the First Machine-Gun Regiment decided that the time had come to topple the Provisional Government, and called upon other radical members of the armed forces and the workers to take up arms. On July 3 a massive demonstration took place in Petrograd. The Bolshevik leaders placed themselves at the head of it. For two days the city was in chaos as loyal troops and insurrectionists clashed. Then reinforced by the arrival in Petrograd of more loyal soldiers, the government was able to put down the uprising. Several Bolshevik leaders were arrested; the Bolshevik Party's official organ, *Pravda*, was suppressed; and Lenin went into hiding.

As a result of the July Days and of political conflicts in the cabinet, Prince Lvov resigned as Prime Minister and was replaced by Alexander Kerensky, who gained the backing of the All-Russian Central Executive Committee of the Soviets. A new coalition government was formed, with Kerensky retaining, in addition to the premiership, his portfolio as minister of war.

He appointed Lavr Kornilov supreme commander, a general of humble origins who distinguished himself in the war, was popular in patriotic circles, and was an advocate of strong discipline in the army. Even a decree restoring the death penalty for certain military crimes was passed, but it was never applied in practice.

The Provisional Government now tried to win support from the moderate elements of society, and in the middle of August it arranged a State Conference in Moscow of delegates from local governments and a broad spectrum of organizations and groups. More than 2,000 persons attended, including representatives from the defunct Duma (488), the co-operatives (313), the soviets (229), trade unions (176), commerce, industry, and finance (150), the municipalities (147), the zemstvos and urban councils (118), the army and navy (117), the peasants (100), and technical organizations (99).

Instead of creating a spirit of *union sacrée* in the deeply disturbed nation, the State Conference brought into the open the deep cleavage between moderate and revolutionary currents. The Duma members, the Kadets, General Kornilov, and the ataman of the Don Cossacks, Gen. Aleksei Kaledin, bitterly complained about the growing anarchy and dwindling discipline in the army, and demanded the reestablishment of order and the power of military command. The representatives of the revolutionary democracy rejected all such proposals, terming them "reactionary," and demanded more effective and rapid "democratization" in domestic life and foreign policy. Prime Minister Kerensky delivered an eloquent and emotional speech, promising to exercise strong government, a speech which his supporters characterized as "historical" and his opponents as "hysterical."

Shortly after the close of the State Conference, the Russian armies suffered a severe defeat. The Germans broke through the Russian northern front and on August 21 occupied Riga. Their offensive, if continued, would threaten Petrograd. General Kornilov did not see how the country could be defended with a disorganized army and a powerless command. In a proclamation issued on August 25, he demanded that decisive measures to strengthen the army and the government be taken, and seems to have relied on the support of Kerensky. However, his dispatch of a cavalry detachment to the outskirts of Petrograd to enforce his demands threw the capital into panic. Afraid of a military takeover, Kerensky deprived Kornilov of his command and denounced him as "a traitor to the fatherland." Details of the "Kornilov affair" and of his political intentions and relations with Kerensky remain obscure and contradictory to this day.

To combat the threat from Kornilov and his supporters, the VTsIK formed the Committee for the Defense of the Revolution, with Bolshevik participation. The Bolshevik leaders arrested after the July uprising were released from jail, and the Military Organization of the Bolshevik party got busy organizing workers into groups of "Red Guards" to combat what was imagined to be a "counterrevolution" from the right. The weak cavalry units sent by Kornilov and commanded by General Alexander Krymov dissolved and retreated without clashing with Petrograd's revolutionary forces. Krymov committed suicide, and Kornilov was arrested soon afterward. Kerensky assumed the post of supreme commander. But the Red Guards did not disband and stood ready to start the real counterrevolution from the left.

The cabinet was once again reconstituted. In a futile attempt to create a strong executive, the Provisional Government created a temporary "directory" consisting of five ministers; Prime Minister Kerensky, Foreign Minister Tereshchenko, Interior Minister A.M. Nikitin, War Minister Gen. V.I. Verkhovsky, and Navy Minister Adm. Dmitry Verderevsky. Prior to that, on September 1, Russia was formally proclaimed a republic.

In the meantime, important changes were taking place in the Petrograd Soviet. On August 31, it voted for the first time for a resolution introduced by the Bolsheviks. As a result, the presidium of the soviet resigned, and the Menshevik Chkheidze was replaced as president by Leon Trotsky, who had recently joined the Bolsheviks.

With the powerful Petrograd Soviet now under control of the Bolsheviks, the Provisional Government attempted to strengthen its support among the more moderate elements of the revolutionary democracy. In the middle of September it convened the so-called Democratic Conference, the composition of which was substantially more to the left than that of the earlier State Conference. Delegates were sent by the VTsIK (100 representatives), local soviets (50), the soviets of peasants' deputies (150), the cooperatives (150), trade unions (100), military organizations (84), various nationalities (59), the zemstvos (50), and other groups. The conference voted in favor of a coalition government with the "bourgeoisie" by 595 to 493, with 72 not voting.

The new (and last) coalition government was formed on September 25. It was headed by Kerensky and included three Socialist Revolutionaries, four Mensheviks, four Kadets, and six members without definite party affiliation.

The principal leaders of the revolutionary democracy, Victor Chernov and Irakly Tseretelli, did not join the cabinet.

To establish a permanent link between the Provisional Government and the organizations of the Left, the Democratic Conference decided to establish a "Provisional Council of the Russian Republic," a temporary legislature generally referred to as the "Pre-Parliament." It was opened on October 7 and remained in session until the Bolshevik takeover. Of the total of 313 members, the cities sent 45 to the Pre-Parliament, the zemstvos 45, the soviets of workers' and soldiers' deputies 38, the soviets of peasants' deputies 38, military organizations 26, national groups 25, лe cooperatives 23, and trade unions 21, the rest of the seats being distributed among various other public organizations. The Socialist Revolutionary Nikolai Avksentiev was elected chairman of the Pre-Parliament. The Bolshevik faction, after a bitter speech by Trotsky against the coalition government, walked out on the first day.

The Pre-Parliament failed to provide the Provisional Government with the strength needed to survive. Permanently in crisis and a state of uncertainty, the government lost its popularity and received active support neither from the left nor from the right. And the parties that constituted the mainstay of the government were also in a weakened condition or undependable.

The Socialist Revolutionaries were badly divided. The center of the party, headed by Chernov, was pressed from the right by the more moderate elements under Avksentiev's leadership and from the left by a strong minority headed by Boris Kamkov, Maria Spiridonova, and others. (After the Bolshevik coup d'état the left-wing faction formally broke away and formed a separate party known as the Left Socialist Revolutionaries, which entered into a short-lived coalition government with the Bolsheviks.)

The Mensheviks could not be depended upon. Influential party leaders like Iulii Martov and Fedor Dan stood not far from the Bolsheviks on questions of foreign policy. Known as the Menshevik Internationalists, they considered "the international bourgeoisie" (not German militarism) to be responsible for the war and accepted the Zimmerwald program of peace without annexations and indemnities. Obsessed by the fear of a counter-revolution from the right, they saw a counterrevolutionary general behind every bush and failed to see the coming counterrevolution from the left. The Bolsheviks they considered to be merely "erring comrades," not enemies of freedom and of a democratic revolution.

The ideological father of Russian Marxism, George Plekhanov, advocated a policy of "revolutionary defensism" with regard to the war, and had certainly no illusions about Lenin in domestic matters. But his newspaper *Unity*, though widely known, had little following among the Social Democrats, and his organization — also named Unity — had few members.

The Kadet Party, under the unquestioned and strong leadership of Paul Miliukov, wanted the victorious conclusion of the war and, therefore, demanded the preservation of order and military discipline in the army. In domestic policy the party insisted that basic decisions on social, economic, and political reconstruction be reserved for the Constituent Assembly and should not be made by the Provisional Government or the soviets. Because of that position, the Kadets were denounced by the Bolsheviks and socialists as the party of the "counterrevolutionary bourgeoisie." The party maintained its following among the intelligentsia and the businessmen in the cities, but its access to the peasantry and to industrial workers was blocked by the acrimonious propaganda of the Left.

Only the Bolsheviks, led by a strong-willed, reckless, and purposeful leader who insistently pushed the party toward one goal, the seizure of power, were growing in strength. Because of worsening conditions and under the influence of skillful, though deceitful, propaganda, most workers in Petrograd and Moscow shifted their sympathies from the Socialist Revolutionaries and Mensheviks to the Bolsheviks, although they were not necessarily ready to support Lenin's ambitions with an armed uprising. The party had no more than about 200,000 members in October 1917, but it controlled the Petrograd and Moscow soviets, which gave the Bolsheviks power far out of proportion to their numbers.

The situation in the army in October 1917 was deplorable. In the eyes of millions of soldiers the protracted war, with all its dangers and privations, no longer made sense, and the Bolshevik promise of a general democratic peace was greeted with understandable sympathy. The military command, deprived of any real power over the ranks, concentrated on trying to preserve the front line from complete disintegration. The majority of junior officers, depressed by the army's disorganization and demoralization, often insulted and humiliated, felt only disgust over and resentment against their peculiar supreme commander, the Provisional Government, and the soviets. But inexperienced in politics and the wiles of conspiracy, the grumbling officers were neither willing nor able to form any real counterrevolutionary organizations.

The population of the cities was restive because of food shortages (caused chiefly by the disorganization of transportation) and the growing depreciation of paper money. In several cities vodka warehouses, which had been sealed at the beginning of the war, were broken into by crowds; hard drinking and riots followed.

In the countryside the lack of manpower was felt as fifteen million young men languished in trenches and barracks. The peasants impatiently waited for the division of the landlords' possessions promised by the Bolsheviks and Socialist Revolutionaries, although in most cases the agrarian disturbances, called a "peasant war" in Bolshevik propaganda, consisted only of the peasants' trespassing upon and plowing up of fields belonging to neighboring landowners.

The fact is that on the eve of the Bolshevik coup d'état no group of the population was satisfied with existing conditions, and very few people were ready to die in defense of the Provisional Government.

S.G.P.
July 1969

FROM THE AUTHOR'S PREFACE

The purpose of my book devoted to the October coup of 1917 is to reconstruct the specific conditions under which the Bolshevik armed uprising and the resistance to it took place. The narrative covers only a short span of time. The "ten days that shook the world" are inserted into the somewhat wider frame of the three weeks which include the preparation for the seizure of power, as well as the revolt itself. My description is predominantly static in character, and I hardly touch upon those problems that pertain to the dynamics of history. This is why it appeared appropriate to include separately at least a brief analysis of some material characterizing sentiments in the countryside, sentiments on which the creators of the October social experiment relied in part.

The first part of my work relates how the Provisional Government in Petrograd was overthrown by fantasts of the politics of violence. From the moment when members of the Provisional Government were incarcerated in the Peter and Paul Fortress, the struggle against the Bolsheviks in fact passed into the hands of the so-called revolutionary democracy. Hence I have called the second part of my work "Under the Banner of Revolutionary Democracy," even though the leader of the former government still played a role.

My narrative is limited to the description of events at the center. Only cursory reference is made to the provinces. To tell how the country as a whole reacted to the act of violence in the capitals would require a separate study.

S.P.M.
March 1939

PART I

The Overthrow of the Provisional Government

By the will of men, not by the force of the elements, did October become inevitable.

KERENSKY

CHAPTER 1

A Scheduled Uprising

I will not deal in depth with the social processes which move history and perhaps partly explain why Bolshevism engulfed Russia. In the thinking of some historians these social processes almost fatalistically predetermined the course of events. In actuality, there is no such determinism, and not every revolution must unavoidably follow a definite path and go through "natural stages." "October" was not the realization of "February." Only the mistakes of those who were able to prevent the seizure of power by the Bolsheviks made it "inevitable."

A REMISSION OF SINS FOR THE BOLSHEVIKS

The last head of the Provisional Government, Alexander Kerensky, is inclined to consider the victory of the Bolsheviks to be the consequence of Kornilov's "rebellion." Without Kornilov's action, he believes, there would have been no Bolshevik uprising. Paul Miliukov, the foreign minister of the Provisional Government and the first historian of the Russian Revolution, has disputed Kerensky's point of view many times. I am not able to discuss this question fully here, but it is true that after the unsuccessful action of Kornilov, there was widespread proliferation of Bolshevik cells and the soviets of workers' and soldiers' deputies were gradually won over by the Bolsheviks. The Kornilov affair struck an irreparable blow to the idea of a coalition government and caused a deep split in the thinking of the leaders of the revolutionary democracy. Moreover, it opened the door to the activity of demagogues from the Bolshevik camp. The measures taken by the government to liquidate Kornilov's movement were more decisive than General Kornilov's actions themselves. Not in vain did Lenin insist on the necessity of changing tactics in a letter written in September to the Central Committee of the Bolshevik party. "We must agitate *this minute,* not so much directly against Kerensky as *indirectly,* demanding active, the most active, revolutionary war against Kornilov. Only the development of this war can lead *us* to power." He urged that Kerensky be presented with certain demands: arrest Miliukov, arm the workers of Petrograd, call the troops from Kronstadt, Vyborg, and Helsinki, dissolve the State Duma, arrest the chairman of the State Duma, Mikhail Rodzianko.[1]

Some of Lenin's demands were met. The Bolsheviks were enlisted in the fight against Kornilov in the name of defending the revolution. A proposal to coordinate their propaganda activity with the actions of other revolutionary organizations was made to the Bolsheviks, and in Moscow this was initiated by the Socialist Revolutionaries and the Mensheviks. Together with government agents and representatives of the socialist parties, the Bolsheviks took the most active part in all temporary organs set up to fight against "counterrevolutionaries." It may even be said that they played the leading role. The Bolshevik party newspaper *Rabochii Put* was not exaggerating when it asserted on September 16 that "in the days of Kornilov the power had already gone over to the soviets."

In effect, the Bolsheviks were given a public remission of sins by the socialist democracy. They were definitely exonerated in the eyes of the masses from the accusations of treason and betrayal that had followed their uprising in July. Trotsky, with biting sarcasm, relates how he, "the Hohenzollern agent," joined the Committee for the Defense of the Revolution immediately upon his release from prison. The most important thing was that the Bolsheviks were legally able to arm themselves. As the Soviet historian of the civil war, A. Anishev, points out, this was one of the most significant achievements of the September "united front." According to one member of the Bolshevik Central Committee, Moisei Uritsky, 40,000 rifles were put at the disposal of the Petrograd proletariat. During the Kornilov affair mass formations of Red Guards were started in the working-class quarters. At the beginning of October, the Red Guard in Petrograd alone, according to the chief of the Bolshevik Military Organization, Nikolai Podvoisky, numbered 12,000 to 14,000 men. After the suppression of the Kornilov movement it was inconceivable to speak of disarming the Red Guards because of the widespread belief in the existence of danger from the right.

During the period of the "September united front" (an expression coined by Soviet historians) attempts were made to extend throughout the country local coalitions with the Bolsheviks and to form a homogenous socialist government. Attempts to form such a government, which would exclude the non-socialist parties, failed, in part because the Bolsheviks refused to pledge their support except for a very short term.

INSURRECTION IN THE "MARXIAN" MANNER

Lenin, who was still underground,* was decidedly opposed to any confusing maneuvers which would dampen, by way of "constitutional illusions," the fighting mood of the proletariat. With all his authority he pressed the party to include "in the order of the day the question about uprisings in Petrograd and Moscow." In his letters of September and the beginning of October addressed to the Bolshevik Central Committee and the Moscow and the Petrograd party committees, he stubbornly besieged the party organizations with his arguments. Besides these official letters, other communications were evidently sent to his confederates behind the back of the party organizations. Otherwise it is difficult to understand why certain letters from the leader were discussed in secret, private group meetings, as was the case, for example, in Moscow. Trotsky definitely asserts that Lenin channeled his ideas about an insurrection to the party "in roundabout ways." It was necessary for Lenin to convince the "Philistines" in the party not to be frightened by a civil war and to think of ways to agitate for an uprising "without saying so in print." With the stubbornness of a maniac under self-hypnosis, he insisted *now or never,* insisted on it as early as the days of the Democratic Conference in September, when talks concerning the united front of the revolutionary democracy were going on. The uprising became an obsession with Lenin. He sketched specific plans for the seizure of power, plans that were frequently rather fantastic and often changed in his own mind.

M.A. Aldanov, in his "Pictures of the October Revolution"** relates an interesting story told by the high-ranking Bolshevik leader Nikolai Bukharin about the unanimous decision of the Central Committee of the party to burn a communication from Lenin that could only have been written in a paroxysm of madness. "You will all be traitors and villains if all members of the Bolshevik faction do not immediately go into the factories and mills and surround the Democratic Conference and arrest all the scoundrels," Lenin had said. The statement was probably made in one of the letters discussed at the September 15 meeting of the Central Committee. The editor of the minutes entitled these letters "The Bolsheviks Must Seize Power" and "Marxism and Uprising." In the printed text the lines quoted by Bukharin do not appear but the essence is there. Trotsky also mentions a letter from Lenin

*Because of the warrant out for his arrest since the July Days.
Eds.

**M.A. Aldanov (Mark A. Landau), *"Kartiny oktiabr'skoi revoliutsii. Den' perevorota"* (Pictures of the October Revolution: The Day of the Coup d'Etat); see the bibliography.

written in "more than energetic terms" about the Pre-Parliament, which is not included in Lenin's collected works.

What did Lenin mean when he talked about an uprising in the "Marxian way"? It was imperative, he wrote, "without wasting a minute to organize a *staff* of insurgent detachments, to distribute forces, move reliable regiments to the most important positions, . . . occupy the Peter and Paul Fortress, arrest the general staff and the government, send against the cadets and the Savage Division* detachments that are willing to die rather than let the enemy move toward the center of the city; we must mobilize armed workers, call them to the desperate final battle, take over immediately the telegraph and telephone, place *our* staff of the insurrection at the central telephone exchange, connect the staff by telephone with all factories, all regiments, all places where fighting is going on."[2]

Allegedly Lenin developed this plan only as an example, an "illustration," but he made concrete proposals — and they were considered as such by the members of the Central Committee who met on September 15. Joseph Stalin proposed that these letters be sent "to the most reliable organizations to be discussed." A decision on this question was postponed until the next meeting of the Central Committee, and the voting was on the question, "Who is for the saving of only one copy of the letters?" For — six, against — four, abstained — six. Thus, there was no agreement. A resolution introduced by Lev Kamenev rejecting the "practical proposals" in Lenin's letters and calling street action inadmissible was voted down. Nevertheless, nobody really supported Lenin's proposals, and members of the Military Organization and of the Petrograd Committee were instructed to take measures against the possibility of any action in the barracks and the factories. Moreover, three days earlier, there appeared in *Rabochii Put* an announcement from the Central Committee of the party stating that the "unknown people" who were going into the factories and urging the workers and soldiers to move on the days of the opening of the Democratic Conference, were imposters. "Any reference to our party is a lie. Their party certificates are falsified . . . . The name of the party is being used by these provocateurs, who are hired by agents of the counterrevolution."

In the meetings of the Central Committee that followed, the question of an uprising was not raised again until October 10, and the members of the committee tried to forget the letters. Evidently, the Central Committee did not feel like spreading Lenin's views, for tactical and security reasons. On September 21 the question of the Democratic Conference was discussed, and despite Lenin's demand that it be boycotted, the committee decided to remain in the conference but not to join the Pre-Parliament, which the

*A cavalry division formed from native Caucasian tribes. Eds.

Democratic Conference decided to form. This last amendment was accepted by a majority of only one vote; therefore, the final decision of the question was handed over to the Bolshevik faction in the Democratic Conference. The faction voted 77 to 50 to take part in the Pre-Parliament — a decision which Lenin termed "shameful." Victor Nogin, a Bolshevik delegate, formulated the opinion of the majority, saying that a boycott of the Pre-Parliament "would be a call for an uprising," a repetition of the July Days. "We have not forgotten the days of July and we will not repeat such stupidity again," added a Bolshevik named Zhukov in a conversation with Fedor Dan that probably expressed the opinion of the average Bolshevik. Three days later, at a conference of the Central and Petrograd committees with provincial party workers who had come to the Democratic Conference, Bukharin delivered a speech on the current situation in which he went no further than to say that "the chain of events, apparently, is leading to open class conflict" and that the party's political slogan should be "all power to the soviets," a slogan which the Bolsheviks were at one time ready to revoke, since they did not have a majority in the soviets. How far this was from Lenin's assertion, now or never! From the minutes of the September meetings of the Petrograd Committee it is possible to conclude that the basic tendency of the leading organ of the Petrograd proletariat was to pursue a program of "peaceful development of the revolution." "It is still too early to speak about a struggle for power," Vladimir Nevsky stated on September 10, for example.

Lenin was still raving. "We're ruining the revolution." He could not reconcile himself to the "indifference" of the party's upper echelons to an uprising. Lenin, of course, could not be satisfied with the "courses for the preparation of personnel" for a future armed uprising which were taught in the latter part of September in Petrograd by the Bolshevik Military Organization. His barrage of letters to party organs demanding an immediate uprising, an immediate seizure of power, did not stop. In a letter dated September 29 the leader announced his withdrawal from the Central Committee in order to agitate in the lower echelons of the party, since his ideas were suppressed and his demands "remained without answer," and he summarized his arguments in favor of an immediate uprising. "To wait for the Congress of Soviets is idiocy, the Congress cannot and will not yield anything . . . . Bolshevik victory *is now assured*: (1) We can (if we don't wait for the Soviet Congress) strike suddenly from three positions, from Petrograd, from Moscow, from the Baltic fleet; (2) We have slogans which assure us the support . . . of the peasants; (3) We are the majority in *the country*; (4) There is complete disintegration among the Mensheviks and the Socialist Revolutionaries; (5) We have the technical ability to seize power in Moscow (which could take the enemy by surprise); (6) We have thousands of armed workers and soldiers in Petrograd, who can *immediately* seize the Winter Palace, the general staff, the telephone exchange, and all large printing presses. We cannot be driven back because agitation in the *army* will be such that it will be *impossible* to fight against this government of peace, of land for the peasants, etc. If we strike immediately, suddenly from three positions, in Petrograd, in Moscow, on the Baltic fleet, it is 99 per cent certain that we will win with fewer casualties than on July 3-5, for *troops will not go* against a government of peace."[3] This 99 per cent also assured Lenin that the Germans would at least agree to a truce, and "to have a truce now would mean to conquer the whole world."

The minutes of the Central Committee do not mention how its members reacted to Lenin's announcement of his withdrawal, which, it is quite obvious, was intended only to influence the undecided, to overcome the tendency of the upper echelons to wait for the Congress of Soviets and oppose an immediate uprising. Only in the minutes of October 3 are there remarks that indirectly shed light on the matter. The committee decided "to propose to Lenin that he come to Petrograd so that there could be a permanent and close liaison." This was a hint that the leader was out of touch with reality. Lenin was also given the assignment to write "a special brochure" treating the question raised in his letters "about the present situation and the policies of the party." The "brochure" turned out to be his famous article "Will the Bolsheviks Retain State Power?"

It is difficult to call the mixture presented by Lenin an ideology. It contains old Russian populistic utopianism, Western European anarchism, and syndicalism, flavored with Marxist terminology affirming that an uprising is possible when the revolutionary party holds a majority in the leading ranks of the revolutionary class. "A real revolution," Lenin said, will awaken "the hidden socialism" of the popular masses, and the "avant-garde of the oppressed classes" will be confronted with only "a hopeless rebellion of a small group of Kornilovists." The victorious proletariat will seize, through the soviets, that "machine of coercion" which will produce a social leveling and will discipline the anarchistic "rabble." In reality Lenin was inclined to be guided in his daily tactics neither by an ideology nor by a Marxist analysis, but by a daring Dantonesque audacity. In a small article published in *Pravda* in 1923 about Nikolai Sukhanov's memoirs of the revolution, Lenin revealed his philosophy with great clarity: "I remember that Napoleon wrote, *on s'engage et puis on voit*." Freely translated, this means, "first you engage in a serious battle and then you see what happens."

Early in September Lenin argued that "thousands of armed workers and soldiers could smash 'the government gang' in Petrograd." But it was not necessary to begin the uprising in Petrograd, the Bolsheviks could wait there. By the end of the month he had developed great hopes for Moscow. In a special letter addressed to the Moscow and Petrograd party organizations at the beginning of October, he wrote: "If it is impossible to take power without an uprising, then we must start an uprising *right away*. It is entirely possible that at this moment we can take power without an uprising, if, for example, the Moscow Soviet *immediately* takes power and declares itself (together with the Petrograd Soviet) the real government. In Moscow victory is assured, and nobody will resist . . . . There is nothing the government can do — except surrender. For when the Moscow Soviet seizes power, the banks, the factories and the [newspaper] *Russkoe Slovo*, it will gain a gigantic base and strength, it will agitate throughout Russia, posing the issue: peace we offer tomorrow, if the Bonapartist* Kerensky surrenders . . . land [will be given] to the peasants right away . . . . If Moscow begins without bloodshed, it will assuredly be supported by (1) the sympathetic army at the front; (2) peasants everywhere; (3) the [Baltic] fleet and the troops in Finland, who will come to Petrograd."[4] An offensive against Petrograd from a headquarters located in Finland was one of the ad hoc possibilities conceived and propagandized by Lenin. In a letter to Ivan Smilga, chairman of the Regional Committee of the Army, Navy, and Workers of Finland, Lenin ordered him to "give full attention to the military preparation of the troops in Finland and the [Baltic] fleet for the impending overthrow of Kerensky. Create a secret committee of the most reliable military men . . . gather the most precise information concerning the strength and the positions of the troops around Petrograd."

The proposals for Finland did not at all detract from Lenin's plans for Moscow — plans based on the most exaggerated and unfounded hopes. "We must turn to our Moscow comrades," urged Lenin again in a letter to a Petrograd party conference in the first days of October, "convince them to take power in Moscow, to declare the Kerensky government deposed, and to declare the Moscow Soviet of Workers' Deputies the provisional government of Russia." "The revolution will perish if Kerensky's government is not overthrown by proletarians and soldiers in the immediate future." "We must mobilize all strength in order to instill into the workers and soldiers the unconditional necessity of a desperate, last, decisive struggle for the overthrow of the Kerensky government." The conference should adopt a resolution to "send delegations to Helsinki, Vyborg, Kronstadt, Revel, to the military units south of Petrograd to agitate . . . for a quick general uprising and the overthrow of Kerensky as the necessary means of opening the way to peace, saving Petrograd and the revolution, and giving land to the peasants and power to the soviets."[5]

One cannot deny Lenin's energy. These insistent, rather confused, and almost hysterical demands finally infected those upper echelons of the party against whose inertia in regard to an uprising Lenin fought with such fanatical

*A "Bonapartist," in Marxist terminology, is a popular leader who takes advantage of his popularity to make himself a dictator. Eds.

ardor. "The sober, clear, daring, brilliant calculation and prognosis of Lenin" won, and the Central Committee step by step was converted to Lenin's policies.

LENIN AND THE OPPOSITION

The Bolsheviks left the first meeting of the Pre-Parliament, declaring that they had "nothing in common" with a government of "national treason" and calling for "vigilance and courage from the workers, soldiers, and peasants of all Russia" because the "revolution is in danger." At a secret meeting of the Bolshevik Central Committee held on October 10 at the apartment of the Menshevik Internationalist Nikolai Sukhanov,* Lenin's tactics were formally sanctioned. Lenin, who was present, insisted on taking "decisive action," although "the most favorable moment had passed." Having learned that Moscow was inclined "to wait" but that Minsk was able "to send troops against Petrograd," Lenin was ready to use the Minsk contingent to begin the offensive against Petrograd. No specific plan was discussed at the meeting, although Trotsky makes the questionable assertion that it was agreed to start an uprising not later than October 15 — that is to say, within five days. The meeting of the Congress of Soviets on October 20 was another deadline that was discussed. Formally, the resolution of the Committee only placed the "armed uprising on the order of the day." Aware that an uprising was "inevitable and fully ripe," the leadership directed "all party organizations to be guided by this fact and to discuss and decide all practical questions from this point of view." For the political direction of an uprising, a seven-man committee consisting of Lenin, Grigori Zinoviev, Lev Kamenev, Trotsky, Stalin, Grigori Sokolnikov, and Andrei Bubnov was elected.[6]

Only two members of the Central Committee, Kamanev and Zinoviev, voted against the resolution, explaining their objection in a special memorandum which they sent to the party organizations. "We are deeply convinced," they wrote, "that to declare an armed uprising immediately would mean to risk not only the fate of our party but also the fate of the Russian and the international revolution . . . . It is said that (1) the majority of the people in Russia is for us [the Bolsheviks] and (2) the majority of the international proletariat is for us. Alas! Neither one nor the other is true, and therein lies the problem . . . . Before history, before the international proletariat, before the Russian Revolution and the Russian working class, we do not have the right to risk now the entire future on an armed uprising. It would be a mistake to think that an uprising similar to that of July 3-5 would, in case of

*It was arranged by his Bolshevik wife, Galina, while he was away. Eds.

failure, have only the same consequences as did that uprising. Now more is at stake. It is a question of a decisive battle, and a defeat in this battle would be the defeat of the revolution. It would be a great historical mistake to put the question of transfer of power to the proletarian party in terms of 'now or never.' No! The party of the proletariat will grow . . . . Only in one way can its progress be interrupted, and that is if it takes upon itself to initiate an uprising under the present circumstances and in this way exposes the proletariat to the blows of the entire united counterrevolution, which is supported by the petit-bourgeois democracy. Against this ruinous policy we raise our voice in warning."[7]

The memorandum pointed out an "extremely important symptom" of the attitude of the soldiers. "Delegates from the front, who are directing agitation against war, bluntly ask our orators not to speak about a revolutionary war, for this repulses the soldiers." Under the circumstances would the front support the uprising?

In October every soldier, in the opinion of Nikolai Podvoisky, was a Bolshevik, but acted "with complete unawareness of the essence of Bolshevism." When it was proposed to send the Petrograd garrison to the front, naturally "the most backward" were ready to rally around the Bolsheviks. "Who is willing to exchange his easy Petrograd life for the dangerous front with its scarce rations?" At that time thousands were trying to leave the front and join the ranks of the privileged. The Petrograd regiments were filled with soldiers not assigned to them. For example, an army captain named Dorofeev stated in his testimony concerning the July Days that in the Third Infantry Reserve Regiment in Peterhof there were 2,000 such soldiers, and that they were the ones who caused most of the "disorganization." As Kamenev put it: "From the Petrograd garrison it is difficult to expect a fighting spirit and readiness to win or die. In the first critical situation the soldiers will leave us and run away." "Large and heterogeneous masses are following us. They are willing to accept our resolutions, but there is a great distance between a voting ballot and active participation in an armed uprising."

The mood of the crowd gathered at a meeting in the People's House *(Narodnyi Dom)*, where Trotsky was speaking, made a very strong impression on Sukhanov. In his memoirs he describes with great enthusiasm an astounding picture of near ecstasy; it seemed that the crowd was almost ready to sing religious hymns. Thousands swore to die for the worker-peasant cause. And the modern Savonarola, Trotsky, castigating evil, declared that the soviet power would give everything in the country to the poor and the unfortunate. You, bourgeois, who have two fur coats, give one to the soldier who is freezing in the trenches. You who have warm boots? Stay at home. A worker needs your boots. The soviet power will bring peace to the world and cure internal disorder. It will confiscate bread from the rich and send it free of charge to the cities and the front.

The living conditions at that time, of course, were most favorable for the acceptance of the crude Bolshevik demagoguery, of which Trotsky gave a striking example at the People's House. There were severe, prolonged labor conflicts, such as the one at the giant Putilov metal works, caused largely by the discrepancy between workers' wages and the rising cost of living. According to figures presented by the Bolshevik faction at the Democratic Conference, food prices increased about 650 per cent but workers' wages only about 350 per cent. This explains the importance of factory committees and their intervention, demanded in part by life itself, in the production and distribution of commodities. Nor did the fact that the last, "save-the-revolution," coalition government included four widely known millionaires, or that a factory owner who was also a government official locked out striking workers, help the situation. But the "unconscious Bolshevism of the masses" alone could not be decisive.

"If all people oppressed by poverty were always ready to support a socialist uprising, we would have reached socialism long ago," Kamenev and Zinoviev pointed out in their memorandum. "The decisive question is this: Is there really such a mood among the workers and soldiers of Petrograd that they see salvation only in a street battle and, therefore, are impatient to take up arms? No. That is not the mood. The advocates of an uprising themselves say that the mood of the workers and soldiers does not even resemble the mood before July 3." Neither in the barracks nor in the factories did there exist that fighting spirit on which the adherents of an armed uprising, and especially Lenin, based their plans.

Five days after the historic resolution of October 10 was passed a meeting of the Petrograd Committee of the party was held with district representatives. Speakers from the districts reported that there was more or less of a fighting mood among workers in only eight of the nineteen districts, and of these eight, three groups – the Latvians, the Estonians, and the Finns – did not represent specific territorial units of Petrograd. In the remaining districts the feeling about an armed uprising was either undefined or even negative (in five districts). It was typical that the representative of the Military Organization, Vladimir Nevsky, considered it premature to put the question of an uprising "as sharply" as the Central Committee had done, for it was necessary first to intensify the work of organization among the masses. The preparations could not be limited to only Petrograd. Nevsky asked, can the Central Committee guarantee the support of Russia? The countryside, in his opinion, would not support an uprising and in case of an uprising would not supply bread. There was no guarantee that the government could not order an army from the front. Nevsky did not believe the words of a resolution in favor of the uprising which purportedly came from the army, since the delegates from the front reported otherwise. Before you begin you must concretely assess your strength, was the consensus. Even ardent adherents of an uprising who considered it inevitable stipulated that "this does not mean that tomorrow we will start to revolt." Andrei Bubnov, a delegate from the Central Committee who had been elected one of the political leaders of the uprising, held contradictory points of view. On the one hand, he said "everything is hanging by a thread," and on the other, "we must not fix the day of the uprising," it "will spring up itself, if the conditions are favorable." If the Bolsheviks do not take power, "the spontaneous wave will sweep over us." It is no wonder that Mikhail Kalinin, who agreed that the Bolsheviks should take a firm stand on an uprising, proposed to postpone it for as much as one year.

During the days that followed the decision to start an uprising, Lenin was visited in the underground by Bolshevik specialists in military matters with the aim of convincing him of the necessity of postponing it for a few weeks and of using this time for the most intensive preparations in Petrograd, in the provinces, and at the front. Party military expert Vladimir Antonov-Ovseenko expressed confidence that the navy would move at the first call, but doubted that it would arrive at Petrograd on time. The very moving of the navy posed, according to Nevsky, "colossal difficulties," since the sailors without officers could hardly succeed in bringing the ships through the minefields and in directing battles. The mood of the soldiers of the Petrograd garrison, according to Podvoisky, was "clearly sympathetic to an uprising," but they must have time to prepare, all the more since those units which rose up in July were demoralized and would move only if they were assured of the participation of other, "formerly reactionary," units, and the readiness of those units to rebel must be verified. Units of "reactionary persuasion" could appear from the front, and the government could be supported by them. All these arguments did not impress Lenin in the least. The government, which is already preparing to meet the uprising, he argued, will be that much more prepared if the action is delayed.

On October 16, at a meeting of the Central Committee with representatives of the city and district committees, the Military Organization, the soviets, the trade unions, and the factory committees, the resolution of October 10 was again discussed — presumably from the point of view of implementing it. But in reality the question was one of interpretation and even possible reconsideration of the resolution. This meeting was extremely significant. Lenin was again present and heard more arguments. A representative of the Petrograd Committee reported on sentiment in the districts: it was a mood difficult to assess, a careless, indifferent mood; there was no desire for an uprising; things were going badly; it was a mood of waiting; there were doubts concerning an uprising — only in the Nevsky district and in Schlusselburg could a mood strongly favorable to Lenin be observed. Nikolai Krylenko of the Military Organization said, "We have sharp disagreements in assessing the mood . . . . The majority believes that we must not emphasize practical questions too strongly, but the minority thinks that we can take the initiative." Moisei Volodarsky of the Petrograd Soviet reported, "The general impression is that no one is rushing into the streets, but following the call of the soviet, all will appear." A representative of the trade unions said, "The mood is such that we should not expect an active uprising." The veteran trade-union leader Alexander Shliapnikov said that in the metalworkers' union, where the Bolshevik influence was dominant, "an uprising is not popular; rumors about it even cause panic."

On the basis of these reports, Vladimir Miliutin, a prominent Bolshevik economist, concluded that the party was not ready to strike the first blow. "We are not able to overthrow and arrest the government in the near future." The impossibility of an uprising was also argued by A.V. Shotman, a member of the Central Committee, who referred to the fact that "at the city conference [of the Petrograd Bolshveiks] and in the Petrograd Committee, and in the Military Organization the mood is much more pessimistic." "If the resolution is an order, it has not been fulfilled," stated Volodarsky. "If it is a question of an uprising tomorrow, then we must say frankly that we have nothing prepared for it." "The results of the week," Kamenev pointed out, "prove that now no conditions for an uprising exist. One cannot say that the resolution only awakened thoughts; it demanded turning words into action. And this has not happened. We have no machinery for an uprising; our enemies have much stronger machinery, and during this week it has no doubt become even stronger."[8]

The defenders of an immediate uprising could give essentially no other arguments than those presented by the trade-union leader Mikola Skrypnik: "All the arguments that have been made here are only arguments for delay. There is no guarantee of victory," but "if we do not have strength now, we will not have more later. If now we do not take and hold power, later it will be even worse . . . we will then not even have strength for defense." It was a gamble, rationalized by Lenin with a scientific-sounding formula: "It is impossible to be guided by the mood of the masses, for it is changeable and cannot be accurately assessed; we must be guided by an objective analysis and evaluation of revolution."* His analysis assured Lenin that with an uprising

---

*There is some evidence of the "mood of the masses" in October. Out of 169 resolutions received by the VTsIK from local soviets prior to the

"we will have the whole European proletariat on our side." The world revolution was ripe. "We are standing on the threshold of the international proletarian revolution," he asserted in an article published on October 7.

It is also very typical of the mood of the October 16 meeting that one after the other, orators from among the adherents of an uprising tried to interpret the Central Committee resolution of the 10th not as an order mandatory for party organizations, but only as a statement of basic tactics "toward an uprising." The purpose of this formulation was to smooth out differences of opinion. Sokolnikov said it was "completely false" to explain the resolution as an "order to rise." If it happens that circumstances cause a delay, then, of course, the party will take advantage of it. "The resolution is not at all an invitation 'to rise tomorrow,' " explained Kalinin, "it only changes the question 'from one of policy to one of strategy.' " "The day of the uprising must be chosen with expediency in mind," only "in this way must the resolution be understood," was the opinion of Stalin. "Now the question is clearer and it is impossible to object to preparations for a revolution," agreed a trade-union representative named Schmidt, who had formerly been with the opposition. Miliutin commented: "The resolution was written differently than it is being interpreted now; it is interpreted as a matter of a long-term policy toward an uprising. This was already planned in September. Nobody argues about the long-term course." The principal opponents at the meeting of the 10th now yielded likewise. "The present· interpretation" is a "retreat," for earlier it was said that an "uprising should take place before the 20th," declared Kamenev. "If the uprising is understood as a future prospect," said Zinoviev, "then it is impossible to object, but if it is an order for tomorrow or the day after tomorrow, then it is simply an adventure." He agreed that if it were a question of long-term policy, then it must be recognized that "an uprising is inevitable."

Even Lenin appeared satisfied. He proposed "to confirm the resolution, to make decisive preparations, and to let the Central Committee and the soviets decide when." Outwardly, the leader made a great concession and gave up his intention to force events. Both Zinoviev and Kamenev tried to formalize this. "We have a duty to explain to the masses that they will not be called upon to rise up during the next three days," said Kamenev. Zinoviev proposed a resolution: "While not putting off preliminary, preparatory steps, we hold it impermissible to take decisive measures before conferring with the Bolshevik

---

convening of the Congress of Soviets, only six conformed to the standard Bolshevik formulation of demands, 31 demanded only the transfer of power to the soviets (which did not necessarily mean to the Bolsheviks), and 58 advocated a coalition government including the Bolsheviks. The remaining 74 gave even less indication of pro-Bolshevik sympathies. S.G.P.

faction at the congress of the soviets." But Zinoviev's resolution was rejected. A resolution proposed by Lenin was accepted nineteen to two, with four abstaining: "The conference fully approves and supports the resolution of the Central Committee. It calls on all organizations and all workers and soldiers to prepare thoroughly and strenuously for an armed uprising [and] to support the center* created for this purpose, and it expresses complete confidence that the Central Committee and the [Petrograd] soviet will indicate in due time the favorable moment and the expedient means to start an offensive."[9]

Upon leaving the meeting, everyone could interpret the accepted decision according to his own understanding and in his own way pacify his political conscience. The party went from attack to defense, but "our enemies could force us to begin a decisive battle." "Objective" conditions could bring the moment of battle closer. In the opinion of Krylenko, one of those who believed it was inexpedient to fix a date for the uprising, an offensive by the enemy in fact already existed and could be taken advantage of. The government was proposing to withdraw the unreliable Petrograd garrison from the city, but the soldiers were threatening to rebel if they were ordered out of the capital. Krylenko argued that the garrison probably would be ordered to withdraw, and that this would be enough to provoke a "battle," for the issue was an emotionally charged one.

As far as Lenin was concerned, it was not even necessary to look for a provocation. He considered himself victorious in his "decisive battle" at the Central Committee meeting, and for him the "critical day" remained the 20th of October. But Lenin fell into a complete fit of rage when he saw the Petrograd newspapers of October 18. In *Novaia Zhizn* he read an article entitled "Kamenev on the Uprising." "I must say," said Kamenev, "that any decision of our party concerning the fixing of any revolution for this or that day is unknown to me. Similar party decisions do not exist . . . . Not a single revolutionary party can reject, or has the right to reject, an uprising." But "at the present moment, given the relations between the social forces, the instigating of an armed uprising independent of the Congress of Soviets and a few days before the Congress [is to convene] would be an impermissible and fatal step for the proletariat and the revolution." An uprising would be "doomed to failure." "It would be an 'act of desperation.' "

"Shamelessness," "impudence," "captious lie," "swindle," "baseness" — such terms are scattered throughout two letters which Lenin sent off immediately to the membership of the Bolshevik party (October 18) and to

*During the meeting a "military-revolutionary center" was chosen from the Central Committee; it consisted of Yakov Sverdlov, Stalin, Bubnov, Uritsky, and Felix Dzerzhinsky. Eds.

the Central Committee (October 19). He never spared "energetic words." This is treason, strikebreaking. "Mr. Zinoviev and Mr. Kamenev" should be expelled from the party. "On the all-important question of battle, two 'prominent Bolsheviks' attacked the 'unpublished decision of the party center' on the eve of the critical day of October 20." "Kamenev and Zinoviev betrayed to Rodzianko and Kerensky the decisions of the Central Committee of their party concerning an armed uprising, the concealing of preparations for an armed uprising from the enemy, and the choosing of a day for an armed uprising. This is fact. No subterfuge can disprove this fact." "Hesitation and confusion are brought" into the fighting ranks. "From far away I cannot judge how much real damage has been done by the strikebreakers." But "the question of an armed uprising, even if the strikebreakers have delayed it for a long time by their betrayal to Rodzianko and Kerensky, will not be dismissed by the party."

An examination of the relationships of the Bolsheviks to each other belongs to party historians. It is important for us to point out only the muddled confusion among the leading conspirators on the eve of the uprising, that ambiguity and uncertainty which characterized the position of the main political staff of the people rebelling against the Provisional Government. This confusion was sufficiently evident when the Central Committee began, at the meeting of October 20, to discuss Lenin's letters of protest. Several "Leninists" (Dzerzhinsky, for example) demanded the complete removal of Kamenev from political activities. Other members of the Central Committee, such as Miliutin, maintained that "in general nothing special has happened." For us today it is curious that none other than Stalin worked for the preservation of party unity, insisting that in spite of Lenin's "sharp tone" "essentially we will remain united in thought." Stalin thought that after Kamenev's declaration in the Petrograd Soviet and Zinoviev's explanatory letter to the editors of *Rabochii Put* the matter would be considered settled. Kamenev's speech in the soviet on October 17 followed the published declaration of Trotsky stating in the name of "the legitimate representation of the Petrograd proletariat and the revolutionary garrison" that "no day for an armed uprising has been fixed by us. But if in the course of events the soviet should be forced to set a day for the uprising, workers and soldiers, as one, would rise up at its call." Kamenev hastened to agree with Trotsky, saying that he subscribed to every word. In the Central Committee meeting not a word was said about excluding Kamenev from the party as Lenin had demanded. All that was expected of Kamenev was to resign his membership in the Central Committee, which he had already done on his own at the meeting of October 16. His resignation was formally accepted by a vote of five to three. But, in fact, Kamenev did not leave the ranks of the Central Committee, and dragged behind the bandwagon of the future victors, taking an active part in the tactics of conspiracy.

The Deceived

THE REVOLUTIONARY DEMOCRACY

The decisions of the Bolsheviks and the differences of opinion among them became common knowledge. This was due primarily to gossip emanating from the Bolsheviks themselves. Of course, the Petrograd newspapers at the time were full of reports that an armed uprising was in the making. But the Bolshevik leaders publicly denied the intention to organize an armed uprising, and endeavored to find cover in the shrubbery of public emotions.

Trotsky traces the "legal" beginning of the revolt back to October 9, when the Petrograd Soviet passed a resolution disapproving the government's proposal to move part of the garrison from the city to defend the approaches to the capital. This proposal was linked to the general decision to evacuate Petrograd. In making it, the government was, of course, motivated more by political than by strategic aims, for Petrograd was not under any direct threat. But with Petrograd officially included in the zone of military operations and placed under martial law, it would be easier for the government to move to Moscow and to convene the Constituent Assembly in an atmosphere less highly charged with political struggle.

The newspapers reported "stormy debates" at a meeting of the Cabinet on October 4. The socialist ministers felt that they should not push the question of moving the government in order to avoid irritating the revolutionary organizations, which might "adopt a negative attitude toward such a move, viewing it as an attempt by the government to escape from under their influence." The government postponed a final decision until there could be a discussion of the matter in the Pre-Parliament, which was to convene on October 7. The Pre-Parliament was cool to the idea of moving the government to Moscow, and the matter was in effect taken off the agenda. Not only the socialists but also the commercial-industrial group, through their spokesman,

N. N. Kutler, raised objections to evacuation, rumors of which were threatening to disturb the "tranquility in Petrograd." At the session of the Pre-Parliament held on October 13, the government reversed itself and announced that if possible the Constituent Assembly would be convened in Petrograd, and that it would abandon the capital only under direct military threat.

Nevertheless, Lenin had no doubts whatsoever. "The Russian bourgeoisie, Kerensky and company" had decided "to turn over Petersburg to the Germans in order to stab the revolution in the back." "Clear preparations are being made for another Kornilov affair." "Only victory gained by us through insurrection will frustrate plans for a separate peace directed against the revolution." This motif ran through the arguments for the necessity of an armed uprising in the resolution passed by the Bolshevik Central Committee on October 10.

The slogan had been formulated, and it was picked up by the entire Bolshevik press, which was endeavoring to play on the patriotic feelings of the masses. Zinoviev wrote in *Rabochii Put* that the counterrevolution was preparing to expose "the front to the enemy" and to conclude a peace pact with Kaiser Wilhelm "at the expense of Russia." He asserted that Kaiser Wilhelm would carve himself out a generous piece of Russian soil. An anonymous article contained in the same newspaper the day after the first session of the Pre-Parliament bore the title "What Awaits Us." The article (which was written by Stalin) claimed that the bourgeoisie and the government intended to "pacify" Petrograd by surrendering it to the Germans and wrecking chances for a Constituent Assembly. On the eve of a meeting of the Bolshevik Central Committee, the Petrograd Soviet, at the proposal of the Bolshevik faction, resolved "at this moment of mortal danger to the people and revolution" to organize "a revolutionary defense committee which . . . would take all necessary steps to arm the workers and thus guarantee the revolutionary defense of Petrograd and protection of the populace against an attack by military and civilian Kornilovs, preparations for which are being made openly."[10] Thus, on October 9 the camouflaged foundation for the future Military Revolutionary Committee (MRC) was laid.

"The government can flee from Petrograd," exclaimed Trotsky pathetically at the Congress of Soviets of the Northern Region, which convened on the 11th of October, "but the Petrograd Soviet and the revolutionary people will never leave. They shall fight and, if necessary, die at their posts." "The plan for surrendering revolutionary Petrograd, concealed behind the evacuation, is dictated by hatred for the revolutionary proletariat and garrison and by the desire to get rid of them." "At this Congress," Trotsky concluded, "we must in a practical and effective manner deal with the question of transferring all power to the soviets — this is the real agenda of our Congress." The following day Trotsky said: "The time for words has passed. Our Congress should demonstrate that we are backed up not only by words but by deeds as well. The time has come for a duel to the death between the revolution and counterrevolution." "The situation prevailing in this country urges us to meet the task facing our nation and take power into our own hands, even at the price of our lives." However, matters did not proceed beyond general resolutions drawn up in the customary belligerent terms and proclaiming the program of the future "soviet government."

The first clash between the Bolsheviks and the parties of the revolutionary democracy took place on October 14 at a joint session of the Central Executive Committee of the Soviets of Workers' and Soldiers' Deputies (VTsIK) and the Executive Committee of the Soviets of Peasants' Deputies. The topic of discussion was "national defense." The representatives of the revolutionary democracy were experienced politicians well acquainted with the Bolsheviks' cunning demagoguery and they were not, therefore, easily entrapped by official Bolshevik pronouncements. The seemingly naive question put by Dan at the joint session — are the Bolsheviks planning an uprising? — was, of course, only a propaganda device designed to produce an effect on the workers in the factories, who were discussing the question of whether "to act or not to act." Calling Dan's question a "prosecutor's trial by ordeal," the Bolshevik David Riazanov took up the challenge. "The ground for an uprising is not being prepared by the Bolsheviks," he declared, "but rather, by that policy which in the seven months since the revolution began has done so much for the bourgeoisie and nothing for the masses. The ground is being prepared by those who are creating among the masses a mood of desperation and indifference. We do not know the day or hour of the uprising, but we say to the masses: prepare for a decisive struggle for land and peace, bread and freedom. If the worker and peasant masses rise as a result of this government policy, we shall stand in the front ranks of the insurgents."

The Menshevik Boris Bogdanov drew a clear conclusion from Riazanov's essentially evasive reply: "The Bolsheviks are preparing an armed uprising and will lead the insurgents." "But," Bogdanov predicted, "any attempt at an uprising will be crushed by the government. Not the masses, but isolated bands, will take to the streets. This will be taken advantage of by the 'counterrevolutionaries.' The city 'is already rife with rumor' to the effect that 'some kind of White Guard is organizing.'" The account of the meeting also mentions a statement by Martov in the name of the Menshevik Internationalists, who agreed with Riazanov that "the soil for rebellion is being prepared by the government." But he went on to say that now is not the time to "reorganize governmental authority"; an uprising would be total "folly" in a "period of revolutionary lull." The assemblage adopted a resolution proposed by Dan stating that an uprising at that time "would be fatal to national defense and would lead to counterrevolution."[11] The People's Socialists criticized the resolution as "too indefinite" — but its wording was dictated by the desire to gain the Bolshevik vote.

At this meeting the basis was laid for the tactics of the revolutionary democracy during all the critical days to follow — the attitude that the Bolshevik uprising was nothing more than a foolish adventure, and the fear of "counterrevolution," the scarecrow on the horizon. Still, none of the cunning attempts by the Bolsheviks to camouflage the insurrectionist nature of their activities could draw the intended victims into the trap. When on the 16th the Petrograd Soviet discussed a draft plan for organizing the Military Revolutionary Committee as a "defense" agency, the Socialist Revolutionary fraction stated unequivocally that it would not even engage in discussing the matter, while the Menshevik M. Broido called the Bolshevik "venture" the setsing up of a "revolutionary headquarters for seizing power." The Mensheviks refused to participate in this "burial of the revolution."

Two days later, at a special session of the soviet, in which delegates of the All-Russian Congress of Factory and Plant Committees participated, Trotsky was forced to declare that the Bolsheviks had not "planned any armed uprising." Trotsky made light of those "facts" reported in bourgeois newspapers pinpointing the "day of insurrection" as the 22nd, which had been designated as the so-called Day of the Soviet, "a day of agitation, propaganda, and consolidation of the masses under the banner of the Soviet, a day of pro-soviet meetings." He particularly cited the newspaper *Den,* which, he said, took the prize for "prophecy," even printing a "schedule" of the uprising and planned routes of march. The stenographic account notes that there was laughter in the hall. "The aim of this campaign is quite clear to us," continued Trotsky. "There is a conflict between us and the government that could become extremely acute. It is the question of troop withdrawal. We do not intend to permit another Kornilov affair, a preliminary step toward which would be the abandonment of Petrograd by its revolutionary garrison. The bourgeois press wants to create an atmosphere of animosity and suspicion among the soldiers and workers of Petrograd, and they want those at the front to feel enmity toward the Petrograd soldiers . . . Another critical matter is that of the Congress of Soviets. [The Petrograd Soviet was to propose that the Congress take power into its own hands.] . . . The present smear campaign is laying the groundwork for an armed attack against the Congress of Soviets . . . All of revolutionary Russia will respond to it with a most vigorous counteroffensive, which will be merciless and which we shall prosecute to the end." Trotsky's assertions were echoed in the Bolshevik press. "We are not so naive," stated *Rabochii Put* on October 19, "as to be the first to plunge headlong into battle, having made known both the day and hour." The Bolshevik organ dubbed the authors of the expose of Bolshevik plans as "slanderers" and "provocateurs." "To whose advantage is it to peddle all over Moscow alarming rumors of a Bolshevik uprising on the 22nd of October?" chimed in the Moscow yes-men of the *Sotsial Demokrat.* "We are not a conspiratorial party which conceals its plans for action. When we decide to act we shall make an announcement to that effect in our newspapers." "Brother Cossacks," rang an appeal by the Petrograd Soviet on the 21st of October, "scoundrels and provocateurs are claiming that the soviet is planning 'some kind of uprising.' Their aim is to provoke bloodshed and to drown your freedom and ours in an internecine bloodbath."

But Trotsky veered from the "wise serpent" policy because of his orator's temperament when, carried away by a wave of eloquence, he replied to the Mensheviks, "They say here that we are setting up a headquarters of a seizure of power. We make no secret of this," but it is pure and simply "a demonstration of the forces of the proletariat."

Apparently no one doubted the possible result of such a "demonstration." Indicative of this were the reactions of the press, regardless of political persuasion. The writer Maxim Gorky, Bolshevik sympathizer, came out on the 18th with an article entitled "I Cannot Remain Silent." He spoke of the imminent repetition of that "bloody and senseless slaughter" of the July Days, which "undermined the moral significance of the revolution through-out the country." "If the Bolsheviks rise they will be crushed," asserted the Kadet paper *Rech* on the 21st. "The masses will not follow the Bolsheviks." Their slogans "are capable of putting only small bands on the street." "We are not witnessing a spontaneously burgeoning movement," wrote B.V. Avilov in Gorky's paper *Novaia Zhizn',* "but rather a definite political campaign which is endeavoring to shape spontaneous moods in the masses, place them within a specific, organized framework and direct them toward a specific objective." *Delo Naroda,* organ of the Central Committee of the Socialist Revolutionary party, no longer entertained any doubts that the Bolshevik uprising would be of an armed nature. But its result could only be a "second Kornilov affair," which in the opinion of the newspaper would be far more dangerous than the first had been.

Several weeks before the uprising, a prominent member of the Socialist Revolutionary party and one of the majority leaders in the Petrograd Soviet, Abram Gots, earnestly told a group of visiting military men, who were worried about the course the revolution was taking: "You exaggerate the role and significance of the Bolsheviks. Who even bothers about them?" Those who were fated to occupy the stage-front of history failed properly to assess the role that could be played in an era of revolutionary ferment by a minority which not only appealed to popular passions, but which unleashed them as well. They ignored the fact that wartime industry had changed considerably the make-up of Petrograd's working class, which had grown from 194,000 to 403,000, and that recent immigrants were the most unstable from a social viewpoint, more susceptible to the enticing and ephemeral slogans of Bolshevik propaganda. Even more unstable was the politically amorphous garrison, where extremist agitation sought support. This is why it was so premature for *Izvestiia,* organ of the then largely non-Bolshevik Central Executive Committee of the Soviets, to say on October 20 that the Bolshevik folly of an armed uprising in Petersburg was finished and that in this abortive affair the Bolsheviks were "totally isolated and have become surrounded not by Kornilov's troops, but rather by the universal indignation of all Democrats, and they are already capitulating." This was self-deception or worse.

An astonishing appeal was made public by the VTsIK on the 17th of October in response to an alarmed mood prevailing in the working-class districts of Petrograd. The appeal was for exposure of that "provocateur hand" which was attempting to transform ferment engendered among the masses "by their pauper status and indignation against the policies of the Provisional Government" into a "reactionary pogrom." "Comrades," it stated, "the forces of darkness are working vigorously to incite riots and pogroms in Petrograd and other cities during the next few days, in order to secure the opportunity to drown the entire revolutionary movement in a bloodbath. Under the pretext of restoring law and order and protecting the lives and property of citizens, they hope to install the same type of Kornilov regime that our revolutionary people have successfully crushed recently. Woe to the nation if these plans succeed. A victorious counterrevolution will annihilate the soviets and military committees, will sweep away plans for the Constituent Assembly, will stop the transfer of land to the peasants, will put an end to all popular hopes for an early peace and will swell the prisons with revolutionary soldiers and workers . . . Any attempt at this time to organize an uprising or demonstration, be it with the most revolutionary aims, would be criminal folly."[12] A similar appeal had been made by the Menshevik Internationalists.

These appeals were somehow bashfully silent about the Bolsheviks. The emphasis had already shifted to the future counterrevolution. Thus, the line of demarcation between the Bolsheviks and their opponents in the socialist camp was blurred. A unified revolutionary front was preserved. Only "reckless political struggle" that was attempting to overthrow the government violently and prematurely was denounced.

Such a fatal psychological atmosphere (sarcastically defined by Plekhanov, "Come forth Lenin, demi-Leninists salute you") drowned out the warning voices of those few "moderate" socialists such as A. Potresov who demanded an unreserved and vigorous struggle against the Bolsheviks and cancellation of the scheduled Second Congress of Soviets. The call to battle was voiced by the right-wing Socialist Revolutionaries in *Volia Naroda*, which recognized as early as the time of the Democratic Conference that there were no paths of agreement with the Bolsheviks, that "postponement of battle" was dangerous, and that one must "with iron hand compel the Bolsheviks to submit." The appeal to battle was also issued by the People's Socialists in *Narodnoe Slovo*, by Plekhanov's *Edinstvo*, and by the Menshevik Defensist *Den*.* The central organ of the People's Socialist party, appealing for organized resistance against the Bolshevik onslaught and for action by society, published the following on October 20: "A threat hangs over the citizens of Russia. Tomorrow or the next day the Bolsheviks will 'act,' and gangsters will break into homes, destroy, and kill. The 'free' citizens of the world's most democratic republic are, in the face of this, manifesting the great depths of their passivity — as if they want to say, what will be, will be. The social psychology of a revolutionary era," the newspaper pessimistically concluded, "apparently differs very little from that of the era of absolutism." Yet none of the moderate socialist groups undertook any organizational action.

THE "KORNILOVISTS"

Such was the mood within the ranks of the revolutionary democracy. Was any attempt to organize themselves made by those who — not only in the eyes of the Bolsheviks — could be capable of establishing order, and did they attempt to "strangle" the revolutionary movement?

We have already quoted above from an editorial in the Constitutional-Democratic *Rech*. This newspaper saw the inevitability of civil war, toward which blind forces were propelling the nation. Day after day it spoke of the "terror" and "disgrace" to which Russia would be subjected. To a certain extent *Rech* pointed to Russian "oblomovism" — the slavish subjugation to an imminent event — as the cause of an absence of opposition in society. It indicted the government and its wait-and-see policy. But it had no doubt whatsoever that the instinct of self-preservation would be awakened in the public as soon as blood began to flow, and that the government would demonstrate a will to act. Of course the Bolshevik uprising would be crushed. But at what price? asked *Rech* on October 18.

However, *Rech* was still merely a daily newspaper, even though it was a semiofficial organ of the Kadet party. Were there doubts in responsible

*The so-called Menshevik Defensists, who constituted a right wing in the Social Democratic Party, strongly supported the Russian war effort, considering the defense of the homeland to be of primary political importance. Eds.

political circles? October was a time of party congresses and conferences, which were forging out tactical directives for the elections to the Constituent Assembly. One searches in vain in the records of these meetings for any direct response to the economic and political troubles being experienced by the country. Nor does one find any indication of an attempt to organize resistance to the Bolsheviks. On the contrary, one perceives not only instances of narcotizing, but even remarkable notes of self-confidence, such as at the Moscow Congress of the Constitutional Democratic party in speeches given by party-leader Miliukov on the 14th and 15th of October.

At the Kadet congress two schools of thought competed on the matter of short-range party policy. One part of the Constitutional Democrats felt that the national situation demanded joint effort by all statesmanlike political elements. For the sake of creating a revolutionary democratic majority, the party should reach agreement with the socialist and liberal groupings close to them, making necessary concessions in the process. This policy of "agreement," "the last attempt to offer opposition to the swelling wave of Bolshevism," was preceded by preliminary negotiations in Petrograd in which the key roles were to be played by Vladimir Nabokov, who represented the Kadet Central Committee, and the Menshevik Tseretelli, the most influential individual on the VTsIK. Nabokov recalls how on two occasions Kadet representatives met at Moisei Adzhemov's apartment with leaders of the revolutionary democracy (Gots, Dan, and Matvei Skobelev; Tseretelli had left for the Caucasus). "Dan replied to our definitive statement that we believed the chief task of the recently established Pre-Parliament was to create an atmosphere of public confidence in the Provisional Government and to support it in its struggle against the Bolsheviks, that he and his friends were not inclined to promise in advance their confidence and support, that everything would depend on the government's manner of action, and that in particular they did not see the possibility of assigning high priority to the struggle against the Bolsheviks at any price." "We adjourned," concludes Nabokov, "with a heavy foreboding, with the awareness that the old runaround was beginning once again . . . that all the effort expended by us . . . had been practically worthless."[13] Evidently Nabokov was trying to achieve too much − the people whom he had been in contact with had not yet abandoned the goal of a "homogeneous socialist government," that is, one including the Bolsheviks but excluding "bourgeois" parties such as the Constitutional Democrats. Perhaps a more realistic type of coalition was proposed by the People's Socialist Alexei Peshekhonov in *Narodnoe Slovo* (semi-official paper of the People's Socialists) on October 4. For him a fruitful agreement could only be reached between those "leftists" who disassociated themselves from the Bolsheviks and those "rightists" who had broken with the counterrevolution. The Socialist-Revolutionary *Narodnoe Delo* countered that under these conditions there was no one with whom to form a coalition.

Miliukov, expressing the minority view on the Central Committee of the Kadet Party and, according to the editor of *Rech*, Joseph Hessen, vigorously setting himself apart from the socialists, came out strongly against "lucid slogans" being sacrificed to "hypocritical phraseology." He emphasized the growing disenchantment with slogans used by the extremist parties throughout the country. In his opinion an "unquestionable change" had already occurred. At the local level there had been a strengthening of statesmanlike elements who would go along with the Constitutional Democratic party.* The democratic center was impotent and consequently useless. A coalition in Russia was unnecessary. "Other groups may reach agreement with *us,* but we cannot make concessions to *them.*" The "deafening applause" which greeted Miliukov's speeches attested to the fact that the congress was inclined to support not the position favoring compromise advanced by Adzhemov and Nabokov, but rather the uncompromising position of Miliukov.

One may wonder at the lack of farsightedness on the part of the contemporaries of the October events. But do not their equanimity and confidence constitute evidence that the actual situation was not tragically hopeless? Minister of Welfare Nikolai Kishkin stated at the Kadet congress that the weakness of the Provisional Government was "to a considerable degree merely a variety of self-hypnosis." The revolutionary government had no "revolutionary daring." If it developed this daring it would find the necessary "machinery," and the "national anarchy would come to an end." Kishkin oversimplified, but we still cannot fully accept the at times doleful voice of contemporary political commentators as a faithful representation of the reality of that period. It has become popular in some historical works to refer to the major front-page article in *Russkie Vedomosti* on October 20 discussing the growth of anarchy within Russia and entitled "Decay." We read: "The crowd, in the negative sense of the word, is appearing on the streets more frequently and is beginning to feel master of the situation, recognizing no authority. Sometimes this is a crowd of the deeply ignorant, acknowledging nothing but crude personal interests, a pack of insurgent

---

*It may be noted that between August 20 and November 12, the Kadet party in Petrograd actually increased its voting strength only from 21 to 26 percent of the vote, while the Bolshevik percentage jumped from 33 to 45. The change was mostly at the expense of the Socialist Revolutionaries. In Moscow the Kadet vote increased between June 25 and November 20 from 17 to 35 percent, while the Bolshevik vote went from 12 to 48 percent. (James Bunyan and H.H. Fisher, eds., *The Bolshevik Revolution* [Stanford, Calif., 1934], p. 348). Eds.

slaves. Democracy is coming ever closer to total disintegration, from which it will no longer be able to emerge under its own power." But a type of pedagogic technique was concealed behind this patriotic alarm. Moscow historian Alexander Kizevetter, in the pages of the same newspaper, argued persuasively in his article entitled "Anarchy and Society" that "the spectre of anarchy will disappear without a trace." It is significant that even on the 25th of October, the day the Provisional Government fell, *Russkie Vedomosti,* a serious liberal newspaper, did not go any further than to draw parallels with the Bolshevik uprising in July. After all, revolutionary Russia, under the guidance of a government which was constantly changing in makeup, reached the elections to the Constituent Assembly and did not disintegrate into district and county "independent republics," as had been predicted by pessimistically inclined political commentators.

At the same time as the congress of the Constitutional Democratic party, a second meeting was held in Moscow of the Conference of Civic Leaders, that heterogeneous conglomerate of civic figures, which the Kadets attempted to draw into the orbit of their influence (for the party's task was the assimilation of "statesmanlike" individuals, not only from the left, but from the right as well). At the meeting there was a highly negative attitude toward the Provisional Government and a tendency to lump all groups of the revolutionary democracy together. The following is a statement made, at least according to the account in *Vlast Naroda,* by the Hegelian philosopher I.A. Iliin, who already occupied a position on the right flank of the Russian public life: "The entire population of Russia can now be divided into two camps, the supporters of order and the party of anarchy, at the head of which stands the prime minister." Almost nothing was said about the Bolsheviks. "Bolshevism," commented Prince Evgeniy Trubetskoy, "is an 'epidemic infection' that will run its course." The speaker believed that signs of imminent recuperation were already evident. On the threshold of the fateful "October Days" the most eloquent speeches at this congress became virtually irrelevant rhetoric. This holds true even for the star performance by Gen. Alexei Brusilov, on whom some public figures counted to head the anti-Bolshevik cause.

The Moscow meeting failed to sound the appeal, the fatherland is in danger! The businessmen participating in the conference did not issue an appeal to "save Russia," as had been the case in August. On the contrary, the rightist press launched a particularly sharp attack against the government for its lack of action against the Bolsheviks. "It is difficult to believe," one reads in *Russkaia Volia,* "that at a time when the insurrectionists are issuing a criminal challenge in such an open manner the authorities beat around the bush, gather information, and wait to see whether or not the Bolshevik threat will materialize."

THE GOVERNMENT

One definite conclusion can be drawn. The majority of both the leftists and rightists made approximately the same assessment of the Bolshevik chances of success in an uprising. In and of itself such an adventure was not dangerous. The government had sufficiently well-organized forces to paralyze a Bolshevik uprising.

Trotsky asserts that the government was totally oblivious to the Bolshevik uprising. Such a claim, if it can be accepted at all, must be taken with major modifications. From the very first to the last day during the period of preparations for the insurrection we hear regular assurances from the prime minister and other government figures: "We are ready and shall permit no uprising." On October 12 the Petrograd correspondent of *Russkie Vedomosti* reported that the Bolshevik action, expected on the 20th (he referred to a "demonstration" which would demand that authority be transferred to the soviets) was cause for no "particular concern" in government circles. This attitude expresses the confidence that this demonstration would have the same fate as that in the memorable July Days. At a meeting between representatives of the government and of general headquarters (Kerensky, Alexander Konovalov, Verkhovsky, Gen. Nikolai Dukhonin, and Gen. V. A. Cheremisov) it was determined that law and order could be maintained in Petrograd by the military.

On the 13th the government, in connection with a report made by Food Minister Sergei Prokopovich, who had returned from a trip through the south, held a special discussion on the struggle against "anarchy." Prokopovich came to the conclusion that "we can wait no longer to show firm authority on the national and local level." Anarchy had to be put down. "We must cease to be the persuaders-in-chief." Kerensky, supported by War Minister Verkhovsky, felt that until the convening of the Constituent Assembly the government should run the country "without physical coercion," which might undermine its moral authority in the eyes of the masses. The government should not stop "at anything to put down . . . armed uprisings menacing the country with civil war." By contrast, "swift but legal measures taken with the sanction of the parliament are essential to fight the anarchy engendered by economic disintegration." The Kadet ministers and the naval minister retorted that anarchy requires "just as vigorous and immediate action as will be required for the Bolsheviks if they decide to engineer a bloody clash in the capital." The members of the government were almost equally divided on this subject. They also discussed the organization of the Military Revolutionary Committee of the Petrograd Soviet. It was decided to take steps to protect the capital and prevent a Bolshevik uprising. "If an uprising occurs anyway it must be put down, without stopping at anything, even the use of the armed forces, in this case acting in close coordination with the Central Executive Committee [of the Soviets]."[14] That same day Kerensky spoke before the Pre-Parliament. "The Provisional Government is well aware of all current speculations and believes that there is no basis for panic — any attempt to counter the will of the majority and the Provisional Government by a minority will be met with ample resistance."

On the 14th, in a conversation with journalists on the possibility of a Bolshevik uprising, the commander of the Petrograd military district, Col. G.P. Polkovnikov, stated: "We do not have the precise information, and we are being fed a steady diet of rumors. I believe that the Petrograd garrison will have the good sense to refrain from participation in an uprising. In any case we are prepared. All steps will be taken to prevent such an uprising." At a session of the cabinet held on the 16th Polkovnikov stated even more explicitly that "the mood of the Petrograd garrison is generally on the side of the Provisional Government, and there is no need to fear active participation by the garrison in a Bolshevik uprising." On the 17th Polkovnikov, speaking at a closed session of the Pre-Parliament's committee on the struggle with the counterrevolution, joined with Assistant Minister of the Interior Saltykov and the government commissar* of the Petrograd municipal government, Rogovsky, to give assurances once again that all necessary steps had been taken to cover a possible uprising and that no such occurrence would be permitted. "And there will be no 'demonstration,' " announced Kerensky himself, reassuring the journalists. "Agitation in favor of an uprising is not enjoying success in military units, nor with the majority of workers. All necessary steps to curtail excesses have been taken, both by the military and civil authorities." "Nor will the Central Executive Committee permit a demonstration," Gots informed the Committee in turn: "We have enough troops to squelch any riot."

Buchanan wrote in his memoirs "Kerensky . . . had in my recent conversations with him more than once exclaimed: 'I only wish that they would come out, and I will put them down.' "[15] Nabokov mentions something of the sort in his memoirs: "Four or five days prior to the October Bolshevik uprising I asked [Kerensky] frankly at one of our meetings in the Winter Palace about what he thought of the possibility of a Bolshevik uprising, a matter which was under general speculation and discussion at the time. 'I would hold a special

*Commissars were appointed by the Provisional Government, the VTsIK, and eventually the Military Revolutionary Committee to various governmental bodies and military commands. They were to act as official arms of whomever they represented and exert as much control as possible. Eds.

church service if I thought it would make an uprising take place,' he replied. 'Are you sure you can handle it?' 'I have more troops than I need. They will be totally annihilated.' "[16]

So two memoirists (Buchanan's are based on a journal kept by him), apparently quite different in both background and position, make the same assertion. Here is an entry from my own journal: "On the 21st of October I was visited in Moscow by an individual of like political persuasion . . . who at the time occupied a responsible post in one of the ministries. He was complaining of the failure by the Provisional Government to act — the only active individual in the government was Kerenksy. He told me 'confidentially' that Kerensky wished for a Bolshevik uprising expressly for the purpose of destroying them."

I certainly do not intend to imply conscious connivance on the part of the head of the Provisional Government. But these intimate and frequently expressed opinions characterize the personal attitude of Kerensky and that confidence which remained with him up to the last. The "painful agony of revolution" in September and October appeared only in his later reminiscences. His real feelings were much closer to that self-confidence with which the head of government spoke at the August Moscow Conference on the strength of a regime which could permit itself "the luxury of uprisings and conspiracies."

V.B. Stankevich, the Government's chief commissar at the General Headquarters [and a close personal friend of Kerensky], relates that when he arrived in Petrograd from the front on October 24, Kerensky met him in an "elated mood." " 'Well, how do you like Petrograd?' I expressed surprise. 'You mean you are unaware of the fact that we are having an armed uprising?' I broke out laughing, since the streets were completely quiet, without a sign of an uprising or demonstration. He also treated the uprising rather ironically, although with some concern. I said that we must put an end to these constant shocks within the government and take vigorous steps to take care of the Bolsheviks. He replied that he was of like mind and that now no Chernovs would help the Kamenevs or Zinovievs . . . as long as we can cope with an uprising."[17] But there were no doubts that an uprising could be coped with.

Kerensky, and others as well, did fail to appreciate the crisis which was coming to a head. Unfortunately, none of the writers of memoirs said specifically what was proposed by that "non-socialist part" of the government which was informally headed by the Kadet minister of social welfare, Nikolai Kishkin, whose specific objective was to shake the government out of its state of "self-hypnosis" and move it onto the path of "daring." We are able to appraise government activity during this time chiefly from fragmentary newspaper sources and equally fragmentary recollections of various ministers. After the disaster Kerensky had the tendency to place the blame on others, while the former members of his cabinet manifested the inverse tendency to justify their lack of action and absence of foresight. The statements of the ministers are characterized by the clear desire to emphasize that they were worried and had inquired about the situation and that they always received the same stereotyped reply: all necessary steps have been taken and there is no danger.

We cannot deny a certain degree of authoritarianism and tendency toward "sovereign rule" (a characteristic noted by the then Minister of Justice Alexander Zarudnyi at the Democratic Conference), which almost inevitably appeared in Kerensky as a consequence of the idolization of which he had been the object during the first six months of the revolution. Perhaps Sukhanov is not so far from the truth when he speaks of Kerensky's faith in his "providential calling." The cabinet became "spineless" in the absence of its indispensable chairman, and A. A. Demianov cites rather striking examples of this phenomenon. With that "game of ministerial chairs" which went on during the crises of the Provisional Government, naturally the ministers could not feel that they were part of a unified team. Nevertheless, all were mature individuals, not puppets, and all must share equally in the historical responsibility.

Explanation of the fact that the Bolsheviks *were* able to overthrow the Provisional Government must be sought primarily in the psychology of the time, which has been sufficiently delineated. Boiled down, it is represented by a piece of soothing advice given by Deputy Minister of Welfare P. I. Palchinsky to an alarmed query by a prominent representative of the industrial community, "Sleep with your mind at ease."

Apparently Kerensky actually felt that all proper steps had been taken against a possible Bolshevik uprising. At least this is what he indicated in an official conversation by direct wire with General Dukhonin at the general headquarters in Mogilev on the night of October 23-24, when he stated: "My arrival in general has been delayed, not by the fear of disturbances, riots and other such things, for everything has been organized to function in my absence. I have been delayed by the necessity of hastily reorganizing the high-echelon administration in the War Ministry." Mentioning merely in passing the activities of the Military Revolutionary Committee, Kerensky added: "I think that we shall have no trouble handling it."[18]

There is no point in dwelling on a detailed enumeration of those rather formal and purely paper measures for preventing disorders that were taken by the government. These were conventional measures derived from the police manual, where the *ultima ratio* for putting down riots was the imposition of "martial law." During the revolution they were ridiculous. They intimidated no one and were unable to yield any practical results. For example, one cannot read without a smile Polkovnikov's instructions that henceforth sidearms could be obtained only with special permit from the municipal authorities. This was at a time when, in accordance with a decision made during the Kornilov days, five thousand rifles were legally released by order of the chairman of the Petrograd Soviet from the Sestroretsky factory to workers for arming the Red Guard.

In the absence of a properly organized police and administrative apparatus none of the preventive measures had great significance, since many of the government's decisions could not be implemented. This fact to a certain degree justified Buchanan in commenting, "The Government possesses only nominal authority." For example, on October 19 the newspapers reported: "Justice Minister Maliantovich, under orders from Supreme Commander Kerensky, instructed the procurator of the Higher Judicial Tribunal to issue an immediate order for the arrest of Lenin, who according to the information of the Provisional Government was hiding somewhere in Petrograd. The procurator requested the commander of the Petrograd military district, the Provisional Government's Commissar for the Petrograd municipal administration, and the chief of the general and criminal militia to instruct their subordinates to cooperate in the detention and delivery of Lenin to Aleksandrov, investigating magistrate for special matters."

There was also an order to arrest those Bolsheviks who had been freed from prison and were actively agitating for an armed clash. The first to be arrested, of course, would be Trotsky, freed in September on 3,000 rubles bail, which had been paid from funds furnished by the Trade Union Council. On October 11 Ensign Raskolnikov was released, along with others on bail, paid by the Kronstadt Soviet. On the following day Raskolnikov spoke at a political gathering in Kronstadt and appealed for a revolt and the overthrow of the Kerensky government. A similar open appeal was made by Raskolnikov on October 20, at a political gathering at the Modern Circus. But nobody attempted to arrest Raskolnikov, let alone Trotsky, who was chairman of the Petrograd Soviet. At a session of the Pre-Parliament's committee on the struggle with the counterrevolution, a Kadet delegate, Maxim Vinaver, asked why Trotsky had not been arrested. Rogovsky, the government commissar for the Petrograd municipal administration, replied that this was "absolutely impossible, because Trotsky sleeps in military barracks and spends every night in a different one." (Trotsky later said he slept at the Smolny Institute, the Bolshevik party headquarters.)

The procurator might have had at his disposal the militia — the theoretical main support of the government — which had been reorganized (it turned out to be of little value during the July events) and brought up to combat efficiency with 4,000 men in its ranks. But even in this form it failed to inspire confidence that "it would be perfectly capable of putting down a

Bolshevik uprising." It is no wonder that when the chief of the militia, Capt. N. Ivanov, received from the government a belated order to arrest the Military Revolutionary Committee, he simply put it away in his pocket. The militia considered itself to be subordinate to the City Duma and had already assumed a "neutral position" in the political struggle. In actual fact, it might as well not have existed, and the Duma was compelled to organize "volunteer civil protection" of its constituents.

It is quite clear that nothing in this area could hinder the Bolsheviks from "legally" preparing an armed uprising, and on October 21 the Military Revolutionary Committee began to operate in the open. The only realistic step the government could have taken to combat preparations for the uprising was an immediate liquidation of the MRC. During the first days of the committee's existence, this measure could have been effected almost painlessly, probably even without armed resistance.

CHAPTER 3

On the Eve

TRAGIC OPERETTA

The conditions under which the Bolshevik uprising began were dubbed an "operetta" by the memoirist Sukhanov. And he was not far wrong. Reporting to the Petrograd Soviet on October 23 about the latest activities of the Military Revolutionary Committee, Antonov-Oveseenko emphasized that the committee's make-up was "purely functional, non-partisan in nature" and that its job was the organization "of an effective defense" of the capital against the Germans. The capital, he maintained, could not be left unsupervised in the hands of military headquarters, which was "linked with the counterrevolution both covertly and overtly." Thus, the Bolsheviks were stealing into power under the banner of defense. When it was expedient they ignored Lenin's assertion that neither the taking of Riga nor the seizure of Petrograd would make "defensists" out of revolutionary internationalists. "We shall become defensists after power is transferred to the proletariat," he said.

Preparations for seizure of power were made behind the scenes by the "Voyenka," party parlance for the Bolshevik All-Russian Bureau of Military Organizations, which was tightly linked with the Military Revolutionary Committee. The "non-partisan nature" of the latter was purely a fiction, even though it was headed by the Left Socialist Revolutionary Lazimir. (The Left Socialist Revolutionaries had not yet made the final break with their party, but because they held sway in the Petrograd branch of the party, they were able to participate in the work of this manifestly insurrectionary organ.) In fact, the MRC was entirely a Bolshevik creature, having as its objective the maintenance of contact with the Petrograd garrison.

Dispatching its commissars to individual sections of the garrison (allegedly 292 of these commissars were sent out), the committee delegated three commissars to "supervise" at the headquarters of the Petrograd Military

District. They were met with a fair amount of hostility. To the announcement by the delegates that henceforth only those orders for the military
district signed by the commissars would be recognized, the commander of the
Petrograd military district, Polkovnikov, responded categorically that he
would not honor the commissars, that the garrison was under his command,
and that he "would and could do anything that is necessary" with it. The
deputy commander, Captain Kuzmin, who was a Socialist Revolutionary,
threatened the self-appointed commissars with immediate arrest, and they
had to leave. The MRC in turn telephoned a proclamation to the garrison
giving orders that only its instructions be carried out, instructions which
would be transmitted through the regimental commissars. Thus, an open
conflict developed between the headquarters of the military district and the
committee. It was on this day, in fact, October 22, that authority passed into
the hands of the MRC and District Headquarters was for all practical purposes
rendered impotent. On this day the Bolshevik armed uprising began.

Initially, Bolshevik actions were not too bold. The game was a simple one
— to drag things out. At the invitation of District Headquarters the MRC sent
representatives on the 23rd for "negotiations." "This was merely for
'reconnaissance,'" asserts Nevsky. They ascertained the conditions of
agreement and departed. The newspapers reported that at a government
session on the night of the 23rd Kerensky demanded the liquidation of the
Military Revolutionary Committee. But in view of a message from Polkovnikov on the resumption of negotiations with the MRC, the government
decided to limit itself to an ultimatum calling for retraction of the telephoned
proclamation to the garrison and a warning that the military authorities
would take vigorous steps to restore order. This decision was influenced by
the mediation of representatives from the VTsIK, who begged Kerensky to
avoid an open clash, hoping to resolve the conflict peacefully by means of
negotiations between members of the VTsIK and the Bolshevik-dominated
Petrograd Soviet. The compromise consisted of increasing the number of
already existing representatives of the revolutionary democracy at District
Headquarters and of including delegates from the MRC, while headquarters
would not raise objections to the appointment of special regimental
commissars on the condition that the commissars would be subordinate to a
single commissar appointed by the VTsIK. Immediately reassuring words
appeared in the newspapers: "Apparently agreement will be reached."
Trotsky, in the *Recollections of the October Revolution* he published in
1918, says that "Vladimir Il'ich," having read this account, was "furious."
"Can this be true?" Lenin demanded. "No," replied the wily Bolshevik Ulis;
"This is merely to camouflage the game."

However, that night the MRC announced a "basic acceptance of the points
contained in the ultimatum" issued by headquarters. The fact is that in spite

of the proud pronouncement in the Antonov-Ovseenko report to the Petrograd Soviet that the government "does not and will not dare touch the MRC," the strategists at the Smolny Institute were extremely worried about the possibility of active intervention by headquarters and fulfillment of the liquidation threat. Prior to the 24th the MRC citadel was almost defenseless. This was acknowledged by Trotsky himself.[19] The Smolny commandant was rather hostile toward the Bolsheviks. The Bolshevik machine gun crew guarding the seat of the committee was totally incapable of putting up any kind of battle, and the machine guns themselves were not even in serviceable condition. A more dependable machine gun unit was not brought to Smolny until the night of the 24th. Counting its forces, the MRC issued a directive merely of a "defensive nature" — to secure the defense of the approaches to Smolny if the "enemy initiates an offensive."

But the "enemy" did not attack. If one is to believe Kerensky, the military authorities were guided by extraordinary moral and pedagogic considerations. "Although everything was at hand to take immediate, decisive, and vigorous steps," the military authorities "thought it essential first to give people an opportunity to recognize their own conscious or unconscious mistake and give them time, if it was a mistake, to withdraw voluntarily." This statement was made by Kerensky twenty-four hours later in the Pre-Parliament. "The government," he went on, "can be accused of weakness and excessive patience, but in any case, nobody has the right to say that the Provisional Government, during my entire tenure in office, resorted to any coercive measures unless the very existence of the nation was in jeopardy . . . . I prefer in general that the authorities act more slowly, more surely, and at the right moment more decisively."

Subsequently, after his sure method had led to catastrophe, Kerensky in his memoirs had a different explanation to offer for the apparent indecision displayed by the authorities before the Bolshevik uprising. The writers of memoirs (here Kerensky is not alone) place the entire blame for the indecision and disorganized action by District Headquarters on the shoulders of the commander of the Petrograd forces. And it is a fact that Polkovnikov failed to display leadership and organizational ability during the confused days prior to the uprising. Moreover, the "non-socialist" part of the ministry had no confidence in Polkovnikov, as the memoirs of the Kadet Vinaver tell us: "Already vague rumors were going about to the effect that Polkovnikov was in contact with the Bolsheviks." There is no doubt that such rumors about Polkovnikov could have been rife in some circles. Not all sympathized with the tactic of negotiating with the MRC, although the initiator of these talks was certainly not the commander of the Petrograd forces, but higher authorities. One can state with assurance that the testimony of Polkovnikov and his colleagues could not but create a most joyless impression on the

Pre-Parliament commission investigating counterrevolutionary activity: "There was no doubt of an impending uprising and that our defense is in unreliable hands," writes Vinaver, and such was the case.

But in Vinaver's memoirs we see once again the personality of the prime minister advancing to stage front. The features of Kerensky's personality seem to mirror the indecision of government policy. Nabokov also describes some of his traits. "Apparently Kerensky at this time was in a period of depression. It was absolutely impossible to move him to undertake any vigorous measures."

The chief political motif was that of watching and waiting, and in this sense Kerensky was by no means alone. An extraordinary elusiveness is manifested by those who understood the danger and were disturbed by the situation in Petrograd. According to Alexander Izgoev the majority of the Central Committee of the Constitutional Democratic party "merely shrugged their shoulders" when Kishkin and Nabokov reported that "all steps have been taken" and that Kerensky "is awaiting a Bolshevik move in order to take care of them once and for all." Buchanan wrote in his journal on the 23rd that three cabinet ministers who had lunched with him, Tereshchenko, Konovalov, and S.N. Tretiakov, "assured me that the Government had sufficient force behind them to deal with the situation." The ministers were usually rather frank with the British ambassador. The American ambassador, David Francis, told a U.S. Senate investigating committee in 1919 that on the very day the uprising was expected Minister of Foreign Affairs Tereshchenko had assured him that it would be quelled.

The government did not act against the MRC because during the twenty-four hours following the committee's proclamation of October 22 "no real effects" of the orders were observed among the troops. Kerensky made a statement to this effect at a session of the Pre-Parliament. Apparently it was possible to discount the de facto seizure of the arsenal at the Peter and Paul Fortress, the organization of military units for the uprising, seizure of the cruiser *Aurora* in direct disobedience of a government order, preparations for the armed defense of Smolny, and so on.

But the moment to act had come. During the night of the 24th the government did take action. We have no stenographic record of the cabinet meeting that night, and must, therefore, limit ourselves to the newspaper accounts. Minister of Justice Maliantovich ordered court officials to begin an investigation of MRC activities directed against duly constituted authorities, and a special courier was promptly dispatched with an appropriate order to the prosecutor's office. According to an account contained in *Novaia Zhizn'*, several ministers had again proposed the arrest of the Military Revolutionary Committee, but this was opposed by the minister of justice, and the matter was temporarily removed from the agenda. However, it was decided to close down the Bolshevik newspapers *Rabochii Put* and *Rabochii i Soldat,* which had incited rebellion, and to institute legal proceedings against the authors of the inflammatory articles. To equalize the blow struck against the Bolsheviks it was decided to shut down simultaneously the most vociferous newspapers of the opposite political camp, *Novaia Rossiia* and *Zhivoe Slovo*, which were guilty, as the prime minister put it, of agitation and propaganda for the immediate dissolution of the Provisional Government and replacement of the existing system with a dictatorship. An appeal to rebellion and mere agitation were thus treated as if they came under the same articles of the criminal code.

It was not difficult to shut down the "bourgeois" papers. But a more active effort was required to suppress the insurrectionist organs. Pursuant to a government order, the commissar of the Third Rozhdestvenskii District appeared at the Bolshevik newspaper printing plant at 5:30 A.M. with a detachment of cadets from the Second Oranienbaum School and confiscated 800 freshly printed copies of *Rabochii Put*, destroyed the type, and closed and sealed the premises. Having completed their mission, the commissar and his detachment left, and no one was left to guard the insurrectionist's central printing facility. Immediately after their departure a company of the Volynsky Regiment arrived with its commissar and broke open the printing plant. There was no one to put up any resistance, and the Bolsheviks were greatly encouraged.

The government began to mobilize its forces, and District Headquarters was given orders to draw up a detailed plan for crushing the insurrection. Unfortunately, we do not know what the plan was and probably never will. Its primary feature obviously consisted of a few protective measures like those taken during the restless days of the 20th and 22nd of October, when it was rumored that the Bolsheviks intended to initiate an armed uprising and the government divided the city into districts, the defense of which was entrusted to the commanders and committees of the Moscow, Grenadier, Pavlovsky, and Finliandsky regiments. Checkpoints set up by these regiments were to prevent "armed groups of insurrectionists" from entering the downtown section. They were to "vigorously" break up any such group "using weapons if necessary." Several detachments of cadets were summoned to the Winter Palace, a few armed checkpoints were placed about the city, and troops were detailed to several government establishments. An innovation was the opening of the drawbridges across the Neva linking the downtown district with the outlying sections. But no steps were taken to hinder water traffic on the Neva, a step the Bolshevik military specialists had feared.

Kerensky gave orders that all commissars appointed by the Petrograd Soviet be removed "until approved by the government commissar" and that "all garrison units remain in their barracks until they receive orders from District Headquarters." Court-martial for armed mutiny was threatened for all those who appeared on the street carrying arms. This order contained a point that had fatal consequences on another day: officers were ordered to remain in the barracks in case of armed mutiny by any military unit. These orders could no longer intimidate anyone, and the last proclamation by Polkovnikov even took on a somewhat humorous character. District Headquarters ordered automobile owners, under threat of "prosecution to the full extent of the law," to deliver their vehicles immediately to the palace square and put them at the disposal of headquarters in order to prevent arbitrary seizures. Not one automobile was brought to the palace square, and on the morning of the 25th headquarters had a hard time finding its own cars.

That was more or less how the government made its preparations. In this case the "verbal psychosis" indeed engendered "lack of will."

"The enemies of the people went over to the offensive last night," rang an appeal from the Military Revolutionary Committee in response to the actions taken by the government. "They are planning to deal a treacherous blow against the Petrograd Soviet . . . . This campaign by counterrevolutionary conspirators is directed against the All-Russian Congress of Soviets on the eve of its reconvening, against the Constituent Assembly, against the people . . . . The MRC is directing *resistance* to the onslaught of the conspirators . . . . All the conquests and aspirations of the soldiers, workers, and peasants are threatened by great danger. But the forces of the revolution are incalculably superior to those of its foes . . . . The conspirators will be destroyed. There are no vacillations nor doubts. Firmness, steadfastness, stamina, decisiveness! Hail the revolution!"[20]

The appeal to "defense" was able to affect neutral and wavering military units. It could be used also to conceal the MRC's own lack of confidence. The committee appealed to all troop committees and their commissars appointed by the Petrograd Soviet to be constantly vigilant, to be "fully combat-ready," and to await further orders. Thus the committee was clearly hoping for some kind of spontaneous demonstration in order to shift from a defensive position to the offensive. A seemingly continuous political rally was being held in the garrison's units. The Red Guard was already openly being furnished weapons from the arsenal of the Fortress of Peter and Paul, the commandant of which had been placed under arrest, and the government was receiving its first ominous warning in the form of a refusal by a battalion of cyclists to stand guard duty any further at the Winter Palace. The battalion had arrived from the front in July and was considered to be the most reliable unit.

But perhaps an even more significant sign of the times was the daylight appearance at MRC headquarters of a delegation from the City Duma, consisting of two Socialist Revolutionaries, one People's Socialist (a former Trudovik), a Menshevik, and two Bolsheviks. A delegation from the City Duma to people who were supposedly subject to arrest! Trotsky reported the visit at a special meeting of the Petrograd Soviet convened for the purpose of "gathering information." "The delegation asked us," reported Trotsky, according to an account of the matter contained in *Izvestiia,* "what steps were being taken by the Petrograd Soviet to establish order in the city and also informed us that the Provisional Government was planning to transfer authority to the Petrograd City Duma. We replied that the Petrograd Soviet was concerned with protecting the residents of Petrograd and found it possible to coordinate its work with the Petrograd City Duma. We also offered them one seat on the MRC. They asked us if an uprising was being hatched. I replied that . . . an armed conflict today or tomorrow did not come within our plans on the threshold of the All-Russian Congress of Soviets . . . . But if the Government wished to utilize that time remaining before its demise — 24, 48, 72 hours — and moved against us, we would respond with a counteroffensive, blow by blow, steel against iron." Trotsky, to the accompaniment of "stormy applause" by those present, proclaimed that "this is defense, comrades, this is defense." Trotsky emphasized, "The arrest of the Provisional Government is not on the agenda as an independent task." The transfer of power could be effected peaceably. Now everything depended on the congress. "If it falters, the revolutionary regiments will come out, but the rest will waver. Our only hope is [the adoption of] a firm policy [by the congress]." According to the account contained in *Rabochii Put,* Trotsky ended his speech by saying: "Tomorrow the Congress of Soviets opens. It is the job of the garrison and the proletariat to place at the disposal of the congress force sufficient to frustrate government provocation. It is our job to present this force to the congress undamaged and whole."[21]

(On the day following the seizure of power, Trotsky, replying to a comment made from the floor of the Congress of Soviets which pointed out the contradiction between the political formula of the revolt — it should have occurred after the Congress convened — and its reality, said: "If the Congress was surrounded by military cadets, how could it take over authority? In order to carry out this task a party was needed which would seize power from the counterrevolutionaries and would say to you, 'Here is power which you must accept.' ")

In fact, to wait for the Congress was to undertake a risk. The Congress could produce undesired results. Lenin pointed this out in a last-minute appeal to local party leaders, bypassing the central apparatus: "Comrades. I am writing these lines on the evening of the 24th. The situation is extremely critical. It is amply clear that to delay our uprising means death.* With all my

---

*We might note as a curiosity that in later Soviet publications (such as *Days of the Great Proletarian Revolution,* 1937) this warning was attributed to Stalin, who, contrary to fact, was portrayed as the chief leader of the October uprising. Trotsky's direct actions were also credited to Stalin. S.P.M.

heart I assure you, comrades, that at the present moment everything is hanging by a thread, that matters are pending which are not resolved by conferences nor by congresses (not even by congresses of soviets), but exclusively ... by struggle undertaken by the armed masses ... We cannot tarry. Tonight, at any price, we must arrest the government." Otherwise, "we may lose everything .... Who should take over authority? This is no longer important. Let it be assumed by the MRC or another body which will promise to hand over authority only to genuine representatives of the people's interests .... All districts, all regiments, and all forces must mobilize immediately and send a delegation to the MRC, to the Bolshevik Central Committee, insistently demanding that in no case should authority remain in the hands of Kerensky and company on the 25th .... History will not forgive delay if we can win today but risk to lose everything tomorrow ... The purpose of an uprising is to take power; its political aim will become clear after the uprising. It would be a catastrophe or mere formalism to wait for a wavering vote on October 25. The people have the right and the duty to decide issues like that by force, not by voting .... The government is tottering. We must finish it off at all costs. A delay in the uprising means death."[22]

The party membership did not respond to the appeal of their leader. In all the abundant Bolshevik literature on preparations for the October uprising there is not the slightest hint of any popular pressure exerted on the Military Revolutionary Committee. And once again on the evening of the 24th the MRC made the following public statement: "In spite of any and all rumors the MRC announces that it does not exist for the purpose of preparing for and carrying out a seizure of power but rather exclusively to defend the interests of the Petrograd garrison and democracy against counter-revolutionary encroachments."

Of what possible use was this fig leaf at a time when the MRC was already feverishly preparing for an uprising, when the "revolutionary forces" in Kronstadt and Helsinki had been sent a telegram with the coded message, "Send charter," calling on them to rise in support of the rebellion, when Committee commissars had already occupied the central telegraph office, and when the cruiser *Aurora* had been brought to Nikolaievsky Bridge after the arrest of its officers? This was a "military stratagem" at the commencement of a "general battle," stated Trotsky subsequently. He expressed himself quite contemptuously on the "semi-authority" which "awaits a sweep by the broom of history to clear room for genuine rule by a revolutionary people." Trotsky was able to quip: "Comrades, I have been warned that at twelve o'clock the electricity may be shut off. There is no coal in the city. Do not think that means Kerensky is attacking us. It will mean only that Kerensky is not able to furnish lights at Smolny Institute for even two extra hours." Nevertheless, Trotsky did fear that the weak enemy would "make a daring attempt to revive his own corpse," would begin to act, and that then the card house of "defense" (which Trotsky publicly called "solid steel") would not be able to withstand the attack. As for the fig leaves, they were not intended to deceive the government. They were designed for the proletariat, which was to be infused with faith that the government was attempting to "thrust a knife into the back of the revolution."

It is indicative of this strategy that an article by Zinoviev that appeared in *Rabochii Put* on the day of the uprising, October 25, was not at all in the nature of a revolutionary appeal, but was structured on the principle of "defense." "They" have moved to the offensive. Perhaps this is why the Petrograd newspapers did not "notice" the uprising and so disappointed Trotsky. "We do not yet know," stated the People's Socialist *Narodnoe Slovo* on the 25th, "the seriousness of the events which are occurring," for example. "The Bolshevik drums are sounding loudly, but this does not yet mean that their deeds will be loud." In the moderately left-wing newspaper *Dni*, the Menshevik Ivanovich appealed to all to join ranks to crush this latest "adventure" by the Bolsheviks, and in stereotype fashion once more warned of the inevitability, in case the Bolsheviks emerged victorious, of a counterrevolution which would wipe out all democratic elements. But the newspaper at the same time assuaged its readers with the assertion that "Bolshevik circles are becoming more and more inclined toward a bloodless and gradual seizure of power," since it was quite obvious that the garrison would be just as inert as it had been in July and that the "Red" army was "infinitesimally small."

A "HISTORIC CONVERSATION" IN THE PRE-PARLIAMENT

While both sides were mobilizing their forces, the prime minister, following a decision by the cabinet, went to the Pre-Parliament for support. His speech was intended primarily to convince the leftists of the necessity of supporting the government in the struggle that had begun with the MRC. Obviously impelled by tactical considerations, Kerensky made a number of statements in the name of the coalition government for which he was hardly authorized. One statement was to the effect that the government was "discussing in its *final* form the matter of transferring land temporarily to the disposal and control of the land committees prior to the Constituent Assembly." Such draft legislation was actually proposed by the minister of agriculture, Semen Maslov, and the Socialist Revolutionary press agitated for it vociferously. But within the cabinet itself objections had been raised to the proposals, and it was reported in *Delo Naroda* on October 18 that the cabinet had decided to treat this draft legislation only as "raw material." At the same time, implementing such legislation would, to a large degree, only sanction an actual state of affairs. A number of land committees had already seized control of landholdings on their own.

The other statement was that the government intended to send a delegation to Paris in order to bring up to Russia's allies the matter "of the necessity of decisively and precisely defining the aims and objectives of the war, that is the matter of peace."

Kerensky went on to give a legal classification of what was taking place in the capital. "I must classify . . . the obvious, definite, over-all condition of a certain portion of the population of the city of Petrograd as a state of rebellion . . . . In actuality this is an attempt to raise the rabble against the existing order of things, to prevent us from holding the Constituent Assembly, and to bare the Russian front before the massed regiments of Kaiser Wilhelm's mailed fist. The Provisional Government," concluded Kerensky with pathos, "proclaims with full consciousness of its responsibility to the state and the future of this country that those . . . groups and parties which dare raise a hand against the free will of the Russian people . . . will be subject to immediate, decisive, and total liquidation. May the people of Petrograd be aware that they will be met by decisive authority, and perhaps at the last hour or minute reason, conscience, and honor will emerge victorious in the hearts of those who have still preserved them. I ask for the sake of the country — and let the Provisional Council of the Republic forgive me — I *demand* that the Provisional Government receive a reply from you today, at this session, as to whether the government can carry out its duties with the assurance of support from this high assembly."[23]

It would seem that the government was speaking with the tongue of authority, conscious of its strength, both moral and physical. At the last hour Kerensky had found within himself the decisiveness "to keep the promise publicly made by him to Russia in Moscow's Bolshoi Theatre" and to crush the "wave of anarchy," a promise of which Plekhanov in *Edinstvo* reminded him many times. Perhaps "for the first time since the revolution," stated the populist-socialist *Narodnoe Slovo* on the following day, "the authorities have found those words they should have uttered long ago."

During a four-hour recess of the Pre-Parliament the factions held caucuses to draw up a resolution. The Left Socialist Revolutionaries, expressing a lack of confidence in the government, walked out of the Pre-Parliament. A few hours later Trotsky triumphantly reported this to the Petrograd Soviet and announced that the Left Socialist Revolutionary faction was officially sending its representative to the MRC. ("We have found each other in the struggle against a common foe, the counterrevolution," he commented.) Out of the discussions held by the remaining members of the Pre-Parliament two competing resolutions emerged, one proposed by the Kadets and representatives of the cooperatives, and the other by the Menshevik Internationalists and supported only by the Mensheviks and Socialist Revolutionaries. The former contained the promise to support the government. The formulation of the leftists indirectly expressed lack of confidence in the government. It read: "1. The armed uprising under preparation in recent days, having as its aim the seizure of power, threatens to cause civil war, is creating conditions favorable to pogroms, and the mobilization of counterrevolutionary forces, will inevitably frustrate the convocation of the Constituent Assembly, and will lead to new military catastrophes and the death of the revolution in a setting of economic paralysis and total national disintegration. 2. Soil for the success of the above-indicated agitation has been prepared, in addition to the objective conditions of war and disorganization, by the delay in implementing urgent measures; and, therefore, it is essential immediately to pass a decree calling for the transfer of land to the land committees and to take a vigorous stand in regard to foreign-policy with a proposal that the allies announce peace conditions and initiate peace talks. 3. In order to combat the active outbursts of anarchy and pogroms, steps must immediately be taken to eliminate these phenomena and set up in Petrograd for this purpose a "Committee of Public Safety" consisting of representatives of the municipal government and organs of the revolutionary democracy acting in concert with the Provisional Government."[24]

The Bolsheviks were not even mentioned in the resolution. In the balloting it received a plurality of eleven votes due to the abstention of several "moderate" socialists. (The abstention was to a certain extent a result of a technical misunderstanding, according to the explanation given by Chaikovsky to Aldanov; and as noted at the time by *Narodnoe Slovo*, some of the so-called Right Social Revolutionaries voted for the decision of their party faction on formal grounds.) In the Bolshevik press this Pre-Parliament resolution was dubbed a "mobilization of the reactionaries." In reality it refused direct support to the government. Of course, the resolution of an "ephemeral" (to use Martov's expression) institution with the high-sounding name of Council of the Republic, of itself could not significantly influence the outcome of the struggle in the streets of Petrograd. The Pre-Parliament did not enjoy great popularity. Only the position of the Central Executive Committee of Soviets, which had retained authority among the masses, was of any significance. The leaders were the same individuals, but the customary label was important. The Council of the Republic was treated with contemptuous indifference even by its creators — as an "abortion" rising from the unsuccessful Democratic Conference. Dan characterized it thus.

Dan relates in his memoirs that in the prevailing situation Kerensky could not count on a different proposal by the leftists. "It was axiomatic to us," explains Dan, "that it was ridiculous to attempt to fight the Bolsheviks purely with armed force . . . simply because at the time the government did not have such forces and had no prospects of acquiring them. It was an axiom for us that if it was possible to counter the Bolsheviks successfully with something, then it had to be a definite policy. A policy could gather forces around the government that would help it to oppose the Bolsheviks." Listening to Kerensky in the Pre-Parliament, Dan felt only sorrow. "It was sad in view of the overall political situation, and I felt sad for Kerensky personally, who with all his good intentions and sincere devotion to the cause of freedom was so obviously and with closed eyes plunging into the abyss." In the Pre-Parliament Dan, replying as the spokesman of the democrats to Kerensky, said: "While desiring to fight the Bolsheviks as vigorously as possible, we at the same time do not desire to be in the hands of that counterrevolution which wishes to play its game in putting down the uprising . . . . We Mensheviks do not wish a government crisis. We are prepared to defend the Provisional Government to the last drop of blood, but the government should make it possible for the democrats to join ranks around it. The government should clearly define its stand on the vital questions of the moment, a stand the entire nation is awaiting with impatience."[25]

We shall never know what the result would have been if Dan's plan had been achieved. Would the rebellion have dissolved if the soil had been removed from under the feet of the Bolshevik demagogues? The judgment of both the politician and historian on what might have been will be equally arbitrary and subjective. Marxian ideology is inclined to establish immutable alternatives. For example, it was clear in Lenin's mind that ahead lay "either a Kornilov dictatorship or a dictatorship of the proletariat." A more rational approach apparently would seek a "middle course"; in this sense Kerensky's position was correct. But sometimes, when the balancing act no longer works, it may be necessary to jump. This Dan understood.

"The thought came to me," writes Dan, "to go immediately to the session of the cabinet and demand from it in the name of the majority of the members of the Council of the Republic the immediate printing and distribution throughout the city that same night of posters announcing that the Provisional government (1) has demanded that the allied powers immediately propose that all belligerent nations cease military operations and initiate general peace talks; (2) has issued orders by telegraph calling for the transfer of all landlord holdings to the land committees until such time as the agrarian question is finally resolved; (3) has decided to hasten the calling of the Constituent Assembly – I do not remember exactly the dates suggested. Gots, to whom I communicated my idea, was quite enthusiastic. We decided that the chairman of the Council of the Republic should join forces with us . . . . Avkentsiev beat around the bush. He basically did not share the viewpoint expressed in the resolution . . . . He finally gave in to our insistence and half-heartedly joined us." Thus, a delegation of the Pre-Parliament was created which subsequently went to the Winter Palace.

The resolution of the Pre-Parliament was a complete surprise to Kerensky and upset him greatly. As usual Kerensky was hypnotized by appearances — the appearances that he himself wished to see. "At the moment of this universal national explosion," he writes in his memoirs, characterizing the atmosphere at the session, "only a few leaders of parties and groupings closely linked with the two extreme wings of Russian society were unable to overcome their burning hatred for the government of the March Revolution. They continued to sit while the whole meeting rose as one man." These "irreconcilables" were the Menshevik Martov, the Kadet Miliukov, and two or three "Kornilov Cossacks." "Confident that the representatives of the nation would ultimately recognize the extreme gravity and seriousness of the situation, I . . . returned to my urgent work which had been interrupted, confident that in less than an hour and a half I would receive a report concerning the decisions and measures that the Council of the Republic had taken to help the government."[26]

Actually the events turned out quite differently, and Kerensky utters many bitter truths about the short-sightedness of the anti-Bolshevik democracy, which "instead of hastily organizing their forces" wasted so much time "on interminable and useless quarrels and debates." Kerensky merely forgets to say that he himself failed to see the tragic nature of the ripening events until the last minute.

The participants disagree in their description of the conversation which took place in the Winter Palace between the prime minister and the "delegation" from the Pre-Parliament consisting of Dan, Gots, and Avksentiev. Kerensky claims that, hearing the text of the adopted resolution and answering it "with an emotional philippic," he stated that "tomorrow morning the government is resigning." "I do not recall," relates Dan, "that Kerensky said that he was resigning, but in any case, it was apparent from further conversation that these words were not a firm political conclusion he drew from the present state of affairs but rather at most an extreme expression of agitation and upset." "Gots and I," he continued, "really did speak of the deception being perpetrated on Kerensky by the 'reactionary [Petrograd] Headquarters.' But we meant that Headquarters was misleading the government, and perhaps, was deluding itself as well when it issued assurances that it still had loyal units in sufficient number to defeat the Bolsheviks in open battle . . . . We also spoke of the useful nature of the resolution by the Council of the Republic and of the turning point in the mood of the masses, but we spoke in the sense that adoption and implementation by the government of our proposal would lead to a turning point in the mood of the masses, and that in such a case one could count on a swift lessening of the influence of Bolshevik propaganda . . . . We also said that the great majority of Bolsheviks did not want a rebellion and feared it, and that, therefore, the acceptance of our proposal could intensify even among the Bolsheviks the tendency favoring cancellation of the uprising. Our conversation did not last very long. Toward the end Kerensky announced with extreme irritation and arrogance that the government had no need of instruction or advice, that it was time not to talk but to act . . . . We demanded that Kerensky inform the cabinet, which was still in session, of our wish to be admitted to the session and heard. A few minutes later he returned and announced curtly that the cabinet took cognizance of our withdrawal of unconditional cooperation and that it would act independently and handle the rebellion alone."

Preference is purposely given here to the Dan version, since Kerensky in his story excessively stylizes the "historic conversation" to agree with his later mood. But even with the Dan text we must make one important reservation. There is no doubt whatsoever that in it a memoirist rather than a contemporary is evaluating the potential strength of the Bolsheviks. In this case Kerensky is more correct when he ascribes to the "delegation" an attempt to convince him that he was exaggerating the Bolshevik danger. It is sufficient to give one example. That same night Dan spoke once again at the special joint session of the VTsIK and Executive Committee of the Soviets of Peasants' Deputies. The session was attended by Bolsheviks, who left it by the time the resolution was passed. Delegates to the future Congress of Soviets were also present. Dan told the meeting: "Armed clashes do not signify triumph for the revolution, but rather triumph for the counterrevolution, which in the near future will sweep away not only the Bolsheviks but all socialist parties as well . . . The counterrevolution has never been as powerful as it is at the present moment. The bulk of the masses are indifferent to politics . . . The reactionary press is enjoying considerably more success at the factories, plants, and garrisons than the socialists . . . The power organized by the Bolsheviks will be immediately overthrown by mass dissatisfaction."[27]

In this spirit, when taking leave of Kerensky, Dan's "delegation" informed the prime minister that "by its acts" the government was depriving the revolutionary democracy "of the opportunity . . . to lend it effective support." Thus rebuffed, the government could have attempted to rely on those groups which did vote for it in the Council of the Republic (Pre-Parliament). But Kerensky the politician was personally incapable of such a step. Kerensky the memoirist later had much to say about the harm of the "obsession with a future counterrevolution from the right," which paralyzed the "top ranks in revolutionary circles" and reduced to nil all attempts to prevent a Bolshevik take-over. But the spectre of a dictatorship which would do away with the "conquests of the revolution" also held firmly at that time in Kerensky's own mind. In his memoirs he stubbornly defends the plan for an immediate struggle "on two fronts."

It is not known whether pressure was exerted on the prime minister by other members of the government to put together a different kind of political base for a purely military struggle against the Bolsheviks. But as a result of the failure to establish any political base the Provisional Government was totally isolated. The conflict with the Bolsheviks was even made to be a kind of personal "Kerensky cause." This was not just the view of those officers who came to Kerensky's former aide Boris Savinkov on the morning of the 25th with an announcement in the name of an undefined group that they would no longer defend the Provisional Government because they did not wish to fight for Kerensky. The Social Democrat Vladimir Woytinsky, commissar for the northern front, approached the matter from a different viewpoint, but with similar reasoning. By direct wire he persistently questioned Tolstoy, deputy chief of the War Ministry Political Administration, whether the struggle against the Bolsheviks was a cause pursued by Kerensky and the group of bold individuals in his entourage or a cause of all democrats.

Almost from the outset the "Kerensky cause" was doomed to failure, for he had no real forces at his disposal.

THE MOBILIZATION OF FORCES

No matter how one looked at it, at the moment there was only one real matter on the agenda, that of resisting the Bolshevik onslaught. It would seem natural that during these decisive hours the military command should have been headed by a man enjoying authority. Perhaps this was psychologically difficult after the Kornilov "putsch," but not impossible. "By rights," comments Aldanov, "leadership should have gone to General Alekseev. But the old general, accustomed to a different kind of war, considered the cause totally hopeless." The fact remains that nobody invited General Alekseev to assume command. If General Alekseev had headed the defense of the government his name alone could have attracted many military units. The newspaper *Obshchee Delo* carried a significant conversation between Alekseev and Tereshchenko that occurred on October 20, and Nikolai Kulman, who was an eye-witness, confirmed in his 1921 memoirs the "absolute accuracy" of the conversation. "Tell the Government," said Alekseev, "that there are at least 15,000 officers in Petrograd at the present moment. If permission is granted, by tomorrow 5,000 of them under my command will be protecting the Provisional Government." Peter Struve, writing later in the journal *Vozrozhdenie,* stated that Alekseev "was spoiling for a fight and if . . . the Provisional Government had appealed to him he would have organized resistance and would have taken upon himself command of the battle. But none of those who still possessed any means of struggle turned to him." There can be no doubt as to Alekseev's attitude. The general, who had been forced to remain inactive during the critical July days, offered his services to the government. "I cannot stand by idle while my country is dying," he wrote Prince Lvov.

What, indeed, happened to the officer corps on October 25? It is hardly likely that many officers would come to the defense of the Provisional Government on their own initiative, since they lacked sympathy for it. In the opinion of General Simansky, the majority "did not see any particular difference between the last two or three months of the Kerensky regime and the approaching hegemony of the Bolsheviks." Colonel Korenev, who was close to the government leaders because of his work on the Special Commission investigating activities of the former Imperial administration, said that during this time individual officers and entire groups of officers returning from the front had come to him and expressed a readiness to act against the Bolsheviks. It was necessary merely to call them together and organize them. Officers from the front continued to lounge about helplessly, filling up hotels and dormitories, not knowing what to do with themselves. or took refuge in their rooms, shrugging their shoulders hopelessly. The situation was somewhat similar among the officers of the local garrison. Some (to borrow Trotsky's expression), wandered about the barracks like "sleep-drugged flies" precisely carrying out the orders of headquarters; others sat it out at home, some voluntarily and others under house arrest. Here is a vignette related by the MRC-appointed commissar of the Guards Reserve Engineer Battalion. Receiving orders to bring his unit to "combat readiness" on the 24th, the commissar called a meeting of the battalion committee. Almost all the officers, headed by the battalion commander, replied that in view of the instructions from their superiors they "could not submit" to the Military Revolutionary Committee, but they would not "interfere." Only two agreed to go along with the Bolsheviks. It was decided to place the officers who refused under house arrest, "each in his quarters," and each was required to sign a statement that he "would not leave until instructed to do so." Finally, there were some who, arranging a cozy sanctuary for themselves in neutral regiments, voluntarily arrested themselves. A frightful picture of drunken orgies is described in the memoirs of Alexander Sinegub, who at the time was an adjutant serving in the Engineer Corps Ensign School.

Finding it impossible to mobilize even one organized military unit for the defense of the government (and were any such attempts made at all?), headquarters had both the time and opportunity at least to prepare the cadets in the military academies. The fact that on October 25 so few cadets appeared on the palace square speaks for itself. There would have been even fewer had some cadets not gravitated to the scene on their own initiative.

Once again the memoirs of Sinegub serve as a fine illustration. A night telegram from headquarters with instructions to move out on the 25th to the

Winter Palace almost took the Engineer Corps Ensign School by complete surprise. Their machine guns had not been put in order; the officer in charge of weapons had not been at the school in two days. The school council on the very eve of the uprising had not even decided what attitude the cadets should have in regard to the "current moment" and toward the Provisional Government. A meeting was held with speeches and resolutions. The school rose to the occasion. Only three out of 800 persons remained behind. The cadets came to the Winter Palace as a combat unit. The huge square was empty. "The slight paleness of the faces and the confused, searching looks revealed more eloquently than words what was going on in their minds . . . . They had expected to encounter something quite different."

General Mikhail Diterikhs, the deputy chief of staff of the supreme commander, talked from General Headquarters in Mogilev with Petrograd on the 25th by the direct line, and expressed puzzlement. "Why are the government forces so infinitesimally small?" These forces, according to information given him by the headquarters commissar, "totaled two and a half cadet schools, a battery from the Mikhailovsky Artillery Academy, and two armored cars." (The Bolsheviks had estimated potential cadet forces at four to five thousand.) "Today I received from the commissar of the Cossack forces," claimed Diterikhs, "the assurance of total loyalty on the part of the First Don Cossack Regiment, and part of the Fourteenth, while only the Fourth Don Regiment fails to inspire confidence. What is the Konstantinovsky School doing, and what about the Nikolaievsky Cavalry School? Surely more will be found. I believe that we can find sufficient forces, but proper organization must be employed until troops begin moving in from the front." It is quite obvious that the cadet schools had not been brought to "combat readiness" beforehand. This explains Savinkov's surprise when on the morning of the 25th he noticed on Nevsky Prospect the usual large number of cadets: "I drew the conclusion that the cadets had not been ordered to remain in their barracks and that they therefore could not be assembled in case of a Bolshevik attack on the Winter Palace." The fact that four days later an active part in the fighting was taken by those very schools (Vladimirsky, Pavlovsky, Nikolaievsky), which were absent during the defense of the Winter Palace on the 25th, would seem to prove the total lack of organization in the defense of the government. Yet the Pavlovsky School was considered by the Bolsheviks to be "number one in its counterrevolutionary attitude." The Nikolaievsky Cavalry School was, according to General Polovtsov, the most "reliable reserve at the disposal of the Government."

There were still the Cossacks, the only part of the Petrograd garrison which had sworn loyalty to the Provisional Government. The greatest hopes rested upon them during these troubled days. But they were perhaps the most wary in respect to the prime minister personally, which was why the Cossack faction in the Pre-Parliament padded its expression of confidence in the government with reservations. Not long before the decisive session of the Pre-Parliament, on October 17 Kerensky was visited by delegates of the Don Cossacks for the purpose of elucidating the relationship of the government with the Cossacks. The delegation, mentioning the lack of Cossack confidence in a government that the soviets were leading around by the nose, demanded that the government reinstate Ataman Kaledin as troop commander with full authority and openly acknowledge the injustice done to the Don Cossacks. Kerensky promised that within the next few days he would make an official announcement reversing his decision on Kaledin and terming his dismissal an unfortunate misunderstanding. But the announcement was not made in time. It was not until October 23 that the special board of inquiry into the Kornilov affair decided that General Kaledin had not participated in the Kornilov putsch. A local incident intensified the dissatisfaction. While at the suggestion of the troop commander a Cossack religious procession planned for October 22 was cancelled, there was no cancellation of the "Day of the Petrograd Soviet" — that is, the pro-Bolshevik demonstration — and the MRC hastened to announce that the Cossack demonstration had been cancelled at its insistence. This showed once again the dependence of the government on the soviets.

In general the attitude of the Cossacks about the imminent Bolshevik uprising was passive. A critical moment came on the night of October 24-25. In spite of repeated demands by the Military District Headquarters, the Cossacks did not saddle their mounts. "At midnight," relates Kerensky, "after the 'historic conversation' with Dan, a delegation from the Cossack regiments, consisting of two or three officers and an equal number of men from the ranks, came to the Winter Palace." The delegation informed him that the "Cossack regiments will defend the government only" if they received personal assurances from Kerensky that "this time Cossack blood will not be shed in vain as it was in July, when sufficiently vigorous steps were not taken against the Bolsheviks." Kerensky reports that "the delegates particularly insisted that the Cossacks would fight only on *my personal* order." Following explanations by Kerensky about what happened in July, the delegates "categorically" stated that "all their regiments in Petrograd would carry out their duty." Kerensky thereupon signed an order commanding the Cossacks to place themselves at the disposal of the district military staff. "At this moment, at one o'clock in the morning on October 25, I had not the slightest doubt that these three Don Cossack regiments would hold to their oath, and I immediately sent one of my adjutants to District headquarters to inform them that they could count on the Cossacks .... Once again I made a bad miscalculation. I did not know that while I was talking with the delegates from the regiments, the Council of Cossack

Troops, meeting throughout the night, came out vigorously for the neutrality of the Cossacks in the struggle between the Provisional Government and the insurgent Bolsheviks."[28]

In Kerensky's opinion the Council's decision was part of a "strategic plan" to overthrow the government by using the Bolsheviks. This conclusion is somewhat hasty. It is quite obvious that the Cossack delegation came to the Winter Palace for the purpose of obtaining information and that it was the impulsiveness of the prime minister which caused him to jump to conclusions. In the situation prevailing at the Winter Palace at the time, the delegation was unable to get a good picture of what forces the government had at its disposal to put down an insurrection. Probably the impression given by the wavering regimental representatives who met with the Council of Cossack Troops that night shifted the balance in favor of "neutrality." Moreover, the wording of the order signed by the district chief of staff, Gen. Yakov Bagratuni, and the VTsIK-appointed commissar at district headquarters, Malevsky, could hardly have made a favorable impression on the leaders of the Council of Cossack Troops. "In the name of freedom, the honor, and the glory of our native land" the Supreme Commander-in-Chief appealed to the First, Fourth, and Fourteenth Cossack regiments to support the "Central Executive Committee of the Soviets, Revolutionary Democracy, the Provisional Government and to save perishing Russia." [In Cossack minds the "honor and glory" of Russia did not mix with the Central Executive Committee of Soviets.]

Publishing his reminiscenses of that period, the acting chairman of the Council of Cossack Troops, Lt. Col. A. Grekov, describes in a somewhat different manner the conditions under which the decision was taken not to act. On the night before the revolt a member of the Council of Cossack Troops, Lieutenant Kalmykov, who was acting as liaison officer with the government, brought the order to act. A council member named Shamshin was sent to the regiments with this order. For a long time the regiments did not render a direct reply. Then a general meeting of the Council was arranged with representatives from the regiments, and the decision was made to act under the following conditions: the regiments must be given a sufficient number of machine guns; the Cossack units located at industrial plants must be recalled to their regiments; armored vehicles must be assigned to each regiment; infantry must act in conjunction with the Cossacks. With these directives Grekov and Kalmykov went to the Winter Palace, where a promise was made to meet all demands. On the basis of this agreement two Cossack cavalry squadrons and the machine-gun squad of the Fourteenth Regiment were sent to guard the Winter Palace. It was assumed that the remaining regiments would act when the demands were met. However, the next day at five o'clock in the afternoon it was decided at another meeting of the Council with regimental representatives to recall the two squadrons and not to participate in putting down the Bolshevik uprising, since the conditions requested by the regiments had not been met.[29] One should bear in mind, that use of Grekov's carelessly compiled memoirs can be made only with great caution. He makes major chronological mistakes. For example, the Cossack's final refusal did not occur until later in the day on the 25th, when the balance of power was clearly no longer in the government's favor. But in general there is evidence to support his version.

The refusal by the Cossacks was tragic indeed, but they were not the only ones to show what Kerensky called "total, almost universal, lack of comprehension of the fatal significance of developing events." In their case, lack of understanding grew from mutual distrust. The French journalist Claude Anet, a direct observer of these events, commented at the time that the Cossacks feared Kerensky and Kerensky feared the Cossacks. In Grekov's memoirs we find indications that the Cossack initiative encountered opposition in the Petrograd military command, and mutual distrust is confirmed by a record made by Buchanan on November 1 of words spoken by Verkhovsky: "He said that Kerensky had not wanted the Cossacks to suppress the rising by themselves, as that would have meant the end of the revolution."

By the time the Bolshevik units began to advance in various districts and to occupy government buildings, the Provisional Government in Petrograd had practically nobody to defend it, except cadets and shock troops from the Women's Volunteer Battalion who had arrived at the palace square on the previous evening. "The government," wrote Buchanan in his journal, "has not taken the trouble to organize detachments for its own protection." The French Ambassador, Joseph Noulens, expressed similar amazement.

It is true that there was the prospect of help from troops that supposedly had already been recalled from the front. This was the general belief, and the MRC was extremely worried by the possibility of such a shift of troops. This uneasiness was expressed in the Bolshevik press and by statements issued by the MRC. Kerensky himself relates that he was not counting on "a garrison totally demoralized by the Kornilov adventure; troops were supposed to be sent on my order from the front as soon as possible, and the first trains from the northern front were to arrive in the capital on October 24."

But one can state definitely that until the night before the 25th of October no real orders were issued for the immediate withdrawal of troops from the front. Speaking by direct wire with General Dukhonin at General Headquarters in Mogilev on the 23rd, Kerensky expressed full assurance that everything was well organized in Petrograd and that they would have no trouble dealing with the Bolsheviks. Their conversation touched upon many subjects. But there was no mention of sending troops from the front. The prime minister asked only that 150 officers be sent to supplement the militia in the provinces. On the following day Dukhonin was informed that he was not to leave his headquarters "until so notified." On October 23 General Cheremisov, commander of the northern front, was summoned to Petrograd to discuss the conflict between the headquarters of the military district and the Petrograd Soviet. The general arrived together with northern front commissar Woytinsky, who, *Den* reported, was "very optimistic in mood." Claiming for himself the initiative of having come, Cheremisov in his brief memoirs states that he was a person in a somewhat exceptional position. By an order issued on October 17, Petrograd, Kronstadt, and Finland were put under the jurisdiction of the commander in chief of the northern front, a goal which Kornilov had tried to achieve earlier. However, authority to guard the capital's security was retained by the government. Cheremisov was worried that Kerensky, a person unacquainted with military details, might err in his timing if he was counting on bringing in some military units in case of a Bolshevik uprising. According to Cheremisov, he received the reply that the government would handle the situation with those troops currently in the capital. It is probable that he would have received approximately the same reply from the cabinet because of the previous decision that it was unnecessary "to assign special troop units to protect the Provisional Government and the city." Noulens assures us that on the 22nd Kerensky, in response to his question as to what steps the government had taken for putting down an insurrection, replied that several divisions were already approaching Petrograd. The ambassador claims that it was obvious from the statement made by the prime minister that nothing at all had been organized. The only troops moving toward Petrograd were those of the Fifth Cyclist Battalion, which was billeted in Proskurov on the southwestern front and this apparently was not in connection with the emergency measures being taken for the expected Bolshevik uprising. It was not until 2:20 in the morning of October 25 that General Levitsky, Kerensky's aide, passed on to Dukhonin an order for Cheremisov that Cossack units in Finland and the First Don Cossack Division on the northern front be sent to Petrograd. In case it was impossible to transfer the troops by rail, they were to be marched in. Dukhonin asked why the telegram had not been dispatched earlier. Levitsky replied, "Only now has it become possible to reach an agreement with the Cossacks."

THE "CONSPIRACY" AT DISTRICT HEADQUARTERS

In the thickening dusk of the 24th of October there was a certain amount of alarm in the city. "High society disappeared from the streets," recalls the Bolshevik Alexander Shliapnikov. In the downtown section armored cars were crawling along, "whistling ominously." Clashes began at the raised bridges between cadet patrols and Red Guards, who appeared under the protection of the cruiser *Aurora* to lower the bridges. These were perhaps the few hours when the capital waited in frozen silence for the coming events. On the next day, on the very eve of the revolution, the Petrograd theaters and movie houses were already choked with people again. "As if oblivious to anything unusual taking place in the capital," noted a reporter from *Narodnoe Slovo*, "the public jammed the sidewalks of Nevsky Prospekt that evening, heading for the theaters and other places of amusement."

A session of government was taking place in the Winter Palace under the chairmanship of Konovalov. Kerensky was absent. It began calmly – perhaps even too calmly – with minor matters and with approval of some articles in an agrarian bill. Midnight was approaching. According to the rules the deputy ministers present should have left – a closed session was beginning, under the chairmanship of Kerensky himself. The chairman was "nervous, upset, kept jumping up from the chair and striding about the hall." In his memoirs State Comptroller Sergei Smirnov described the last session of the government in an epic manner by saying almost nothing about it at all. Kerensky's pronouncements, he noted, did not serve to calm all those present and "many of us were seized by alarm for the imminent future." This is all the minister was able to say. Reading Smirnov's brief memoirs, it is quite impossible to picture the "tense, nervous atmosphere at that night session" about which Kerensky speaks. Smirnov admits that "some of the so-called rightist members of the government quite harshly criticized the 'indecision' and 'passivity' of the higher military authorities, totally ignoring the fact that we had to act all this time between the hammer of the rightists and anvil of the leftist Bolsheviks." One should note that these severe critics did not make the slightest attempt to participate actively in organizing a struggle against the growing uprising.

The session ended between one and two in the morning, and all the ministers left for home. On the way, the minister for religious affairs, Anton Kartashov, and the chief of administration, Galperin, were detained by troops from the Pavlovsky Guards Regiment, which had posted checkpoints on Millionnaya Street. Only the prime minister and his deputy remained in the Winter Palace.

To help round out the picture of events at this time in the Winter Palace, we can draw upon the brief comments contained in the diary of P. I. Palchinsky, a deputy minister who was put in command of the defense of the Winter Palace on the 25th. Written for the benefit of the author himself, these entries are too brief to make it possible for us to know exactly what was happening, but they do enable us to shade in certain lines essential to revise and correct Kerensky's memoirs. Palchinsky notes the total lack of any plan for defense of the government and the hopelessness of the commander of the Petrograd military district, Colonel Polkovnikov. All of Polkovnikov's hopes were pinned on the assumption that the enemy would not take a "reckless step." District Headquarters kept its eyes on the Winter Palace and awaited orders from Kerensky. In short, things were in a complete mess. Attempts by Palchinsky to introduce order and system into the leadership failed. Apparently Palchinsky insisted on the removal of Polkovnikov. No decisions were made, and Palchinsky headed homeward about two in the morning with a feeling of hopelessness.[30]

"Immediately after the Government session was over," recollected Kerensky, "the military commander came to me accompanied by his chief of staff. He proposed that an expedition be organized to seize Smolny, the Bolshevik headquarters. Of course this plan received my approval at once, and I insisted that it be implemented immediately. During this conversation I paid closer attention to the strange and ambiguous behavior of Colonel Polkovnikov . . . to the glaring contradiction between his extremely optimistic and reassuring reports and the sad reality with which I was already acquainted." Perhaps Kerensky was displaying unaccustomed acumen. Obviously the plan for an expedition to seize Smolny could have been devised at headquarters only because Kerensky himself had assured headquarters that it "could rely completely on the Cossacks." In the prevailing situation three Cossack regiments meant a lot, if not everything. But was headquarters really fully confident that the Cossacks would act? This may be the reason for that "ambiguity" seen by Kerensky.

Kerensky himself names the source that opened his eyes. While he was conferring with Polkovnikov, Rogovsky, the government commissar attached to the municipal administration, appeared with "exceedingly alarming news." A large number of ships from the Baltic Fleet had entered the Neva in a battle formation, and the Nikolaievsky Bridge had been taken by a group of insurgents, who were moving toward the Palace Bridge. "Rogovsky communicated to me in private the observation made *time and time again* by him: headquarters . . . was watching the events as they took place with total indifference, displaying no action whatsoever." (We should not forget that the Socialist Revolutionary Kuzmin was the deputy commander at headquarters, and Palchinsky's diary notes the "obvious vacillation on the part of the VTsIK commissar and his fear of taking active part in any measures.") Kerensky continues, "Not a moment was to be lost." Kerensky and Konovalov set out for headquarters. "The headquarters building was filled with officers of all ages and ranks, and by delegates from various military units. Here and there among the crowd of military men civilians whom nobody could identify were darting about." A "detailed report" by Polkovnikov on the state of affairs finally convinced the ministers that it was no longer possible to rely on the commanding officer nor on the majority of his staff officers. "I had to take command immediately, but no longer for offensive operations against the insurgents, but rather to defend the government itself." Kerensky speaks quite vaguely in his memoirs about his reorganization of headquarters. Apparently Polkovnikov was in fact removed from command, which was transferred to Kerensky, who began to telephone all those whose presence seemed essential to him. Then Kerensky "decided to call in the military organizations of the parties, particularly the rather large Socialist Revolutionary organization."[31]

In a state bordering on hysteria, which was apparently caused by extreme nervous tension and fatigue, Kerensky himself was responsible for the disorganization at headquarters (at least that's the impression given by his own memoirs). And is it not primarily the actions of Kerensky himself that explain the tense atmosphere created at headquarters by morning? According to Kerensky, he "subsequently" found out that some of the officers, "at the instigation of Polkovnikov," had begun to agitate for the arrest of the prime minister. "An insane idea captured many minds at the time: without Kerensky we shall be able to take care of the Bolsheviks more easily and rapidly, and we shall be able without difficulty to finally create that so-called strong government. And there is no doubt whatsoever that during the entire night Colonel Polkovnikov and several other staff officers from the district were in constant contact with anti-government rightist organizations, whose activities in the city had become intensified at that time." We do not know where Kerensky obtained this assailable information. It is impossible to unearth any corroborating data. Proof of that intense activity by "anti-government rightist organizations" remains particularly elusive. If such did exist, it was only the small Purishkevich conspiratorial military-monarchist organization, which was soon exposed by the triumphant Bolsheviks. One thing can be said about the Purishkevich organization: its members, as we shall see, fought in the ranks of the few defenders of the government and, consequently, they could not have directed a "strategic plan" for letting the Bolsheviks overthrow the government — a plan which was in fact born in the tired imagination of a politician and supported by a self-justifying memoirist. The attempt by a headquarters dispirited by Kerensky to make contact with organizations "in town" should have been viewed by him in a positive light, for if it had been successful it would have dispelled that ominous atmosphere of total isolation which enveloped the government.

The practical steps taken by the prime minister led to a situation as a result of which several hours later the headquarters building was almost empty, whereas just the night before it had been jammed with officers of all ages and ranks and delegates from various military units. The young defenders of the Winter Palace became alarmed by the "stifling atmosphere" (Kerensky's words) of distrust. Their "firmness of spirit" was wavering. Yet another disappointment awaited Kerensky. "Party combat forces not only failed to appear at headquarters," Kerensky reports, "but even in town they failed to display any activity. This fact, puzzling at first glance, is quite easily explained. The party centers, carried away by interminable negotiations with Smolny and placing considerably higher expectations on the authority of 'resolutions' than the force of bayonets, were tardy in finding the time to issue appropriate orders." But, perhaps, they neither wished nor could do so? According to the secretary of the Military Commission of the Central Committee of the Socialist Revolutionary party, Broun, the Central Committee issued no instructions calling for action against the Bolsheviks. Stankevich claims that when he spoke in the corridors of the Mariinsky Palace about the necessity of organizing civil defense among the university students, the Mensheviks began to avoid him like the plague. As far as the party combat forces are concerned, one can only say that they probably either existed only on paper or, more likely, in the imagination of memoirists. But even if they did exist, at this moment total confusion reigned in the Central Committee of the party to which the prime minister belonged. After all, the Petrograd organization of the Socialist Revolutionary party, which was the only organization actually capable of furnishing the required troops, had just proclaimed itself neutral in the struggle with the Bolsheviks. There was nobody to mobilize. According to Semenov, there were no more than eighty "armed volunteers" in the Socialist Revolutionary party even when the party subsequently was preparing to defend the Constituent Assembly.

Kerensky later delivered many philippics against the party "adepts," who had spent the entire night "in endless debates about various formulas which could constitute the foundation for reconciliation and for the liquidation of the uprising." "I must confess that the Bolsheviks acted at that time with greater energy and with no less skill. At the time when the uprising was in full swing . . . several Bolshevik leaders, specially appointed to do so, not unsuccessfully endeavored to force the leaders of the revolutionary democracy to look and see nothing, to listen and hear nothing."

These vague hints, along with Trotsky's boasting about the skilled policy he was conducting, "rocking to sleep" with legalisms both the government and the "stellar chamber" (that is, the VTsIK leaders), led to the birth of a legend, which appeared in a later edition of Miliukov's study, about last-minute negotiations during the night of the 25th conducted by the Socialist Revolutionaries and Mensheviks with the Bolsheviks. There were never any such talks. The wizards of the revolutionary democracy spent the night at an emergency session chaired by Gots of the VTsIK and the Executive Committee of the Soviets of Peasants' Deputies.

KERENSKY'S DEPARTURE

The morning of October 25 finally came. Exhausted by their nerve-racking work throughout the night, Kerensky and Konovalov returned to the Winter Palace at 7:00 A.M. to get some sleep. Two hours later they were on their feet again. An urgent message had arrived. Telephone communications between the Winter Palace and the city had been interrupted, and the Palace Bridge, under the windows of the rooms where Kerensky was resting, had been seized by armed sailors. "Nothing had changed" at District Headquarters, Kerensky says. The approaches to the palace and to headquarters "were totally unprotected," which explains why the locks of the armored vehicles disappeared so easily that night. "Panic broke out." According to Kerensky, a delegation of cadets guarding the palace appeared with the announcement that they were prepared to carry out their duty only if "there is some hope that some kind of reinforcements will arrive." Under these conditions, "there was only one thing to do: to set out, without losing a minute, to meet the columns of troops which had bogged down somewhere near Gatchina and to prod them onward to Petrograd . . . . I resolved to make my way past the Bolshevik armed checkpoints. After some thought we decided to stake all on one ploy. In order to lull to sleep any suspicions we decided to act quite openly. I ordered my excellent open touring car to be brought from the garage," and "for the last time shaking the hand of Kishkin, who had taken over direction of the defense of the capital during my absence, I walked out with a look of great unconcern into the headquarters courtyard, accompanied by my companions." There follows a description of Kerensky's departure. "Red patrols and detachments were everywhere. Of course everyone on the street − passersby and soldiers − recognized me immediately. Military personnel stood at attention as if in truth nothing had happened. I saluted as always, somewhat casually and with a slight smile."[32]

At the moment of Kerensky's departure, supposed representatives arrived from the British and, as far as Kerensky could recall at the time he wrote his memoirs, the American embassies, and told him that the envoys of the Allied Powers would like the ministerial automobile to proceed "under the American flag." Kerensky "accepted this proposal with gratitude, as proof of the interest of the Allies in the Russian Provisional Government." But since the American flag could only attract quite undesired attention to the travelers, an officer who was to keep at a "respectable distance" went along with the flag in an automobile "which just happened to be American."

In these pages of reminiscences there is, as we have seen, a certain emphasis, whereas in reality the departure of the prime minister was of a somewhat different character. Even the details are different. Miliukov deals at length with the matter of the automobile and cites the memoirs of American Ambassador Francis, which attest that nothing had been said by the Allies about making an automobile available to Kerensky. Some officer "seized" the automobile of the embassy secretary for Kerensky's needs, a fact which was confirmed by Kerensky himself when the owner of the car went to headquarters for an explanation. The embassy secretary bowed to the inevitable and contented himself with a protest against use of the American flag.

The officer who drove the American automobile, Ensign Knirsha, a lawyer, was later arrested by the Bolsheviks and related the entire incident in detail. His story is not without interest. It turned out to be exceedingly difficult to obtain two automobiles for Kerensky's journey to the front. The headquarters quartermaster, General Paradelov, had already tried unsuccessfully to obtain automobiles for commissar Malevsky and for the representative of the Soviet of Peasants' Deputies, Mazurenko, who were to meet the troops proceeding to Petrograd. Polkovnikov suggested that a vehicle be obtained at one of the embassies. Knirsha appealed to the Italians, but they had no cars. He went empty-handed to the chief of the militia, Prince Sidamon-Eristov, and together they set out to search further around Petrograd, as a result of which they acquired an automobile that was standing in front of the American embassy. From that point on the story corresponds to the Francis version, which is almost identical to Buchanan's account. Kerensky was, in fact, given an automobile assigned to the War Ministry Political Office. Its delivery was not accomplished without difficulty, however. The vehicle could not be moved due to an empty tank. "Then," testifies Knirsha, "I went into the headquarters courtyard, filled a can with gasoline myself, and sent the motor pool clerk in a cab with the gasoline to the Political Office." According to Knirsha, those persons driving the ministerial Pierce-Arrow insisted that the vehicle sporting the American flag should head up the procession, but this was impossible due to ignorance of the route to be followed. Along the way the American flag came loose, and Knirsha hid it away.[33]

Kerensky succeeded in leaving town. There were no military trains from the front in Gatchina, so it was decided to travel on to Luga, in the direction of Pskov. "As if heeding some inner voice," Kerensky ordered that they set out immediately. The behavior of the commandant in whose quarters they were stopping over seemed "extremely strange" to him. "We left in time. Five minutes after our departure an automobile bedecked with a red flag drove into the courtyard. It contained members of the local military revolutionary committee, who had come to arrest me. It appears that there were traitors in Petrograd, at headquarters, who had succeeded in informing Smolny of my departure for Gatchina." Apparently Kerensky was told this later. Nobody on his staff betrayed him. An arrest order was indeed sent out, but much later — to Pskov, where Kerensky had gone.

Kerensky's departure from Petrograd not only had a more prosaic character than portrayed by the author of the memoirs, but there was even a shade of excessive haste, creating a negative impression on some ministers. That day Nabokov visited the Winter Palace. "Tretiakov," he relates, "sat next to me on the sofa and said indignantly that Kerensky had abandoned and betrayed them."

Kerensky had left to meet the troops proceeding to the capital from the front. The first column comprised cyclists from the western front, who had almost reached Petrograd and had stopped or been detained some forty miles short at Peredolskaia station. Nobody had come out to meet them, although Dukhonin and Diterikhs considered it "essential" to send out particularly reliable persons to meet them two or three stations from the capital. That evening Commissar of the Northern Front Woytinsky reported that the cyclists "were met by nobody, contrary to my instructions, and we have information indicating that their condition has taken a sharp turn for the worse."

CHAPTER **4**

The 25th of October

A PLAY "FROM THE SCORE"

On the night of October 24-25 the Military Revolutionary Committee initiated open action "following a prearranged plan." The revolt was conducted "from the score." "Each gear of revolutionary power was brought into movement and placed in the appropriate spot."

The above quotations were written by a supposedly authoritative memoirist and one of the chief actors in the preparation and conduct of the Petrograd uprising – Nikolai Podvoisky. But even Trotsky in his history of the revolution confesses that the treatment in Soviet literature of military operations conducted during those days is "not critical" but rather "apologetic" in nature. It is strange that a carefully prepared plan would be so completely forgotten in its very first stages, and that at subsequent "evenings of recollections" the leaders of and participants in the uprising would be so uncertain about the timing and main events. Trotsky himself could not recall what the final plan was.

We shall, however, let the "apologists" tell about the plan. A special three-man committee consisting of Podvoisky, Antonov-Ovseenko, and G.I. Chudnovsky was appointed by the MRC to direct military operations against the government. They planned to surround the Winter Palace with a cordon of reliable troops during the night session of the cabinet on October 24-25 and to arrest all the ministers. In case of resistance they were to compel the government to surrender by directing artillery fire on the Winter Palace from the cruisers *Aurora* and *Dawn of Freedom,* as well as point-blank fire from the Peter and Paul Fortress. Podvoisky gives us a detailed topographic diagram of the proposed movement of "dependable" regiments and battalions and an exposition of tactical assignments given to various units. But the plan of a night attack was not carried out, due to "defects inevitable in all large-scale operations in which a major role is assigned to enthusiasm."

"Improvised troop control, lack of communication, and many other circumstances made it impossible to begin the first troop movements toward the Winter Palace before six or seven o'clock the next morning."

The "many other circumstances" consisted of the fact that there were no dependable units in the Petrograd garrison. At the MRC session held on the day of the uprising, Podvoisky himself listed the numerous units that had declared their neutrality: three Cossack regiments, the artillery, the cavalry regiments, the Semenovsky, Izmaylovsky and Preobrazhensky infantry regiments, a regiment of engineers, a cyclist battalion, an armored car detachment, and others. In the accounts of the memoirists – including Podvoisky himself – the Preobrazhensky and Izmaylovsky regiments figure among those active in the uprising, and the Preobrazhensky barracks even became one of the three insurgent headquarters. But the true attitude of the Preobrazhensky has been more accurately outlined in the journal of a volunteer named Militsyn. Listening to conversations on the days preceding the revolt, Militsyn came to the conclusion that "among our soldiers there are almost no Bolshevik partisans at all, nor will they support the Provisional Government. The name of Kerensky is too hated." "It is strange," Militsyn observed, "that [Kerensky] is particularly accused of sleeping in the Tsar's bed. Somebody spread gossip to this effect, and it has been quite effective . . . the soldiers are indignant. 'Maybe he himself aspires to be Tsar. He has surrounded himself with cadets and women. Apparently he does not trust us.' " Career officers, according to Militsyn, had "only one desire – to keep the regiment from participating in the uprising. They will play it by ear from there."[34] According to eye-witnesses, the Preobrazhensky regiment took no part in the events of October 25.

But even the active participation of other regiments in the uprising was to a considerable degree a bluff. An army communique spelled out the situation: "The infantry units are not executing any orders, but they are not rebelling either." Not one entire regiment took part, only individual soldiers or sub-regimental units – at best – and many of them were in no mood to fight. The MRC's own commissars attested to these facts. The 180th Infantry Regiment, considered to be "Bolshevik," displayed "astounding inertia and indifference" in regard to the defense of the "proletarian cause." On the eve of the uprising the regimental commissar noted an "extremely vacillating" mood in the armored battalion, which had adopted a resolution of total support for the MRC; the drivers and machine gunners were deserting their vehicles one after the other. The grenadier regiment, which at any moment, under the leadership of the famed Commissar Dzevaltovsky, could offer "1,000 bayonets," and the chemical flamethrower battalion, totaling "400 fighting men," were still counted in the "reserves" – the grenadier regiment perhaps because the insufficiently reliable Left Socialist Revolutionary regimental committee was still obviously in charge there. Nor did the Keksgolmsky Regiment have anything to show for itself, although a resolution by the regimental committee on October 21 solemnly proclaimed: "We are all prepared to emerge victorious or die at our posts." Or take the Pavlovsky Regiment — "our revolutionary support," maintained Antonov. It had set up checkpoints on Millionnaya Street and had made arrests. Apparently its active role in the uprising ended with this. Besides, the Pavlovsky checkpoints were not very insistent and were easily swayed. They released not only Minister for Religious Affairs Kartashov, who had been arrested after leaving the night session of the cabinet, but also acting War Minister General Manikovsky, who was stopped on the way to meet Kerensky at the palace on the morning of the 25th. Later the Pavlovsky checkpoints ("bunches of soldiers," to quote one of the Bolshevik leaders) blocked Nevsky Prospect and prevented access by strollers to the palace square. These were all rather passive functions. The extent of the active role played by the Pavlovsky on the night of October 25-26 can be judged by the official report of the regimental commissar: "At three o'clock in the morning our units began to move toward the Winter Palace" — but by that time the Winter Palace was no longer a strategic point. And in the final analysis the garrison of the Peter and Paul Fortress, which voiced support for the insurgents, also remained rather neutral in fact. Only one platoon of the regiment of machine gunners, who, according to Anatol Lunacharsky, "were itching to fight," could be considered "combat-ready."

Thus the "truism" about the role played by the garrison in the October Revolution (inspired by the idea of bringing the war to an end, the "army rose up against the Provisional Government and crushed it") should definitely be removed from the category of axiom and relegated to the realm of hypothesis. An edifying debate about the role played by the garrison on October 25 broke out among the ranks of the Bolsheviks themselves. According to Trotsky's historical interpretation, the common soldier occupied the front of the stage. This interpretation was followed uncritically by the émigré military historian Gen. N.N. Golovin, who claimed that the corrupted army of the rear enabled the Bolsheviks to seize power. A foreigner, General Niessel, chief of the French military mission, noted in his memoirs, in greater agreement with reality, that the majority of the troops in Petrograd and Moscow were neutral. This is also attested to by French Ambassador Noulens.

Stressing the role of the soldiers depreciates the role played by the proletariat, maintains the Marxist historian Mikhail Pokrovsky, who vigorously protests such an emphasis, referring among other things to the testimony of military authorities from the opposing side. "The skilled eye of the military" received a more "realistic" impression of the rebellion than that of some of its "participants and even leaders." Pokrovsky cites a later (November 10) communication from General Marushevsky to Dukhonin: "From those military operations, if they can be called military, I draw the conclusion that only sailors and armed workers were fighting here in the streets, while the men from the reserve regiments were apathetic and it seems were obviously sparing themselves and did not wish to take a particularly active part."

The soldiers were peasants; it was the sailors who, in the class concept of Bolshevik Marxism, represented the proletariat, declassé to be true. Yet, mass participation of genuine workers in the operations of the 25th cannot be claimed either, though in theory factory and plant committees were to spearhead the rebellion. Thus, on the morning of the uprising work at factories and workshops did not shut down. One worker at the Baltic shipyards recalls that work went on and meetings were held only by the party committees. Finally 235 workers from this shipyard did participate in one way or another in combat operations. The numbers were even smaller elsewhere. At the Putilov steel works, where there allegedly were 1,500 organized Red Guards, it was possible to raise a contingent of only eighty men, who participated in the attack on the Winter Palace. We do not know what happened to the 10,000 Red Guards claimed for the industrial Vyborgsky district, or to most of the 50,000 claimed for the city as a whole. There were actually only a few of the latter; Peshekhonov, in an article published the following day in *Narodnoe Slovo*, spoke of "insignificant groups" of Red Guards.

If the MRC indeed had at its disposal all those Red Guard units and regiments of the Petrograd garrison which had been counted on by the leaders of the uprising, and if the seizure of the government "by frontal assault" was the central point of a carefully worked out plan, it is probable that no chance circumstances would have hindered the insurgents from taking the weakly defended Winter Palace during the night of October 24-25 or on the morning of the 25th, whereas, in fact, the encirclement of the palace did not begin until 4:30 in the afternoon. Interestingly, one of the younger "revolution-aries," Sergei Uralov, claims that the entire tactical plan for the 25th — "to seize the Winter Palace, to arrest the ministers and imprison them in the Peter and Paul Fortress," — was hastily drawn up the morning of the uprising, under the direct guidance of Lenin. "Everything was done within 10 or 15 minutes."[35]

The balance was tipped by sailors of the Kronstadt naval base, tested in combat during the July Days, and Baltic fleet sailors from Helsinki who arrived in Petersburg in the afternoon. It is difficult to say just how strong these contingents of sailors actually were. Lenin demanded that the entire fleet be brought in, but the sailors did not want to leave the German front bare. According to the figures of one naval officer, I. I. Rengarten, author of one of the most significant personal journals of this time, 1,500 men left Helsinki (1,800 according to Antonov). The total number of "Kronstadters" apparently did not exceed 2,000.[36] The sailors were a real force, which the young workers of the Red Guard could support. The importance of the sailors is fully confirmed by Antonov-Ovseenko himself in his later sketches entitled "In 1917." According to him, the infantry was to carry out the passive role of neutralizing the Cossacks and cadet schools; the main blow of the attack on the Winter Palace was to be launched by a column of Kronstadters.

The initial scheme was to start the uprising in the outlying Vyborgsky worker district, and then gradually move toward the center with the help of the Baltic sailors. The MRC planners even conceived of the possibility that Smolny would be seized by government troops, in which case the headquarters of the insurgency would move to the Peter and Paul Fortress. But since government resistance did not materialize (the Cossacks announced their neutrality and no troops arrived from the front) — it was possible to gamble on seizing the Winter Palace directly, with a small force.

The uprising spread very rapidly throughout the city during the early morning, if one can call the takeover of government offices an uprising. Possibly there were a few scuffles. But these first "military operations" rather resembled "a changing of the guards," to use Sukhanov's apt words. The MRC commissars simply occupied key offices. Even on the eve of the uprising two unarmed commissars were able to take such an important point as the Central Telegraph Office. The insurgents operated with complete freedom. It was "child's play" — an observation was made by Sukhanov and others. The French newspaperman Anet painted a similar picture in his reports to Paris. Summarizing events on the following day, the acting government commissar at General Headquarters, Lt. Colonel Kovalevsky, sent the following communication to the government commissars of military districts: "The actual relationship of forces is such that the uprising proceeded without bloodshed until late in the evening. The insurgents seized government posts without any resistance. . . . . Initially the insurgents did not display great decisiveness, but sensing the absence of resistance, they began to seize in rapid order all the main offices." Everything took place so simply, so "harmoniously," to quote Kovalevsky, that it seemed unquestionable to him that the "plan for the uprising had been worked out ahead of time." But is not Sukhanov more correct when he employs a different term to define the mentality of the leaders of the insurgency: encountering no resistance, they "simply were having their fun"?

Thus began the uprising — "ominously" in a historical perspective, but not at all so in the perspective of the day. Life in the capital continued almost as if nothing had happened. "The crowds in the streets and streetcars show astounding indifference," stated Kovalevsky in his report. "It seemed that the entire city was taking a constitutional on Nevsky Prospect," recalls the Bolshevik-sympathizing American correspondent John Reed, who wrote the rather fantastic "epic of the great revolution," *Ten Days That Shook The World*. At eleven that morning State Auditor Smirnov, summoned to an emergency session of government, drove calmly through town, and the everyday look of the streets in no way foretold an imminent catastrophe. It was not until he had reached the Winter Palace that he learned that "the situation in the city has greatly deteriorated." Almost identical is the testimony of Col. S.A. Korenev: "On the morning of October 25 a carriage was brought to the hotel as usual. I set out for the [Winter] Palace with a presentiment of something bad, but I noticed no signs of anything imminent. Everything on the streets was quite normal, and I saw the familiar crowd on Nevsky Prospect, the same mixed crowd of idlers and persons on business; the streetcars were crowded as usual, and the stores were open for business . . . . I saw nowhere a sign of troops or armed detachments in general . . . . Only in front of the palace itself did I notice an unusual stir . . . . . From outside, the palace had taken on a martial appearance; all its exits and passageways leading to the Neva were occupied by cadets. They were also seated by the Palace gates and doors, shouting, laughing, and chasing one another along the sidewalk. There were about 400 of them."[37] A member of the defunct State Duma, Shidlovsky, was also wandering through the streets to check on the action. He saw none at all. Nor could he hear gunfire. Everything was "exceedingly quiet and calm." The crowds on the streets were laughing and joking. There were no clashes. Only on the corner of Nevsky and Bolshaya Morskaya did the former deputy encounter two unfriendly patrols. Peshekhonov, who walked along the streets and questioned patrols, gives a similar impression. Another characteristic eyewitness account is given by the engineer V. A. Auerbakh. At eight o'clock in the evening Auerbakh went out walking with a friend: "Things were very quiet, somehow, and we encountered few people in the streets," he says in his memoirs. On Gorokhovaya they "encountered a militiaman who was continuing to guard law and order at his post." At eleven in the evening Auerbakh and his friend went out once again, and near the municipal offices they saw an artillery piece with its muzzle pointed toward the Winter Palace and about twenty soldiers who paid no attention to them whatsoever. "We walked along Gorokhovaya and Morskaya to the corner of Nevsky, encountering no one on our way." There they saw another artillery piece, a couple of machine guns, and about fifteen soldiers and sailors who were preventing curious onlookers from proceeding onto Nevsky Prospect. The streets seemed "totally deserted." The entire struggle was limited to the besieged area.[38]

One must really possess a great imagination to follow Podvoisky's lead and liken Petrograd on October 25 to a "military camp," with armored vehicles at stragetic points, cavalry patrols throughout the city, and heavily manned military checkpoints guarding the approaches to the capital. As early as the 23rd, according to Podvoisky, several "regiments," or rather companies of fighting men, stood "in solid ranks at the checkpoints," and military assistance from without could reach the government only over their "dead bodies." On the 25th the approaches to the capital were, in fact, occupied by "checkpoints" of Red Guards instead of regiments. These checkpoints, in spite of all their "solidity," were easily pierced by the ministerial roadster carrying the commander in chief, Kerensky. "The mood of the soviet sentries is certainly not bellicose," observed Pavel Tolstoy on the 25th to Woytinsky.

An incident noted by Sukhanov serves as confirmation. Shortly after noon Sukhanov left for the Mariinsky Palace, where the Pre-Parliament was convening. His path lay across Nevsky Prospect and the Moyka river. The streets were lively, but there was no trouble. Suddenly he came to a cordon; pedestrians were not being permitted to pass. Sukhanov presented his Pre-Parliament identification card. The cordon opened, and the officer in charge said: "I don't get it. They told us to act. Why? I don't know. We are being pitted against each other. Strange." There were no doubts in the mind of the leftist politician — these troops were in no mood to fight, they would scatter and surrender at the first round of blanks fired.

Let us assume that this was illusory. But to a certain degree it determined the tactics of those who were inside the Winter Palace.

Why did the cabinet choose the "silly, almost hopeless" position of waiting things out in the Winter Palace? Almost nothing had been done to prepare for an actual defense of the Winter Palace. There were neither provisions nor ammunition. The cadets who had been summoned that day could not even be supplied with dinner. It all happened in a natural, spontaneous way: the cabinet was meeting in the Winter Palace, and in the Winter Palace it remained in expectation of the arrival of troops from the front. Kerensky says that upon his departure he instructed Kishkin to stand in for himself temporarily as commander in chief. Other ministers recall the situation somewhat differently. According to Smirnov the matter of appointing Kishkin was brought up at a cabinet session. To leave the defense of Petrograd in the hands of Polkovnikov, in whom the government had no confidence, was too risky. Even though it was late in the game, they had to find a worthy individual who could be entrusted with the struggle against the Bolsheviks. The choice fell on Kishkin, who was appointed "governor-general." The investment of Kishkin with emergency powers for establishing order in the capital, including the subordination to him of the military and civilian authorities, was effected with all due formality. Yet, at the most critical moment there were several hours during which there was a vacuum of authority, a fact extremely indicative of the disorganized state of affairs when the prime minister left town. Polkovnikov, who, in fact, had been removed from his duties by Kerensky,* began to take an extremely pessimistic view of the situation. We have the text of his report to Dukhonin, timed 10:05 A.M.: "I report that the situation in Petrograd is ominous. There have been no riots or disorders, but a planned, peaceful takeover of government offices and railroad stations is proceeding, and arrests are being made. No orders are being carried out. The cadets are surrendering their sentry posts without resistance. The Cossacks, in spite of a number of orders issued, have not yet left their barracks. Recognizing the critical situation, I report that the Provisional Government is in danger of losing its authority, and there are no guarantees whatsoever that there will be no attempts to seize the Provisional Government.**

The newly appointed Kishkin, to cite Miliukov, attempted to "inspire District Headquarters with confidence," but he "had to admit that the military district authorities lacked this confidence." Then "in anger" he formally removed Polkovnikov from his post and returned to the palace in order to "organize resistance" from that vantage point. The functions of troop commander were handed over to General Bagratuni. Of course, Kishkin's functions as "governor-general" at this time were very modest. It was no longer a question of governing the capital, but rather of self-defense of the Winter Palace. It is possible that Kishkin and the aides he appointed, Palchinsky and Rutenberg, displayed much courage and bravery that day. But what could be accomplished in a few hours by the ebullient energy of Kishkin and his unquestionable organizational talent? His practical experience lay in quite another area of public service – he was a medical doctor. Kishkin is reported to have recognized himself that he could not handle an unfamiliar job and to have accepted the appointment only because the acting war minister, General Manikovsky, had vigorously refused to direct the defense of the Winter Palace. What happened during the morning hours in the Winter Palace remains unclear.

*One should bear in mind that the night telegram to General Headquarters prescribed that troops sent from the front be placed under Polkovnikov's command, but all subsequent orders were issued in the name of Polkovnikov's chief of staff, General Bagratuni. S.P.M.

**This telegram is timed 10:05 in the morning of the 25th in the *Red Archives;* in the Hessen Archives [Arkhiv Russkoi Revoliutsii (Archives of the Russian Revolution), edited by I.V. Hessen; see the bibliography] it is timed fifteen minutes after midnight. Judging from its contents it is more likely that the telegram should be assigned to the morning. Of course it takes on more significance if it is assigned to the earlier time, when Polkovnikov was giving Kerensky his optimistic report on the number of troops that could be relied upon. S.P.M.

Kishkin and his aides were unsuccessful in creating order out of that unbelievable confusion which marked the government camp. A symbol of organized activity at the Winter Palace were those piles of logs, stacked by chance at the main entrance, with which the cadets had hastily constructed barricades. A small detail — they forgot not only to post guards, but even to lock the exit from the palace to the Winter canal. Perhaps they were simply unaware of the existence of this exit, since the newly appointed building commandants were ignorant even of the internal topography of the palace. By evening soldiers, sailors, workers, curious onlookers, and opportunists began to enter the palace through these forgotten doors. The organizers of the uprising subsequently utilized this blunder by the palace defenders for an ideological argument: "The denizens of the palace basements, in their class hatred of the exploiters," opened up "secret" entrances for the Bolsheviks, through which passed MRC agitators, who decimated the ranks of the defenders. Of course, these men from the MRC were not described as scouts who chanced into the palace, but as special emissaries.

During the morning the members of the cabinet apparently did not sense the tragic nature of their position. Gradually, shock units from the Women's Battalion,* a detachment of Cossacks with machine guns, and a battery from the Mikhailovsky Artillery School arrived to reinforce the cadets from the Peterhof and Oranienbaum schools who were guarding the palace. The Engineer Corps Ensign School arrived, and volunteers gathered (so newspaper accounts noted). In brief, there was gathered together a certain military force, supposedly sufficient to hold firm until troops arrived from the front. Constant statements from General Headquarters gave assurances that the troops were moving in that day. The government, hypnotized by the passivity of the attackers, felt comparatively safe.

"Perhaps some active initiative against the insurgents could have shaken the Cossacks and some of the garrison troops out of a state of indecision and vacillation," belatedly opines Maliantovich in his memoirs. But nobody intended to display such activity. Even without Kerensky, who presumably paralyzed its will to "venture," the cabinet continued to consider its main task to be that of swaying public opinion. It made a number of belated, useless appeals, appeals which probably never reached the intended ears — appeals to the public, signed by Deputy Chairman Konovalov, and appeals to the garrison in the name of VTsIK Commissar Malevsky and his assistant,

---

*The Women's Battalion of Death was formed in early June of 1917, at a time when signs of the demoralization of the Russian "male" army were quite apparent. The idea was initiated by the Simbirsk League for Women's Equality. The participants were great admirers of Kerensky, "the world's first minister to allow the formation of women's military units." Eds.

Skalov. It is characteristic that the government in its appeals attempted to cover itself primarily with the authority of the VTsIK and the Pre-Parliament. It was allegedly in agreement with them that newspapers preaching civil war were closed and that it was decided to arrest the main agitators appealing to the troops to rebel against government authority and the higher organs of the revolutionary democracy.

The government appeals threatened armed reprisal from the front. The moment of struggle has come, stated one appeal. "Offer vigorous resistance to treasonous agitation and stop outrages on the home front." How could this be done? "Citizens, organize yourselves around the Provisional Government," stated another appeal. But how could they organize and give help? "I appeal to all to remain perfectly calm," announced Malevsky, as if in reply. "Carry out the orders only of the Petrograd Military District Headquarters." Not only the authority of the VTsIK was evoked, but even that of the gathering Congress of Soviets, which was to proclaim a change in rule. "Comrade soldiers! The counterrevolutionaries are merely waiting for that moment when the uprising inevitably becomes transformed into a pogrom"; an armed uprising at the moment the Congress of Soviets convened could only frustrate the Congress. Obviously, such cheap demagoguery was unable to kindle the hearts of those who could have come to the government's defense.

That evening, summarizing his impressions of a day spent in teletype conversation with Woytinsky, Tolstoy said: "He will rule who gathers even a small, concentrated force; I believe there may be a few days of interregnum, and then everything will be up to Russia and the front." The Bolsheviks succeeded in creating "a small, concentrated force" in Petrograd formed of sailors from the Baltic Fleet and several Red Guard units. The government did not even think of doing the same kind of thing, and, of course, the extremely heterogeneous 1,000 cadets without officer leadership could not form the required force.

The defenders of the government lacked any enthusiasm. All testimony seems to agree on this point. The Oranienbaum cadets, who were the first to be summoned to guard the Winter Palace and were clearly counted among the government's most loyal troops, announced through their delegates at a garrison meeting held at the Smolny Institute on October 18 that they would act only under orders of the VTsIK. Replying to an inquiry from Dukhonin on the state of the cadet schools, General Levitsky on the morning of the 25th was merely able to say that the cadets would not be active. What was happening in the palace could not improve the fighting ability of the defenders and would rather worsen the morale of those who were intending to offer armed resistance to the Bolsheviks. Total inaction in the face of myriad rumors (such as that the prime minister had fled disguised as a Red Cross nurse), the lack of information (at first for some reason even the fact of the cabinet's presence in the palace was concealed), and a gradual weakening of faith in the arrival of the troops from the front (the conviction was growing that these assurances were merely a tactical device and that the defenders were being deceived), could not but demoralize those who vacillated. In accordance with the custom of the time, they began to hold meetings. The most tenacious were precisely those groups who had inspired so much suspicion during the pre-dawn hours of that fateful day, those cadets who were prepared to fight and put down an uprising, as Rengarten stated in his journal, but who did not want to "defend Kerensky or his government." It was they who defended the Provisional Government up to the last minute, even if it was "without enthusiasm," as Palchinsky noted in his journal.

It still seemed to a few vigorous individuals close to the government that available forces could be effectively employed. For example, Headquarters Commissar Stankevich attempted to recapture for the government the Mariinsky Palace, where the Pre-Parliament sat, and the telephone exchange, and he asked for a company of cadets. The Mariinsky Palace was guarded by an armored car, so he picked ten men to enter the telephone exchange, which could be seized without bloodshed. At that moment, a few shots sounded in the distance and the cadets ran for cover. On the way back to the Winter Palace Stankevich lost half his company, which was peacefully disarmed by "neutral" troops. His attempt may have been valiant, but perhaps he would have been more helpful had he kept his promise to Supreme Headquarters, and met the troop transport of cyclists from the western front, who were sitting idly forty-six miles away . . .

The City Duma, limiting itself to a protest against "all displays of violence and armed force" and appealing to the public to unite around the "authorized representative body" for the purpose of "subordinating brute force to law" actually maintained a neutral position. There were too many of these "neutrals" on October 25.

The cabinet could not help but sense its isolation, which was increasing with each passing hour. The Winter Palace, which was gradually being encircled by the insurgents, was isolated in the full sense of the word. Nobody showed up to lend aid and to share responsibility with the ministers. Perhaps this was merely because nobody yet recognized the threat of approaching danger and nobody foresaw catastrophe. An attempt was made from the Winter Palace to generate a reaction in the capital artificially and to round up "live forces" that could be grouped around the government. Stankevich claims credit for the initiative in calling to the Winter Palace delegates from various civic organizations after the government refused to take his advice, supported by Minister of Labor Gvozdev, to move to the Duma, where "public-spirited citizens" were gathering. Deputy Chairman Konovalov sent emissaries out in all directions with an "urgent invitation" in his name to come to the Winter Palace. Unfortunately, we do not know to which civic organizations Konovalov's emissaries were sent. Nabokov mentions members of the Pre-Parliament – an institution directly connected with the government. Judging from several subsequent newspaper accounts (see, for example, a report of events by an *Utro Rossii* correspondent on November 8), one can draw the conclusion that essentially only the presidium of the Council of the Republic was summoned (the Socialist Revolutionary Avksentiev, the Kadet Nabokov, the People's Socialist Peshekhonov, and the Menshevik Krokhmal).

Yet, the Council of the Republic itself was liquidated at one o'clock in the afternoon, in a fashion that was, considering the spirit of the day, by no means spectacular. As usual, the presidium of the Council met at eleven o'clock in the morning. "The Mariinsky Palace," says Nabokov, "was already rather crowded; a confused, agitated, and helpless mood prevailed. The Socialist Revolutionary faction was totally absent; there were also few Social Democrats. Avksentiev, chairman of the Council of the Republic, did not know what to do. At this time the Council sergeant at arms reported that Kerensky had just crossed the square and was headed toward Voskresensky Avenue. *Nobody knew anything* about where the other members of the Provisional Government were or what they were doing." How characteristic the phrase is of Nabokov's memoirs.

Perhaps equally characteristic is the account written by Captain Second Grade Zhdan-Pushkin (a People's Socialist) in the Moscow paper *Vlast Naroda* on the following day, that is, on October 26. Zhdan-Pushkin was to see Avksentiev at the Pre-Parliament on army business. At about twelve o'clock he was received by the chairman. "Calmly hearing us out, Avksentiev said to us with even calmness: 'At this very moment Bolshevik troops are occupying the palace. The government has gathered in the Winter Palace, guarded by cadets and groups of officers. I do not know what the outcome will be. The government has no forces here. In the next few days it will be impossible to do anything, for we are powerless.' " This account differs somewhat from Nabokov's but the impression he gives of what was taking place is approximately the same.

Nabokov continues that in order to decide what to do, Avksentiev called a meeting of Pre-Parliament faction leaders, during which meeting Kuskova informed the body that a detachment of soldiers headed by an officer had arrived, that all exits to the square were occupied, and that the officer wished to see the chairman. "A reply was given that a meeting of faction leaders was taking place and that when it was over he could talk to the chairman." Sometime later Kuskova again informed them that the officer in charge of the detachment requested that all those present immediately leave the Mariinsky Palace; otherwise vigorous steps would be taken, including the use of firearms. This created a staggering impression. In response to the ultimatum a stereotyped resolution was hastily drawn up. It mentioned the use of force against the Council of the Republic and declared that it would be reconvened at the first opportunity. "The time of the meeting will be posted and announced in the newspapers," stated the chairman, according to a reporter from *Delo Naroda.* The Council members calmly proceeded past the lines of armed men. The Bolshevik detachment did not seem to display great animosity. Nabokov was sure that he would be arrested. And it seemed to him that the naval officer who was allowing the Council members to pass through to the street hesitated when he glanced at Miliukov's card — "but in any case, it only lasted a second." They saw the "characteristic figure" of General Alekseev, "saw him in heated argument with the chief of the guard," recalls Denikin. Only the Menshevik Dubois was arrested at the Mariinsky Palace, because he was deputy minister of labor.

Apparently nobody even considered going to the Winter Palace. It was not until four o'clock that Nabokov, learning that a messenger from Konovalov had come to his apartment in his absence, and surprised at the invitation, headed for the Winter Palace. He went as far as the palace square by streetcar. The square was already cordoned off, soldiers having taken up widely spaced positions around it. There was quite a crowd present. "It was difficult to comprehend what was happening, the purpose of these troops." Nabokov silently showed the first soldier his old pass to the Winter Palace and was immediately allowed through the line. But Nabokov was the only one to respond to the invitations that had been sent out. "Of course," he writes in his memoirs, "my presence was totally useless. I could do nothing, and when it became clear that the cabinet did not intend to act, but was merely waiting things out, I preferred to leave the premises."[39]

It is possible that the mood of the cabinet members would have changed if there had been a response from outside. There was no response. "We were left to our fate," concludes Maliantovich: "They sympathized with us in words and yet turned us down in deeds." Actually a historian would have some difficulty in uncovering even "verbal sympathy." Isolated voices do not create a public mood. "All the talk factories went into action," scornfully noted the minister of justice. Actually, they were silent as the hours slowly dragged by in the vegetating Winter Palace. "Every hope has been tried and exhausted," wrote E. D. Kuskova in her moving article, entitled "Night," which was the first published comment by an eyewitness to the "great crime" committed during the historic night of October 26. Her husband, Minister of Food Prokopovich, in turn later related that he "had made every effort to organize in Petrograd a movement to defend the Provisional Government." He was arrested on the street at ten o'clock in the morning by a group "of eight or nine armed men," who had stopped his automobile. He was taken to

Smolny, then at five o'clock in the afternoon was released. He communicated with the Winter Palace and began organizing public opinion. "By seven or eight o'clock in the evening it became obvious to me that . . . the Provisional Government had no forces whatsoever on its side."

No one has yet given concrete information about what the Russian public attempted to do on that day to aid the government. Some hints can be found in the testimony of Doctor Feit at the Moscow trial in 1922 of the Socialist Revolutionaries. Feit, who was administrator of the party central committee, attempted to summon troops from the barracks. When Feit spoke over the telephone to those units which a few hours before had been "quite ready to defend the Provisional Government," they now "refused to go to the Winter Palace square."

Nobody acted. The Russian public was almost completely absent on that tragic day. Izgoev wrote in his memoirs: "The regime was going under in the face of universal disgust. It was clear that nobody would move a finger in its defense." Izgoev was not the only one to say this. Zinaida Hippius, whose salon was one of the focal points of literary life at that time, wrote in her diary that it was clear to her, too, and that she had become "bored and disgusted." "At this moment there is no camp with which one must side." In the Winter Palace there was an increasing sense of doom. This is clearly seen in the memoirs of Maliantovich: "Doomed men, abandoned by all, wandered about in that immense mousetrap, from time to time gathering together or in separate groups for brief conversations."

The sense of doom was felt not only by the ministers themselves, but by all those around them. Despairing of the possibility of a display of action by the "doomed men," Stankevich hastened back into the city, climbing "over unguarded barricades by the palace gates." He was stopped at Aleksandrovsky Park. He showed his old officer's identification papers and was allowed to pass. The chief commissar headed toward the City Duma, where he found "a seething center of anti-Bolshevik activity by public-spirited citizens." "It was pleasant," he recalled, "to feel oneself once again among men who were not doomed. All the rooms were crowded. Many meetings were being held. Many proposals were being made. There was much energetic, vigorous talk and many confident faces."

SIEGE OF THE WINTER PALACE

It is difficult to maintain a high degree of accuracy about details and at the same time relate what occurred during the last hours in the Winter Palace. The observations of eyewitnesses are too subjective, and their testimony is too contradictory. But details cannot alter the general picture.

We do not even know the precise number of defenders of the Provisional Government. The Bolsheviks numbered them between 1,500 and 2,000. By evening the ranks of the defenders had thinned out significantly and seemed pitifully small in the immense palace building. The palace was being abandoned by those who were starving for a meal. An attempt to send in provisions had been a failure, and the cadets sent out with a truck for foodstuffs were taken prisoner, although on the initiative of Kuskova and others baskets of provisions were obtained from the Ministry of Food. The dispirited and disillusioned were leaving individually and in groups. Perhaps the most important instance of this was the departure of the artillery; it had a depressing effect on many. At about six o'clock in the evening the cadets from the Mikhailovsky Artillery School abandoned the Winter Palace at the order of the school commandant. Not all the cadets followed orders. Some broke discipline and refused to obey. According to the Bolshevik version, the order to leave the Winter Palace was issued by the school commandant "under pressure" from the Military Revolutionary Committee. Actually, the artillery was removed as a result of deception by the political commissar at the school, who had been appointed to the post during the period of the Kornilov "putsch." He himself wrote in the journal *Byloe* about how he had played the role of wolf in sheep's clothing in the Winter Palace. Upon leaving the Palace gates the cadets were arrested (apparently by one of the checkpoints set up by the Pavlovsky regiment) and sent back to the school. According to Sinegub, the Cossacks also left, extremely disturbed by the fact that the only infantry at the disposal of the government consisted of "women with guns." Before leaving they wished to talk with the cabinet — they wanted to know just what the government was counting on. This conversation was recorded by Maliantovich in his journal. The government gave the Cossacks the same answer it had given the cadets: it could not issue the military order to fight to the last man; perhaps bloodshed would be useless, and therefore, it was offering freedom of action. The Cossack colonel "said nothing" and merely "sighed." The Cossacks left — "it seemed to me" with a look of bewilderment and yet, perhaps, with "decision."

The day passed in waiting. Isolated shots were heard from time to time. By evening they rang out with greater frequency. "We were told that our guard ... replied to the shots or fired when Bolsheviks moved on the palace," Maliantovich recalls. "They fired into the air. For the time being this was sufficient; the crowd retreated." Then a cannon was heard. "Ours or theirs?" Maliantovich asked Admiral Verderevsky. "Ours," the latter replied. "Probably into the air, to scare them." Palchinsky reported that a cannon had been fired into the air and the crowd had scattered. But the moment was approaching when "it will be necessary to issue a brief, decisive order. What will it be? To fight to the last man, to the last drop of blood? In the name of what? If government authority was not being defended by those who organized it, was this regime worth defending? They came to us and asked us these questions. We could not issue an order to fight to the last man because perhaps we were already defending only ourselves. Nor could we give the opposite order — to surrender, because we did not know whether the moment had come when capitulation was inevitable . . . . What military order could we give? None at all." In this manner "we offered freedom of choice to our protectors to link their fate with ours."[40] This, according to Maliantovich, was approximately the reply given to the cadets by himself, Konovalov, Kartashev, and Maslov, when a delegation from the defending forces appeared and insisted that the government act.

"Some cadets left," Maliantovich jotted in his journal, as if making a mental notation. The same entry is repeated over and over again, the last time at twelve o'clock that night: "Some of the cadets from the Oranienbaum School have left." At six thirty that evening two cyclists arrived at District Headquarters from the Peter and Paul Fortress, presenting an ultimatum signed by Antonov-Ovseenko which demanded the surrender of the Provisional Government and the disarming of all its defenders. Twenty minutes were given to think it over, after which the beleaguering forces threatened to open fire with the heavy guns at the Fortress of Peter and Paul and from warships standing in the Neva. The ultimatum was rejected by the cabinet; or to be more accurate, they decided not to enter into any negotiations with the MRC. Instead, the cabinet resolved to appeal to the City Duma for moral support. Simultaneously an intensified search began for some kind of physical support. This was done over the telephone, which had not been disconnected. Several times Nikitin called friends with the request to inform all democratic organizations about the current situation and to point out the necessity of bringing in at least some troops to support the tired palace defenders. The energetic Kuskova was also engaged in continuous telephone conversations with Nikitin, Maliantovich, and Tereshchenko. All were appealing for aid. But they found none. "The democracy, or rather the spurious democracy provided no assistance," noted Kuskova bitterly in her article, "Night." A few went over to the City Duma, announcing to the various factions that a tragic denouement was approaching and that it was necessary to come to the defense of the government and to issue an appropriate appeal to the public. Miliukov recalls that Kishkin, too, attempted to get in touch with Kadet party headquarters in order to request reinforcements. What kind of a party is it that "cannot even send us 300 armed men?" But Kishkin himself was one of the main organizers of his party. One can find in the newspapers of the time many public announcements in the name of the military commission of the Kadet party. But it did not show itself on the day weapons were deciding the country's fate. And one involuntarily recalls the speech made by Miliukov at the Eighth Congress, when he spoke of the effect of the "application of force in those cases when people appear who are consciously in the service of Germany." The party leader confidently stated that the revolution could "be stopped if this . . . is necessary for the good of Russia."

We know of only one real attempt to aid the government. This was organized by Savinkov, the energetic former terrorist of the Socialist Revolutionary party. According to Savinkov, during the afternoon he went looking for General Alekseev in order to discuss with him what could be done to help the government. He first visited the Socialist Revolutionary Filonenko, the government commissar at General Headquarters, who advised him "not to undertake anything against the Bolshevik uprising, arguing that the Bolsheviks would be easier to defeat after they, having taken Petrograd and seized power, have displayed a total incapability of running the government." "I did not find General Alekseev until that night," relates Savinkov. "We decided to make an attempt to liberate the Winter Palace. It was one o'clock in the morning. I went to the Council of the Union of Cossack Troops, and I succeeded in persuading representatives of the Cossack regiments and military schools to gather at least a small armed force in order to attempt to offer battle to the Bolsheviks besieging the Winter Palace. At one thirty General Alekseev received a delegation of cadets, and, talking with them, outlined a plan of military operations. These operations were never to be carried out. At two o'clock in the morning, before the Cossacks and cadets had time to organize, the Winter Palace was taken by Bolshevik troops."

Denikin, quoting a person close to Alekseev, Captain Shapron, denies Savinkov's version. Indeed, Savinkov that evening had appeared at the secret hideout where friends had taken Alekseev to assure his safety. Savinkov appealed to Alekseev in a very theatrical manner and with great pathos to do his duty and go to the Cossacks. Then Shapron began arguing the senselessness of such an adventure, which could only lead to Alekseev's capture by the Bolsheviks, and Alekseev reportedly rejected Savinkov's suggestion as hopeless. Savinkov was inclined to both theatricality and pathos. Yet I cannot imagine that in his memoirs he altered the situation to such a degree. Shapron may not have been fully informed, since he was not sympathetic to the undertaking. Savinkov's version deserves to be believed, since it was contained in an article published in *Russkie Vedomosti* shortly after the event, on November 21. Grekov's memoirs partially confirm Savinkov's version and, in any case, attest to the fact that lengthy and serious negotiations took place between the Cossacks and Alekseev. Grekov states flatly that the chairman of the Council of Cossack Troops, Anikeev, and his deputy returned from "a secret meeting" called by General Alekseev. A joint journey by Alekseev and Savinkov to meet General Krasnov's Third Corps was supposedly discussed at a second meeting.

Lacking any help from the outside, the beleaguered forces in the Winter Palace began to take real steps to defend themselves in order to hold out until morning, when troops were expected from the front. First, all forces were moved into the palace. The headquarters building across the square was abandoned. (It is therefore no wonder that it was taken by a Bolshevik detachment totaling only fifty men. Quartermaster General Paradelov and several persons with him were arrested at headquarters.) General Bagratuni refused to assume the responsibility of being commandant. Lieutenant Colonel Ananin, commandant of the Engineer Corps Ensign School, was therefore placed in charge of the defense. The school, as the most highly organized unit, was fated to become the main support of the besieged government. The defenders' assignments in case of assault were defined, and the machine guns left behind by the Cossacks were placed on the barricades.

The military authorities did not prevent wavering and doubting cadets from leaving the palace. A cohesive minority was a better support than a scattered mass susceptible to enemy propaganda. And the propaganda came in various ways. The situation can be characterized by the following event: at about eight o'clock in the evening the Bolshevik Chudnovsky, one of the leaders of the siege, easily made his way into the Winter Palace, which was already in a state of battle alert in expectation of an attack. He arrived at the invitation of a delegate from the Oranienbaum Cadet School to discuss "surrender." The cadets "on their word of honor" guaranteed Chudnovsky full immunity. Chudnovsky and the cadet who invited him were arrested on Palchinsky's orders, but were released on the insistence of the cadets. With them left some of the cadets who no longer wished to fight.

The situation still did not seem hopeless. At seven o'clock in the evening Quartermaster General Diterikhs spoke from General Headquarters with Lieutenant Danilevich. After transmitting a telegram from the government for the Chief of Staff of General Headquarters containing a request to speed up the dispatch of troops, Danilevich added on his own: "Rather sporadic firing is and has been going on, caused, I believe, by nerves, since no attack has yet been made, and the Bolsheviks are acting comparatively passively. During my conversation with you there have been only three or four artillery shots fired, which, judging by the sound, emanated from our camp. The Provisional Government is presently in toto in the Winter Palace and is not even considering leaving until the end of the conflict .... Little by little organization and leadership of those few troops we do have is shaping up. I personally believe that if that which we have is utilized the situation of the government is not hopeless." Diterikhs, discussing the Cossack regiments that were to arrive in Petrograd in the morning and evening of the 26th, expressed full confidence that "the difficult situation will practically resolve itself."[41]

At nine o'clock in the evening, the government directed the following appeal to the public: "The Petrograd Soviet of Workers' and Soldiers' Deputies has announced the demise of the Provisional Government and has demanded transfer of authority to itself under threat of bombardment of the Winter Palace by the guns of the Peter and Paul Fortress and the cruiser *Aurora*, which is anchored in the Neva. The government can transfer authority only to the Constituent Assembly, and, therefore, has resolved not to capitulate but rather to place itself under the protection of the people and army, to which effect a telegram has been sent to General Headquarters. General Headquarters has replied that troops are being sent. May the country and its people respond to the insane attempt of the Bolsheviks to mount an insurrection in the rear of our army engaged in war." At about the same time, a blank shell was fired from a gun at the Peter and Paul Fortress as a signal, and the actual assault on the Winter Palace began. Initially, the attack was limited to rifle and machine-gun fire directed at the palace. Armored vehicles in the hands of the government were forced to leave the square because of the lack of gasoline. The intensive fire and return fire by the beleaguered forces continued for about one hour. Then the firing died down. The executive committee of the Postal-Telegraph Union sent out a communique: "The first attack on the Winter Palace at 10 o'clock in the evening has been repulsed," and the government announced "for your information" that "the situation is viewed as favorable . . . . There is an exchange of fire at the palace, but only rifle fire, without any results. It has been ascertained that the enemy is weak."

The actual picture was approximately as follows: "Disorderly crowds of sailors, soldiers, and Red Guards would now surge forward toward the palace gates and now fade back." This is the description given by Antonov-Ovseenko. Palchinsky emphasized in brief comments in his notebook that the troops present were sufficient to defend the palace, but command personnel were tragically absent — there were only five "active" officers. This led to disorganization.

The first assault on the Winter Palace had as its result the surrender of the shock troops of the Women's Battalion. They could not withstand the fire, claim Bolshevik sources. Maliantovich simply jotted down: "The Women's Battalion went out." During the next few days the papers contained fantastic accounts of the Women's Battalion at the Winter Palace. For example, *Vlast Naroda* on the 28th quoted reliable witnesses arriving in Moscow from Petrograd who reported that after the departure of the cadets the palace was selflessly defended only by the Women's Battalion, which was subjected to machine-gun fire from armored vehicles, and that the battalion lost 500 women. This is highly improbable, of course. It is unlikely that there were that many women in the palace. Il'in-Zhenevsky's claim that there was a total of 200 female shock troops is probably more correct. Apparently, by the time of the actual seizure of the palace, there were no female troops left.

At eleven o'clock in the evening the guns of the Peter and Paul Fortress began shelling the Palace. Why were the Bolsheviks so slow in seizing the

Winter Palace? That morning Antonov-Ovseenko had prepared the ultimatum that had been handed to the government via District Headquarters at six o'clock in the evening. At ten o'clock that morning the MRC had announced the following: "The Provisional Government has fallen. Power has been taken over by the MRC, the organ of the Petrograd Soviet of Workers' and Soldiers' Deputies." At 2:35 that afternoon Trotsky announced at a special session of the Petrograd Soviet that "the Provisional Government no longer exists" and that a radiogram had been sent to the active army informing it of the fall of the regime. "The fate of the Winter Palace," he said, "should be decided within the next few minutes."

Lenin appeared openly for the first time in more than three months at this meeting of the Petrograd Soviet and gave a speech on the tasks of the new Soviet government. Until this moment Lenin had remained hidden in the back rooms of Smolny in disguise. "He was wrapped with a kerchief as if he were suffering from a toothache, was wearing huge glasses and a cap which was much the worse for wear," recalls Trotsky. "He gave a rather strange appearance," but Dan, who happened to pass by and who had an "experienced and sharp" eye, saw through the masquerade, "nudged Skobelev with his elbow, winked, and continued on his way. Vladimir Ilyich also nudged me with his elbow: 'The bastards recognized me!' But this was not dangerous, for at that moment we were masters of the situation." If it were not dangerous, why was the masquerade necessary (according to other accounts Lenin even had make-up on his face) in the impregnable Bolshevik citadel, Smolny, which was supposedly guarded by one hundred machine guns? (The Finnish Bolshevik Eino Rakhia, at whose home Lenin had spent the previous night, relates in a picturesque way how he and the leader stealthily made their way to Smolny on the evening of the 24th. They did run into a cadet patrol, which took Lenin, who was dressed in the worst clothes, to be a drunk.)

The minutes calculated by Trotsky passed one after the other, hours went by, while not only was the Winter Palace not taken, but attempts were not even made to seize it. In expectation of the imminent fall of the Provisional Government the convening of the Second Congress of Soviets was postponed. It was to be presented with a fait accompli. Persistent orders came from Smolny to seize the Winter Palace immediately. MRC headquarters designated three o'clock as the final deadline. Then the deadline was put off to six o'clock, and an ultimatum demanding capitulation was presented to the government. The twenty minutes allowed in the ultimatum for a reply passed, and the deadline was magnanimously extended ten minutes "at the insistence" of the beleaguered forces. An exchange of fire began, but the Winter Palace still was not taken.

The Second Congress of Soviets finally convened at 10:40 P.M. Lenin did not appear. He paced back and forth in the little room adjoining the convention chamber like a caged lion and "cursed." From this room he sent one note after another to Podvoisky, Antonov, and others. Trotsky claims that he and "Ilyich" lay down on the floor in the room to rest, but from time to time Trotsky would go out into the convention hall to give a cue to one or another speaker. Meanwhile, at the Congress, which was opened by Dan and in which the Bolsheviks had about 52 percent of the registered delegates' votes,* the usual factional delays occurred. The representatives of the Socialist Revolutionaries, Mensheviks, Jewish Social Democratic Union (Bund), and groups from the front issued special statements of protest against the conspiracy and seizure of power. The protesters walked out of the Congress. They were followed by the Menshevik Internationalists, headed by Martov, who had proposed that the agenda of the Congress be suspended until a peaceful solution to the crisis could be worked out by establishing a completely democratic government. The Left Socialist Revolutionaries remained in the Congress, coming out in favor of a "united revolutionary front," but opposing a resolution introduced by Trotsky, who called for a vote of welcome for the "victorious uprising."

The Winter Palace had not yet been taken. The Congress, at which only kindred spirits had remained, recessed. Why? Obviously the conspirators did not have much faith in the firmness of spirit of the rank-and-file delegates. To use Trotsky's expression, they were afraid of "making the Congress nervous." They were afraid that a psychological isolation of the Bolsheviks could develop at the Congress. Only a true denouement, the actual fall of the Provisional Government presented to the Congress as a fait accompli, could

*Neither the total membership nor the party composition of the members of the Second All-Russian Congress of Soviets of Workers' and Soldiers' Deputies can be determined with any certainty. The number of Bolshevik delegates at the Congress is variously given as 250, 300, or 390 (see a table in James Bunyan and H. H. Fisher, ed., *The Bolshevik Revolution 1917-1918* [Stanford, Calif., 1934], p. 110). A note in volume twenty-three of Lenin's collected works (2nd ed., 1928), p. 577 states that "at the Second All-Russian Congress of Soviets there were no accurate lists of delegates, data on the mandates of some delegates were absent from questionnaires, and the lists included a number of comrades with an advisory vote and guests; the party affiliation of some of them is unknown." According to a recent work by the Soviet historian E. N. Gorodetsky, *Rozhdenie Sovetskogo Gosudarstva* (Moscow, 1965), p. 62, there were "not less than 859 delegates at the Second Congress of the Soviets, but data on party affiliation is available on only 648 [registered] delegates; 338 of them [52.1 percent] were Bolsheviks." According to Vera Vladimirova *(God sluzhby sotsialistov kapitalistam* [Moscow, 1927], p. 18), the 390 Bolshevik delegates usually referred to included "fellow travellers who signed up with the faction."

After the delegates of the Mensheviks, the right-wing Socialist Revolutionaries and the army organizations walked out of the Congress, the Central generate enthusiasm and compel the Congress to follow the "leader" blindly. Until such a moment the success of the uprising would still be in question.

With such attitudes prevailing it is difficult to comprehend why the insurgents were slow about seizing the Winter Palace, if they actually had the force. The Smolny headquarters continued to demand action against the Winter Palace. Local "revolutionary staffs" produced impressive forces in comparison with those defending the Winter Palace. Chudnovsky's "cordons," including artillery, armored vehicles, machine guns, and infantry, advanced to the palace walls; the Peter and Paul Fortress, where Podvoisky had dug in, was threatening an artillery bombardment; the *Aurora*, surrounded by destroyers, threateningly trained its six-inch guns on the palace, under the vigilant supervision of Antonov-Ovseenko. Nevertheless, something kept them from seizing the Winter Palace by frontal assault.

One can hardly believe that they held back their advance due to sentimental feelings, wishing not to kill the members of the government and the defending cadets and wishing to avoid destruction of the palace. This flimsy myth was subsequently supported by Lunarcharsky, who was inclined at times to inappropriate buffoonery. Nor can one accept Podvoisky's explanation that the slowdown was dictated by the attempt to bring about the surrender of the Winter Palace, to compel its defenders to lay down their arms and humiliate the government. Such a tactic does not correspond to the furious and impotent snarlings of Lenin at Smolny. We must also reject the version according to which the delay in carrying out the last act of rebellion

---

Executive Committee of the Soviets (VTsIK, inherited from the First Congress) published a declaration asserting that after the departure of these groups those assembled "can call themselves what they please" but in fact represent only the Bolshevik faction (F.A. Golder, ed., *Documents of Russian History 1914-1917* [New York and London, 1927], p. 619). In its appeal to the local soviets, the VTsIK announced that under conditions created by the Bolshevik armed uprising, the legal All-Russian Congress of the Soviets was unable to function, and that the meeting in progress represented a "private conference of Bolshevik delegates," the decisions of which should be considered illegal and void *(Krasnyi Arkhiv*, vol. VIII, 1925, No. 1, p. 154). The prominent Bolshevik historian of the October Revolution, I. I. Mints, still asserts that the Second Congress of Soviets "was the genuine forum of the majority of the population, an authoritative and plenipotentiary popular assembly." (I. I. Mints, *Istoriia velikogo oktiabria* [Moscow, 1968], vol. II, p. 1100). Yet, on subsequent pages Mints has to admit that "there is no documentary data on the work of the Congress, neither stenographic records, nor minutes, nor even secretarial notes" (p. 1102). In fact, a crowd dominated by Bolshevik cheer-leaders may be a more accurate description of the Congress. S.G.P.

was caused by the wish to avoid those hundreds of heroic deaths among the "Reds" which would be inevitable in a storming of the palace. And the suppositions expressed by General Levitsky in a conversation that morning with Dukhonin seem to have missed the mark. He ended his conversation with the comment: "The indecisiveness of the Bolsheviks, who have long possessed the ability to take care of all of us, enables me to assume that they will not dare act counter to the wishes of the army at the front and will stop at that point."

Something else put sand in the gears. Certain accidental elements injected themselves into the orders and commands. At times these were even petty and of a comic nature. It was, for example, arranged with Blagonravov, the Bolshevik commandant of the Peter and Paul Fortress, that upon encirclement of the Winter Palace a red lantern would be hoisted on the fortress mast. Blagonravov was unable to hoist the miserable lantern, because he had neglected to make preparations ahead of time and nowhere in the Peter and Paul Fortress could a red lantern be found. Then Blagonravov received an order to initiate an artillery bombardment from the Peter and Paul Fortress. But the guns would not fire. Certain components were missing. So a search was instituted – not so much for the missing components as for other gun crews. Two sailors were sent in. They fired the cannons, but the projectiles missed the target zones. Only two out of thirty-five shells hit the target, and both of these struck along the roofline. "I walked out this afternoon," wrote Buchanan the following day, "to see the damage that had been done to the Winter Palace by the prolonged bombardment of the previous evening and to my surprise found that, in spite of the near range, there were on the river side but three marks, where the shrapnel had struck. On the town side the walls were riddled with thousands of bullets from machine guns, but not one shot from a field gun that had been fired from the opposite side of the Palace Square had struck the building." (Buchanan, II, p. 208)

Trotsky had to confess that apparently even the most loyal artillery crews deliberately aimed high. When they wanted to put the six-inchers on the *Aurora* into action, it turned out that the cruiser was unable to fire at the Winter Palace due to its position. All they did was fire a warning blank. This is how the "bass voices of the *Aurora* informed the world of the birth of a new era," to quote the Soviet novelist Ehrenburg.

I have run somewhat ahead of events. The artillery fire did not commence until eleven o'clock in the evening, after the Congress of Soviets had convened at Smolny and when it seemed that the last hour had come for completing the plan lest it be threatened with failure. Let us return to our chronological account of events.

At the very moment when the machine-gun and rifle fire on the Winter Palace began, that is at about nine o'clock, the City Duma convened.

Stankevich found there a "vigorous and confident" atmosphere. It is probable that another eyewitness was more correct when he described the atmosphere at the Duma as "alarmed." During the day neither the Duma nor the political parties guiding it had been able to organize any assistance to the government, in spite of the existence of a centralized organization of residential committees with district commissars. "The revolutionary democracy is talking and the revolutionary government is perishing," commented Minister of Interior Nikitin bitterly in a telephone conversation with a friend.

When the Duma convened, Mayor Grigori Shreider announced that a bombardment of the Winter Palace would begin in a "few seconds." The Duma resolved to send out three delegations for the purpose of averting a catastrophe – one to the cruiser *Aurora* (headed by Countess Sofia Panina), one to Smolny (Shreider himself), and the other to the Winter Palace (Duma Chairman Isaev). The Duma session was recessed. Two hours later the delegations returned; they had been stopped by patrols. The Duma session reconvened. The galleries were jammed with onlookers, and civic leaders and representatives of the district Dumas filled the corridors. The Socialist Revolutionary Bykhovsky "ran" up to the rostrum and announced excitedly that he had just spoken by telephone with Minister of Agriculture Maslov in the Winter Palace. Maslov requested that he announce that the situation at the Palace was critical, that the ministers were about to be cut down, and that his, Maslov's, last words before dying would be, "a curse on that democracy which appointed me to the government and now has betrayed it." His announcement in view of the nervous atmosphere had a "crushing effect." With their effusive women's temperaments, Panina and Nechaeva made an emotional appeal to the Duma to go out and die together with their elected representatives in the Winter Palace. The Duma passed a resolution to proceed to the palace; the resolution was adopted overwhelmingly with sixty-two votes in favor, and only the fourteen Bolsheviks voting nays and three abstentions.

One and one-half hours passed after the adoption of the resolution to die together with the government. Calls were placed to party organizations, the Executive Committee of the Soviet of Peasants' Deputies, and other groups summoning their members to the palace square that night to die. They communicated with the palace, agreed on the order of procession, and determined signals. (If they waved a lighted lantern three times, etc.). The charged, exultant atmosphere, bordering on heroic ecstasy, gradually dissipated. The mood became more gloomy. By the time they set out on their march there was neither enthusiasm nor inspiration. According to Vladimir Zenzinov, they proceeded in even files, singing the Marseillaise. They advanced two hundred paces and were stopped on Kazan Square by a patrol. The cortege probably had assumed a rather amorphous shape; bystanders had joined the Duma procession. And it is hardly likely that this night "demonstration of impotence" headed by Prokopovich and Shreider could have impressed the patrol which stopped the procession. After milling about for an hour, shivering and soaked, they returned to the City Duma.

Aldanov, in his "Pictures of the October Revolution," speaks with great irony about the "historic and hysterical" scene at the Duma when the resolution was passed. This large group of intellectuals was probably as subject to mass psychosis as any crowd. Revolutionary phraseology is identical in all epochs. Too frequent mention was made of the readiness to die, without the recognition that such words could create some kind of binding obligation. Nekrasov spoke of death at the Kadet Congress on March 28, Miliukov during the April crisis, Avksentiev at the Moscow Conference, Kornilov at General Headquarters, Kerensky at the Pre-Parliament and even earlier, and Dan at the Congress of Soviets; after the Bolshevik Revolution, Skobelev in the Committee for the Salvation of the Country and the Revolution and Tseretelli in the Zemsky Sobor were prepared to lay down their lives. Representatives of the Soviet of Peasants' Deputies promised at the Moscow Conference to give their lives for the Provisional Government. Probably all spoke sincerely and with feeling. And at the Duma on the 25th, awareness of the magnanimous act that was to be performed inspired tears of rapture.

However, the Duma resolution did infuse the beleaguered forces in the Palace with hope. An objectively meaningless gesture was transformed into a positive factor. Persons going to their death always need moral support; this constituted that moral support for the defenders of the Winter Palace. The night "demonstration of impotence" by the Duma also had other, more far-reaching results. It brought about a turning point in the attitude of some members of the rank and file of the anti-Bolshevik revolutionary democracy and made it possible for further resistance to the Bolsheviks to be conducted under its flag. Alongside the idea of isolating the insurgence, the idea of armed resistance to the uprising also became possible.

When the Duma procession arrived at its point of departure at about three in the morning, representatives of all the organizations that had adopted a resolution to organize a "Committee for the Salvation of the Country and the Revolution" were gathered there. These included representatives of the Duma, of the old VTsIK, the Executive Committee of the Soviet of Peasants' Deputies, the factions of the Socialist Revolutionaries and Mensheviks that had left the Congress of Soviets, various other socialist parties, representatives of the Pre-Parliament, committees of the front, and trade union organizations. It was decided to make a national appeal to oppose the Bolsheviks and restore the Provisional Government — a government that would be new in composition, to be sure. Yet what an immense distance lay between the

Committee of Salvation and the Duma Security Committee, which was negotiating with the Bolsheviks and in the political struggle tended to take a neutral position! "The Duma should not mix in the political struggle," the Socialist Revolutionary Kapitsa had stated several hours before, according to a report printed in *Delo Naroda*. The Duma had no basis for defending "personal interests," those of Kerensky in particular.

The "posthumous" message of Maslov from the Winter Palace was fated to constitute the last straw that upset the emotional equilibrium of a great many representatives of the revolutionary democracy – even that wing that did not participate in the subsequent struggle. The message even penetrated into the Smolny Institute. During a recess of the Congress of Soviets, the Menshevik Internationalists (Martov's group) passed a resolution censuring the "military conspiracy." The rumble of artillery reached Smolny, and Martov went into "hysterics," to quote Bolshevik observers. A Bund group headed by Abramovich also became alarmed. Abramovich suggested that they, too, head for the Winter Palace to "perish with the government." And it is perhaps somewhat unexpected that we encounter on board the minelayer *Amur*, which was supposed to begin bombardment of the Winter Palace in lieu of the *Aurora*, a delegation from non-Bolshevik members of the Petrograd Soviet with aims similar to those of the delegations from the Duma which were dispatched almost simultaneously. The delegation, which consisted of two Left Socialist Revolutionaries and two Menshevik Internationalists, endeavored to dissuade the sailors from firing on the Winter Palace, explaining that it also sheltered socialist ministers. One member of the delegation announced "with a tremor in his voice" that "Maslov was cursing the democracy." At this moment a messenger ran in with an order to begin the bombardment immediately. Another group from the Soviet headed for the Winter Palace. It reached the headquarters building and from there tried to telephone the Winter Palace in order to "reach an agreement without bloodshed." "These delegations left Smolny to the accompaniment of 'guffaws and jeers' on the part of the throng of Bolsheviks," recalls the Bolshevik writer Vladimir Bonch-Bruyevich.

We do not know whether the *Aurora's* six-inchers or the guns of the minelayer *Amur* would have been fired. Execution of the order was delayed. "We decided to wait another fifteen minutes, instinctively sensing that things might change," reported one of the leaders of the attack. Envoys of the insurgents, headed by Chudnovsky, carried a new ultimatum to the beleaguered forces. It was decided to surrender the Provisional Government's citadel; this was the decision of Palchinsky. The final moment arrived. Once again Nikitin got in touch with his friends by telephone and through them sent "greetings" to the democracy.[42] The next conversation could no longer take place – only a "wild din" was heard at the other end of the line.

One should read the extremely able memoirs of Sinegub, which, though outwardly confused, nevertheless portray with striking vividness the atmosphere during the last hours of the Winter Palace. Their chaotic character was merely a literary device employed by the author. With genuine brilliance, Sinegub portrays his own state of mind bordering on hysteria, the feelings and thoughts of the defenders of the government, and the chaos all around. The halls of the palace swarmed with sailors and Red Guards, who were infiltrating through the rear entrances. It was frequently impossible to distinguish which forces were which. The sailors were disarming various groups of cadets. Palchinsky, the most effective commander in the Winter Palace, appeared with pistol in hand, surrounded by a dozen cadets. Some of the conquerors were taken prisoner. But beyond the walls were thousands, while in the palace there were only a few hundred disorganized men, sometimes without leadership and without officers.

A din penetrated from the outside. This was an "accompaniment to the silence," that frightful silence reigning in the ministerial chamber, writes Sinegub. Then "a terrible clatter broke out in the palace itself." Thirty to forty men appeared from nowhere. Exploding grenades sailed through the air. Silence returned. Again a throng surged into the palace. This one was larger, about one hundred men. Palchinsky reported that the cadets mistook them to be the delegation from the Duma. The intruders were disarmed. "Suddenly a noise became audible, swelled in volume, and drew nearer. The noise sounded different than before." "They are launching a frontal assault," Maliantovich noted.

The Bolshevik memoirists — that is, those who directed the siege of the Winter Palace — were not satisfied to use such prosaic phrases in describing the "heroic moment of revolution," the "beautiful," "unforgettable" seizure of the Winter Palace. It is pathetic how they endeavor to exalt the "feats of the Red heroes" on the night of October 25-26. Artillery projectiles whistle through the night, shells burst, and the crackle of machine guns is heard. The assaulting forces "vault" the barricades. The defenders are crushed. The courtyard is seized. The heroes break through to the palace. They scatter the government defenders. The cadets throw down their arms. A search is launched for the "guilty parties." The locked doors of palace rooms are broken down. Here is a door at which cadets are standing rigid with terror, chained by their duty. The cabinet! Fix bayonets — away with them! The throng surges into the room . . . . All are arrested. The captured politicians "babble about protection from the masses." This is approximately how Podvoisky reminisced in 1920 about that evening.[43] It is difficult to imagine how with such a "frenzied" attack the seizure of the Winter Palace cost the assaulting forces "only six lives." This was announced semi-officially after the insurrection by Zinoviev and later (on November 1) was confirmed by the

Military Revolutionary Committee: "Several wounded on both sides and six killed among the MRC forces." (The real figures may have been somewhat different. For example, the leaders of the workers' detachment from the Baltic shipyards also reported six casualties. And six were reported by the forces from Kronstadt.) To an outside observer this "frenzied" assault would not appear to have been a real battle. And, of course, he would be more correct in his appraisal. "There was . . . no organized defense, and the casualties on either side were but few in number," wrote Buchanan, who watched from the windows of the British Embassy during the very height of the bombardment, at eleven o'clock in the evening, while streetcars continued calmly crossing Trinity Bridge.

Trotsky, in his history of the October Revolution, did not entirely conform to the version of the Bolshevik apologists. In his version of the operations around the Winter Palace one can see the influence of "White Guard" sources. Nevertheless, he does say that the "Palace did not surrender, but was taken by storm," though at a moment when the "resistance of the beleaguered forces was exhausted." He repeats Maliantovich's account of how a hundred enemy troops, whom the demoralized defenders mistook to be the deputation from the Duma, burst into the corridor, not by way of the secret passageway any more, but by way of the defended courtyard. What probably happened is that an armed group forced its way in after the truce envoys and thus broke through the "barrier of bayonets and fire" between the attackers and defenders; the throng from the square began to pour into the courtyard, then from the courtyard into the palace, spreading up the staircases and through the corridors. "Phantasmagoric encounters and clashes took place in the corridors. All were armed to the teeth. Raised hands brandished revolvers. Hand grenades hung from their belts. But nobody fired and nobody threw grenades, for the defenders and attackers were so intermingled that they could not separate themselves." Here was the door where the cadets had frozen in their last pose of resistance. They were disarmed. The victors broke into the ministerial chamber. "Members of the Provisional Government, I place you under arrest," proclaimed Antonov-Ovseenko in the name of the MRC. It was 2:10 A.M., October 26. "The members of the Provisional Government bow to superior force and surrender in order to avoid bloodshed," replied Konovalov. The inescapable part of the ritual had been observed.

Corrections must be made in Trotsky's account. These corrections are furnished by Sinegub. The commander of the defending forces sent Sinegub to warn the cabinet that he was compelled to surrender the palace and that a promise had been made to spare the cadets' lives. The envoys with the ultimatum refused to discuss the fate of the government. A surrender conference was held by the ministers. The crowd accompanying Antonov stopped in front of the cadet guards, and Palchinsky took only Antonov into the ministerial chamber. Palchinsky then came out and announced the cabinet's decision to the cadets – to accept terms of unconditional surrender, bowing to superior force – and he suggested that the cadets do likewise. The latter had to be persuaded by Palchinsky, Konovalov, and others, who tried to prove that further resistance would lead only to a senseless loss of life. The cadets remained silent while Antonov-Ovseenko frantically appealed to the attacking crowd to maintain "revolutionary discipline."

The theatrical staging that both Trotsky and Antonov attempt to depict is, to a great degree, false. The ministers sat around a table, as if a normal meeting of soothsayers was taking place – but frightened soothsayers. The scene has been described by Maliantovich. "Let us take seats at the table," said Kishkin. "All thirteen sat frozen around the table, merging into one single, pale, trembling face." Sinegub's account contains more truth and vitality: "The members of the Provisional Government, some seated, some standing, gazed with a great calmness, which can be manifested only by men marked by fate." "We have not surrendered and have merely bowed to superior force, and do not forget that your criminal adventure has not yet met with final success," bravely announced one of those present.

There was neither confusion nor hesitation. Nevertheless, it was a fearful moment. It was not a revolutionary cohort of the Bolshevik host that had forced its way into the palace, but an ill-assorted mob, in the full sense of the word, with a mob's inherent excesses and violence, a mob aroused by the martial atmosphere of gunfire, powder, and bursting shells. Hooligan elements looted the palace – this is denied neither by Bolshevik memoirists nor Soviet historians. Probably gathered in the palace was that entire "demoralized *okhlos*" which some researchers of the Russian Revolution are inclined to place in the forefront of their description of the events of October. Five days after the assault a special commission of the City Duma made an investigation of the destruction in the Winter Palace and established that the loss of valuable works of art had been small, although wherever the looters had gone there was vandalism – eyes had been pierced through in portraits, leather armchairs had been slashed, oaken chests containing china had been pierced with bayonets, and valuable miniatures, icons, books, and other items were lying about the floor.

Unequivocal threats of violence were made against the ministers. Yet Maliantovich, Sinegub, and Kartashev do point to a certain kindly attitude and bewilderment in the relations between individual representatives of these two seemingly different worlds. The guards and prisoners exchanged comments, which developed into conversations. Even Antonov-Ovseenko notes that Tereshchenko argued with a sailor from the *Aurora*. How are you going to get along without the intellectuals? he demanded. Kartashev practically held a theological debate with a sailor. A third sailor, an anarchist, was assuring everybody that the Bolsheviks had seized power only temporarily and was insisting that power should be in the hands of the anarchists, who were against power. He found supporters among the guards. That class hatred which Bolshevik literature has so assiduously attempted to find was not in evidence. Very characteristic is the way Sinegub was able to escape from the palace at the last moment. He was led out by a factory worker who had come with a friend to "see how they take the palace." (The friend remained in the palace wine cellar.)

The ministers were to be taken to the Peter and Paul Fortress. Guarded by twenty-five men, they were led out to the courtyard. They made their way across the battered barricades. The guards lost track of their prisoners in the darkness. Maliantovich was forced to take hold of the sash of the sailor guarding him in order to avoid being left alone in a new and unfriendly mob. Somebody struck Liverovsky, the minister of railroads. Two sailors were guarding Kartashev, the minister for religious affairs; one of them kept leading him off toward the wall, as if wishing to do away with him, while the other protected his recent opponent in the religious discussion and gave Kartashev his name. The prisoners were led out of the palace grounds onto the square, where they were surrounded by the guards. The crowd in the square was not so large as Bolshevik descriptions make it seem. There were not thousands of people jamming the palace square and surrounding the palace in a solid wall, but rather "small groups," according to Smirnov, which were lost in the immense square and unexpectedly popped up out of the darkness. There were many drunks in the crowd, reported Minister of Labor Gvozdev and Minister of Agriculture Maslov in accounts published later in *Delo Naroda*. "The mood was getting ugly," says Maliantovich. At one point the crowd broke through the cordon, and, according to Nikitin's account in *Rabochaia Gazeta*, the consequences could have been fatal if it were not for the vigorous intercession of Antonov-Ovseenko. The crowd angrily looked for Kerensky, on whom so much hatred and irritation were focused as a result of all the propaganda and demagoguery. If Kerensky had been among the ministers arrested it is possible that mob justice could not have been avoided. This was the impression of the prisoners themselves. They were threatened with violence again on the Trinity Bridge when they encountered another mob, this one consisting of perhaps only a few dozen people. Provocateurs or genuinely enraged voices cried out: "Into the water with them, bloodsuckers, traitors, selling Russia to the Germans." "Hey, you, onward to victory! Drown them all and have done with it." "A miracle saved us," asserts Maliantovich. An armored vehicle began firing at the bridge "due to a misunderstanding." The crowd dispersed. The guards and their prisoners dropped to the ground for cover. Finally they reached the Peter and Paul

Fortress, in which the new authorities imprisoned the members of the Provisional Revolutionary Government.

These ministers, who had been unable to organize the resistance to the Bolsheviks, who had been unable to defend themselves and the state, attested to a truth of history: those who are incapable of bearing the burden of power do not possess the moral right to take upon themselves responsibility in times of revolution. Yet through their courage and dignified behavior, they succeeded during the last tragic hours in writing a truly worthy page in the chronicle of history. And their deed was praised by their contemporaries. A city-wide meeting of 350 Menshevik defensists held on October 27 praised the "unshakable courage displayed by the ministers of the Russian Republic, who remained at their posts right up to the end under artillery bombardment, demonstrating a magnificent example of genuinely revolutionary valor."

Nevertheless, everyone who reads what Aldanov said about that "terrible evening on the palace square," that "there is nothing for which the Russian democracy should be ashamed," will rightly ask: what did the democracy have to do with it? The organized democratic forces are perhaps more to blame than the others for the fact that the "terrible evening" of October 25 passed with the Provisional Government in such total isolation, and that the honor of democracy and the fate of the nation were defended by shock troops from a women's battalion, two or three companies of young cadets, and forty disabled wearers of the Order of Saint George headed by a captain on artificial limbs.

What was the fate of the young people who defended the palace? Testimony recorded in the days following the surrender of the Winter Palace is contradictory. For example, in *Delo Naroda*, a cadet named Rizin told about some cadets who were mauled in the assault on the Winter Palace and then were brought to the barracks of the Pavlovsky Regiment. When the cadets attempted to escape, the soldiers fired at them and "many were killed." But Rizin was one of those who escaped, and in his agitated state, he could not have been an objective witness. Militsyn reported that some of the cadets who had been led away to the training compound of the Preobrazhensky Regiment immediately began to be released in groups. Some sailors learned of this, came to the barracks, and beat up the initiator of the release. "The men of the regiment, to their own shame, did not stand up for him." There were many rumors of atrocities, but one could find direct denials of them in the press. For example, *Narodnoe Slovo* explained that rumors about the execution of cadets at the Peter and Paul Fortress had sprung up as a result of a clash between a "mentally deranged" cadet and the guards. The latter threatened to use their weapons. The newspapers carried accounts of only a few isolated, random cases of mob justice. Ambassador Buchanan recorded one incident. "In the evening [of the 26th]," he wrote, "two officer instructors of the women's battalion came to my wife and beseeched her to try and save the women defenders of the Winter Palace, who after they had surrendered, had been sent to one of the barracks, where they were being most brutally treated by the soldiers." Eventually, the female shock troops were freed at the insistence of the British Embassy — General Knox made a special trip for this purpose to the Bolshevik Headquarters at Smolny Institute.[44]

We must be objective. All those rumors of violence and reprisals following the surrender of the Winter Palace, those rumors that caused such public agitation, rumors that appeared in the columns of those socialist papers that continued to publish after the revolution and that were later recorded in private journals (for example, the journal of Hippius), should be attributed to overworked nerves. "These were awful days," wrote Militsyn. "The city was full of rumors of bloody Bolshevik reprisals against the cadets and the women from the death battalion. Sailors and the Red Guard were on the rampage." Trotsky was right when he said in his history of the revolution: "There were no executions and due to the mood of both sides there could be none during that period." This was substantiated in essence by a special investigatory commission appointed by the City Duma.

[When news of the capture of the Winter Palace reached Smolny, Kamenev made the announcement to the Congress of Soviets. It was 3:10 A.M. on October 26. Representatives of the Left Socialist Revolutionaries and of the Menshevik Internationalists protested the arrest of the socialist members of the government. Overriding their objections, a resolution was adopted stating that the Provisional Government was deposed and that the Congress of Soviets "hereby resolves to take government power into its own hands." At about 5 A.M. the Congress adjourned, to reconvene at 9 P.M. that evening.

By then its agenda had been decided by the Bolshevik Central Committee, and Lenin proposed to the Congress a resolution calling for immediate peace negotiations (it was adopted unanimously) and a decree abolishing large landed estates and providing for the distribution of the land to the peasants (adopted by an overwhelming majority). The decree on land was lifted virtually verbatim from the program of the Socialist Revolutionaries. This, he said, "does not matter"; he was willing to grant "full creative freedom" to the peasants, even though he disagreed with their demands for small, equal holdings.

Next, Kamenev presented Lenin's plan to form a "provisional government of workers and peasants" to rule the country until the meeting of the Constituent Assembly and to be known as "the Council of People's Commissars." Representatives of non-Bolshevik leftist groups raised their voices again, this time in favor of a "homogeneous" coalition government of all the socialist parties. The Left Socialist Revolutionaries refused to enter a predominantly Bolshevik cabinet. The Menshevik Internationalists introduced a resolution proposing that at least those parties that remained in the Second Congress of Soviets jointly appoint an executive committee to form a new government. Representatives of the All-Russian Executive Committee of the Railroad-Workers Union (Vikzhel) likewise opposed the idea of a one-party government. The Vikzhel, with its power to allow or to stop troop and supply movements by rail, was to play a prominent role in the days to come, as we shall see later.

Trotsky brushed proposals for a "coalition" aside as serving only to weaken the revolution. The list of people's commissars proposed by the Bolsheviks was put to a vote and overwhelmingly approved. Lenin was the chairman of the Council, Alexei Rykov was commissar of the interior, Trotsky commissar of foreign affairs, a triumvirate composed of Antonov-Ovseenko, Nikolai Krylenko, and Pavel Dybenko was to run the army and navy, and Stalin became commissar for nationalities. Then a new, predominantly Bolshevik, Central Executive Committee of the Congress of Soviets was elected, and nominally, the government was made responsible to the VTsIK. At 5:15 A.M. on October 27 the Congress adjourned. S.G.P.]

PART II

Under the Banner of the Revolutionary Democracy

No one will ever take away that freedom which was won by all the people.

KERENSKY

CHAPTER **5**

At the Front

KERENSKY AND CHEREMISOV

"The soldiers and workers together have emerged victorious in an uprising without bloodshed," read the salutation sent by the MRC to the front on the day of the coup, October 25.

The troops expected from the front – the one hope of the besieged forces in the Winter Palace – failed to materialize. The prevailing view seems to be that the delay in bringing in troops to aid the Provisional Government, a delay which had such fatal consequences, was caused by General Cheremisov's cancellation of Kerensky's orders, a step the general took on his own initiative. Kerensky, of course, elaborated this version in his memoirs. Arriving in Pskov, about 175 miles southwest of Petrograd, around eight o'clock in the evening on October 25, Kerensky stopped at the quarters of his brother-in-law, Quartermaster General Baranovsky, and summoned Cheremisov, the commander in chief of the northern front. He tells us that Cheremisov attempted to demonstrate that he could not spare any troops from the front and that, in addition, he could not be held responsible for the personal safety of Supreme Commander Kerensky in Pskov. At the same time, Cheremisov, not hiding the fact that he did not wish to link himself with the fate of the doomed government, supposedly announced that he had already countermanded Kerensky's order. Cheremisov was to attend a session of the local military revolutionary committee. He promised Kerensky a final report on the state of affairs after the session and promised to send him General Krasnov, who, at the head of the Third Cavalry Corps, was to move toward Petrograd and was expected in Pskov "at any moment."

History does not have objective methods of psychological analysis that enable one to read the hidden thoughts of an individual and determine the inner motives impelling him to act in a certain way. Cheremisov was considered a protégé of the revolutionary democracy and had even been

97

mentioned among the top candidates for the post of supreme commander during the days of the Kornilov affair. His candidacy had been advanced again at a later date, because the VTsIK felt that it was appropriate to have a military specialist occupy the top military post. V. L. Burtsev waged a bitter campaign in his newspaper, *Obshchee Delo,* against Cheremisov in the days preceding the October coup d'état, accusing him of an excessively "friendly" attitude toward the Bolsheviks. To speak of such sympathies is rather far-fetched. In many subsequent talks with representatives of front organizations during October the commander in chief of the northern front always clearly emphasized the "hopelessness" of the Bolshevik position and their total isolation from the rest of the democratic parties. Cheremisov's fate disproves Burtsev's accusations. When the Bolsheviks came to power his career did not prosper, as did General Bonch-Bruevich's, and he was one of the first to be arrested by Krylenko, the new commander in chief. During the "Petrograd difficulties" Cheremisov was inclined toward the semi-neutral position characteristic of a considerable segment of the revolutionary democracy and fairly representative of the attitudes at the front. Moreover, personal impressions gained by him in Petrograd weighted the scale on the side of neutrality. As Cheremisov saw it, the "Petrograd difficulties" would run their course without his interference.

Prior to Kerensky's arrival, Cheremisov had already been informed of the state of affairs in Petrograd by General Bagratuni. They held a laconic teletype conversation: "The government has lost its last vestige of authority and an attempt may be made to take over the government," said Bagratuni. "What are the Cossacks doing?" "In spite of a number of orders received by them, the Cossacks would not budge from their quarters all night." "You mean they refuse to carry out your orders?" "So far, they have not carried them out." "All right, thank you. Goodbye." Obviously Cheremisov concluded that the Provisional Government was absolutely powerless. Besides not wishing to get involved in its "difficulties," Cheremisov, of course, could have been guided by the immediate interests of the front. The northern front was threatened by a possible German offensive, and the situation was very unsettled in respect to the mood prevalent in some army troops. According to the French general Niessel, the northern front was "*le plus mauvais de tous.*" A civil war among the Russian soldiers at the front could bring about a total collapse of the army. And what then? "Then," Cheremisov replied to General Boldyrev on November 1, "the Germans will sweep Russia from the map of Europe." For Cheremisov the "real enemy" had always been, as he put it, the "Berlin Germans." Cheremisov, who somehow was able to cope with the soldier organizations at the front and keep them within the bounds of at least external discipline, wished to prevent "internecine strife," which would "fatally affect military operations." The order from Kerensky to withdraw troops from the front, an order not coordinated with the local command and counter to the plans made at the conference in Petrograd on the 23rd, constituted an unnecessary and untimely disturbance at the front.

Some light is shed on Cheremisov's failure to send troops by the actions of the government commissar at the northern front, Woytinsky. Woytinsky unconditionally sanctioned the order from Kerensky and Lieutenant Colonel Grekov summoning the First Don Cossack Division to Petrograd from Ostrov. "Let the deserters, entrenched in the rear, rage against the Cossacks," he wired in reply on the 25th. "But the Cossacks shall carry out their duty to their country to the end." However, although Woytinsky fulfilled his obligations, he was plagued by doubts. This can be seen from his subsequent conversation by direct line with P. M. Tolstoy, deputy chief of the War Ministry's Political Administration. "I am interested most of all," began Woytinsky, "in one thing: What is the attitude of the Central Executive Committee of the Soviets toward recalling armed forces from the front, and what are the present relations between the Provisional Government and the VTsIK?" Woytinsky then explained that the use of the armed forces boiled down to one question: "Is this step an act of self-defense by bold individuals grouped around Kerensky or is democracy [represented by the VTsIK] using a certain method to defend its position against encroachments? All depends on the answer to this fundamental question. If you are politically isolated in Petrograd, no efforts whatsoever will be able to muster support for you at the front." Woytinsky then elaborated: "Today's evening papers say that certain factions in the Congress of Soviets have spoken out against resolving the conflict by force of arms. This vote puts ... matters in a new light, for now we can act only in the name of the VTsIK. It has been proven to me today that references to the Provisional Government can have no effect whatsoever." Woytinsky eventually replied to Tolstoy in the affirmative: Petrograd could count on his support. We do not know whether Woytinsky attempted to persuade Cheremisov, as Tolstoy requested. But if he did it could not have been prior to Kerensky's talk with Cheremisov, because the conversation ended with a statement by Tolstoy: "The entire Duma has left for the Winter Palace." Consequently, *this conversation occurred no earlier than eleven o'clock in the evening,* October 25. During the conversation, Woytinsky mentioned that "troops are moving but it seems that the commander in chief of the northern front has decided to halt them, since he considers the attempt to be a failure already."

Woytinsky continued to have doubts after his conversation with Tolstoy. They were dissipated only when he spoke with the Socialist Revolutionary leader Gots and received directly from him corroboration of the position taken by the VTsIK. This was late that night, after the Socialist Revolutionary and Menshevik factions walked out of the Second Congress of Soviets and the Committee for the Salvation of the Country and the Revolution was organized.

Meanwhile, earlier that same evening Woytinsky's assistant, Savitsky, announced at a meeting of the Pskov military organizations that "since we have received from Petrograd the rather strange information that Kishkin, Palchinsky, and Rutenberg have been appointed to important posts, the commissariat of the northern front has decided *not to* send troops for the time being." The meeting appointed a "Northwestern Revolutionary Committee," the purpose of which was to oppose the orders to send troops. At a session of this special committee, close to midnight, Woytinsky announced that he was resigning in view of the fact that only one of the three armies he had communicated with was in favor of sending troops to aid the government. But on the following day Woytinsky appeared at the meeting of the military organizations in "a totally different mood" and resumed his post, announcing that he would heed only the orders of the VTsIK, which was insisting that troops be sent. During a subsequent interrogation by the Bolsheviks, Woytinsky explained that he had submitted his resignation in ignorance of the fact that the Central Executive Committee of the First Congress of Soviets had disavowed the Second Congress of Soviets and the Bolshevik-controlled Central Executive Committee elected by it. "Receiving more accurate information, I hastened to retract my statement of resignation, since I felt it was inadmissible to shun participation in the struggle initiated by the first VTsIK." Thus the matter of not sending troops goes far beyond the framework of any personal intrigue by General Cheremisov.

Let us now return to the meeting of Kerensky and Cheremisov. This has created a historical knot that must be untied. Three memoirists – Kerensky, Cheremisov, and Krasnov – contradict one another, and their testimonies are in disagreement with records we have of talks by direct wire between General Headquarters in Mogilev and Northern Front Headquarters in Pskov.[45]

According to Kerensky, Cheremisov informed him during their first conversation – that is, between eight and nine o'clock in the evening on the 25th – that he had cancelled his order to send troops to Petrograd. One is amazed at the equanimity with which the impulsive supreme commander received such a fateful piece of news. It would seem he merely asked Cheremisov: "Have you seen General Krasnov? Does he agree with you?" "General Krasnov will arrive here any minute from Ostrov," Cheremisov replied. "In that case, General, send him to me immediately."[46]

One cannot help but wonder how Cheremisov's order did not come to the ears of Commissar Woytinsky if it had been issued before Kerensky's arrival. In his conversation with Tolstoy, which could not have taken place earlier than 11 P.M., Woytinsky only mentioned Cheremisov's *intention* to halt troop movements. One must also bear in mind that all orders issued by the commander in chief of a front had to go through the hands of the commissar to the front, in this case Woytinsky, not only due to the prevailing conditions of life in the army at the time, but also because according to the instructions of August 30 the commissar constituted an official organ of the government. The "statute" on commissars stated quite clearly that the "use of armed force for other than regular military operations shall not be permitted without the knowledge of the commissar" (Paragraph 24). The commissar had the right to "stop an order" issued by command personnel which ran counter to instructions from the government.

Finally, Kerensky's version is convincingly denied by written evidence – a wire sent on Cheremisov's instructions by Lukirsky, chief of staff of the northern front, to Dukhonin, General Headquarters chief of staff, informing him that the commander in chief of the northern front had at ten o'clock in the evening cancelled all orders to dispatch units to Petrograd. Consequently, the final decision was made *after* the conversation with Kerensky.

In a subsequent conversation between Dukhonin and Cheremisov, the latter gave the following answer to Dukhonin's question about what motivated the cancellation: "It was done with the consent of the supreme commander, received by me from him personally." What came next was even more sensational: "The Provisional Government no longer exists in its previous form. Authority has been transferred to the [Military] Revolutionary Committee. This evening someone, apparently rightist elements, appointed Kishkin governor general of Petrograd. His affiliation with the Kadet party is well known at the front; this appointment has abruptly changed the mood of the front troop organizations, [which are no longer] in favor of the Provisional Government . . . . *Kerensky has stepped down from his position* and has expressed the wish that the position of supreme commander be transferred to me. This matter will probably be decided today. Please order any shift of troops to Petrograd stopped if such is occurring on the other fronts."[47] "Where is the supreme commander right now?" asked Dukhonin. "He is here. Would you like me to tell him anything?" "Can he come to the teletype?" "Impossible, in his own interests." Cheremisov tried to break off the conversation, claiming that he was late for an appointment and promising to call Dukhonin ninety minutes later to inform him about "decisions on certain matters." Nevertheless, Dukhonin attempted to use persuasion on Cheremisov. "The Provisional Government is still in existence. The arrival in Petrograd of troops loyal to the government could show results, considering the passivity of the troops who have rebelled against the Provisional Government. An indication of this is the extreme sluggishness and indecision on the part of the Bolsheviks. If Kishkin's candidacy is not acceptable, we can ask the Provisional Government to replace him with someone else, a military man. If Supreme Commander Kerensky proposes that the job be given to you, I implore you in the name of our beloved country to permit me to inform the Provisional Government, with which I am in contact about this. I also beseech you not to countermand the orders calling for troops to be sent to Petrograd. I firmly believe that with proper organization matters can be settled without much bloodshed, while the inviolability of the front will be maintained, and you as future supreme commander will not have to deal with very serious . . ." At this point Cheremisov interrupted once again. "For the time being keep everything to yourself, but bear in mind that there is no longer a Provisional Government in Petrograd . . . . In two hours I shall need to call you urgently." "Two hours from now I shall be at the teletype," replied Dukhonin, "but the contents of the tape are known to the [All-Army] Committee,* which is here with me in this room." "This is no secret from the Committee, I mean your relations with those members of the Provisional Government remaining in Petrograd." Cheremisov did not call again and had no further contact with Dukhonin, although the latter waited for his call "all night."

At 11:45 P.M., just before he talked with Dukhonin, Cheremisov had communicated with General Baluev. He informed the commander in chief of the western front of the state of affairs in Petrograd ("The Provisional Government no longer exists in its previous form") and of the appointment ("without Kerensky's participation") of Kishkin, and stated that he was against sending troops, considering it not only a "pointless" but also "harmful" act, since "obviously the troops will not support Kishkin." The commander in chief of the northern front proposed to his colleague on the western front that they combine the operations of both fronts "in order to avoid anarchy." "Things are still calm on the northern front," added Cheremisov, but the resolution of the front organizations "will not favor the Provisional Government as it was," although "seizure of power by the soviets will also fail to meet the support of the majority." Baluev replied sharply: "It is a pity that your troops are participating in politics. We swore allegiance to

*After the Petrograd Soviet issued its "Order Number 1" on March 1, elected committees of soldiers, with possible participation of officers sprang up in all lower-level military units (companies, battalions, squadrons, regiments) to protect the economic, civil and political rights of soldiers. Later, similar committees were formed at the level of a corps, an army, and a front. Representatives from the latter two formed the All-Army Committee, which was attached to the General Headquarters in Mogilev. The political majority in the committees of the larger units belonged to the Socialist Revolutionaries and the Mensheviks. The All-Army Committee was headed by Socialist Revolutionary Perekrestov. Formally, the activity of the committees was regulated by the "Statute on Army Committees" issued on August 30.

the Provisional Government, but it is not our job to argue about whether Kishkin or someone else is the Governor of Petrograd."[48] As to combined operations: "According to law, in the absence of the supreme commander, all orders should be issued by the General Headquarters chief of staff." "We do not have any right to shun politics," retorted Cheremisov, "nor to fail to consider the political moods of the masses . . . in order that the front not be exposed to the enemy." The "politician" and the "soldier" could find no point of agreement. Baluev immediately reported his conversation with Cheremisov to General Headquarters in Mogilev and requested that Dukhonin hold "the commander in chief of the northern front within proper bounds by swift and vigorous action." A short time thereafter, Baluev proclaimed his "political neutrality," and Dukhonin reproached him for drifting with the current and knuckling under to the demands of the MRC. Eventually General Baluev went over to the Bolsheviks and served in the Soviet army and General Cheremisov became an émigré.

In memoirs published in the émigré newspaper *Golos Rossii*, Cheremisov gave his own version of Kerensky's readiness to resign. At about midnight Cheremisov returned to Baranovsky's quarters to inform Kerensky of the talks he had held with the troop committees. Having heard Cheremisov out, Kerensky ushered him into an adjoining room (apparently somebody was present during the conversation) and said: "I have decided to turn over the supreme command to you, to go to Petrograd and resign as prime minister. Please tell me what you think about that, General, and be absolutely frank." In his "memoirs" Cheremisov of course turns down the job of supreme commander and convinces Kerensky that it is out of the question to make any changes during a moment of crisis. "I advised Kerensky to proceed immediately to General Headquarters and to gather reliable regiments there in order to advance on Petrograd. I then offered the opinion that another government should be set up at General Headquarters . . . otherwise Kerensky might end up playing the same role Kornilov had played." Kerensky "agreed" with this argument and decided to proceed to Mogilev. Cheremisov supposedly left to get some sleep, and it was not until ten o'clock on the morning of the following day that he learned that Kerensky "was fighting the Bolsheviks near Gatchina." Cheremisov said absolutely nothing in these reminiscences about his order cancelling the dispatch of troops or about his talk with Dukhonin.[49]

The bias in these memoirs is quite obvious, but even Kerensky admits that Cheremisov recommended that he proceed to General Headquarters. The commander in chief of the northern front obviously wished to rid himself of his nervous guest as soon as possible.

Be that as it may, there is no need to wade through all the controversies and the voluntary and involuntary errors made by both memorrists. We have established one unquestionable fact: the order to send troops from the front to Petrograd was cancelled *after* Kerensky arrived in Pskov.

In order to reconstruct what must have taken place at Pskov, we have to understand Kerensky's state of mind. Almost all observations made at the time—both friendly and unfriendly to Kerensky—mention Kerensky's depression during the October days. There is nothing strange in this. A man's nerves are not of iron. Kerensky had gone through a lot in the frothing caldron of revolution between February and October. During that period occurred the February Revolution, numerous government crises, the June offensive, the Bolshevik insurgency in July, the Kornilov affair, and, finally, the confusion of events prior to the October uprising. In addition, Stankevich testifies that at the beginning of October Kerensky was "dangerously ill." Sukhanov recalls his "pale, exhausted figure." During a conversation at the Winter Palace on October 24 Kerensky impressed Dan as a "thoroughly exhausted individual." Although his nerves had already become accustomed to sleepless nights, the night of the 24th must have had an effect on the low spirits of the prime minister. Cheremisov was probably not far from the truth in his description of his meeting with Kerensky: "Kerensky looked like a broken man. He was lying on a couch. 'Greetings, General,' he said to me, and extended his hand, rising up slightly and apologizing." Three or four hours later Cheremisov found Kerensky in the same posture: "He was still lying on the couch, evidently thoroughly shaken and exhausted by all that he had gone through in Petrograd and on the long automobile trip."

The degree of Kerensky's nervousness is indicated by the account of one of those "friends" who subsequently helped Kerensky escape arrest at Gatchina. This friend was the Socialist Revolutionary Veiger-Redemeister, who later left the party and effected a rapprochement with the Communists. But this was no reason to fabricate the episode he related in his essay entitled "With Kerensky at Gatchina." Kerensky was handed a telegram from Dukhonin in Gatchina on the 27th. Reading it, Kerensky "stood up and exclaimed, 'All is lost,' and sank limply into his armchair. Everybody wondered why Kerensky had reacted that way, because Dukhonin had proclaimed 'support of the Provisional Government with all his forces,' and when Kerensky came to they explained to him that he had misunderstood the telegram. The telegram was indeed quite simple: "All orders issued. Personally assured comm chief north today that your order to be carried out to the letter . . . . Situation calm on other fronts. Organizing further consolidation of your forces together with the committee and commissars."

In his memoirs, which were written too soon after the events, Kerensky does not mention the names of those "friends" whom he had seen and with whom he had taken counsel, in order to protect the persons involved. He also fails to mention Woytinsky. When did their meeting in Pskov take place? Of great importance is a statement made by Cheremisov in a telegraphic exchange with Dukhonin on November 3. He said that during the conversation with Kerensky on the night of the 25th he advised cancelling the order to send troops, "foreseeing that [to send them would be] impractical and would only lead to a situation whereby Kerensky and those troops which he could personally lead would become entangled in a difficult and perhaps hopeless situation." Cheremisov added: "Witnesses to this conversation were Baranovsky, Kuzmin, and Woytinsky. Kerensky agreed with me at the time and cancelled the orders . . . but as I was leaving at five o'clock in the morning Woytinsky arrived again with Krasnov." It is thus possible that Woytinsky was present during the second conversation between Kerensky and Cheremisov. In view of his vacillating position prior to his talks that night with Gots, he certainly could not have inspired Kerensky with confidence in the support being given the government by the revolutionary democracy. On the contrary, he could have caused Kerensky to waver. It is also possible that Kerensky did not speak directly in favor of cancelling the order to send troops. In his state of mental prostration he did not speak in definite terms.

Some contemporaries were almost positive that Kerensky himself had cancelled the order to send troops to Petrograd. This was the opinion of V. V. Vyrubov, deputy chief of staff of General Headquarters, when he arrived in Petrograd from General Headquarters. I noted it in my diary on December 4, 1917.

Apparently Vyrubov's opinion was also held by General Headquarters, although an official report to General Headquarters on the 26th by Lukirsky, chief of staff of the northern front, stated quite clearly: "Yesterday, after issuance of the order cancelling the movement of troop units to Petrograd, Alexander Fedorovich [Kerensky], who does not share the opinion of the commander in chief of the northern front, arrived. . . But it was impossible to transmit an order reconfirming the dispatch of troops to Petrograd, since members of the revolutionary committee organized in Pskov stood watch at the telegraph keys." The copy of this document published in *Red Archives* contains a notation, which one must assume was made by Cheremisov: "The order cancelling the transfer of troops to Petrograd was made with the consent of the supreme commander, who arrived in Pskov not subsequent to, but prior to the cancellation. The second order to dispatch the Third Cavalry Corps was issued by the supreme commander directly to the commander of the Third Cavalry Corps."

THE GATCHINA CAMPAIGN

Thus the commander of the Third Cavalry Corps, General Krasnov, appears on the scene accompanied by his memoirs, which must be used with extreme caution. This is not only because they were written by a novelist with the tendency to reproduce past events in a more or less fictional form, but also because the memoirs were published just after the "cornet undertaking, dashing at first glance, but essentially representing an ill-conceived adventure" (thus Cheremisov characterized the Gatchina campaign) ended in failure. One instinctively uses caution in approaching a memoirist who, in two variants of his memoirs under differing political conditions (in Russia and as an émigré), has given us two radically different versions of the end of the Gatchina venture.[50]

Krasnov was to lead the first detachments sent to the aid of the government. "Fate would have it," commented Kerensky, "that my last attempt to save the nation from Bolshevism was linked with the Third Cavalry Corps — that same unit which, under the command of Krymov, was used against the Provisional Government by General Kornilov." Fate had nothing to do with it, since units of the Third Corps had been selected by Supreme Commander Kerensky himself without a prior agreement with Cheremisov, obviously because these units, demoralized though they were by the Kornilov affair, were still considered to be the strongest in respect to their anti-Bolshevik sentiments. The emergency dispatch of units from the Third Corps emphasizes the lack of deliberation manifested during those days in government circles. The Third Corps was scattered along the entire northern front. General Krasnov saw in this a malicious intent. He states that in September he had made vigorous attempts to station the corps close to Petrograd in order to support the government. But since the "soviets" insisted that the corps be removed from the environs of Petrograd, it was placed at Cheremisov's disposal. The scattering of the corps along the front apparently was not a deliberate or "premeditated" act, but rather a natural sequence of events. The Cossacks were dispatched here and there at various times in anticipation of disorders along the front. They forgot about this fact in Petrograd when they designated the regiments of the First Don Division for the job of going to the aid of the government. On the 24th four regiments of this division had been sent to Revel "to disband an infantry division which had refused to carry out combat orders." Krasnov was able to collect only ten undermanned *sotni* (Cossack squadrons) of 70 men each, that is a total of 700 cavalrymen, only 460 of whom would count as an armed force if they had to fight in dismounted formation. Due to the absence of the commander of the First Division, who was on leave, command was assumed by Kerensky himself, who intended to concentrate his troops in Luga, half way between Petrograd and Pskov, and march from there in order to "avoid repeating Krymov's mistakes." At about eleven o'clock in the evening on the 25th, Krasnov received the order cancelling the march, and he proceeded to the headquarters of the northern front in Pskov in order to clarify how to act in the face of two conflicting orders.

Then at 5:30 A.M. on October 26, Kerensky, after having discussed the matter with Krasnov, issued an order countersigned by Government Commissar Woytinsky directing that the transfer of the Third Corps continue. "What is the decision of the commander in chief of the northern front [Cheremisov]?" Dukhonin asked Lukirsky that morning. "He has ordered the 'revolutionary committee posts' to be removed and units of the Third Cavalry Corps to continue proceeding by railroad," answered the chief of staff of the northern front.

Simultaneously a general order to the army was issued under Kerensky's signature: "For the time being, until and if a new government is formed, every man must remain at his post ... and I shall remain at my post of supreme commander until the will of the Provisional Government of the Republic is expressed." This order caused some confusion. For example, Iordansky, commissar of the south-western front, informing Vyrubov that the front was quiet ("the majority are behind the Provisional Government") and that he was prepared to send a detachment in order to provide at least "moral satisfaction," said: "One sentence [in the order] is puzzling, the mention of a possible new government; if this means a readiness to compromise with Petrograd, it is a mistake. The slogan should be restoration of the government and the convening of the Constituent Assembly at the appointed time. . . . We view the situation as the inevitable moment to liquidate Bolshevism and would be quite disturbed if the half-measures of July 3 through the 5th were to be repeated." Kerensky's phrase about a new government was a concession to the mood of the VTsIK, about which Gots informed Woytinsky. The struggle against the Bolshevik seizure of power was to proceed under the banner of the revolutionary democracy and not of the Provisional Government.

After signing the two orders, Kerensky proceeded with Krasnov from Pskov to Ostrov, about thirty miles to the south, where Third Corps Headquarters was located. In reading Kerensky's memoirs one learns that it was only his "personal appearance among the troops that did away with ... all concealed and visible obstacles" in the way of moving out. According to Krasnov's memoirs it was only his energy and initiative that achieved the objective. The troop trains departing from Ostrov to the accompaniment of "shouts and threats by unruly conscripts" steamed past the Pskov railroad station, where unfriendly masses of armed soldiers had also gathered on the platform. The swiftness of events once again prevented Dukhonin from talking directly with Kerensky.

Toward evening, when the trains were approaching Luga, about halfway between Pskov and Petrograd, Kerensky learned of the taking of the Winter Palace. "Now I believe," he wrote in his memoirs, "that [accompanying Krasnov's detachment] was an irreparable blunder. If, on the morning of the

26th I had known that the Provisional Government had been seized by the Bolsheviks, I probably would not have embarked on this risky plan." Of course, even in Luga it was not too late to alter the plan, but the communique received through Baranovsky seemed improbable at the time and Kerensky decided that the news had been fabricated by Bolshevik agents.

Gatchina, an outer suburb some twenty-four miles south of Petrograd, was taken without a shot at dawn on the 27th, just as the Second Congress of Soviets was adjourning. Pro-Bolshevik troops that had been sent from Petrograd (according to Kerensky they were numerous and possessed artillery and armored vehicles, but according to Krasnov they consisted of two companies and a group of sailors) ran without offering battle. According to MRC records 100 sailors and 1,500 soldiers from the Semenovsky and Izmailovsky regiments were sent to Gatchina. They supposedly retreated "in order to avoid bloodshed with their deluded Cossack brothers." Local troop units were passive and neutral. Inspired by this initial success, Kerensky demanded an immediate advance. Krasnov would have preferred to wait in Gatchina until help arrived. After all, the garrison at Tsarskoe Selo, the next obstacle on the way to Petrograd, totaled 16,000 men, while Krasnov's detachment was joined only by a troop train from Novgorod carrying 200 Cossacks. But "civil war is not war," comments General Krasnov in his memoirs. "Its rules are different, calling for decisiveness and offensive pressure." At two in the morning Krasnov, who had now been appointed by Kerensky commander of all armed forces in the Petrograd area, advanced toward Tsarskoe Selo. He moved cautiously, "parleyed" where possible, arriving at agreements with some of the enemy forces. Relinquishing the personal direction of the troops and following his rule of "non-interference" with the orders of persons assigned to carry out given tasks, Kerensky stayed in Gatchina. But he was unable to remain idle and soon went out into the very thick of the "concentration of government troops." Krasnov explained to the supreme commander that the delay in the advance was due to the small size of the government detachment and the organization of the defense at Tsarskoe Selo, which was better than he had foreseen: "We are still haggling," he said. Krasnov begged Kerensky to leave the battlefield, since his presence hindered the operation and made the officers nervous. Kerensky returned to Gatchina.

Time passed. Tsarskoe Selo still had not been taken. At dusk Kerensky went out to the field once again with the "firm resolve to participate in combat operations." Kerensky had no doubt that the "sudden paralysis that had seized all units of the Third Cavalry Corps was not military but rather political in origin." (Many times subsequently Kerensky asserted in articles that Krasnov "had been slipped orders" telling him to remain neutral.) After acquainting himself with the situation on the spot, Kerensky sent Krasnov written orders to begin combat operations immediately. At this moment

Stankevich, who had come from Petrograd with the most optimistic information about the state of the "combat forces" prepared to support Kerensky, arrived on the field of battle. Krasnov's hesitation came to an end. In his memoirs he provides us with a bit of colorful detail. Becoming impatient, Kerensky plunged into a crowd of wavering soldiers and launched into agitated oratory from his automobile. The situation became quite confused. The outcome was decided by a Don Cossack artillery squad. They fired one or two rounds, and "it seemed they had wiped away this sea of heads and flashing bayonets. The field became deserted." Tsarskoe Selo was taken. The MRC announced that "two regiments had fought heroically, but were forced to retreat under the pressure of superior forces." Soviet historians later claimed that the Bolsheviks had made "one more attempt to avoid bloodshed."

"Victory was ours, but it consumed us entirely," Krasnov was forced to admit. During the entire day of October 28, only 300 men from the first Amur Cossack Regiment arrived to help them, having taken over the armored train "The Invincible." But, according to Krasnov they announced that "they would not participate in a fratricidal war." A regiment proceeding from Luga by rail was fired upon by sailors and scattered. Kerensky had the "firm hope of finding fresh troops" when he returned to Gatchina. He found only telegrams.

Krasnov's small force drowned in the sea of the disintegrating "neutral" garrisons of Tsarskoe Selo and Gatchina. In order to hold his handful of Cossacks at the necessary level of discipline, the solidarity of command personnel was necessary. This was lacking from the very beginning, and not only due to the unnatural combination of two persons of such differing political views and such differing personalities as Kerensky and Krasnov. Kerensky himself was compelled to acknowledge that the officers of the detachment considered themselves "Kornilov men" and were hostile toward him. Krasnov described the following scene: Lieutenant Kartashov, arriving from Petrograd, informed Krasnov near Luga about events in the capital. Kerensky entered the compartment and extended his hand to Kartashov (in keeping with the supreme commander's democratic custom to "greet all identically"). Kartashov stiffened to attention, but did not offer his hand. "I am sorry, sir, but I cannot offer you my hand, I am a Kornilov man." Kerensky also recalls this episode, but assigns it to a later time, when intriguers arrived from the Union of Cossack Troops, instigating hostility toward the Provisional Government and demanding that Kerensky be done away with, and when Krasnov began definitely to throw off the guise of loyalty.

The negative attitude toward Kerensky increased as the isolation of the detachment became more obvious and the hope of assistance waned. The hostile attitude of the officers could not but be passed on to the rank-and-file

Cossacks. Kerensky was accused of responsibility for what was happening. Kerensky himself emphasizes very strongly that the demoralization of the Cossacks was due to clever Bolshevik propaganda, which made use of "old regime" statements by the officer corps and at the same time represented Kerensky as a "counterrevolutionary." In any case, the atmosphere in the detachment was tense. According to Krasnov, an extremely agitated delegation of Cossacks came to him with the demand that Kerensky be removed from the detachment immediately because he was "betraying" the Cossacks.

Who made up the intimate and not very numerous group of persons around Kerensky at Gatchina, and what did they attempt to do? As has been pointed out, in his memoirs Kerensky deliberately omits to mention the names of those whom he calls his "friends." Apart from the people who had accompanied him from Petrograd, this intimate group consisted primarily of Woytinsky, who took up quarters in Gatchina on the 27th. He himself in testimony given to the Bolsheviks defined his main functions as the "prevention of any excesses and of any utilization by the counterrevolutionaries of the advance detachments." "I did not permit the formation of military-revolutionary courts, mass arrests, or other violence," he testified. He had the detachment adopt "a definite platform of a conciliatory and strongly democratic character." Stankevich, as a valued advisor and the principal official intermediary between Gatchina and Petrograd, also participated closely in the events of Gatchina. Guest appearances were put in by the Socialist Revolutionaries Gots, Feit, and several others. Chernov also appeared. They all endeavored to organize, rather unsuccessfully, propaganda in the Gatchina and Tsarskoe Selo garrisons. Their failure was partially due to confusion among the propagandists. According to Veiger's testimony, some were defending the necessity of combating the Bolsheviks, while others were rejecting this view, basing their stand on the idea of a united front of socialist democracy. Thus they could hardly inspire unity in the ranks. At best the propagandists helped create a situation in which the soldiers preferred to maintain a status of neutrality since they were also antagonized by the importunate Bolshevik propaganda. Stankevich, who was a participant, described a remarkable scene in his memoirs. Arriving in Tsarskoe Selo from Petrograd on the 26th, he observed the local garrison running "in terror" from an enemy that had not yet appeared. The idea came to Stankevich to sway the soldiers to the side of the government. He exercised his eloquent oratorical ability before a crowd at the Tsarskoe Selo railroad station. But, the memoirist recalled, "I had hardly stopped talking, confident of success, when an old soldier spat and began shouting in angry indignation: 'Everything is so damn confused, I understand nothing; to hell with all speechmakers.' "[51]

Everything was quite confused indeed, and the entire social and domestic muddle was clearly represented by this variegated conglomeration of men and moods at Gatchina.

ATTITUDES IN THE ARMY

Success in the Gatchina campaign depended entirely on a rapid movement of troop trains from the front — at a moment when the front was in an uncertain mood.

Help was coming, but it moved with "a strange and puzzling" sluggishness. General Headquarters in Mogilev dispatched telegrams in all directions, and so did Krasnov and particularly Kerensky. "Subsequently," said Kerensky, "we received an explanation of this mystery: on the one hand we were being 'sabotaged' by some headquarters, such as that of Cheremisov; on the other hand, the Bolshevik railroad workers and telegraph operators were employing a sit-down strike." "General Headquarters was idle, paralyzed," Krasnov charges. But aside from all these causes there was one more, which was noted by Cheremisov.

"The first thought," recalls Cheremisov, "was, of course, immediately to move whatever possible to Kerensky's aid."* But supreme commander Kerensky did not wait for local initiative. He proceeded on his own. Northern Front Headquarters began receiving telegrams from Kerensky containing categoric instructions to send such and such a regiment to Gatchina. Orders from the supreme commander could not be knowledgeable about troop locations or the relative reliability of any given regiment. This mistake had immediate consequences. The orders brought objections from the commanding officers in the field. One reported that the requested regiment had just been deployed. Another reported that the requested regiment could not move out for two days. And so on. Cheremisov's account can be corroborated by a considerable number of examples taken from army teletype communications that have been published.

One example is rather typical. On October 31 several units of the Seventeenth Dragoon Regiment left Kaluga to aid the government forces in Moscow. After they left an "extremely urgent" telegram was received from Kerensky in his capacity as supreme commander. It was addressed directly to the regimental commander and ordered him to transfer units "by passenger

---

*It is very doubtful that such an idea guided Cheremisov. All the subsequent behavior of the commander in chief of the northern front does little to bolster such an assertion. "In four days," claims Budberg, a corps commander on the northern front, "the troops in Dvinsk received from Cheremisov merely a telegram saying that 'politics are of no interest to the army.' " S.P.M.

train" to Gatchina. As a result, the departure of the rest of the regiment for Moscow was delayed. Cheremisov explains that this confusing tactic was due to the interference of Woytinsky, who as commissar of the front, claimed to have knowledge of what troops were available.

The task of securing reinforcements was complicated by the endeavor to send Kerensky units that were sufficiently "revolutionary" rather than ones that were "rightist." The commissar of the Eighth Army, Vendziagolsky, arriving in Gatchina on the 28th with the news that an entire corps, the Seventeenth, just transferred from the Rumanian Front and deployed in the Nevel area, was coming to lend assistance, was amazed by the fact that in Gatchina they did not have the slightest idea of troop deployment along the northern front. Equally characteristic was the fact that they were trying to deprive Vendziagolsky, who was suspected of collaborating with Savinkov, of any position of command. He was named commissar of an armored train, which, in Woytinsky's opinion, was to play "merely a morale-boosting role." Later it was proposed that he be assigned as agitator to some weak units, with instructions that "if they are too far to the right, step on their tail," to quote Woytinsky.

It is amazing that Kerensky displayed no initiative in consulting directly with his chief of staff. All attempts made by Dukhonin to consult with Kerensky were fruitless. This lack of communication also probably explains to a certain degree why General Headquarters did not display more initiative. Headquarters maintained the position it had taken on the 26th, when it sent telegrams to all the fronts declaring that it would extend "full support to the government," a decision based on the fact that the majority of army committees spoke out against the Bolsheviks (nine out of the eleven armies). Dukhonin was telling the truth when he informed the supreme commander on the 31st: "I am doing everything possible in view of the present situation to put down the Bolshevik movement and support you, and I am persistently endeavoring to surmount all unexpected obstacles in the way of carrying out these measures." He had the full cooperation of the All-Army Committee, as evidenced by the fact that Dukhonin, his deputy Vyrubov, Government Commissar Kovalevsky, and the chairman of the All-Army Committee at Headquarters, Perekrestov, jointly sent the following telegram from Mogilev on October 30: "As spokesmen for the army and navy we demand that the Bolsheviks immediately cease acts of violence, give up their armed seizure of power, and subordinate themselves unconditionally to the Provisional Government acting in full agreement with the plenipotentiary democratic bodies, since only the Provisional Government is capable of bringing the country to the Constituent Assembly, master of the Russian land. The active army will back up this demand with force."

"General Headquarters lives on illusions and has itself come under the influence of political parties," said Cheremisov, persistently continuing to pursue a policy of noninterference and still considering the "involvement of the army deployed along the front in a political affair" "to be a major government blunder."*

General Headquarters dealt with matters theoretically. It calculated and combined abstract values, whereas on the northern front real troop units had to be dealt with. The position of the commander in chief of the northern front — aside from the personal views of the person who occupied the post—was extremely difficult in view of the fact that it was in his territory and among his units that a civil war was breaking out. Under such conditions a posture of political neutrality was sometimes almost compulsory for the commander.

Such was also the case in the Baltic Fleet. The officer corps advocated non-interference in politics in order to persuade the Helsinki-based sailors not to go to the aid of the Bolsheviks in Petrograd. When the first telegram from the supreme commander requesting aid to the government arrived, there was nothing the officers could do but reply that the instructions "can not be carried out." They resorted to subterfuge and said that the telegram "cannot be deciphered." Two days later Lenin demanded that ships be sent from Helsinki because "the situation is critical and the troops of the Petrograd garrison are exhausted." The navy commander issued a statement saying that he could not continue to exercise his authority if the armed forces were drawn into "politics."

The situation in Pskov was quite unique from the very beginning — a military revolutionary committee with Bolshevik participation, and vacillating government commissars. Here is how Cheremisov characterizes the political positions of the commissars: "One of them, the internationalist Shubin, eventually sided with the Bolsheviks; another, former Bolshevik Woytinsky, took Kerensky's side; the third, Savitsky, opposed both the Bolsheviks and Kerensky." As soon as a purely Bolshevik committee separated from the military revolutionary committee, a tense atmosphere developed in Pskov. On the 26th Woytinsky informed Vyrubov "for the time being a bloodless war is

*Of course, Cheremisov was endeavoring primarily to influence Dukhonin. Since other units were protesting the departure of the Third Cavalry Corps and were willing to be sent to Petrograd in defense of the MRC, there was a threat of civil war at the front and of its disintegration. Cheremisov requested Dukhonin to cancel the dispatch of troops from the northern front, other than those already dispatched personally by the supreme commander. ("You agreed not to send troops, but then altered your decision," Cheremisov reminded Dukhonin in a conversation on November 3.) Then the commander in chief of the northern front issued the following order to his armies: "The political struggle taking place in Petrograd should not concern the army, whose task remains unchanged — to firmly hold those positions presently occupied, to preserve order and discipline." Nevertheless,

being waged between me and the [local] MRC, which has taken control of all teletype machines but mine; they are attempting to stop troop trains and plan to arrest me." On the morning of the 27th Woytinsky's house was surrounded by a Bolshevik guard, but Woytinsky was no longer there (he had been replaced by Savitsky).

One must admit that Cheremisov did succeed in avoiding major excesses. But at what price? This is the heart of the matter. Passive loyalty delayed the possibility of putting a swift end to the "Petrograd affair." For Cheremisov the "only correct policy for the military authorities" was dictated by the confidence in a swift self-liquidation of the Bolshevik venture. "The Bolsheviks," he assured the Chairman of the Revel military revolutionary committe on the 29th, "have become totally isolated and have proved unable to actually seize power." The same Cheremisov teletyped the following to General Boldyrev, commander of the Fifth Army: "None of the other political parties has taken the side of the Bolsheviks, who have seized power in Petrograd; therefore, apparently the incident will die out by itself when the Bolsheviks release power. They naturally understand that in a time of revolution authority cannot remain in the hands of a party which expresses the political views of the minority."

Each day of delay increased tension along the front. "The wave of Bolshevism proceeding from the rear," Dukhonin informed Kerensky on November 1, "is gradually approaching. . . . If the crisis drags on another two or three days it will be impossible to guarantee calm on the front." On the southwestern front, where the mood was "most favorable" to government, bloody clashes took place. "In Vinnitsa," reported Dukhonin on October 31, "a bitter clash took place, with both sides employing armored vehicles and airplanes." By evening the Bolsheviks had been "put to flight." The most noticeable event on the northern front was the decision of the army committee of the Fifth Army to dispatch twelve battalions with field pieces and machine guns from Dvinsk to Petrograd to settle the conflict. This

---

Cheremisov himself officially maintained a loyal posture in respect to Kerensky. All orders received by him were sanctioned with the reasoning that "all who believe that an army should be an organized army and not a disorganized mob understand that orders from the supreme commander and General Headquarters should be carried out without question." This explanation was given by Cheremisov on October 29 to representatives of the Pskov military revolutionary committee. But his loyalty was of a rather formal nature — a desire not to bear any responsibility for Kerensky's acts. Cheremisov's position was ambivalent indeed, but this ambivalence did not mean that "Cheremisov's headquarters had clearly taken the side of the Bolsheviks," as Denikin claimed in his *The Russian Turmoil*. S.P.M.

expedition, which supposedly had a "neutral objective," did not materialize, though, because General Boldyrev vigorously stated that he would use arms to prevent a detachment being sent from the Fifth Army to support the MRC.

The attitudes that had developed in the Fifth Army may be of particular interest. This army, the closest one to Petrograd, had, according to Alexei Budberg, responded "enthusiastically" in July "to the appeal against the Bolsheviks," but in October it became a "bulwark of Bolshevism." In his vivid journal,[52] Budberg, who was in command of an army corps, provides us with the material for forming a judgment. (But one should not forget that as a memoirist Budberg was very impulsive and that he felt very keenly the disintegration of his corps, which "up till now," he noted on October 14, "has been considered a happy exception in respect to maintaining order.") Noting cases of fraternization with the enemy, refusals of army units to occupy combat zones, announcements of abandonment of the front "in a week," etc., all of which were quite common at the time, Budberg believed that his "very steadfast corps" had been ruined by replacements arriving from the rear in October, replacements that he had "begged" headquarters not to send. "They brought to the front cowardly companies which had no desire to fight or work, companies which . . . intensified the food crisis that had prevailed at the front for quite some time already." On October 15 he wrote: "Right now the entire strength of the Bolsheviks" resided in those third-rate divisions. Budberg considered disbanding these units and leaving at the front only volunteers, with whose aid it would be possible "to hold on to the last stake — elections at the Constituent Assembly." According to Budberg his plan did not find favor at Northern Front Headquarters, where they were not so pessimistic in assessing the situation and were even drawing up, in October, a plan for an offensive.

(Actually, as can be seen from the report by Deputy Commissar Sviatitsky to the War Minister on October 22, the question of reorganizing corps so they would be homogeneous in respect to nationality and of the creation of volunteer regiments was advanced at the Council of Government Commissars of the Northern Front among the measures outlined for combating demoralization in the army. By this time an entire draft plan had been developed at General Headquarters for a "volunteer army," in which Dukhonin, to quote the author of an article published in *Golos Minuvshego* in 1918, saw Russia's "sole salvation." This plan, presented by Vyrubov to Kerensky, was ratified on October 16.)

Budberg's conclusions on the eve of the October uprising were extremely pessimistic: "There is no doubt whatsoever that the denouement is drawing closer, and there can be no doubt as to the ultimate result; on our front there is no longer a single unit (other than two or three shock battalions, and possibly the Ural Cossacks) that are not under Bolshevik control." The corps commander called himself a "fallen scarecrow." Yet from Budberg's own account it is easy to see that he still enjoyed great moral authority among his men, and from the daily entries in his journal one can sometimes obtain data for making substantial revisions in the joyless picture sketched by the pen of this pessimist. I shall not introduce these corrections. Let us merely turn our attention to an event which is in itself remarkable.

It would seem that Bolshevik headquarters in Petrograd would have learned of the mood of the Fifth Army through its emissary, Skliansky. Yet Lenin's military advisors, recalling the July Days, feared most of all that Kerensky would be able to transfer units of the Fifth Army from the front to Petrograd. The "sober-minded" army committee of the Fifth Army had sent a telegram to Petrograd stating that "the bayonets of the Fifth Army are ready to restore order on the home front." Budberg, mentioning this telegram, adds: "All this was merely boasting and idle talk; it is self-evident that under the pretext of pacifying the rear everybody is ready to abandon the front, but when they arrive home one must think about how to pacify them and with whom."

Apparently the MRC had a different assessment of this possible rush from the front. Budberg's entries for the days of the October revolution seem to attest to the fact that the Bolshevization of the Fifth Army, particularly of Budberg's own corps, was a relative thing. Here is a comment made on October 26: "There is great rejoicing in all units because of the overthrow of Kerensky and transfer of power to the soviets. But in spite of all the Bolshevik indoctrination, the majority of the men are against Bolshevik power and would like merely that power be handed over to the Central Executive Committee of the Soviet of Soldiers' and Workers' Deputies [VTsIK]. The appearance of Lenin at the head of the new government flabbergasted the majority of the inert soldiers; this figure, with its German stamp was so odious that even Bolshevik agitation proved powerless to whitewash it. In our corps committee the leader of our Bolsheviks, a veterinarian's assistant, said to the chief of staff with great anxiety: 'Is it really Lenin? Is this possible? What will happen now?' ... This appointment so affected the corps committee that by a majority of twelve to nine it rejected a discussion of a resolution favorable to the Petrograd Soviet."[53]

"The day went by in a generally calm atmosphere; the mood in the units was one of waiting; all wanted to see how things would develop," writes Budberg in his diary under October 27. At the front a decree calling for "immediate peace" was received. The telegram "had an immense effect everywhere and evoked great joy. Our last possibility to save the front was gone." These were the circumstances in which the new Bolshevik Army Executive Committee discussed the order from Petrograd to send reliable units to lend help. The Army Executive Committee "rather cleverly escaped from its ambiguous position," deciding not to send troops, because "security of the front makes it impossible to send large numbers, and it is not worth it to send only a few." Thus Army Commander Boldyrev was not compelled to "test the loyalty" of his shock troops and cavalry units, with which he intended to prevent troops from being sent to aid the MRC; according to Budberg's pessimistic forecast, they would have refused to carry out pacification. "In view of the fact that in one part of the army sympathy is on the side of Petrograd [Bolsheviks] and in another it is on the side of the Central Committee [VTsIK]," said Lieutenant Captain Sediakin, head of the local military revolutionary committee to Cheremisov, "the Army Executive Committee will take a neutral position and will take all steps necessary to prevent fratricidal slaughter among the troops of the revolutionary parties, but will release all troops at its disposal to fight counterrevolution." "This is a right decision. I welcome it wholeheartedly," replied the commander in chief of the northern front. "Fearing civil war between the political parties at the front, I have asked the supreme commander to cancel his order to send troops to Petrograd from the northern front, except for those units under his own personal command, and it seems that my request has been complied with." Such was the situation in the most "Bolshevik" army during the Petrograd "affair."

I shall mention a few features characteristic of the Twelfth Army, which according to its commander, General Iuzefovich, was "in an exceptional position" because it was deployed on Latvian soil, and because earlier, in May and June it was the target of intensive Bolshevik propaganda: it was here that Roshal published his *Okopnaia Pravda*. At the July Congress of Bolsheviks the representative of the Baltic region stated: "We shall be able to turn the Twelfth Army into a Red Army." "In Riga eight Latvian regiments, that is 48,000 bayonets, support us." According to the Bolsheviks, the Riga front was notified about the impending takeover in Petrograd, and indications were that the Twelfth Army would fully support it. But quite unexpectedly, at least for some, it was precisely the Twelfth Army, one of three, which immediately responded to the appeal of Commissar Woytinsky for support of the Provisional Government. Apparently the German breakthrough at Riga had a great effect in the army, and its "recovery" began. In the October 3 issue of *Izvestiia*, organ of the VTsIK, one could read the appeal to the nation from the Twelfth Army Congress of Soldiers' Deputies, which stated that "there is no immediate way out of the war," and therefore, "brothers, gather your last strength, get rid of your disappointment and weakness of spirit and give all to defend our nation, without vacillation." This appeal called upon the enlisted men to "join with your officers" and demanded that all segments of the population sacrifice all for defense needs. This same Congress came out against convening the Congress of Soviets on October 20 and urged the Petrograd garrison not to support "the insane agitation of liars and demagogues." The first days of nervous waiting at the front following the revolution went by. The front commander reported to his superior on November 1 that "the situation is extremely acute in the Latvian brigades." But in spite of the entire "arsenal of provocation" and demagoguery the Bolsheviks were unable to emerge triumphant at the Riga front. An agreement was reached at the army congress: full neutrality in regard to dispatching troops to Petrograd, cancellation of all orders issued by the MRC, and the return of Latvian units that had deserted from their positions. A new *Isposol* (Soldiers' Executive Committee) was formed, consisting of twenty-three Bolsheviks and twenty-three non-Bolsheviks, with two chairmen. But in a statement issued on November 5 in Petrograd the MRC maintained that no agreement had been reached. "Civil war" could be expected at the Riga front.

What position did General Iuzefovich consider it necessary to take in this complex situation? "I am making every effort," he telegraphed to Cheremisov, "to avoid that first shot. I am assuring my men that no troops will be sent from this army to Petrograd. Under these conditions nothing can be pulled out, while at the same time Kerensky's plenipotentiary has arrived — a representative of the Union of Armored Car Crews — to take the Fifth Armored Division. I have forbidden it categorically, but he is holding talks with Pskov, attempting to seize the vehicles arbitrarily and dispatch the division. All these meddlers in army affairs will get out of it all right, and we shall be left here holding the bag. I believe the army cannot be run with all this meddling. I believe we must think about what can be done if civil war breaks out within the army. We are sitting on a powder keg."

This was essentially the position taken by General Cheremisov also. It is characteristic of Budberg, a man very removed from "revolutionary careerism" but not adhering to the "right" either, that he too was inclined to take a similar position. At a conference called by Boldyrev in Dvinsk (on the 26th) he seemed to be repeating Cheremisov's argument, when he noted in his diary: "Boldyrev is undecided, and as he told me himself, he is afraid to remain between two chairs. I replied that if we do not launch into politics there is no reason to fidget, for we have a single chair — our responsibility to hold our combat sectors; we cannot leave this post, while the struggle between parties, in which we do not and cannot participate, is not our affair; right now we are merely professionals, guarding the remnants of the dam, a German breach in which can destroy Russia. Of course there is still another solution: We can use shock units to arrest the Army Executive Committee and enter into the power struggle; but under the circumstances this would be senseless in respect to the balance of forces, and it would be fatal to the interests of the front, since the front would be immediately drawn into the struggle. At the present time we are obliged firmly and decisively to hold our combat positions and demand that all political organizations, without exception, vigorously support the disciplinary order and the combat capability of our troops. Let the soviets, committees, and commissars engage in politics and graze their unruly herd as they will." "I myself," adds Budberg, "have little faith in the success of all this, but such policy is the only possible one for us." (A.R.R. XII, 230-231.)

Thus the pessimist Budberg and optimist Cheremisov agreed on one professional tactic. Such a political position constituted an external, rather forced neutrality, and it was not only command personnel who adhered to it. The general mood of the troops and their officers, particularly after the days of initial confusion, is perhaps reflected in the resolution of the Sixth Army Committee passed on November 1: "Not one man to Kerensky, and not one man to the Bolsheviks."

But this attitude certainly did not constitute an immutable postulate. "The make-up of the former government," stated the commissar of the Rumanian front, Tizengauzen, immediately upon receiving news of the revolution, "is not particularly popular among the men and as such holds little interest for the troops. . . . There is scarcely a possibility of moving troops from the front to protect the members of the government. . . . Yet there is no question but that the entire front will come to the defense of the Constituent Assembly." However, Tizengauzen did say that "perhaps there could be . . . found one unit which would go unquestioningly." He was correct. When shock troops from the Seventeenth Corps arrived in Luga on November 1 they were in a mood for battle. "Loyal" units such as these were also to be found at the front. They readily responded to the appeal to offer resistance to the Bolsheviks and proceeded conscientiously and without compulsion. For example, Woytinsky was definitely not pleased by the fact that "a mood of enthusiasm, even too enthusiastic," could be observed among the Cossack troops. (The quote is from a conversation with Vyrubov on the 26th.) Hardly an empty gesture was the announcement of the 28th committee for forming shock battalions that a total of "thirty-six revolutionary shock battalions in full battle readiness await orders from the supreme commander of the Russian Revolutionary Army and the Provisional Government to proceed to Petrograd to put an end to the aspirations of an irresponsible gang of anarchist-Bolsheviks." (On a copy of the announcement there is a note by Dukhonin: "We must sent at least one battalion each to Petrograd and Moscow.") Still, according to Dukhonin even some of the most reliable units vacillated. For example, the Fifth Cavalry Division decided to carry out all operational orders, but not to participate in political actions. The Seventeenth Cavalry Division proclaimed itself "neutral" and decided to act only to stop excesses. "The mood of the masses is fickle, [and their] view of the situation [is] frequently changing," Dukhonin reported to Kerensky on the 31st, relating how military units of a Seventh Corps infantry brigade which initially expressed "a voluntary desire to proceed to Petrograd" balked during loading operations, and it was necessary to send other troops that "today expressed their unanimous desire."

The situation on the western front was quite characteristic. It seemed "worse than ever" to its commander Baluev who, in a conversation with Dukhonin on the 29th, compared himself to a person "sitting on a powder keg with the fuse lit." In reality things were not nearly as bad. An important role was played here by the "Committee to Save the Revolution" in Minsk. The tactics of this committee became clear on the 26th, when a local congress of soldiers and peasants had passed a resolution stating that it "has heard with profound sadness that one segment of the democratic forces is once again attempting in Petrograd to seize power on the eve of the Constituent Assembly." The congress "categorically proclaims that it will permit no one to seize power in this republic by force without the consent of the majority of the people, and *if necessary*, will use force to curb those who choose to ignore it." But at the same time the congress proclaimed that "regardless of the magnitude of errors committed by one segment of the revolutionary democracy, the army shall not permit these errors to be used by the counterrevolution for its own aims." These tactics were inspired by the local Social Democrat *Bund* group, as well as by Socialist Revolutionary leader Chernov, who put in an appearance during his visit to the western front at the end of October. Then on the 27th the Minsk Committee to Save the Revolution reached an agreement with the local military revolutionary committee not to permit troops to be dispatched to the capital. The courtship took place through the mediation of the Mensheviks and had succeeded because after an unsuccessful attempt "to seize power," the military revolutionary committee had been forced to recognize that armed struggle with existing forces (against hostile cavalry units present in the area) would only lead to the "crushing defeat of the [military revolutionary committee]." It was also agreed to form a united socialist front and establish a joint committee. A venomous and perhaps somewhat simplistic description of the joint committee was given by General Valter, chief of staff of the western front, in a conversation with Diderikhs on October 31: "The committee is made up partly of well-intentioned elements and partly of Bolsheviks. It was formed because the Socialist Revolutionaries and Mensheviks, generally well-intentioned, are not sure that their military strength would provide sufficiently firm support against the Bolsheviks, and at the same time they are not sure how the struggle in Petrograd will end. Hence, the selfish fear of stating one's own views in the committee clearly and distinctly, and, in addition, the fear that vigorous steps taken against the soviet would cause an outburst of violence at the front. The Bolsheviks are vigorously implementing their policy, while the moderates . . . do not desire vigorous action against the Bolsheviks. All are holding the tuning fork to

Petrograd. As soon as the knot in Petrograd is untied in favor of the Provisional Government *all influence* by the soviet and the Bolsheviks will immediately disappear. To this one must add a total lack of affection for Kerensky," concluded General Valter.[54] Nevertheless, in spite of the absence of "affection" for Kerensky and in spite of the agreement not to permit troops to be sent to the capital, the Finland Rifle Division passed through the front without particular difficulty on its way to Petrograd to aid the government.

In reading materials characterizing the attitude at the front about the Bolshevik coup one comes out with an impression differing somewhat from the traditional view. It is apparently not true to say that in October the armies at the front had practically disintegrated and were held together only by inertia. If the representatives of the revolutionary democracy at the front had been able to take a definite, unambiguous position, they apparently could have carried with them the bulk of the troops without any particular difficulty. The attitude of the army and front organizations toward the Bolshevik takeover was generally negative. For example, an official communique to General Headquarters on the 28th definitely indicated that Bolshevik propaganda "is enjoying no success" on the Caucasian front. In his interesting memoirs, entitled *Defense of the All-Russian Constituent Assembly*, the Socialist Revolutionary Sokolov comes to the conclusion on the basis of his own personal observations of the attitudes of the soldiers in the Special Army (southwestern front) that the front was "still the most healthy organ in the country."

After all, between the 25th and the 31st of October, despite the uncertain, wait-and-see attitude that prevailed in the army, up to fifty troop transports started moving toward Petrograd to help the government, and virtually none to help the Bolsheviks. One troop train with 500 infantrymen did arrive from Finland on November 1, but instead of supporting the Bolsheviks it began to "fraternize" with the Petrograd garrison. It is quite clear now that when the Bolsheviks organized the coup in Petrograd, they had virtually no direct organizational links with frontline troops. Efforts to "organize" the front were begun essentially on October 26, the day after the coup. In response to these efforts, some Latvian riflemen from the Northern front began filtering toward Petrograd as individuals, but many of them were intercepted and stopped in Pskov. It was not until November 22 that the Sixth Latvian rifle regiment arrived in Petrograd, 2,500 strong, and not until the 26th that a special Latvian company took over guard duty at Smolny. From then on, it would no longer be the sailors who constituted the main armed support of Bolshevik rule, but the new praetorian guard of the Latvian riflemen.

CHAPTER 6

After the Coup

THE COMMITTEE OF SALVATION

Let us now see what took place in Petrograd the day after the Provisional Government fell.

We shall begin with the account of Stankevich, who was the provisional government commissar at General Headquarters at the time. His memoirs are amazingly straightforward in depicting impressions and attitudes. "The next evening," writes Stankevich, "the news burst upon us that Kerensky was approaching Petrograd with troops. . . . This bit of news improved the mood. Vigorous attempts to organize the struggle against the Bolsheviks began. These same rumors led to depression in Bolshevik ranks, evident in their street patrols. . . . Confidence in early elimination of the Bolsheviks grew hour by hour, particularly since news began filtering from the barracks that the garrison was dissatisfied with the new masters, and offers to participate in an armed action against them *literally rained in*. There were reports of confusion within the MRC. The City Duma and the Peasant Soviet quarters in the Law School were entirely in our hands and became the center for preparing political and military action against the Bolsheviks."[55]

These preparations were directed by the All-Russian Committee for the Salvation of the Country and the Revolution, which had been created by various supporters of the government on October 25 at the emotionally charged night session of the City Duma. The Committee of Salvation represented a broad democratic front. From the very beginning it included the presidium of the Pre-Parliament, representatives of the City Duma, the old VTsIK, and the Executive Committee of the Soviet of Peasants' Deputies, the factions that had walked out of the Bolshevik-dominated Congress of Soviets, and a group from the railroad and postal-telegraph unions. The central committees of the Socialist Revolutionary, Menshevik, People's Socialist, and Plekhanov's "Unity" parties were also represented. They were joined by delegates from Tsentroflot (the All-Navy Committee), which had taken a position against the uprising. The Committee of Salvation was swelled by representatives from other organizations. It was headed by Avksentiev, the chairman of the Pre-Parliament, which, in a sense, established succession from the Provisional Government. Its first act was to issue an appeal to the public not to recognize or carry out the orders of the usurpers, to rise to the defense of the nation and revolution, and to support the Committee of Salvation. "Preserving the succession of unified government authority," the Committee "will assume the initiative of reconstituting the Provisional Government," which, based on the forces of democracy, would lead the nation to the Constituent Assembly and save it from counterrevolution and anarchy. Clearly, it had in mind a new government formed on principles of coalition different from those reflected in the government that had just left the stage and the members of which were presently being held in the Fortress of Peter and Paul almost to a man.

Simultaneously with the appeal of the Committee of Salvation, participating organizations issued their own separate appeals. A sufficient quantity of vigorous words were spoken regarding the Bolsheviks. These words were of varying force and were combined in various ways. An analysis of these documents might be of considerable interest in characterizing the attitudes and moods of the Russian public. I shall mention only two features.

Not one political group issued a direct and open call to oppose the Bolsheviks with arms. But there were hints. The appeal of the military commission of the Central Committee of the Socialist Revolutionary party proposed "full cooperation with military organizations, commissars, and command personnel in putting an end once and for all to this insane venture." The right-wing Menshevik Defensists, headed by Alexander Potresov, "enthusiastically" praised the "courage" of the ministers who had remained "at their posts" under the guns of the "usurpers" and ended their appeal as follows: "Hail the Provisional Government! Assist the Provisional Government and Comrade Kerensky." In these words could be seen a call to arms. *Narodnoe Slovo*, organ of the People's Socialists, and *Volia Naroda*, organ of the right-wing Socialist Revolutionaries, demanded reconstitution of the Provisional Government, with restoration of all its authority. But the organs of the dominant socialist groups did not even mention giving aid to the government.

Another feature distinguished all the appeals that emanated on this and the following days from the camp of the "implacable" opposition. The spectre of an approaching counterrevolution stood before them like a *memento mori*. An appeal issued by the Central Committee of the Socialist Revolutionary party on the 26th already spoke in specific terms of a "triumphant counterrevolution" that would deprive the people of "land and liberty." In a joint session of the groups making up the committee, the Menshevik Skobelev put the cards on the table: "There are rumors," he said, "that there are generals in the provinces who wish to make use of the events taking place to march on Petrograd, naturally not to save the revolution but with quite different aims and objectives." Skobelev was alluding to General Kaledin. "Let us swear, comrades," exclaimed the speaker pathetically, "that the revolution shall be saved or we shall perish along with it."

With the aim of "restoring revolutionary order and preventing fratricidal civil war," the committee resolved to enter into "negotiations" with the Provisional Government and the central committees of the socialist parties for the purpose of "organizing democratic authority," which would assure "rapid liquidation of the Bolshevik venture by methods guaranteeing the interests of democracy, and a vigorous quashing of all counterrevolutionary attempts." A firm guarantee preventing the replacement of "extremists of the left" by "extremists of the right" was seen by the committee in the implementation of the program outlined by the majority of the Pre-Parliament prior to its dispersal by the Bolsheviks. The last point in the program rings with self-assurance: "*to demand* that the MRC immediately put down its arms, give up the power usurped by it, and appeal to its loyal troops to submit to the instructions of the Committee for the Salvation of the Country and the Revolution." The committee spoke like an authoritative master of the situation, although, as Tolstoy and Kovalevsky reported to General Headquarters, it "has no force whatsoever to back it up."

AFTER THE SEIZURE OF POWER

The Bolshevik leaders could hardly have been shocked by their political isolation. They could have expected nothing else. On the 26th, Bolshevik delegates at the City Duma meeting were greeted with invectives like "Murderers!" "Rapists!" "Get out!" "To the gallows!" Some delegates smiled in response, but in general the victors felt that their position was by no means secure. Suffice it to say that at the Second Congress of Soviets, despite its pro-Bolshevik make-up, only about half the army representatives were in favor of rule by the soviets, according to the answers given a questionnaire distributed by the Bolshevik faction. Lenin was counting on the hypnotic attraction of the decrees on land and peace passed by the Congress on October 26. But slogans do not have the swiftness of lightning. Only a Podvoisky was capable of thinking that victory would be theirs the minute "the regiments were given the right to speak of peace directly and to deal with their enemies." At best they might be able to say with some reservations, what Chernov said later: "Through its decree on peace Bolshevism has secured itself against any pacification expeditions from the front." And as a result of the decree on land Bolshevism "fenced itself off from the village" in some measure.

But not even the most astute of the Bolsheviks foresaw the extent of the mass sabotage, planned by no one and cropping up quite spontaneously, with which they had to cope.

This strike by the working intelligentsia, the "little people" — civil servants and the like — who refused to knuckle under to the yoke of violence, is one of the most beautiful pages in the history of the revolutionary period. It stands as a symbol of the civic honor of the public-spirited Russian. Universal among the intelligentsia was the conviction that the Bolsheviks would be unable to create any authority on their own.

It was inevitable that opposition to the "policy of revolutionary daring" and the blunt tactics of the Leninists would appear within the ranks of the very party that had seized power through chance and violence. The opposition was born spontaneously — first of all in that very city where the revolt had taken place with such ease. We have an interesting document concerning this — a summary of reports by Bolshevik party district commit-tees in Petrograd submitted in the days immediately following the uprising (October 28-30). The document echoes the voice of rank-and-file Bolsheviks. From these reports one does not get a sense of the confident victor. Noted were "signs of exhaustion" among the workers; the successes of Menshevik-Defensist propaganda; statements to the effect that "bloodshed is in vain," that the civil war should be stopped "peacefully."[56] A week later the Petrograd committee was forced to acknowledge an almost "total indiffer-ence among the worker masses" to the Bolshevik cause. The mood rapidly became critical among the workers who had not participated actively in the uprising. An official delegation of workers from the Obukhov Works unequivocally threatened to "take care of" all those guilty of wreaking the "chaos."

October 25 provided the Bolsheviks with a graphic illustration of the fact that in reality they had at their disposal a very limited military force. "The unwarranted exaggeration of revolutionary mood became quite clear a couple of days after the overthrow of the Provisional Government," Trotsky was forced to admit. This was the man who prior to the uprising eulogized the revolutionism of the Petrograd garrison. But the garrison, according to Antonov-Ovseenko, who assumed the position of commander in chief of Petrograd, began to disintegrate catastrophically and caused him considerably more worry and anxiety than the seizure of the Winter Palace. First of all, many of the garrison soldiers deserted, and only small remnants were left in the capital; for example, only 380 men were left in the Semenovsky Regiment, according to official figures. Antonov places particular emphasis on the "drunken madness" that seized the garrison, the memorable riots. According to Solomon, everyone at Smolny "panicked," including Lenin. "In the many years of our acquaintance I had never seen him like this. He was pale, and his face was seized by a nervous twitching." "Here you have a

Russian mutiny," he told Solomon. It was not only a matter of moral disintegration, however. The soldiers were beginning to emerge from a state of passive obedience to the directives of the MRC, and it became even more difficult to lead them into battle than it was on October 25. Militsyn, commenting on the attitude of his fellow soldiers in the Preobrazhensky Regiment after the revolution, wrote in his diary: "It suddenly came to me that I had not yet encountered a single defender of Bolshevism." In the records of the MRC an account is given of the significant episode: at a garrison meeting held on October 31, the plenipotentiaries of the Litovsky Regiment brought up the question of conducting negotiations with Kerensky's troops for the purpose of reaching a peaceful solution to the struggle. They unilaterally decided to send delegates to both Kerensky and the Committee of Salvation. The MRC was forced to go along with this, since the representatives of the guards' regiments (including the Semenovsky, Izmailovsky, and Volynsky) stated unequivocally that "the Petrograd garrison does not wish to be a tool of civil war and demands the formation of a coalition government."[57]

One could not rely on these regiments to go into action against the advancing Krasnov detachment. After the fall of Gatchina Lenin was in "an unusually severe nervous state," recounts Raskolnikov, who was dispatched to Kronstadt to mobilize the sailors "to the last man." "The revolution is in mortal peril," said Lenin. "Kerensky and his bands will crush us." Lenin demanded ships and men from Helsinki. "The revolution is in greater danger in Petrograd than on the Baltic Sea," he argued indignantly, encountering opposition on the part of the sailors, who feared to leave the front open to the Germans. Even John Reed talks about the sense of hopelessness holding sway among the Bolsheviks. The trade-union leader Lozovsky said to him: "What chance have we? All alone. . . . A mob against trained soldiers!" Another Bolshevik stalwart, G. I. Petrovsky, commented: "Tomorrow maybe we'll get a sleep — a long one."

The confusion was increased by the absence of command personnel. At a garrison conference held on the 29th, with Lenin and Trotsky participating, not one of the officers dared even hint that they did not want to repulse Kerensky. Trotsky drew from this the somewhat hasty conclusion that the majority of these "old officers" were for the Bolsheviks and that their hatred of Kerensky made them wish for his downfall. But nobody agreed to accept responsibility for directing the operation against the Krasnov Cossacks, and following unsuccessful attempts to recruit regimental commanders, the choice of the MRC fell upon Colonel Muraviev, "a showoff and a big mouth" in the opinion of Trotsky. On the following day a special garrison meeting was called for the purpose of political agitation. Scarcely half of the regiments were represented at this meeting.

The Kronstadt sailors – "the militant order of the revolution," as Trotsky called them – continued to be the only real support the Bolsheviks had. Groups of sailors raged in the streets brandishing the "revolutionary bayonet at the bourgeois scum." What psychology can explain the behavior of these ungovernable freebooters? What explains that unquestionable group psychosis that overcame so many sailors during the months of the revolution? In an article entitled "The Bizarre in the Revolution," Vladimir Bonch-Bruevich, who at one time collected a lot of material on Russian mystical sectarianism, has written a strikingly vivid vignette about the life of a group of sailors headed by the anarchist Zhelezniakov and his brother. He describes scenes of frenzied zeal, of "satanic" songs and "death" dances among effigies of people who had been strangled, dances characterized by bloody cries and threatening gestures.[58] This is definitely a picture of some kind of pathology, which was acted out in real life as well.

The excesses of the Kronstadt sailors abated after the 26th. In the general atmosphere of perplexity, the unbridled sailors, the "pride and joy of the Russian revolution," quieted down, and many were eager to return to their homes.

At the news of Kerensky's approach, "the bourgeois became insolent in the streets." Petrograd had been placed under martial law and all street gatherings had been prohibited, but on the 28th a reporter from *Narodnoe Slovo* noted "extraordinary animation" on Nevsky Prospekt – large crowds, everywhere "fleeting political meetings" taking place among armored vehicles, which were darting to and fro. According to this reporter, it was not only the "bourgeoisie" that was being impertinent. A sailor was loudly reading proclamations in the name of Kerensky. Here is an authentic fact, recorded in an official document: on Nevsky Prospekt on the 28th a crowd disarmed fifty Red Guards. This act was perpetrated by a "mob" of workers from the Municipal Electric Power Plant and the Government Printing Office.

Such was roughly the situation during the first days following the Bolshevik seizure of power, and paradoxically it weakened the active will of the anti-Bolshevik camp. Again illusions lulled vigilance, and spectres of the future acted more convincingly than reality.

A leftist political commentator, writing under the pen name of S. An-sky, recalled the excited mood prevailing in the City Duma during the continuous session" of October 26-28 – the flaming speeches and resolutions expressing protest – and he notes that the mood, "in spite of all the awful rumors," was "optimistic." "Nobody believed in the ultimate victory of those who had accomplished the coup, and the Bolsheviks believed in victory least of all." An army of news hawkers spread rumors of the "desperate position of the Bolsheviks," giving assurances that the new regime would hold out "a couple of days at most." The "criminal venture" hatched by the Bolsheviks and crowned "by sucess, to the shame of Petrograd, is already losing ground," asserted *Narodnoe Slovo* on the 27th. The Bolshevik rulers would be "caliphs [only] for an hour." They were "in a hurry to leave and set sail for Helsinki." "The end of a risky venture," stated a headline in *Delo Naroda* on the 29th over a section devoted to the "Bolshevik conspiracy." The conspiracy would finally be quashed, "if not today, then tomorrow," and the paper issued an appeal to join in the struggle against Bolshevism "with hands folded across the chest." The newspaper *Den* had no doubt that the Bolshevik government would last only a few days. The Menshevik *Rabochaia Gazeta* was convinced that the Bolshevik leaders themselves would halt, horrified by the work of their own hands. One after the other, people of different political camps tried to prove to themselves and convince others that this venture of ignorant demagogues, who had worked up the passions of the crowd at political meetings, would be ephemeral (Sukhanov). According to Gorky the venture would be at an end within two weeks. As early as September the sagacious Tseretelli was predicting that the Bolsheviks would hold out "two to three weeks at the most." Nabokov and his friends "did not believe for one minute in the strength of the Bolshevik regime and expected its early demise." Izgoev, a member of the same circle, added that few believed that the operetta would last more than two or three weeks. A writer for *Rech* recalled twenty years later how two days after the revolution "the cream of the intelligentsia gathered in our editorial offices – professors, civic leaders, political commentators" – and speculated on when it would end. "The majority," related the memoirist, "remained firmly convinced that it would last no more than two weeks." The minority attempted to press the view that it might last until spring. Two or three pessimists (including A. S. Izgoev) expressed timid doubts, amid general indignation. "Who knows, perhaps it will last up to three years." "There is not now and it is scarcely likely that there will be a new power structure; the victors feel like they would after a Pyrrhic Victory," Tolstoy said to Vyrubov on the 26th.

The notion of a "Pyrrhic Victory" spread along the front, from one headquarters to another. On the 30th General Baranovsky related to General Dukhonin Woytinsky's words to the effect that victory would ultimately come either to the revolutionary democracy or to the Cossack ataman, Kaledin. "There is no third possibility." "We have no basis," stated Baranovsky, giving his own evaluation, "for an argument about whether the victory will be ours or Kaledin's; the important thing to us is that victory does not come to the Bolsheviks. The primary task is to save Russia one way or another." On the morning of the 27th Avksentiev assured the British ambassador almost officially that the Bolsheviks "will not last long." This optimism was even transmitted via radiotelegraph to the Paris *Matin*, which reported that liquidation of the Bolshevik adventure was a matter of a few days and perhaps a few hours. The only prophetic dissonance to be heard in the general choir of optimistic forecasts was the voice of Kadet Shingarev (who was later killed by the Bolsheviks in a hospital). It would not be "ten days," but "ten years," he said.

Quite a few Bolsheviks themselves thought that under the circumstances they would not last two weeks. Only if we take this into consideration, along with the confusion and chaos that characterized the period right after the revolution, when there was no real authority, is it possible to understand the somewhat unexpected tractability of the new government. They were aware of the force that the rest of the socialist democracy could represent if united. On the day after the coup, the Bolsheviks emphatically stated that the events of the preceding day should not be viewed as an action directed against those elements of socialist democracy who were represented in the coalition government. Martov had merely to knock at the Bolsheviks' door with a petition on behalf of the socialist ministers interned in the Peter and Paul Fortress for them to be set free. Not only Martov knocked. On the day following the arrest of the ministers a protest was presented at the Congress of Soviets by the representative of the Third Army, supported by peasant delegates. The army representative viewed the act committed against the ministers as "illegal." "If they are harmed in the slightest," he said, "responsibility will lie on the shoulders of those who have perpetrated this act." Trotsky, as spokesman of the MRC, was compelled to issue an official promise to take steps to free the socialists from the fortress as soon as possible and place them instead under temporary house arrest.

The uncertainty of the Bolsheviks is illustrated by an incident related by An-sky. The new authorities decided to take three million rubles out of the State Bank to cover current expenses. "I remember," writes An-sky, "the agitation caused in the City Duma by the news that the Bolsheviks were demanding the keys to the State Bank from its director. Shouts rose from the floor of the Duma that the Bolsheviks would rob and pillage the state treasury and that they should be given the keys under no circumstances whatsoever." The intimidated bank director was compelled to come up with the keys, but the Bolsheviks "did not dare go to the bank alone and requested that the Duma send representatives to be present during the opening of the vault." The Duma sent delegates.[59]

At first the new authorities did not touch the socialist newspapers, even though according to Trotsky, they constituted a "solid chorus of wolves, jackals, and rabid dogs." The People's Socialist *Narodnoe Slovo* bore the slogan: "Down with the Bolsheviks. Save the country and the revolution." But this freedom lasted only a few days. While not closing down the socialist newspapers formally, the new authorities in fact subjected them to the most "loathsome" form of persecution, to quote Ivanovich. They mounted night sorties against editorial offices and printing plants, dismantled and smashed type, damaged machinery, and put printed copies to the torch (see the memoirs of Argunov and Ivanovich). The editorial offices of *Narodnoe Slovo* were vandalized on the 29th, and the newspaper was unable to resume operations until November 3. Somewhat later the newspapers were compelled to change their titles almost daily. The "People's Word" became the "Unceasing Word," the "Day" became the "Night," the "Midnight," "the Coming Day," etc.

The City Duma, the majority of the members of which were socialists, not only resounded with "flaming speeches" against the violent acts of the Bolsheviks, but even endeavored to act as an organ of authority. An-sky explains the "privileged position" of the Duma by the fact that in its hands was concentrated the entire food-distributing machinery of Petrograd. "The Bolsheviks did not dare touch it." On the 26th the people of Petrograd read a unique appeal issued by the Duma "security committee." "The City Duma, in view of recent events, has resolved: to decree the inviolability of citizens' homes; to call upon the population, through the apartment house committees, to offer vigorous resistance to any and all attempts to break into private quarters, resorting if necessary to the use of weapons in the interest of the self-defense of citizens." The security committee, which the Duma insisted was a "neutral" body, appealed to the MRC to be assigned troop units to protect the public, but with the condition that MRC commissars not interfere with instructions issued by the committee. The Duma felt it necessary to take these steps in view of expected pogroms, which in the absence of duly constituted authorities, might get out of control. The newspapers contributed to the spread of alarmist rumors by printing stories about "an unprecedented influx of deserters . . . jamming railroad stations" and the arrival in Petrograd of bandit gangs, which, sensing profits to be made, filled "the cheap cafes and thieves' haunts." Many of these reports were gross exaggerations, of course.

THE FIGHTING ORGAN OF
THE REVOLUTIONARY DEMOCRACY

The Committee of Salvation was deliberately created to fight against the violent seizure of power, yet it was not touched by the authorities. It organized freely and acted openly. At its well-attended organizational meeting a representative of the Luga Soviet assured the audience that the 30,000-man Luga garrison stood ready to support the Committee of Salvation in its struggle with the usurpers of power. "The time for resolutions is past," stated the speaker. No time should be wasted. It was essential "to begin creative work immediately." The Committee of Salvation resolved to offer "vigorous resistance" to the Bolsheviks. Although the meeting was surrounded by sailors and Red Guards, none of them entered the building. And the committee swung into action.

Under the conditions prevailing at the time, "vigorous resistance" could only mean armed resistance. The only real force the committee could count on for the time being was Krasnov's small Cossack detachment, which was proceeding to the capital under the banner of the Provisional Government. On the 27th the committee delegated a Socialist Revolutionary member to proceed to Luga to coordinate operations and to find out when Krasnov's troops would reach Petrograd. "I am marching on Petrograd at eleven o'clock tomorrow morning," replied Krasnov. A delegation from the Duma – Gots, Zenzinov, Kapitsa, and others – was to have left earlier, and officially, its objectives were more conciliatory: to determine what had happened in Gatchina and to forestall new bloodshed. But in his memoirs Zenzinov admits that in reality he and Gots had decided to join up with Kerensky. Both Gots and Zenzinov were arrested at the Baltic Railroad Station.

Meanwhile, the decision of the committee to act in concert with Kerensky was so wrapped in fog that it did not constitute a formal agreement to act in behalf of the government. "The criminal uprising undertaken by the Bolsheviks," stated an appeal made by the committee on the 27th to the soldiers of the Petrograd garrison, "has already borne its bloody fruit. . . . But all is not lost. Revolutionary troops led by the All-Army Committee are now approaching Petrograd. These troops are being led by elected soldier committees. They will not permit blood to be shed in vain." The omission of any mention of Kerensky and Krasnov was not just "creative propaganda." From its very first day the Committee of Salvation endeavored to hold itself aloof from the unpopular Provisional Government.

"Strangely enough," recalls Stankevich, an active member of the committee, "in fighting with the Bolsheviks, everybody was afraid of being linked with the government. [When the committee was] formulating [its] political aims, I [suggested] stating that the aim of the struggle was to restore the government overthrown by the Bolsheviks. But not one voice spoke out in support. Everybody pointed out that since the government was unpopular it was better not to mention it at all."[60] What Kerensky in his memoirs considers a "legend" is an unassailable fact: the name of the government was not capable in itself of moving troops from the front into Petrograd.

This fact was attested to by the military authorities. Baranovsky, who was stationed at the northern front, told Dukhonin: "I should make crystal clear to you the attitude of the [soldiers'] committees. It is obvious that the committees are not going to support the former government and do not wish to send troops to Kerensky. A public announcement must be made about just what the Committee of Salvation is and what part Kerensky plays in it; it is better to be able to use the name of the committee than that of the latter. Otherwise nothing will come of it, and in the meantime the house is on fire and must be saved."[61] Learning that the First Army Committee had reversed its initial decision and was now determined to support the Provisional

Government, Cheremisov ordered that appropriate infantry units be chosen "immediately" and sent to Gatchina (an example of the fact that Cheremisov did not always limit himself to passive loyalty). On October 29 the chief of staff of the First Army reported that the army committee "is not at all inclined to support the Provisional Government, but rather the Committee of Salvation. Is this one and the same thing?" Lukirsky explained that the Committee of Salvation was an "open enemy of the Bolsheviks and was firmly committed to giving all-out support to the Provisional Government."

While some people on the committee merely wanted to hush the unpopular name of the Provisional Government for tactical reasons, others genuinely remained aloof from it and wanted only to retain the fiction of association. Kerensky's name was necessary to preserve the "succession of authority." But Kerensky had been eliminated in advance as a candidate for ministerial positions, just as had the possibility of forming a coalition government with the bourgeoisie. If Kerensky the victor decided to play the role of a "white general" and permit reprisals, the Committee of Salvation would oppose him as it would oppose any reactionary military dictatorship. (This was reported in a rough account given by Vompe, one of the leaders of the Vikzhel – the All-Russian Executive Committee of the Railroad Workers' Union – of a conversation he had with delegates from the Committee of Salvation.) Buchanan, an astute observer, noted in his memoirs: "Kerensky is utterly discredited with all parties, and the troops, if they do come to Petrograd, will not fight to restore his government, but to support the Socialist groups who have turned against the [Bolshevik] revolution" (II, 211). The semi-official organ of the Central Committee of the Socialist Revolutionary party, *Delo Naroda*, picturesquely formulated its attitude toward the Provisional Government in the issue of October 28: the Bolsheviks were a "soap bubble," but a government overthrown by a "soap bubble" was not worth restoring.

Because of the committee's disregard of the lawful government the anti-Bolshevik action taken by it was sometimes depicted by outsiders as the notorious position of "neutrality." This undermined the authority of the committee in the eyes of its sympathizers and potential followers and weakened the struggle against the Bolsheviks. "The position of the Committee of Salvation is a neutral one," Rengarten wrote in his journal without any qualifications. He was in Helsinki at the time and based his judgment on rumors, newspaper accounts, and the stories told by new arrivals. The position of the Committee of Salvation was not "neutral." It was implacable in its opposition to the Bolsheviks. But in the final analysis it was only this hostility that held the different organizations in the Committee of Salvation together. Each group interpreted the goals of the alliance in its own way. Hence the indefinite and contradictory nature of the actions taken by the committee. It never defined its position in sharp and clear-cut terms, and if only because of this, the Committee of Salvation was unable to pursue an effective policy, in spite of the sympathetic response in the country.

In theory the Committee of Salvation had become the headquarters of the struggle against the Bolsheviks, which was being conducted under the banner of "revolutionary democracy." There was no government. There was no, or almost no, social basis for the creation of a coalition. The "bourgeois" community had disappeared somewhere after the revolution. The revolutionary democracy had entered the arena with an anti-Bolshevik battle cry, but this cry was muted by a psychology that considered real struggle against the allegedly bankrupt "criminal venture" less urgent than a concentration of revolutionary political forces for future tasks. Under these conditions, any genuine revolutionary enthusiasm that the Committee of Salvation may have had initially dried up in a matter of a few days. Peshekhonov, summarizing the committee's activities in an article published on November 3, noted a significant fact: on the first day of its existence the committee sent out one hundred twenty agitators, seventy on the second day, only twenty on the third, and none at all on the fourth. It seemed to Peshekhonov that all the activity of the committee boiled down to information and talk.

From the very beginning the committee had a three-faceted image. In the eyes of the men at the front, it was the General Headquarters of the armed struggle, a headquarters curiously nestled inviolably in the very backyard of the MRC. For Petrograd it was an organ crystallizing democratic public opinion, which encompassed a variable range of oscillating moods and political evaluations. (Thus, the striking civil servants were also represented on the committee.) Finally, somewhere within the committee, clandestine, undercover work was going on, which had direct links with Kerensky's front and with the local garrison. Persons from the internationalist camp put in guest appearances at general meetings, seeking ways to reconcile the warring camps of social democracy, while in the undercover activities, people of opposing political persuasions worked together, joined in the belief that the use of force would eventually be needed against the Bolsheviks.

The resulting situation was difficult to explain in terms of conventional party logic. The first to sense the ambiguity in the posture of the Committee of Salvation were the Mensheviks, whose central committee did not wish to lend support to the new regime but also rejected an armed struggle against it. Their position was extremely difficult, as the émigré journal *Sotsialisticheskii Vestnik* subsequently explained: "In view of the social kinship of these segments of the population on which both the Bolsheviks and the Mensheviks relied, armed struggle inevitably led to a fratricidal war within the working class." Representatives of the Menshevik central committee left the committee. Officially this took place later, on November 8, but prior to this date they had already refused to attend some meetings and attended others for the sole purpose of gathering information.

The small Kadet group (Nabokov, Panina, Obolensky) that came to the committee from the City Duma felt ill at ease and lost in this leftist environment. The presence of a Constitutional Democratic faction on the Committee of Salvation was to a certain extent the result of a misunderstanding, because when the committee was founded a precondition for membership was set that in effect ruled out participation by nonsocialist elements. "Non-labor and nonsocialist representation on the committee was not permitted," Gots, one of the leaders of the committee's conspiratorial activities, testified at the trial of the Socialist Revolutionaries in Moscow. This was absurd from the viewpoint of expediency, since in armed combat it would be necessary to count on cadets, shock troops, and Cossacks and to rely on the sympathy of command personnel at the front. Representatives of the Kadet party neither participated in nor were aware of the conspiratorial activities of the committee. "They concealed from us everything that was going on in the Executive Committee," said Obolensky in his memoirs. The open meetings of the Committee of Salvation quickly became nothing more than "talk factories" concerned with whether to set up a coalition government of socialists and "bourgeoisie" or a homogeneous socialist government and whether the Bolsheviks should be included. Naturally, Nabokov was depressed by the "purposelessness and fruitlessness of the meetings, where first-day illusions died."

THE VIKZHEL

The Committee of Salvation was discussing a specific plan for organizing a government, a plan that had been proposed at a political conference organized by the All-Russian Executive Committee of the Railroad Workers' Union, or the *Vikzhel*. (This word became so meaningful! The verb *vikzheliat'* came to mean duplicity bordering on the betrayal of principles, or in Peshekhonov's words, "political blackmail." In assessing the role played by the Vikzhel, Bolshevik historians split. For some the Vikzhel "objectively" played a counterrevolutionary role, while for others it "wholeheartedly promoted the Bolshevik cause."[62]) On the day after the Bolshevik uprising, the Central Committee of the Vikzhel left Moscow as a body for Petrograd and took the side of the Bolsheviks. In theory it was against the seizure of power by a single party. "Recognizing its power ...which should be used only...by the revolutionary democratic majority and under no condition can serve any minority or single political party, the Central Committee of the Union of Railroad Workers has resolved to support the C[entral] E[xecutive] C[ommittee] of the Soviet of Workers' and Soldiers' Deputies, in both its present membership and that which will be elected by the Congress of Soviets," read the Vikzhel appeal to the nation. But there was the "danger of victory by the counterrevolution, when under the pretext of putting down the Bolsheviks troops may be moved to Petrograd and all soviet institutions may be wiped out." Therefore the Vikzhel resolved: "All Cossack troop movements toward Petrograd must be immediately stopped," and a special five-member bureau was to be elected for establishing contact with the MRC and the Congress of Soviets. The sailors from Helsinki arrived in Petrograd on the 27th without any difficulty because they encountered no opposition whatsoever from the railroad workers.

Events progressed with dizzying swiftness. Dual political allegiance by the Vikzhel was becoming impossible. The old VTsIK declared the new VTsIK to be illegal, and the revolutionary democracy split into two camps. The Vikzhel tried to assume a position of strict "neutrality," which meant taking "feasible steps" to oppose the advance of troops proceeding in the name of the revolutionary democracy and "decisive steps" against troops being sent to "destroy the socialist parties." Vompe notes quite correctly that each member of the Vikzhel in effect pursued his "own neutrality" locally, a neutrality that was determined by his party affiliation. But quite independent of various "connivances," neutrality primarily meant undermining the force of the anti-Bolshevik movement. The rescue of the Provisional Government depended on the rapid advance of troop units from the front, and it was precisely against this that Vikzhel agents were to take not "feasible" but "decisive" steps.

Gradually, the Vikzhel shifted toward a position of "complete unity" with the socialist parties that had left the Second Soviet Congress — with those people who sought ways to achieve reconciliation within the ranks of the quarreling democrats. These groups called on both camps to come to an agreement in the name of creating a homogeneous democratic government capable of offering resistance to the counterrevolutionary coalition of the propertied classes, so that "the revolution will not bog down in the blood of the soldiers, workers, and peasants." The appeal was signed by the Menshevik-Internationalists, the pro-Bolshevik faction of the social democrat "uniters," the Left Socialist Revolutionaries, the Polish Socialist party, and the Jewish Social Democratic Labor party (*Bund*). The semiofficial organ of this seemingly amorphous bloc was Gorky's *Novaia Zhizn'*, the organ of "groomed Bolshevism," as Potresov described it at the time. On the 29th the Vikzhel issued a manifesto "to all, all, all": "There is no authority in this country. . . . Each belligerent side is trying to create this authority by force of arms. A fratricidal war is going on. At a time when an external enemy is threatening the freedom of our nation, the democratic parties are resolving their internal differences with blood and iron. . . . We must create a new government that will enjoy the confidence of all democratic parties and will possess the moral strength to hold this authority in its hands until the Constituent Assembly is convened. Such authority can be created only through intelligent agreement by all democratic parties, but certainly not with arms." The Vikzhel took the initiative by proposing the formation of a homogeneous socialist government ranging from People's Socialists to Bolsheviks. The Vikzhel stated that in order to implement its decision it would go as far as to stop all rail traffic at midnight on October 29. The Railroad Workers' Union declared that it considered all those who "continue to resolve domestic difference by force of arms" to be "enemies of democracy and traitors to the country."[63]

Representatives of the quarreling factions and neutral organizations convened at the Vikzhel headquarters on the 29th at seven o'clock in the evening. Present at this meeting were delegates from the Bolshevik party, Social Democrats of all shades, Left Socialist Revolutionaries and plain Socialist Revolutionaries, delegates from the old VTsIK, the Council of People's Commissars, the City Duma, the Soviet of Peasant Deputies, and the Committee of Salvation. Missing were representatives of the People's Socialist party, which first proposed the unification formula for establishing a government, although as a result of some sort of mix-up, one member was present as a representative of the Committee of Salvation. (The Central Committee of the party turned down the Vikzhel plan by a vote of thirteen to one.) The Vikzhel political conferences dragged on for almost two weeks, surviving various crises. These meetings were not only an expression of the position taken by the majority of the revolutionary democracy. Opposition elements within the ranks of the Bolshevik party saw the possibility of a way out of the impasse through an agreement with the other socialists, although for the "Leninists" the talks were merely a diplomatic game played to gain time.

CHAPTER 7

Bloody Sunday

The negotiations going on at Vikzhel headquarters stood in sharp contrast to the clandestine activities of the Committee of Salvation's "Military Commission." The leadership on this commission was assumed by representatives of the Socialist Revolutionary party. Only in this sense can one accept a subsequent statement by Zenzinov: "What were the revolutionaries to do? To resist violence with arms. This we did." We must accept with even greater reservations the words flowing from the exuberant pen of the journalist Osorgin on the day following the Bolshevik coup. He wrote in the Moscow *Vlast Naroda*: "Let the Bolsheviks with their uprising frighten the cowardly bourgeois. . . . They will encounter not only cowardly liberals but also old wolves of the revolution."

These "old wolves" proved to be very few in number, and the youths comprising the party combat forces were also extremely few in number. The members of the united socialist front were compelled to rely primarily on those very military cadets — the "child heroes," as veteran revolutionary Vera Zasulich called them — who defended the Provisional Government and the Winter Palace. Of course, one cannot present the wartime schools for cadets and ensigns "in a Marxist light," as caste institutions. This could only be done at Bolshevik "evenings of recollection," where it was asserted that only "sons of the nobility" — "landowners' kids," as Bukharin dubbed them in his articles — could be cadets. These young members of the intelligentsia were, in fact, quite diverse both socially and politically — that is, they included socialists, "cowardly bourgeois," and individuals of "liberal psychology"; united by a consciousness of military duty, they were practically the only ones who put up a struggle against the Bolsheviks on Sunday, October 29.

Certain circumstances associated with the armed uprising of the cadets gave rise to a flood of idle talk, which found expression both in Miliukov's "history" and, particularly, in Kerensky's memoirs. Testimony at the

137

Bolshevik trial of the Socialist Revolutionaries in Moscow has scotched these rumors. (Unfortunately a full stenographic account of the trial has not been published.) Here are Gots' concluding remarks, which were published in the émigré *Revoliutsionnaia Rossiia* and according to the editors, were reprinted from the transcript of the trial. "The [Central Committee] authorized me to organize resistance," stated Gots, "and naturally in embarking on a struggle against dictatorship by a single party I had to issue an appeal to rebellion, not in the name of any single party, but in the name of the committee, which united all the forces of democracy and socialism. . . . The Committee to Save the Country and the Revolution began this movement on October 29 and never disavowed it subsequently. I assigned Colonel Polkovnikov to direct the movement. . . . We considered him to be the most capable and eminent military leader."[64]

Another participant in the organizing of the uprising, Broun, secretary of the Socialist Revolutionary party's Military Commission, testified that the following plan of action was adopted at a joint meeting of the military commissions of the Committee of Salvation and the Socialist Revolutionary party on the 28th: "First we shall seize the telephone exchange and the Mikhailovsky Riding School, where the armored cars are parked, and start an uprising at the Nikolaievsky Engineers' Castle. Another center of the uprising will be on Vasilievsky Island; the boys from the Vladimirsky and Pavlovsky cadet schools are to seize the Peter and Paul Fortress, where we have been in contact with the cyclists. Then we shall join forces and take Smolny." In view of the "approach of Kerensky and the Gatchina Front," asserted Broun, "it was decided at the same meeting to begin the uprising immediately." And the rebellion did begin on the 29th. Of course this was "without the knowledge" of the Committee of Salvation's plenary body.

An order issued by Polkovnikov, dated two o'clock in the morning, instructed each military unit to send a representative in the name of the Committee of Salvation to the Engineers' Castle and to arrest the MRC commissars in all garrison units. Several appeals were issued that same day in the name of the Committee of Salvation calling upon the troops to fight with weapons in hand against the "insane Bolshevik venture." One of these appeals, directed "to the soldiers," called upon "all troops loyal to the Revolution" to proceed to the Nikolaievsky Engineers' School to "gather around" the Committee of Salvation: "Go in regiments, battalions, companies, go in groups and individually." "Help is near," the appeal concluded. "Troops loyal to the Revolution are approaching Petrograd, guided by their elected regimental and division committees. Together with them is the leader of the S[ocialist] R[evolutionary] party and the entire Russian peasantry, Chernov." No mention is made of Kerensky, let alone the Provisional Government.

At about four o'clock in the morning insurgents seized the Engineers' Castle, where Polkovnikov had set up his headquarters. The "political leaders" of the rebellion, headed by Gots, arrived at the headquarters. An accidental arrest of Bruderer, one of the rebels, on whom military papers signed by Gots were found, gave the MRC an early warning about the rebellion. Nevertheless, it was successful initially, and that morning the following item appeared in Bulletin Number One of the Committee of Salvation: "The troops of the Committee to Save the Country and the Revolution have freed almost all cadet schools and Cossack units, have seized armored and artillery vehicles, have seized the telephone exchange, and the forces are organizing to take the Peter and Paul Fortress and the Smolny Institute, the last refuges of the Bolsheviks. We order all military units that have recovered from the intoxication of the Bolshevik adventure to proceed immediately to the Nikolaievsky Engineer School. Any delay will be viewed as a betrayal of the Revolution and will cause extremely vigorous measures to be taken." This document bore the signatures of Avksentiev for the Council of the Republic, Gots for the Committee of Salvation, Sinani (a member of the Unity group) for the Military Commission of the Committee of Salvation, Broun for the Military Commission of the Socialist Revolutionary party, and Shakhverdov for the "military section" of the Menshevik Social Democratic Labor party.

On the following day *Delo Naroda* published letters by Gots and Avksentiev denying that they had signed this appeal. Disavowal of one specific document (it had been edited in an extremely unfortunate manner, with somewhat vainglorious overtones) could not per se discredit the entire movement, but in the prevailing situation such a repudiation could not be viewed other than as an attempt to remain aloof from the rebellion. And many took it to mean just that. In court Broun testified that he and Sinani had placed the signatures of Gots and Avksentiev on the published appeal, which Broun and Sinani had written. "In the original we left them a space for their signatures, since at that moment (3:30 in the morning) they were not present, and we certainly did not doubt that they would sign, since they were the actual leaders of the rebellion." Gots emphasized quite strongly in court that his disavowal of his signature on the "apocryphal document" meant nothing more than just that, the fact that "I did not see and did not sign this document."

The Bolsheviks had no difficulty in dealing with the premature insurrection. None of the military units of the garrison came to the assistance of the insurgents. The Cossacks, to whom Avksentiev and Chaikovsky had been sent in the name of the Committee of Salvation, did not act either. Nor do the annals of the day make any mention of the participation in the uprising of "party combat teams," even though they had been "mobilized," according to

Kerensky. Gots accurately called them "pitiful groups," and the role played by them was completely insignificant. The cadets were joined by a few dozen male and female shock troops, as well as by a few odd officers, the majority of whom were possibly, as Bolshevik historians claim, adherents of the military-monarchist organization headed by Vladimir Purishkevich, which was exposed soon after the uprising.

From the testimony of members of this monarchist organization, who were brought to trial before a revolutionary tribunal on January 3, 1918 (the sentences were actually very mild – Purishkevich, for example, was sentenced to four years of socially productive labor in custody), one can determine quite precisely both the objectives of the organization and its connections. It arose prior to the October ccup. Captain Dushkin of the Izmailovsky Regiment testified that he had been present at a meeting at which Purishkevich had presented a "program for restoring the monarchy in Russia." Purishkevich "developed the idea that one should not speak openly at the present time of restoring the monarchy. There are still too many enemies of the monarchy among the intelligentsia and the public at large. Therefore, without mentioning restoration of the monarchy for the time being, we should mobilize all our forces to consolidate statesmanlike political groups into one channel for the purpose of combating anarchy." He hotly defended the idea of close consolidation and common action among the monarchists, the cadets, and the right-wing group of Socialist Revolutionaries headed by Savinkov. Purishkevich particularly insisted on close connections with Savinkov and his followers, explaining that the monarchists alone were too weak to achieve success and would be doomed to destruction unless they had the support of Savinkov's people and other right-wing Socialist Revolutionaries.

As a witness at the trial Dushkin had the following to say about the organization: "Purishkevich's organization contained many cadets, but the organization was set up on the masonic model, in groups of five, so that the members of the different groups were not acquainted with one another. But in each cadet school there was a person who united all groups. It is quite possible that the members of these groups of five, blindly following the instructions of our organization's headquarters, really had no conception of the nature and the true aims of our organization."[65] Actually the Purish- kevich organization was small. In a letter to Kaledin, which was seized by the Bolsheviks, he spoke of the "fantastic inertia on the part of a substantial part of the officer corps" and the public.

After the Bolshevik takeover Purishkevich tried to convince the organiza- tion that it was essential to act immediately in order to seize power and restore the monarchy, because the Bolsheviks had not yet consolidated their power, and Kerensky and the Socialist Revolutionaries had not yet completely surrendered their authority. To this end it was necessary to enter into the conflict against the Bolsheviks, but when victory over the Bolsheviks was gained, power should be given over to no one and resistance should be offered to all claimants to authority, be they Kerensky or anyone else. "I know," testified Dushkin, "that as a consequence of these decisions by Purishkevich the majority of the members of his organization participated actively in the seizure of the Mikhailovsky Riding School and the telephone exchange by the Committee to Save the Country and the Revolution." According to Purishkevich, the cadets at the disposal of the organization were sent to seize the telephone exchange, the Mikhailovsky Riding School, and the Engineers' Castle contrary to his orders. They had obeyed "the provocatory orders of Colonel Polkovnikov and the Committee of Salvation, with which I personally had no connection whatsoever." But is clear that the Committee of Salvation headquarters was linked through one of Polkovnikov's aides with the secret military organization. In any case, Purishkevich's followers could not have played an important part in the events of the 29th.

"All the workers, soldiers, and sailors of Petrograd" rose as one man against the insurrection, the Bolsheviks claimed afterwards. New "miracles of revolutionary enthusiasm" were displayed. The military cadets, even those who did not come forth, were surrounded in their schools, and the Vladimirsky School, which offered the most resistance, was crushed by artillery. By evening everything was over. The Bolsheviks had dealt mercilessly with the insurgents. According to Sukhanov's figures, both sides suffered about 200 casualties, including dead and wounded. Obviously the main casualties were among the cadets, who were arrested, beaten up, and led off to prison. Even the official "bulletin" (November 2) of the Central Committee of the Bolshevik party acknowledged that "there were many casualties."

The failure of the carelessly organized rebellion was, according to Kerensky, due primarily to the ill will of traitors and provocateurs: "All battle-ready Bolshevik forces were swung into action before we (in Gatchina) were able to give support or at least take advantage of the uprising in Petrograd to attack the Bolshevik troops at Pulkovo." Was it really ill will? Neither Stankevich nor Gots, who reported to Kerensky about the failure of the uprising on the next day, say anything in their memoirs about traitors and provocateurs. Late in the evening of the 28th, after returning from Gatchina, Stankevich went to the Committee of Salvation. It turned out that "during the day" organizational work had made "tremendous strides." "The Military Commission had connections with almost all units and considered itself the possessor of a *solid* armed force." The question of an uprising came up at the meeting, but it was "unanimously decided to wait at least another day. Each day increased our strength and organization; in addition, my information that

Kerensky's detachment apparently would not start its march on Petrograd any sooner than the following day also helped sway opinion toward the side of waiting to deal a coordinated blow." According to Miliukov, Avksentiev corroborates this version. Although Avksentiev "did not participate in the council of war," he was in the building where the meeting was being held, presumably attending to his duties as Chairman of the Soviet of Peasant Deputies. He left together with Gots, and the latter told him that "nothing has been decided for tomorrow, and the day will be without incident." The next day "I learned," writes Stankevich, "that after my departure Polkovnikov and someone else came to the committee with the news that the Bolsheviks had decided to disarm the cadets on the following day.... Naturally, we had to anticipate this stroke. It was therefore decided to begin the offensive immediately."

It is still difficult to extract a clear picture from this confused situation. One cannot determine precisely at what time the Bolsheviks arrested Bruderer and found the papers he had with him showing the disposition of the insurgent forces. This could have forced the hand of the insurgents. The uprising could also have been precipitated by rumors of the imminent disarming of the cadets — there was a precedent in the disarming of the Pavlovsky School on the 27th. An MRC decree to this effect is in existence, but it is dated the 29th and refers to an hour of the day when the insurgency had already been crushed to a significant degree. Whatever the reasons, the time of the uprising was finally decided upon at the night session, and to one degree or another there was general consent. Bruderer's arrest merely made it easier for the Bolsheviks to crush the insufficiently planned and prepared insurrection. Very characteristic in this respect is the testimony given by a nineteen-year-old cadet of the Nikolaevsky Engineering School, Duke Leichtenbergsky, an active member of the Purishkevich organization. "We cadets," he said, "were ordered to sleep fully clothed and with our rifles by our beds. At four o'clock in the morning we were suddenly awakened and ordered up. We were issued cartridges and lined up. Colonel Muffel spoke to us in the name of the Committee of Salvation.... Muffel announced that Kerensky's troops were expected in the city by about eleven o'clock that morning, and that the cadets, in anticipation of the arrival of those troops, were instructed by the Committee of Salvation to maintain order in the city and were therefore to occupy Mikhailovsky Castle and the telephone exchange.... Muffel announced that those cadets who due to their own political convictions felt that they could not carry out these instructions could remain behind, but only one such individual stepped forward."[66]

They were fully confident of Kerensky's advance. While the MRC officially announced that Kerensky was advancing with 5,000 Cossacks, in opposition circles a conviction held sway that an entire corps was approaching Petrograd. (Buchanan was informed of this on the 27th by a special delegation, which included Nabokov, and similar assertions were made on the floor of the City Duma.) Stankevich, who had returned from Kerensky's field headquarters, corroborated this version, as he himself acknowledges in his memoirs: "I did not feel I had the right to ask in detail about the condition of the detachment, since the conversation was held in the presence of too many persons." But Stankevich reported his impression that Krasnov had "*at least* an entire cavalry corps." In addition to Cossacks, Kerensky had the support of 30,000 men from the Luga garrison, who were prepared to act in support of the Committee of Salvation. Nor is there any doubt that in a number of units of the Petrograd garrison a turning point was close, where the "watching and waiting" mood could shift to an active one. (The MRC minutes for the 29th note, for example, that the mood of the Semenovsky Regiment was "not good.") The Committee of Salvation was already able to hold several political meetings in the barracks, and its speakers were sometimes successful in contending with the Bolshevik demagogues before the audiences of soldiers. The changed mood of the garrison and some organizational contacts were interpreted by the optimistically impulsive to represent an actual possibility of support by a "solid armed force."

The cadet uprising was easily crushed, but it was not quite as easy to destroy the spirit of youth. A few days later the entire student body protested in the name of the thirteen higher educational institutions of Petrograd against the "acts of barbaric violence" committed by the Bolsheviks. At the time, Trotsky was threatening that the jailed cadets would be sent to Kronstadt as "hostages" and that "we shall exchange each worker for five cadets." Forty-four cadets were in fact transferred to Kronstadt. But as a result of a "petition" – that is, demands – presented by a delegation from the student organizations of the socialist parties, including representatives of the Bolshevik group, the MRC agreed to free all "cadet-socialists" on the 31st.

Why was no support given by the Cossacks, with whom "preliminary talks" had been held and whom Avksentiev and Chaikovsky had tried to persuade to participate in the uprising on the 29th? Just as on the 25th, the main cause was the indecisive mood of the Cossack regiments in the Petrograd garrison, with their badly deteriorated morale. No wonder the delegates from the First Don Regiment in Petrograd who came to Krasnov seemed to the general to be more like scouts from an enemy camp than fellow travelers. The mood could easily change if there was a successful offensive by the Krasnov "corps." But for the time being the majority of the Cossacks in Petrograd preferred to continue to play the waiting game.

The wing of the Council of the Cossack Troops that adhered to the tactics of the waiting game and endeavored not to become entangled in the

Petrograd "affair" acted chiefly from a desire to preserve three Cossack regiments for transfer to the Don Region, where in the opinion of Kaledin a healthy national movement was taking shape under his command. Such a tactic was shortsighted, and at the same time naive and erroneous. It was naive, for one could hardly assume that the Bolsheviks would try to free themselves from dangerous neighbors with their clearly unreliable "neutrality" by sending them to the Don. It was erroneous, for with their "neutrality" the leaders were strengthening the Bolsheviks and demoralizing their own Cossacks. Smolny gave its reply a month later, on the night of November 28, when the Cossack council, as a result of its having passed a resolution protesting the sending of "punitive detachments" to the Don Region, was broken up by a detachment of Latvians and seven of its members (out of thirty-three) were imprisoned in the basement of the Smolny Institute.

One can assume that at least some members of the Council of Cossack Troops would have agreed to the uprising on the 29th had the council not considered the revolt to be a "risky venture." The council must have known what mediocre forces Krasnov had at his disposal, because it had its own delegates at Krasnov's headquarters and was also briefed by delegates from Cossak troops in Gatchina. And the Cossacks may have preferred not to join in the game yet — after all, the three Cossack regiments in Petrograd apparently totaled only several hundred men. These are possible explanations.

It is dangerous to generalize about the Cossacks, though. There was no unity even among the Cossack leaders. The General Cossack Congress of the Front, which was meeting in Kiev at the time, passed a resolution proclaiming its readiness "to die to the last man" and on the 25th issued a call "to arms to defend the motherland and freedom." The congress pressured the council in Petrograd to join in the uprising, and it took particular pains to bring its resolution to the attention of Kerensky.

CHAPTER 8

The "White Adventure"

ON THE PULKOVO HEIGHTS

While the cadets were fighting in Petrograd, Tsarskoe Selo and Gatchina were taking a breather. Kerensky was active though, his enthusiasm enhanced by the all-too-easy success of the previous day and by the excessively optimistic report of the envoy from the Committee of Salvation on the attitudes in Petrograd. On the evening of the 28th Kerensky hastened to send a telegram to General Headquarters: "Bolshevism is disintegrating, has been isolated and *no longer exists* in Petrograd as an organized force."[67] The Bolsheviks "are perishing," recorded Vyrubov, deputy chief of staff of General Headquarters, quoting Kerensky. The morning bulletin of the Committee of Salvation on the 29th featured a telegraphed order from the Gatchina Palace: "No orders or instructions coming from persons calling themselves people's commissars or commissars of the MRC shall be carried out, no dealings shall be had with such persons, nor shall they be permitted to enter government offices."

Unfortunately, Kerensky forgot again that Krasnov did not have at his disposal a corps, but only a few hundred Cossacks. According to Stankevich, Krasnov, encouraged by optimistic reports about Petrograd, asked him during a meeting on the 28th if it was possible to "wait one more day before we continue the offensive, since his Cossacks were tired and it was necessary for him to wait for the infantry." "It was my opinion," said Stankevich, "that if there were insufficient forces for an immediate offensive we could wait." According to Kerensky, Stankevich insisted on speeding up "our advance" on Petrograd and "lent him major assistance in his disagreement with Krasnov." Clearly, Krasnov's "passivity" was due primarily to the limited size of his detachment, which, moreover, was disoriented, surrounded as it was by mass "neutrality" in Gatchina and Tsarskoe Selo. And perhaps even the easily enthusiastic Krasnov was afraid to rely merely on the "heroism of the brave."

He probably does not exaggerate when he claims that it was with the greatest difficulty that he overcame the unwillingness of the Cossacks to advance without the infantry and persuaded them to conduct only "battle reconnaissance" on the 30th to determine the degree of enemy resistance.

The "battle" of Pulkovo began on the 30th. *Pravda*, which succeeded *Rabochii Put* as the Bolshevik party organ, enthusiastically portrayed the "majestic picture of revolutionary enthusiasm" displayed by the pro-Bolshevik troops heading for the Pulkovo Front. In regiment after regiment marched troopers from the Petrograd garrison, Red Guards, and sailors with heavy artillery. All the young people were sent to the front. According to the Bolshevik Raskolnikov, Petrograd became deserted, and so did Kronstadt. Thousands of workers, accompanied by their wives and children, went not only to dig trenches but also to fight for the revolution. "The struggle for freedom has approached a critical moment," proclaimed an MRC order. The memoirists are equally picturesque in their descriptions: "Blackened, spattered with mud and blood, these fighters for the revolution advanced and battled like lions, in spite of the fact that their comrades were perishing on all sides. We experienced veterans of the front were amazed at their fearlessness." Kerensky's troops had to stop in the face of such "selfless bravery."

The actual situation was somewhat different. Although Raskolnikov asserts that all the regiments of the Petrograd garrison, except for the Izmailovsky (and the Moskovsky, adds Antonov), were prepared to "do battle with Kerensky" at a moment's notice, he admits that the first regiment sent out, the Volynsky, passed a resolution demanding that the carnage be stopped and that the belligerent sides come to terms. "Everybody is scattering at Pulkovo," commented the Bolshevik naval commissar Dybenko. Soldiers at Gatchina told John Reed: "Frankly, we ourselves have no idea what is going on." "Dejection" set in at Smolny, acknowledged Vladimir Bonch-Bruevich, who had been appointed chief of "staff." "The gaping corridors were deserted, and there remained only a handful of men to conduct and direct operations of the military staff." Number one in this "handful of men" was, of course, Lenin. According to Podvoisky, his intervention sobered the confused ones. "Vigorous work" done by the Putilov and Obukhov plants "to equip the defense of Tsarskoe Selo" played a decisive part, but in order to obtain from the Putilov works the armored platforms that were needed at the front, Lenin had to go there in person and bring his powers of persuasion to bear on the workers. According to *Delo Naroda*, on the 28th the workers of the Petrograd Ordnance plant rejected by a vote of 2,000 to 20 the Bolshevik request for active assistance.

In the MRC appeals (to say nothing of the bulletins of the Central Committee of the Bolshevik party) the utmost demagoguery was brought into play. Designed to appeal to all kinds of mob tastes, they certainly did not reflect confidence in the revolutionary sentiments of the people. Kerensky was proceeding toward Petrograd "at the demand of the nobility, landowners, capitalists, and profiteers" in order to "return the land to the landowners" and in order to "renew the deadly, despised war." Kerensky had run from Petrograd, dooming it to "surrender" to the Germans, "to hunger and bloody carnage," Kerensky was coming with Kornilov, and so on. The MRC "Bulletin" of October 30 even carried this sensational fabrication: "Michael Romanov is in Gatchina with the Cossacks. He is waiting for Kerensky to open him the door to the Winter Palace."[68]

The Bolshevik forces at Pulkovo were infinitely superior in numbers to Krasnov's "handful." Krasnov joined battle with 600 Cossacks, 18 artillery pieces, an armored car, and an armored train. An analysis of reports sent to General Headquarters on October 31 reveals that Kerensky had in addition an infantry force consisting of 700 cadets from the Northern Front Ensign School and school for aviators and 110 guerrillas from Luga. The cadets apparently only stood guard duty and refused to participate in active combat against the Bolsheviks. One can get an idea of the size of the Bolshevik forces from MRC documents containing demands made on the 29th by Colonel Velden — one of the few officers to participate actively in the Bolshevik military operations — for provisions for 8,000 men per day.

According to Krasnov's account, the battle resembled army maneuvers, right down to the audience that had come to watch it. The adversaries were separated by a ravine, through which ran Slavianka Creek. The Red Guard occupied the center, on Pulkovo Hill, and the sailors occupied the flanks. Krasnov's strength was in his artillery: "I am holding the enemy at a respectful distance with artillery fire." A large column of troopers was moving to Krasnov's rear: "I sent an armored train and thirty mounted Cossacks." Thirty minutes later came a report that the Izmailovsky Regiment on the Bolshevik side had fled in disarray to a man after the first burst of shrapnel. A hundred Orenburg Cossacks, who had been inactive because of a shortage of rifles, took the initiative and, completely unsupported, rushed into an attack on the village of Suza, which was occupied by sailors. A crowd of black figures fled in utter confusion. They were Red Guards. The sailors stubbornly held their position. The Cossacks encountered a drainage ditch and the attack came to a halt. Men were falling from shots fired at practically point-blank range. The hundred Cossacks, hastily dismounting, beat a swift retreat on foot. The losses were not as large as might have been expected. The commander was killed and about eighteen Cossacks were wounded. Forty horses were killed. (*Pravda* reported that "the entire Cossack squadron was mowed down by machine guns.") "From a standpoint of morale," adds Krasnov, "this unsuccessful attack was very disadvantageous to us. It demonstrated the staunchness of the sailors. And the sailors were more numerous than us by more than tenfold." This last impresssion was obviously somewhat erroneous. The Bolsheviks numbered their sailors at 3,000.

Dusk began to fall. The battle lessened in intensity – the Cossacks were running short of artillery shells. Unrestrained by artillery, the sailors advanced. Krasnov gave the order to withdraw to Gatchina, where his troops were to take up a "defensive position." The "battle reconnaissance" demonstrated that he did not have sufficient forces to take Petrograd. The Cossacks began withdrawing along the Gatchina highway, in perfect formation, taking with them all their artillery and the supply train. The Bolshevik units were "itching to fight," but they did not pursue Krasnov to Gatchina, even though the Cossack withdrawal was supposedly in the nature of "disorganized flight." The victorious MRC report claimed that Kerensky's losses amounted to 1,500 wounded and dead, while the Bolsheviks had suffered about 200 casualties. The Bolshevik commander Muraviev figured his losses at 400 men. Krasnov calculated his losses at only three dead and twenty-eight wounded. After the defeat Kerensky had "700" Cossacks left. "Kerensky and Krasnov have been thoroughly trounced," announced Muraviev to the army in the field. "The night of the 30th-31st will go down in history," announced Trotsky from Pulkovo at two o'clock in the morning, speaking in the name of the People's Commissars. "The soldiers, sailors, and workers of Petrograd have shown that they have the skill and desire to maintain with weapon in hand the will and power of democracy."

BEHIND THE SCENES

Battles of a kind were also under way at Gatchina Palace. They took the form of agreements or violent discord, depending on the adversary.

Late in the evening of the 29th Kerensky was visited by a deputation from the Vikzhel, which brought with it an "insolent ultimatum" demanding that he enter into peace talks with the Bolsheviks and threatening a rail strike if he did not. "A stormy scene ensued," recalls Kerensky. Other participants in the discussion testify to Kerensky's excited state of mind. The delegation claimed in the pages of *Novaia Zhizn'* that Kerensky did not officially reject the ultimatum. He demanded that representatives from the Committee of Salvation and ministers be allowed to visit him in order to discuss the matter, and that a locomotive be furnished to take him to Mogilev so that he could confer with army representatives. As a condition for peace talks Kerensky demanded that all the ministers be freed from the Peter and Paul Fortress.

Evidently Gots and Stankevich arrived from Petrograd that night immediately after the departure of the Vikzhel delegation. One must assume that Gots arrived with a definite aim in mind. "After the failure of the undertaking on October 29th," Gots testified in court, "we saw that we lacked the necessary strength for the immediate removal of the Bolsheviks by force of arms, and we changed our tactics accordingly. The new tactic was to isolate the Bolsheviks gradually from all socialist and democratic forces and from the masses. At the same time, striving to unify the democracy, we did everything in our power to extinguish the civil war by means of negotiations and agreements. By that I mean the talks initiated by the Vikzhel and the talks in Mogilev." According to Gots this was the position assumed by the Socialist Revolutionary party, which dominated the Committee of Salvation. As a result, the anti-Bolshevik action taken by the Committee of Salvation was to become more vacillating and ambivalent. It was to follow party chairman Chernov's tactics, which, initially, consisted of an attempt to replace an armed suppression of the insurrection with a demonstration of armed strength before which the Bolsheviks would be willing to concede.

This line of thought was present within the inner recesses of the Central Committee of the Socialist Revolutionary party from the very outset, but it was not subscribed to by those active in the Committee of Salvation — the peace-loving views were rejected primarily by the veteran Socialist Revolutionary terrorists, among whom "leanings toward the right" could be observed. One must assume that Gots himself did not shift from one position to the other with such agility and grace. His thinking seems to have passed into another stage of evolution (a rather short-lived one, like everything else during those stormy days), which the November 3 issue of *Delo Naroda* defined as follows: "The [Socialist Revolutionary] party should not be a party of civil war against a government of Bolsheviks, since it is not in conflict with those workers and soldiers who are temporarily siding with the Bolsheviks. It should defeat Bolshevism by revealing to democracy its entire inner lie."

The impressions of October 29 led to another milepost, on which stood the name Gatchina. "The rebellion is finished. The unexpected weakness of our forces and the unexpected energy displayed by the Bolsheviks seemed devastating to us," writes Stankevich. "The only hope remaining was Kerensky's detachment." And Gots arrived with a mission, perhaps not fully formulated — to persuade Kerensky to bring down the banner of the Provisional Government and hoist the flag of the revolutionary democracy above Gatchina Palace.

Stankevich and Gots urged Kerensky to proceed to General Headquarters, where one could plan the organization of a large-scale struggle. Kerensky raised objections, but Stankevich refuted all his arguments and with the aid of Gots persuaded Kerensky to agree to leave for General Headquarters on the following day. Since the trip represented a certain risk, Stankevich persuaded Kerensky to name a successor. "Taking advantage of the arrival of a group of friends from Petrograd," Kerensky puts in his memoirs, not mentioning the above conversation, "I gave them a letter addressed to Avksentiev, transferring to him, just in case of 'possible necessity,' the authority and duties of prime minister and requesting that appointments be made immediately to augment the Provisional Government." That is to say, "just in case of 'possible necessity.' " authority was delegated to the chairman of the Committee of Salvation, and not to a member of the Provisional Government. Kerensky attributes his decision to leave Gatchina to the impossibility of remaining in an atmosphere of intrigue. Kerensky did not proceed to General Headquarters, however. He merely went to meet the approaching troop trains in order to expedite the arrival of infantry assigned to Krasnov. Then he returned to the palace.

During the night of the 29th Chernov, chairman of the Central Committee of the Socialist Revolutionary party, also arrived in Gatchina rather unexpectedly on his way from the western front to the northern front. Kerensky was displeased. "Kerensky," relates Stankevich, "asked me to meet Chernov and persuade him to continue on immediately, without coming to the palace if possible, at least without attempting to play a part in affairs at Gatchina. This seemed to me to be an excessive suspiciousness and distrust. I quartered Chernov in my room and even insisted that Kerensky receive him. Their talk did not last long, but it was held in a rather calm tone." This meeting is described by the Socialist Revolutionary Veiger, who was in charge of the "civilian section" at Gatchina. He found Kerensky in a state of "extreme agitation" after his talk with Chernov. Kerensky informed him that the central committee of the party was implementing a "policy of disapproval" of his actions and that Chernov, insisting on the formation of a homogeneous socialist government, considered Kerensky's "military operations" to be out of place. Veiger recommended that the supreme commander issue "orders for Chernov's arrest." But "apparently Chernov's point of view . . . impressed Kerensky. Our conversation boiled down to my defending my viewpoint that it was essential to rely on General Headquarters and in no way to permit discontinuities of policy . . . . Kerensky in reply brought up the Kornilov affair and expressed the fear that he would again be deluged with accusations of 'Kornilov tactics.' In general, Kerensky failed to give me one direct reply," concludes Veiger.

Chernov's appearance in Gatchina was hardly fortuitous, for his name was prominently featured in the martial appeals issued on the 29th by the Committee of Salvation. After the cadet rebellion was crushed, *Delo Naroda* published another proclamation by the Committee appealing to the public not to dig trenches or take other defensive measures, because V. M. Chernov, leader of the Russian peasantry, "is coming with the troops."

It is quite obvious that on October 30 an attempt was made under a plausible pretext to remove Kerensky from Gatchina and thus depose him as head of the "anti-Bolshevik action." Kerensky was the symbol of an unpopular government. The advance of a detachment headed by Kerensky signified the restoration, even if temporary, of a government that had ceased to exist. Kerensky was marching in defense of the coalition government. The Bolshevik demagogues placed a sign of equality between Kerensky and the Cossack ataman, Kaledin; both were leading reactionary "Kornilovist gangs." For the "Socialist Revolutionary Bolsheviks" of *Delo Naroda*, as Potresov called the Chernov group shortly before the October Revolution, the "Kaledin reaction" was less acceptable than the Bolshevik adventure. Chernov was hardly inclined to link his name too closely with Krasnov's Cossack detachment. He was the leader of a policy of "isolation," not "repression."

But Gots, who was in Gatchina at the same time as Chernov, was not yet ready to divorce himself from the Krasnov detachment. We see him together with Savinkov on the field of battle among Krasnov's Cossacks. We see him at a political meeting in Tsarkoe Selo, when an infantry regiment threatened to attack the Cossacks' rear — not in support of the Bolsheviks, but rather to put an end to the conflict that was upsetting the Tsarskoe Selo garrison. Gots succeeded in convincing the regiment to adopt a position of passive "neutrality."

Woytinsky, more than all others, also linked his fate with Krasnov's detachment. All his hopes were centered on its success. At his initiative the detachment passed a declaration emphasizing the democratic nature of the intentions of the troops advancing on Petrograd and the impossibility of detachments being used for counterrevolutionary purposes. The detachment was acting in full agreement with the organ of the revolutionary democracy, the Committee of Salvation. The declaration, which was signed by Woytinsky, Krasnov, and twenty-three Cossack representatives, was published on November 1 in *Novaia Zhizn* .

Considering the social atmosphere at Gatchina Palace, it is quite easy to understand Kerensky's confusion. The Vikzhel, friends and advisors from Petrograd, and Chernov all arrived on the same night. Nevertheless, some kind of agreement was reached, for at 3:20 in the morning of the 31st a circular telegram was sent from Gatchina Palace, bypassing General Headquarters, to all army committees, commissars, and army commanders: "The Temporary Council of the Russian Republic, the All-Russian Committee of Salvation, and C[entral] E[xecutive] C[ommittee] of Peasants', Soldiers' and Workers' Deputies appeal to the armies in the field to send troops immediately, at least one infantry regiment from each of the nearest armies as swiftly as possible, finding the most effective means, stopping at nothing; express trains should be used to transfer troops to Luga and Gatchina. The entire weight of responsibility for delay will fall on the shoulders of the tardy."[69] The telegram was signed by Kerensky, Avksentiev, Gots, Woytinsky, Stankevich, and Semenov, who was a member of the Socialist Revolutionary battle organization. The signature of party chairman Chernov, who was supposedly "coming with the troops," was lacking. Also notable in this collective appeal was the fact that the name of the defunct Council of the Republic (i.e. Pre-Parliament) was introduced, while the Provisional Government was no longer mentioned.

THE END OF GATCHINA

Kerensky's proposed departure from Gatchina did not take place. "We were already ending our preparations for departure," relates Stankevich, when Savinkov arrived "unexpectedly" and vigorously opposed the move, insisting that Kerensky should remain "until the battle is decided." Kerensky acceded and not only cancelled his departure but even appointed Savinkov to direct the defense of Gatchina, in the face of protests from Stankevich, who considered the name of Savinkov to be odious in leftist circles.

It is hardly likely that Kerensky was easy in his mind about leaving Gatchina. He must have realized that his departure was tantamount to giving up his leadership. Also it must have been clear to him that attitudes would change depending on the prevailing state of affairs. In view of Kerensky's tendency to fluctuate and his extreme exhaustion, any unpleasant bit of news must have disheartened him and weakened his will to resist. The Krasnov detachment was becoming demoralized. Everybody felt this, and the commander himself portrayed to Kerensky the loss of combat capability and the confusion of his men. On October 31 and November 1 Gatchina resembled the Winter Palace on October 25. Both were being besieged; both languished in the hope that troops would arrive from the front; both, doomed to inactivity, were seized by panic. But there was one essential difference. Gatchina was not cut off from the front. On the evening of the 31st, when Gatchina appeared to be surrounded, Savinkov and Vendziagolsky (commissar with the 8th Army) traveled unchallenged to Luga, encountering along the road nothing more sinister than an elk. Help was coming, in spite of all obstacles, and the first trainload of infantry was passing in high spirits through a seething Pskov. During the next two days six troop trains arrived in Luga. Now everything might take a turn for the better. But the beleaguered forces no longer believed in such a possibility and felt that they had been betrayed. The rank and file on both sides were inclined to reject a "fratricidal" war. Enforced procrastination was draining away all enthusiasm from those who were supposed to deal the swift blow.

On the 31st Kerensky called a "council of war." In addition to those officials known to us, it was attended by Stankevich and representatives of the Council of Cossack Troops, which the supreme commander speaks of with such repugnance in his memoirs. There is a fair degree of agreement in the recollections of the participants in the "council of war" about the discussions. "The line of debate was immediately defined," relates Stankevich: "Savinkov insisted on fighting, at all costs, agreeing in an extreme case to negotiations merely as a military stratagem in order to gain time . . . . I promoted the opposite viewpoint, arguing that a further continuation of the conflict would lead to the total disintegration of the front; we had to find an organic agreement with the maximum possible concessions."

"All the military, without exception," testifies Kerensky, "were unanimous: in order to gain time it was necessary to begin negotiations immediately. Otherwise we could not guarantee that the Cossacks would remain quiet. Although this was an extremely difficult and odious thing for me to do I supported the majority."

Stankevich was sent to Petrograd to arrange talks; he went straight through Tsarskoe Selo, which was not even guarded by Bolshevik patrols. He was bearing, as Kerensky put it, "my terms" of truce. Kerensky does not remember them well: "At any rate those conditions were not acceptable to the Bolsheviks." This is quite understandable, since according to Kerensky the fundamental demand called for the "Bolsheviks to put down their arms at once and submit to a renewed National Provisional Government." There was no such demand, at least in such a categorical form, in the declaration which was addressed to the Committee of Salvation and was taken by Stankevich to Petrograd, where it was published in the newspapers. Speaking on behalf of the Provisional Government, Kerensky called "once more" for struggle, but declared that the "government is prepared to suspend suppression of the insurrection and negotiate about ways to restore legal revolutionary authority with the leading public organizations and parties," provided it is allowed to meet in a full quorum. In supplementary telegrams sent to the Committee of Salvation and the Vikzhel (in case Stankevich would not reach Petrograd), Kerensky stated that he had issued the order to stop military operations in accordance with the wish expressed by the Committee of Salvation.

A thoroughly dignified declaration was also sent to the Committee of Salvation from the Krasnov detachment, which had remained loyal to the legal government. Krasnov does not mention it in his memoirs, although naturally his signature appears above all the others. Apparently the general had little interest in the "political prospects" (Stankevich's comment). It was proposed in the declaration that the cabinet members who were under arrest be freed and that the legal government be restored, since it had already entered into talks with the representatives of all parties for the purpose of organizing governmental authority and convening the Constituent Assembly, which alone could resolve the problems of land and war. At the same time Krasnov sent a truce proposal bearing his own signature to Bolshevik headquarters. It was logical for the military to conduct the actual truce talks, but unfortunately the Cossack delegation which volunteered its services for this purpose and was approved by Krasnov was not a responsible one. This had catastrophic consequences.

Simultaneously with the peace initiative from Krasnov, another peace initiative originated from the MRC. The MRC was forced into it at the insistence of eight Petrograd regiments and several other troop delegations, which demanded an end to the slaughter and that the sides come to terms. In the Petrograd Soviet Zinoviev reported that a delegation had been dispatched, explained that the MRC was certain of its "failure" and was inclined to view the proposed gesture as "a military stratagem on the part of our enemies." "At any rate," explained Zinoviev ironically, "the delegation will remember that 'the armed conflict is over, and peace terms are the only subject for discussion.' "

The two delegations met in a spirit of fellowship in Tsarskoe Selo and arrived in Gatchina at 6:00 A.M. on November 1. The dashing sailor Dybenko was the dominant personality. A committee began working out the peace terms, and after six hours of debate in a picturesque homespun atmosphere a unique and equally naive agreement for a truce was drawn up. One of the points read as follows: "Comrades Lenin and Trotsky, until they are proven innocent of treason, shall participate neither in a ministry nor in public organizations." On the other hand, "Kerensky shall be handed over to the Revolutionary Committee for public trial [and shall be] guarded by three Cossack representatives, three representatives from the party, and three representatives of the sailors, soldiers, and workers of Petrograd . . . . Both parties pledge their word of honor that no acts of violence or mob law will under any circumstances be perpetrated on him or anyone else."

Thus Kerensky's Gatchina headquarters was seized by fraud, and the last chance of Cossack resistance was eliminated. Later in the day on November 1, Northern front headquarters received the following telegram from Krasnov: "Supr comm chief disappeared at 15:00 hours from Gatchina palace in unknown direction. Gatchina occupied by Bolshevik troops." In his later memoirs Kerensky related how he escaped, disguised as a sailor, toward Luga, and went into hiding on a lonely farmstead that belonged to his chauffeur. His disappearance from the political arena seemed to signify an end to the armed conflict.

Krasnov, who was also a novelist, describes in vivid detail the situation in Gatchina after the signing of the pact – the appearance of the swaggering commander of the Bolshevik troops, Muraviev, the subsequent appearance of Trotsky himself, and Krasnov's removal to Smolny for interrogation. In an official report, Krasnov informed Cheremisov: "The mood here is quite alarming . . . . Our relations with the Bolshevik troops are permeated with mutual distrust. We are surrounded by them and are under double sentries, theirs and ours . . . . Right now the soldiers are disarming the Cossacks. This morning talks were held between the committees — the division committee and that of the revolutionary organization. Command officers were excluded. The following resolutions were passed: to end the bloodshed, to permit the Cossacks to return to the Don, to make no arrests, to commit no arbitrary acts, and to arrest Kerensky. After this our sentry posts were approached by the Finliandsky regiment with artillery and a white flag. They removed our sentry posts and entered Gatchina. Then delegates and the regimental commander, under the pretext of negotiations, left for Petrograd, and nonfulfillment of the treaty is already beginning. Soldier committees are meeting and who knows how all this will end."[70]

Very characteristic of Cheremisov's position is the manner in which he reacted to Krasnov's report: "Kerensky is to blame for everything. I told him how all this would end . . . the results are evident." The status of the Krasnov detachment was of interest to him exclusively from the viewpoint of the situation at the front. The departure of the Cossacks for the Don would disorganize all units and lead to spontaneous demobilization. "Your units should return to their positions without delay." "That will be very difficult," replied Krasnov, "for we are at present virtually prisoners of the Bolsheviks, who will hardly allow my orders to be executed."[71]

During his interrogation on November 2 at Smolny, Woytinsky stated that the agreement between representatives of the Petrograd garrison, the Council of People's Commissars, and the Cossack representatives, an agreement officially called a "truce agreement," "was essentially and unquestionably an agreement calling for cessation of civil war, and it was precisely as such that the agreement was understood by both parties. Believing every additional hour of civil war to be disastrous, I dispatched a telegram to Northern Front Headquarters, to the commissars and all, all, all, informing them that the civil war had come to a truce reached between the opposing sides, and that all hostilities should cease immediately, including preparations for such and the further progress of troop trains heading for Petrograd."[72]

Woytinsky took too much upon himself in sending out this telegram, which disorganized the struggle. The first person to receive it had fundamental doubts about its authenticity. At 5:10 Lukirsky transmitted to Dukhonin a text of the telegram he had "just" received from Woytinsky: "An agreement has been reached between the troops concentrated near Petrograd and representatives of the Petrograd garrison, an agreement based on Kerensky's deposition. See that all troop trains moving toward Petrograd are stopped immediately and that all operations connected with forming a military detachment for Kerensky cease." "This telegram," commented Lukirsky, "must be treated with the greatest caution, since it is known that Woytinsky is in Luga, while this was received by teletype from Gatchina." Lukirsky then added: "Is it possible for you to give us right now a telegram ordering the following quantity of shells and cartridges to be sent from Pskov to the commander of the Third Corps: high-explosive shells, 20,000; shrapnel shells, 20,000; 15 million rounds of rifle cartridges; 2,000 rounds of ammunition for armored cars . . . . The acceptance officer has come for them, but in the absence of an official order coming from the supreme commander or you, the commander in chief of the northern front will not permit this ammunition to be shipped out." Dukhonin: "The order will be sent immediately. I think the order is too large, however. We must cut it substantially."[73]

Dukhonin was a long way from believing that the civil war had come to an end. Having attempted to establish Kerensky's whereabouts from persons who had been acting in Pskov "on the instructions" of the supreme commander, and receiving no information whatsoever, Dukhonin issued an order, which was published in the bulletins of the All-Army Committee: "Today, November 1, the troops of General Krasnov, gathered at Gatchina, concluded a truce with the Petrograd garrison in order to stop the bloodshed of a civil war. According to the report from General Krasnov, Supreme Commander Kerensky has left the detachment, and his whereabouts are unknown. In view of this and in conformity with the regulations on field command, I have temporarily assumed the duties of supreme commander and have ordered the further dispatch of troops to Petrograd stopped. Negotiations to form a provisional government are presently under way between the various political parties. In expectation that the crisis will be resolved, I hereby call upon the troops at the front to calmly carry out their duty to their country, in order not to present the enemy with an opportunity to take advantage of the confusion that has broken out within our country and to penetrate even farther into the interior of our native land."[74]

Apparently Dukhonin was acutely aware of the demoralizing effect on the northern front caused by the confusion arising when on the 31st the army was asked in the name of the revolutionary democracy to send troops to Luga and Gatchina by express train, while on the following day the end of the civil war was announced. What would the rank-and-file soldiers think?

CHAPTER 9

On a New Track

THE PETROGRAD "TALK FACTORY"

Meanwhile, the interparty conference proposed by the Vikzhel was taking place. It convened on "Bloody Sunday," October 29.

The Bolsheviks had readily agreed to the conference. Clearly, the verbal exercises at the Vikzhel conference could only help them. At the most critical moment the attention of their adversaries would be focused on conciliation and not on struggle; as an inevitable result, anti-Bolshevik activity would be weakened and anti-Bolshevik agitation among the masses, who were inclined toward peaceful solutions, made less effective. The Bolsheviks were gaining time. The Bolshevik Central Committee accepted the Vikzhel proposal almost without debate, but in the absence of Lenin and Trotsky, who were the true masterminds of the October coup. Their absence was hardly accidental, and it was probably not because both were busy mobilizing forces to repel Kerensky, who was advancing on Petrograd. More likely, they were holding themselves back so they would be able in due time to nullify any compromise that might be reached. For their vacillating opposition within the party was inclined toward compromise, believing that an agreement between the Bolsheviks and the socialist parties that had walked out of the Congress of Soviets was the only way out of the situation created by the coup.

In any case, at the first session of the Vikzhel conference,[75] the official representatives of the Bolshevik Party, Kamenev and Sokolnikov, acknowledged that agreement was not only "possible" but even essential and proposed that the other socialist parties share power with them, provided they recognize the accomplished facts. The Socialist Revolutionaries and Mensheviks took a position that at first glance seemed uncompromising. Gendelman from the Socialist Revolutionary party stated quite emphatically that he had not come to the conference to enter into negotiations with the Bolsheviks but rather to set forth "the party's viewpoint"; he stated that at times it is necessary to resolve problems with arms. Dan suggested that the Bolsheviks capitulate — disband the MRC and recognize the Second Congress of Soviets as null and void. According to him, agreement was possible only on the program of the Committee of Salvation, that is homogeneous socialist rule without Bolshevik participation in the government, since their participation would deprive the government of authority and of recognition by the country at large. Martov, naturally, favored compromise: democracy did not have the needed strength, and if the crisis were to intensify, democracy would be crushed by "a personal or oligarchic dictatorship." If the Bolsheviks are eliminated, seconded the Bolshevik Sokolnikov, "a Cossack dictatorship" is inevitable. Thus a bridge between the negotiating sides was in the offing: "We can jointly struggle against the counterrevolution," the representatives of the revolutionary democracy seemed to reply, but the first condition was that the insurrection come to an end.

The conference, which was attended by twenty-six delegates from eight parties and nine organizations, elected a conciliation commission in order to draft, after comradely discussions, a specific proposal to be submitted at the following session. (I have deliberately employed the term "comradely," for it was commonly used at this conference of adversaries who to some extent were even prepared to go at each other with weapons in hand.) The commission included a representative of the Socialist Revolutionary party, apparently in contradiction to the basic stand taken by that party. The commission worked through the night, but nothing came of Martov's appeal to come to "a bold agreement by both camps." One reason was that the Bolshevik representatives abstained from voting on the question of a truce between the warring factions, and thus the first and fundamental demand of the Vikzhel was left hanging.

The second session began somewhat tempestuously and had some rather interesting features. Dan, Martov, and the Socialist Revolutionary Filipovsky lodged a protest against the order issued by the MRC to place the Committee of Salvation under arrest. Kamenev explained that no such order existed. The only persons facing arrest were those involved in the cadet conspiracy, Avksentiev and Gots, who had issued the arrest order against the members of the MRC. "The Committee of Salvation," said the Bolshevik Riazanov, "is maintaining a stubborn silence about its connections with the insurrection, but the link is obvious." "What happened yesterday is the same kind of adventure as yours," parried Filipovsky, acknowledging that the order to arrest the MRC had been "inappropriate." After passing a resolution against the use of terror and special courts, the conference moved on to discuss the matter of forming a government. Tactics were flexible, and quite unexpectedly the Socialist Revolutionary Rakitnikov proposed a compromise formula. In order to "satisfy" the Bolsheviks he proposed that a coalition of parties be replaced with a combination of individuals, including Bolsheviks. But the Bolsheviks objected, saying that constituting a government by means of individual combinations and not by party representation was unacceptable. Nevertheless, another commission was elected to study the setup of a new government.

This commission, too, worked through the night, and finally came up with the idea of a "Provisional People's Council," to which the government would be responsible. The City Duma and the old VTsIK were proposed as starting points for the formation of the council, but the Bolsheviks objected. Debate began on the subject of how many persons and who would be given seats on this council. Then the nomination of candidates for the future government began, and the Bolshevik delegates did participate most directly in this political cookery. "Agreement" was eventually reached by passing a flexible resolution: the government should include specialists, independent of party affiliation. Names were mentioned — old and new ones within the framework of the formula "from the People's Socialists to Bolsheviks."

What were the attitudes that influenced the position of the revolutionary democracy and impelled some of its central leadership to go the way of conciliation? The representative of the City Duma at the Vikzhel conference explained that the willingness to compromise was due to the precarious position in which Kerensky found himself: "we were forced to agree to all sorts of concessions merely to reach agreement and stop the civil war." Others made reference to Kerensky's telegram to the Central Committee of the Socialist Revolutionary party, read at the Vikzhel conference on October 30, in which he authorized the Central Committee to conclude a truce under conditions that it would find acceptable. Somewhat in conflict with this, fears of reprisals against workers, supposedly inevitable if Cossacks were to enter Petrograd, persisted. As late as the 31st, the Mensheviks and Socialist Revolutionaries at the Vikzhel conference guaranteed to the Bolsheviks that "if Kerensky enters Petrograd with his Cossacks," they would "not allow his detachment to enter the worker districts," in order to preclude "a rout of the working class."

Not all the revolutionary democracy went along with this spirit of compromise. The All-Army Committee at General Headquarters in Mogilev maintained an unbending position. In the words of its chairman, the Socialist Revolutionary Perekrestov, "We do not admit neutrality, which can only help the [Bolshevik] insurrection. We want the Committee of Salvation to have the force of arms at its disposal." In Perekrestov's view, only an active anti-Bolshevik policy could prevent casualties, which would occur if the Cossacks were allowed to engage in repressions.

But the leaders of the Vikzhel belonged to groups to which the position of the All-Army Committee was unacceptable, and, therefore, when the committee appealed to the Vikzhel representative at General Headquarters on the 31st to assist in the movement of troops in order to "equalize the opposing forces and force the Bolsheviks to come to an agreement" and in order to "create a force that can be relied upon in case the Bolsheviks refuse to agree," the Vikzhel representatives vigorously refused to help move troops that could be used for counterrevolutionary purposes. As if balancing their argument for the sake of neutrality, the Vikzhel representatives also gave as a reason the possibility that the troops might go over to the Bolsheviks and consequently reinforce their indisposition to compromise. In the meantime, another force favoring conciliation entered the Vikzhel negotiations.

During the night of the 30th a twenty-man deputation of workers from the Obukhov works appeared at the meeting in a greatly agitated state. In threatening tones they demanded that the work of the conference be concluded as soon as possible in order to bring the civil war and general chaos to an end. The deputation expressed itself forcefully in word and gesture. The speech "made a powerful impression on all conferees," relates An-sky. "An agitated Riazanov began screaming hysterically that the Bolsheviks had been ready to come to an agreement from the very beginning and would make all possible concessions, but that the other delegates, particularly the representatives of the Duma, were impeding peaceful resolution of the conflict." "Devil knows which of you is right," angrily shouted one of the workers. "None of you are worth a plugged nickel. You should all hang from the same tree — the country will quiet down by itself."[76] In other accounts, the workers scream, "Kerensky, Lenin, Trotsky — all should be hanged from the same tree. Down with the parties and party leaders — they can do nothing for us."

The colorful episode shows that the mood of the workers at the Obukhov works was very different from that depicted at the time by the Bolshevik press, which published a resolution passed by the factory workers wholeheartedly supporting the Bolshevik position. This is an example of how very wary one must be in respect to the workers' resolutions that were published in such a large number. It is possible that draft resolutions of an organized Bolshevik minority were sometimes presented to the press as if they were resolutions adopted by all the workers. In any case, the adoption of resolutions demanding an end to the civil war "by any and all means" swept through plants and factories between October 29 and the 31st in the wake of the cadet uprising and the "battle" of Pulkovo. Such resolutions were passed at mass meetings of workers at the Baltic and Putilov works, the shipyards, munitions and ordnance plants, and the Arsenal, not to mention such craft unions as the printers and the union of postal-telegraph employees. The cry was almost universal. "All together," read the resolution of the postal-telegraph employees' union, "must present a categoric demand to the belligerent sides to call an immediate truce in order to resolve the matter of organizing a government."

There is no doubt that the direct intervention that night by delegates from the Obukhov works influenced the course of the Vikzhel conference. Not only did the conferees' speeches become shorter, but the question of a truce was concretely advanced once again. The Bolshevik representatives agreed to it in principle, assuming that the party was in favor of a truce.

News of this so-called agreement reached Kerensky. On November 1, the Vikzhel received the following telegram from him: "Your proposal accepted. Yesterday my representative Stankevich was sent out. Am awaiting reply."

In reality, the conference so far had been nothing but a talk factory. No true agreement was reached with the Bolsheviks, despite Kamenev's conciliatory personal attitude. The possible composition of a cabinet remained uncertain, since in general the parties were just briefing each other, and each side expressed tacit agreement to the list of candidates presented by their opponents. The only candidates removed were Lenin and Trotsky, which caused indignation among the leaders' followers. It was this generalized talk that was reported by the organizations participating in the conference to their central bodies. In expectation of competent replies, the Vikzhel meetings were adjourned until November 2.

Consequently, there were no talks at Vikzhel on November 1. The participants in the conference were filtering draft agreements in their central committees. The attitudes of the workers, expressed so forcefully at the Vikzhel meeting, had a powerful influence on the Mensheviks. The Central Committee of the party retreated decisively from the position that Dan had taken at the first Vikzhel meeting. It spoke out in favor of a coalition government including the Bolsheviks "no matter what the cost," since "all other considerations are secondary in view of the necessity of preventing continuation of bloody internecine strife among the workers and destruction of the labor movement." The decision of the Central Committee caused a split in its own ranks — eleven prominent members of the committee walked out, saying that negotiations with the Bolsheviks on such a plane would be "disastrous."

Equally characteristic of the situation was the position adopted by the City Duma. It too was in favor of continuing the talks, in spite of the vehement protests by Shingarev, who stated: "The experiment of coming to an agreement with persons of that sort will not result in a truce, for Russia will never bow to these lunatics and will continue the struggle without us conciliators . . . The Kadet faction will not participate in an agreement with those whose hands are stained in their brothers' blood." The instructions received by the delegates indicated with sufficient clarity that attempts at conciliation were totally useless. The Duma "vigorously" objected to Bolshevik participation in a new government and instructed its delegates "to insist that in order to preserve the succession of authority it is essential first of all to declare the composition of the Provisional Government unchanged, and to take steps immediately to free the jailed ministers and in general all those who have been deprived of freedom in connection with the political events now taking place."

The Bolsheviks also announced their decision, but this time with the direct participation of Lenin and Trotsky. The minutes of the meeting of the Central Committee on November 1 clearly reveal the split among the Bolsheviks themselves. Lenin demanded action and not talk. The talks were to serve only as a "diplomatic cover for military operations." Troops should be sent to the aid of Moscow, and victory would be secured. But Lenin commanded only four votes. Ten members voted to continue the talks. "If we cease negotiating we shall lose those groups that support us, and we are not in a position to retain power," said Rykov. "We cannot stand a protracted civil war," asserted Miliutin, who believed that an agreement with the right-wing socialist groupings was inevitable. Others, including Trotsky, retorted that power should not be permitted to be wrested from those who had carried out the revolt. "The Bolsheviks are not usurpers and are prepared to accept those who walked out of the congress if they recognize the decrees of the Second Congress, responsibility of the government to the VTsIK and the struggle against the counterrevolution." And a resolution was passed to this effect.[77]

After two days and nights of general meetings and conciliation-commission sessions, the talks at the conference returned to their initial stage. One major change took place. The discussions widened and deepened the psychological breach dividing those who had united around the Committee of Salvation to resist the Bolsheviks. Those present at the plenary session of the Vikzhel conference could only testify to the futility of the fictitious "agreement" reached as a result of the talks of October 29-30, and the parties affiliated in one way or another with the Committee of Salvation recalled their representatives. They left, however, confident in the belief that in the end agreement would be reached, since "the ground was after all gradually slipping out from under the feet of the Bolshevik leaders."

THE FINAL SPASMS

The above characterizes the situation that Stankevich, carrying with him the points of agreement proposed by Kerensky, was to find in Petrograd on the night of October 31. Apparently, Stankevich did not understand what the atmosphere in Petrograd signified. According to his own testimony, he ran around from one party central committee to another and made speeches, even to the Vikzhel, and everywhere encountered the same stereotyped reply: "We shall discuss it." The talks at the Vikzhel conference were of considerably more interest to the leaders of the dominant parties of the revolutionary democracy than was the immediate fate of Kerensky's military detachment. During the talks they felt themselves to be in the congenial political marketplace where they had transacted their business throughout the period of the Provisional Government. As far as they were concerned, armed conflict with the Bolsheviks was already a thing of the past.

Gatchina fell to a detachment of Bolshevik sailors, and this fact took care of the matters raised by Stankevich. Even the "immediate action" which Chernov was discussing with Dukhonin at the very same time that Stankevich was carrying out his Petrograd mission on behalf of Kerensky was completely out of the question now. This "immediate action" was to liquidate the Pskov military revolutionary committee and thereby put pressure on the Bolsheviks in the Vikzhel negotiations to make concessions in regard to the composition of a new government. Dependable combat troops from the front were to accomplish this task.

It has already been shown that a tense atmosphere prevailed in Pskov as a result of the activities of the Bolshevik-controlled military revolutionary committee. On November 1 the long-awaited infantry contingents finally reached the Pskov railroad junction. "At one o'clock in the afternoon," General Lukirsky reported to Chief of Staff Dukhonin, "the first trains passed through carrying the Third Finland Division and the Thirty-fifth Division from the Seventeenth Corps." By evening the first shock battalion and a detachment of special forces that "had fled from Valk with the blessings of the commander of the Twelfth Army" had arrived, having commandeered rolling stock and having "ejected negative elements from its midst" as a precautionary measure. "They are in an excellent mood," reported Lukirsky. The shock battalion was kept in Pskov by the military authorities in order to provide cover for the trains containing the Third Finland Division, which were passing through; the day before, Bolshevik-oriented units of the Pskov garrison had attempted to seize the railroad station.

The moment the Vikzhel talks broke down, however, the proposed armed demonstration in Pskov lost its political significance. Demonstrations had to give way to action — that is, they had to proceed along the path proposed by Kerensky, a path branded unacceptable by those in the revolutionary democracy who rejected armed conflict as a "means of freeing the revolution from the Bolshevik disease." (Subsequently, at a Socialist Revolutionary party conference on November 18, Chernov stated that while "rushing along the front seeking to avert civil war," he had realized that there was no "possibility of offering active resistance.") The program of the All-Army Committee, as has been noted, provided for the possibility of taking action in case the Bolsheviks refused to come to terms. According to its chairman, the All-Army Committee had the same point of view as the Committee of Salvation; they both accepted active armed intervention as a policy-implementing tool. Chernov and his group did not agree with the position taken by the Committee of Salvation, but nevertheless acted as spokesmen for it as they maneuvered behind the scenes at General Headquarters. And how natural it was that the new intermediaries between General Headquarters and the revolutionary democracy shied away from the direct use of force upon learning that the talks in Petrograd with the Bolsheviks had broken off. They proceeded to Mogilev to hold talks on organizing a new government. Its basis was to be the All-Army Committee, switched to a new track leading toward appeasement.

As we have seen, on November 1, Dukhonin had issued an order halting the movement of troops from the front toward Petrograd. But something compelled the acting supreme commander not to be rigoristic about implementing it. On the following day Dukhonin issued an order to concentrate units of the Third Finland Division and Seventeenth Corps, which had been moved toward Gatchina, in the Luga area; six troop trains carrying an infantry regiment and a shock battalion had already reached there.

Quite justifiably, the commander of the northern front, Cheremisov, saw this to be a contradiction of the spirit of the order of November 1 and opposed such a troop concentration. Cheremisov endeavored to convince Dukhonin that in view of the threatening situation at the front he should shift all military units away from the Luga area immediately, particularly since these units "will very rapidly change their color and possibly head for Petrograd themselves, but for a purpose quite different from that which you have in mind ... I have become so exhausted lately," said Cheremisov, terminating his teletype conversation, "that I would resign my post with the greatest pleasure, and I shall do so as soon as this political donnybrook comes to an end, one way or another. As for the present, if you do not rescind your order to move troops through Pskov I shall be forced to resign, whereas if you do cancel I shall stay here for the time being and use all my influence to keep the front from disintegrating. I beg you ... to forget that gossip and those rumors which I know are being spread about me here and at General Headquarters."[78]

"I did not for a minute think of moving the Third Finland Division and units of the Thirty-fifth Infantry Division to Petrograd after the events at Gatchina were over," replied Dukhonin, "but I made use of the emerging situation and of troop movements already in progress to carry out tasks of strategic significance."

What Dukhonin meant, apparently, was that he wanted to counteract the movement of Latvians in the Twelfth Army. According to General Iuzefovich, commander of the Twelfth Army, the Latvian units were carrying out an organized plan to seize power and take over the major railroad junctions. He believed that it was not completely out of the question that this might be a cleverly elaborated plan by the German General Staff, and the Latvians might be merely a blind tool in German hands.

Cheremisov believed Dukhonin, or at least pretended to believe him. At any rate, on the following day he recommended that Iuzefovich announce to the army that "no units are proceeding to Petrograd for civil war – this will reassure them." Everything must be done to "avoid making it possible for the Germans to overturn our front." "I have always been vigorously in favor of nonintervention by the army in politics, since this can end in disaster for the state. The Germans would come, liquidate all parties, and set up their own government." One sentence in the conversation with Iuzefovich is extremely characteristic of Cheremisov: Let the political parties "believe whom they like and worship whom they like, but they should assist us . . . in our operational task. If they see things differently, there are only two possibilities . . . either they must be removed, or we must leave, depending on our forces and theirs. There is no middle path."

These words, divorced as they were from reality, can serve as an epilogue to an account of the position taken by Cheremisov in regard to the "Petrograd squabble." In view of a subsequent conversation between Dukhonin and Cheremisov on November 13, it would seem that the latter was prepared to make some kind of compromise with the Bolsheviks in the interest of preserving the front. Cheremisov expressed the desire to retire from the scene, since he was "useless"; but "if you insist that I remain at my post, I shall remain, in order not to be a deserter, but please bear in mind that in the very near future I shall either be removed by force or shall be compelled to act quite independently of Headquarters, thinking only of the good of Russia as I see it . . . There are times," added the commander of the northern front, "when it is impossible to prevent evil [and] one can merely attenuate it . . . permitting a small evil in order to avoid a greater one." Cheremisov apparently was not thinking of the utopian possibility of continuing the war under Bolshevik authority, but rather of participation by the military authorities in preliminary peace talks.

This idea took firm root in the minds of many as a result of the November 9 radiogram from the Council of People's Commissars calling upon the "regiments in the field" to elect "representatives empowered to enter into formal truce negotiations with the enemy." "Soldiers, peace is in your hands," stated the appeal. "You will not let the counterrevolutionary generals sabotage the great cause of peace." Under these circumstances the "Committee to Defend the Nation and Save the Revolution" in the Special Army protested the refusal of Dukhonin to engage in truce talks. "Locally," stated the committee, "there can no longer be any question of continuing combat operations, and in order to avoid the most terrible consequences we must

insure ourselves against action by the enemy." The committee stated that a
language-trained staff officer was instructed to go to Dvinsk to join the peace
delegation which had left Petrograd "so that he may be present during truce
talks in order to protect the interests of our front and that of our allies." We
now know that the preliminary conditions drawn up by the Russian military
experts were drafted with the direct participation of representatives of the
Allied military missions.*

Doubts can be entertained that the reasons given by Dukhonin for the
November 2 order to concentrate troops near Luga fully corresponded with
his intentions. At the time he apparently was playing somewhat of a waiting
game and did not wish immediately to disband the detachment gathered at
Luga with such difficulty, a detachment that could be used to fight the
Bolsheviks. The situation might change. It is apparent from a conversation
between Tolstoy of the War Ministry Political Administration and Baranovsky, quartermaster general of the northern front, on November 5, that the
part of the Committee of Salvation that was not in favor of negotiations with
the Bolsheviks had not abandoned the idea of using the troops concentrated
in Pskov and Luga for active combat. "We prefer," said Tolstoy, "to clench
our fists at that point, threatening Petrograd from that distance, in order not
to dissipate our forces and to wait for better circumstances, both in the sense
of reinforcements from the south and in respect to the internal disintegration
of Bolshevism and disenchantment with it, which is presently taking place
even more rapidly than one could have expected." Baranovsky's rejoinder was
extremely pessimistic: command personnel were abolutely powerless; the
front had adopted a neutral posture — "our armies [that is, of the northern
front] have definitely objected to the sending of troops to either side."[79]

The situation was approximately the same on the western front. On
November 5 General Baluev telegraphed: "In Minsk the Committee to Save
the Revolution has fallen apart. The commissar has resigned. A M[ilitary]
R[evolutionary] C[ommittee] has formed. It has taken upon itself the job of

*The commander of the northern front was subsequently arrested
and imprisoned in the Peter and Paul Fortress. Later, during the Brest-Litovsk
peace negotiations, when the Germans were launching an offensive and
Petrograd was in immediate danger of being taken, the new rulers consulted
with the old military leaders to determine whether it was possible to
counteract this offensive. General Cheremisov was one of these experts
invited to confer with the People's Commissar for Military Affairs on
February 7, 1918. At that time many felt it essential to cooperate with the
Bolsheviks in the face of external danger. A few days later another meeting
was held, this time at Smolny, in the presence of Lenin himself. What was the
role of General Cheremisov? Judging from the minutes of the meeting, it was
that of a silent observer. S.P.M.

maintaining order. Our present task, as the authorities, should consist of holding the front and preventing internecine and fratricidal clashes among the troops."

Savinkov attempted to organize further armed struggle, but the fall of Gatchina took the ground out from under his feet. He was able to act essentially only as a private citizen. For three days and nights Savinkov displayed immense energy. He went to Nevel, where the headquarters of the Seventeenth Corps was located, and visited Pskov and Luga. He endeavored to work on Cheremisov, threatening the general that he would be held personally responsible if he did not cooperate. He appealed directly to Dukhonin. Through a delegated officer, Savinkov informed General Headquarters of the favorable mood among the troops concentrated in Luga and urged Dukhonin to move troops to the defense of the "legal authorities," while two to three infantry divisions with artillery could still reach Petrograd "without [meeting] great resistance." By that time, however, many persons in the revolutionary democracy who were quite hostile to any "adventure" on Savinkov's part gathered at General Headquarters. Dukhonin urged Savinkov to come to Mogilev, but Savinkov would not go to headquarters, claiming that such a trip was an impossibility. But such matters are not decided by correspondence. Savinkov's appeals proved futile.

Denikin in his memoirs asserts that Dukhonin had become "hopelessly confused in the abyss of contradictions generated by the revolution." But in many cases wavering does not mean that the vacillating individual has become confused. One must acknowledge the exceptional difficulty of the situation in which Dukhonin found himself (we have seen that even in the military command there were many different viewpoints), and we must realize that to a considerable degree any other course meant for him taking a path of political adventure, for which one must assume moral responsibility. Dukhonin himself obviously had no intention of playing the part of a home-grown Napoleon, and perhaps he lacked the requisites to do so.

Meanwhile, from his hideout Kerensky sent in his resignation to the remnants of the Provisional Government, backdating his decision to November 1. The matter was discussed on November 5, and Prokopovich was elected acting prime minister. The disappearance of Kerensky presented Dukhonin who, as acting supreme commander formally took his place, with a complex task. The "legal authorities" about which Savinkov had spoken had in fact ceased to exist, since the cabinet ministers who had organized themselves as the "underground" Provisional Government failed to assert themselves publicly. The indefinite position taken by the Committee of Salvation, in recent days unexpectedly represented at the front by Chernov, could hardly arouse great feelings of sympathy on the part of command personnel. We quote a statement made by Cheremisov in a conversation with

Iuzefovich: "The ill-fated Committee of Salvation, affiliated with a party which for about eight months ruled Russia and baited us in the military command as counterrevolutionaries, has now hidden its tail between its legs, has started slobbering, and demands that we save them."[80]

To advance on Petrograd under such conditions, without organized political support and when it was quite probable that one would encounter the hostile opposition of a considerable portion of the revolutionary democracy, would not promote the disintegration of Bolshevism (which seemed to be disintegrating), but instead would strengthen it. Should they be guided by the advice Kornilov had given on November 1 from his cell in the Bykhov prison? Kornilov wrote to Dukhonin: "Fate has placed you in a position where a change in the course of events depends upon you. For you is coming the moment when men must either act boldly or retire completely, for otherwise they will bear the responsibility for the nation's ruin and the disgrace of the final disintegration of the army." But Kornilov's advice was unrealistic in Dukhonin's eyes, as can be seen from his gloomy notations on Kornilov's letter (they are referred to by Denikin in his memoirs). Kornilov's plan was based on the idea of getting support from the Czechoslovak corps and Polish troops. But Dukhonin believed that an attempt to implement Kornilov's program, at least at the moment, would be premature and would lead to total disintegration of the front. General Headquarters remained strong only because of its agreement with the All-Army Committee, and it was only their solidarity that offered the possibility of balancing the political scales while preserving the front. Dukhonin had not lost hope entirely.

The prisoners at Bykhov were extremely pained by the new national misfortune, and their being in prison under such conditions was truly unbearable. But apparently they did not fully comprehend the situation. According to Denikin, Kornilov was endeavoring to make direct contact not only with General Headquarters but also with the Council of Cossack Troops, General Dowbor-Musnicki, commander of the Polish units, and Kaledin, the ataman of the Don Cossacks. His "threatening and sharp message to General Headquarters" served merely to complicate things. General Headquarters would have been able to adopt a definite position only if political authority were to appear alongside military authority, if the remnants of the "legal Provisional Government" were to come to Mogilev. This is essentially what Cheremisov had advised Kerensky to do. But we cannot discuss what might have been.

A last episode in the fighting connected with support of the Provisional Government in the Gatchina area was the clash between one of the trains carrying shock troops to Gatchina and certain Bolshevik units. From the hyperbolic memoirs of Dybenko we learn that he uttered one word and a grand total of 3,000 shock troops surrendered at Luga. These shock troops sent a delegation to Petrograd to learn of events there. This was a strange delegation. According to *Pravda,* it appeared at Smolny on November 5 and threatened that the troops gathered at Luga would move against the MRC. The delegation was permitted to leave. They returned to Luga "with the intention of persuading their units to return to the front," stated a bulletin of the Central Committee of the Bolshevik party; the next bulletin reported that 300 out of the 1,000 shock troops in Gatchina had deserted. However, as a precautionary measure the Bolsheviks dismantled the railroad tracks in Luga — in order to prevent the "absolutely peace-loving" shock troops (to quote Antonov-Ovseenko) from proceeding to Petrograd after all. Several such delegations from various units advancing from the front toward Petrograd visited Smolny in those days.

On November 4, Dukhonin confirmed his order of November 1, stopping the transfer of troops from the front to Petrograd. According to one memoirist, he "responded to pressure from his staff." Thus, in effect, the armed struggle with the Bolsheviks at the front was officially brought to an end. "Our victory is secure," stated Lenin at the night session of his party's Central Committee on November 1.

CHAPTER **10**

Wager on Disintegration

THE DESERTERS

The end of the armed conflict did indeed insure victory for the Bolsheviks, because the passive tactics that counted on their disintegration in a sea of "anarchy and chaos" could not possibly intimidate them, or force them to abandon soon their destructive "policy of the revolutionary phrase" (Lenin). The fact that such a policy threatened the nation with a catastrophe was of little concern to men who thought themselves primarily responsible for the fate of mankind. Trotsky gives an amazing confession of their notions of responsibility when he relates with some satisfaction how creators of the new society "improvised" solutions to problems on which "hung the fate of the nation throughout an entire period of history." Taking a "great leap forward," they "improvised" because they knew from their Marxist analysis that their path had merged with the "steps of history." They did not suffer from "uneasy hesitation."

Only a physical obstacle could restrain their fanatical will. Confidence in the "inevitable" self-liquidation of the Bolshevik adventure deprived Russian society of the prerequisites for setting up such a physical obstacle. Self-hypnosis led to paralysis. Nobody pondered how to make the liquidation occur.

Lenin had his own interpretation of the "inevitable": "tomorrow" socialism would emerge victorious throughout the world. (Later, when the Leninist eschatology had faded somewhat, his disciples endeavored to interpret "tomorrow" as merely a pedagogic technique for influencing the masses, a means of inspiring faith in the Bolshevik cause and in its historic mission.) But the fanatic was a realist in his tactics, knowing not only when to advance but also when to retreat. It is unquestionable that in Lenin a sectarian impatience went arm in arm with "proletarian revolutionary" opportunism.

170

Lenin implanted his fantasies not only in the minds of the masses but also in the minds of those at Smolny itself. In the Council of People's Commissars, according to Trotsky, he "invariably" asserted that "in six months we shall have socialism." And the party parrots repeated the "great slogans" of imminent "world revolution" and followed their leader with remarkable ease in accepting "historical responsibility for the fate of mankind." The "great executor of the behest" of Marx became most irritated indeed on those infrequent occasions when he was "inappropriately" reminded of certain social democratic principles by "deserters" and "strikebreakers" in the party like those members who had been so unfortunate as to predict the failure of the rebellion, and who were now concerned about the consequences of the "policy of the revolutionary phrase."

A few days after the takeover "deserters" were trying once again to resist the "will of the people." They included that weak-nerved People's Commissar of Education, Lunacharsky, who on November 2 had abandoned his post, accompanying his resignation with an official statement to the *Sovnarkom*:* "I have just heard from eyewitnesses what has taken place in Moscow. The Church of Basil the Blessed and the Cathedral of the Assumption are being destroyed. The Kremlin, where the greatest treasures of Petrograd and Moscow are now gathered, is under bombardment. Victims number in the thousands. The struggle is assuming the proportions of bestial rage. What will be next? Where should we go from here? I cannot take it any longer. I have just had too much. I am powerless to halt this reign of terror. It is impossible to work under the pressure of these insanity-provoking thoughts. I recognize the seriousness of this decision, but I cannot go on."[81] (On the following day, Lunacharsky retracted his statement, since the People's Commissars considered it "inappropriate," and he informed "all the citizens of Russia" of his decision.)

The "deserters" did not consist only of "gradualists" hostile to the "maximalist insanity," who believed that the "nonsense" going on could not last long but dared not express their "sentimentalism" publicly. Solomon, an old Bolshevik close to the Ulianov family, said that Krasin had expressed himself as follows: "They will continue for a while behaving like vandals, commit a number of stupidities, and then they all will escape abroad again." Solomon tells of his attempt to convince Lenin of the aimlessness of the undertaking, which was doomed to be a fiasco. "There is no Utopia here," Lenin retorted sharply. "It is a matter of creating a socialist state. . . . The point is not Russia; she, my dear sirs, can go straight to hell – this is merely a stage through which we are passing toward the world revolution."[82]

*An acronym derived from the Russian words for Council of People's Commissars, *Sovet Narodnykh Komissarov*. Eds.

Following the Bolshevik Central Committee resolution which in effect rejected any agreement with the other parties represented in the Soviets of Workers' and Soldiers' Deputies about forming a joint "Soviet Socialist government," five members of the Central Committee (Kamenev, Rykov, Miliutin, Zinoviev and Nogin) resigned. They saw that in the public mind a soviet socialist government was not a one-party government, but one representative of all the soviet parties. "We believe," they wrote in a statement on November 4, "that the creation of such a government is essential to avert further bloodshed, the approaching famine, the crushing of the revolution by the Kaledinists, and to secure the convocation of the Constituent Assembly . . . We cannot assume responsibility for the disastrous policy pursued by the Central Committee *contrary* to the will of the vast majority of the proletariat and soldiers."[83] Following on the heels of the resignation of the Central Committee members was the resignation of several People's Commissars and heads of various departments from the cabinet. In their protest statement, they also took the position that it was "essential to form a socialist government consisting of all the Soviet parties." "We assume," they continued, "that outside this there is only one means of preserving a purely Bolshevik government – the means of political terror. This is the path chosen by the Council of People's Commissars. We cannot and *do not wish to follow* this course."[84] The statement was signed by Nogin, Rykov, Miliutin, as well as Teodorovich, Riazanov, Derbyshev, Arbuzov, Fedorov and Larin, who handed in their resignations. Shliapnikov and Iurenev also signed, but considered it inappropriate to leave the cabinet. The statement was issued after the VTsIK rejected by a vote of thirty-four to twenty-nine the proposal of the Left Socialist Revolutionaries to end political repression of the press and to rescind a temporary repressive decree passed by the Congress of Soviets on the 27th. "He who feels himself to be a true representative of the will of the people will not fear the weaker minority or he will believe that his viewpoint is weak," said Karelin, in justifying the proposal. Not wishing to participate in lighting the torch of civil war, the Left Socialist Revolutionaries withdrew their representatives from the MRC, although they remained in the VTsIK to protect the interests of the workers and peasants.

Perhaps the most striking individual protest lodged against the Bolshevik faction in the VTsIK was that of the trade union leader, A. Lozovsky, who was a member of the Bolshevik party. Extremely interesting is this last echo of the past, of intellectual traditions from which the Bolsheviks were to become liberated by entering the path of political terror. Lozovsky's letter is also a concentrated summary of the first days of Bolshevik rule: "I consider it impossible to remain silent in the name of party discipline," stated Lozovsky, "when I feel with every fibre of my being that the tactics of the Central Committee are leading toward isolation of the vanguard of the proletariat, to civil war within the working class, and toward destruction of the great revolution. I cannot . . . remain silent about the administrative ecstasy of such representatives of the MRC as Lieutenant Colonel Muraviev, who issued an order calling for mob ˙ rule and the confiscation of privately owned businesses — an order worthy of Shchedrinesque* generals. I cannot remain silent . . . in face of the annihilation of the non-Bolshevik press, searches, arbitrary arrests, and persecution, which are generating an ominous echo throughout the populace and are causing the toiling masses to think that the regime of bayonet and sword is the dictatorship of the proletariat about which the socialists have preached for many long decades. I cannot . . . remain silent when one of the people's commissars is threatening to send striking civil servants to the front and is demanding obedience on the part of postal and telegraph workers under the threat of withdrawing their bread ration cards. . . . I cannot . . . remain silent and assume moral or political responsibility when the responsible leader of our faction issues statements that we shall kill five of our enemies for each of us [who is killed] — statements similar to one made by Hindenburg, who promised to burn three Russian villages for every Prussian one . . . . I cannot . . . conceal the incipient dissatisfaction of the worker masses who had struggled for soviet rule, which, due to reasons that elude their comprehension, has proved to be purely Bolshevik rule. I cannot . . . remain silent when Marxists, contrary to logic and in defiance of reality, do not wish to come to grips with objective conditions, conditions that are imperatively dictating to us, under threat of failure, that an agreement be reached with all socialist parties which would immediately end the warfare within the revolutionary democracy and unite all forces for a struggle against Kaledin. I cannot . . . give in to the cult of personality and base political agreement . . . on the tenure of a given individual in a ministry and continue bloodshed for even one minute due to such consideration." Lozovsky demanded that a party congress be held to decide the following question: "Will the Russian Social Democratic Labor party (Bolshevik) remain a Marxist party of the working class or will it definitely embark upon a course having nothing in common with revolutionary Marxism?"[85]

Lenin asserted his will with characteristic tenacity. He pursued his objectives with a relentless intransigence which, according to Vera Zasulich, who knew him well, was like a "death grip." The majority of his "retinue" — or "Lenin's schoolboys," as Potresov dubbed his retainers — were not distinguished by a high degree of intellectual strength and swayed easily under the forceful pressure of their leader. This was hypnosis in the full sense

*Shchedrinesque, adjective from Shchedrin (M.E. Saltykov-Shchedrin, 1826-89), a distinguished Russian satirist who poked fun at the generals and bureaucrats of his time. Eds.

of the word, and arguments based on reason and a sense of obligation to society retreated before it. To get his way, Lenin often relied on personal pressure and the power of suggestion. He would summon each member of the Central Committee individually to his office and request that he sign a prepared statement. This is how Lenin's "majority" was created — more correctly, his party dictatorship. At Lenin's insistence, the Central Committee of the party issued an ultimatum to the opposition — to submit to the decisions of the Central Committee and to cease and desist from "sabotage" and "disorganizing activities," under threat of expulsion. "All the doubters, vacillators, skeptics, and all who have permitted themselves to be intimidated by the bourgeoisie or who have submitted to the shouts of its direct and indirect accomplices should be ashamed of themselves," stated a proclamation to party members issued on November 7 in the name of the Central Committee but written by Lenin. "There is *not a shadow* of vacillation in the *masses* of Petrograd and the Moscow workers and soldiers." "We shall not submit to any ultimatums by groups of the intelligentsia, who are not supported by the masses and behind whom, in fact, are only the Kornilovists, the Savinkovists, the cadets, etc."[86]

The "ultimatum" he referred to was a statement issued by the Left Socialist Revolutionaries at a VTsIK meeting on November 2: "The news received from Moscow, where our comrades stand in part on one side of the barricades and in part on the other compels us once again to bring up the matter of organizing government authority. All factional strife should cease in the face of the blood flowing in the streets, and all should unite around a government which will be supported by all segments of the democracy. We as victors should . . . present democracy with more acceptable conditions of agreement." This statement by the Left Socialist Revolutionaries caused "perplexity" in the Bolshevik faction and impelled it to introduce minor changes in a Central Committee resolution dealing with the question of what proportion of government personnel should be Bolsheviks and suggesting names.

Another "ultimatum" was issued by the Menshevik Internationalists Martov and Abramovich at the "Vikzhel" conference. They insisted that the "first condition for further talks" with the Bolsheviks be that they cease using terror and armed force. *Novaia Zhizn'* came out sharply in defense of freedom of the press, protesting against the fact that the Bolsheviks, already poisoned by the "rotten venom of power," were "dishonoring the revolution [and] disgracing the working class" by endeavoring to introduce in Russia "a socialist system using the Nechaev method."*

---

*Sergei Nechaev (1847-82) was an exponent of the use of terror for revolutionary purposes. Eds.

The opposition, however, came to naught, and the only thing that happened was the replacement of Kamenev as chairman of the VTsIK with Sverdlov. Practically the first to beat a hasty retreat was Zinoviev, who rationalized his reversal by explaining: "We prefer to make mistakes together with the millions of workers and soldiers and die together with them rather than take to the sidelines at this decisive moment in history." "There must be and will be no split in our party," asserted Zinoviev. Buchanan made the following entry in his journal at the time: "The Bolsheviks make up a solid minority of decisive individuals who know what they want and how to achieve it." Trotsky, sometimes a competitor and sometimes a talented yes-man for Lenin, defined the party's policy in regard to the civil war toward which the country was being pushed, as follows: "We cannot waver. It is dangerous to hold talks and fatal to sit and wait."

Of course, objective conditions were not in favor of the extremists. Later, in 1920, Lenin himself — not because of his "scientific conscience," about which he had once spoken, but because of the disastrous situation in the country — was forced to acknowledge that Russia did not yet possess an economic basis for social revolution. But in the fall of 1917 the social psychology prevailing among their opponents gave the Bolsheviks all the opportunities.

THE COLLAPSE OF THE VIKZHEL

Under the circumstances it made no sense to continue negotiations at the Vikzhel meetings. On November 4, a critical day for the Bolsheviks, when the resignations from the Central Committee and the cabinet occurred, the regular participants in the conference met once again, at three o'clock. But the Bolshevik representatives did not show up. Evidently they had more important things to do. The conferees waited for the Bolshevik delegates until dawn and dispersed, acknowledging that their mission "had failed." Nevertheless, the proponents of the united front had not yet lost all hope. A split among the Bolsheviks should weaken the position of the "Jacobins" and "improve chances for agreement in the ranks of democracy," at the very least among the members of its left sector. These prospects were depicted in a statement made by the Left Socialist Revolutionary Karelin: "Either Lenin and Trotsky will dare to impose their own dictatorship, or the initiative will pass entirely into the hands of the moderate Bolsheviks, Left S[ocialist] R[evolutionaries], and Menshevik Internationalists. Now we Left S[ocialist] R[evolutionaries] are pursuing a definite policy to isolate Lenin, while not isolating the Bolsheviks as a whole." Karelin expressed confidence that an agreement to set up a government including every party from the People's Socialists to the Bolsheviks would still take place because the masses would influence the moderate Bolsheviks. But Lenin got the better of his admirers.

Once again, at midnight on the 6th, a conference of socialist parties convened at the Vikzhel offices – this time without representatives from the Socialist Revolutionaries and Mensheviks. The content of the previous meetings was faithfully repeated: the Bolsheviks from the VTsIK insisted on immediate agreement to the terms proposed by them. Representatives of the Congress of Peasants' Deputies favored, as usual, the organization of a government without Bolshevik participation. Debates raged on the question of who was delaying negotiations. Zinoviev and Riazanov, who had just come close to being expelled from the party, claimed that the Bolsheviks "sincerely" wanted agreement. A resolution was passed to invite the absent Socialist Revolutionary and Menshevik representatives to the session. The former refused to come, and the latter decided to come in order to show once again that they were not "rejecting negotiations and would continue them at a favorable opportunity," but they did assert that under the present conditions they could not participate in the conference and would remain only for the purpose of being informed about developments. The Left Socialist Revolutionaries suggested that the decision be postponed and that another meeting be held. They debated until morning. Apparently this was too much even for the Vikzhel, and its representatives announced that they were returning to Moscow.

The Bolsheviks wrote a demagogic epitaph: "They made agreement impossible," "they" being those individuals who "for seven months were in agreement with the Kornilovist landowners and capitalists, those who hoodwinked the nation with false promises of land and freedom." "These born compromisers wished no compromise with the Bolsheviks. Why? Because the Bolsheviks would not permit them to deceive the people with empty promises." A month later the Vikzhel was dissolved by the Bolsheviks. In an article entitled "Retribution," which was published on December 7, the Petrograd newspaper *Den* commented upon this with its own epitaph: "Judas, you did not even receive thirty pieces of silver."

THE MOGILEV TALKS

Similar fruitless talks in a different environment continued to be held at General Headquarters in Mogilev by representatives of the revolutionary democracy, who had gathered there early in November. This was a gathering of individuals of quite different political persuasions. They had not come together simply for the purpose of discussing the formation of a government, but also in order to establish a government supported by the authority of the All-Army Committee. After the collapse of November 1, attention naturally shifted to Dukhonin's General Headquarters and to the All-Army Committee. This self-organizing center became the last hope of anti-Bolshevik action, the nature and significance of which was taken by each

in his own way. For some it was another attempt to organize a military force
to continue the active struggle against the dictatorship of Lenin and Trotsky.
For others it was another form of the Vikzhel agreement on organizing a
coalition government. Among the "names" mentioned by sources as having
been present at the large meeting were former War Minister Verkhovsky;
Avksentiev, Chernov, Gots, Feit, Gernstein, and Rakitnikov, all representing
the Central Committee of the Socialist Revolutionary party; the Mensheviks
Bogdanov and Skobelev; and the People's Socialist Znamensky. Present also
was the General Headquarters commissar, Stankevich, who, according to him,
played just about the most important role at the talks. "Political representatives" had met at his quarters and conducted negotiations, and he
participated in the formulation of the concrete proposals that were later
carried to the general sessions of the All-Army Committee.

These talks on setting up a government evoked a response for the first time
from the remnants of the Provisional Government who had been endeavoring
to preserve its organizational forms on an underground basis. On November 9
the Council of Ministers heard a belated report by Tolstoy on what was going
on at General Headquarters. At Prokopovich's suggestion, apparently made in
connnection with this report, a decision was made to send two representatives
to the meeting with instructions to keep the Provisional Government
informed and to speak out against forming a new government at General
Headquarters and against a homogeneous socialist government with Bolshevik
participation. The minutes of the cabinet meeting on the following day
contain a comment by Prokopovich, who replaced Kerensky as president of
the Council of Ministers: "Cancel the sending of representatives from the
Provisional Government to General Headquarters." Perhaps the Council of
Ministers had already received information that the work at Mogilev was
nearly finished. Or perhaps this was a manifestation of the lack of agreement
among the ministers of the underground government. Two basic ways of
thinking were in conflict. The minority were in favor of the government's
coming out in the open and said that the masses, who had begun to "sober
up," should be given support in their inclination to take action. The majority
favored refraining from official and open acts, considering their task to
consist of preserving the apparatus of government, and argued that the
underground government's sphere of activities should be limited to supporting political sabotage.

The objective of coming out into the open in connection with the Mogilev
talks could not be achieved, of course. It was too late. The ministers could not
count on united efforts in Mogilev, and at General Headquarters itself, at least
according to Stankevich, the conviction was developing that because of the
"lack of clarity and lack of agreement on a concrete plan of action," they
must abandon any thought of engaging in an active struggle against the

Bolsheviks, but rather must "struggle against them passively, maintaining control of the army in spite of them." There was consequently no hope of success for belated plans advanced in some circles of the Committee of Salvation to create a military "fist" and wait for the appropriate moment to act. Such a plan was developed by Chaikovsky and Skobelev. On November 7 they visited the American and British ambassadors to discuss their plan. Buchanan describes it as follows: "They told me that a Socialist Government, exclusive of the Bolsheviks, was about to be formed, that it would include representatives of the Cossack democracy, and that it would be supported by the Kadets. On my asking how they proposed to put down the Bolsheviks, they replied — by force! They could, they asserted, count on certain troops, sufficient for the purpose, as the army cared nothing for the Bolsheviks and only wanted peace. Russia was worn out and could not fight any more; but if they were to succeed, they must be authorized to tell the army that the Allies were prepared to discuss peace terms with a view to bringing the war to a speedy conclusion. Such an assurance would, they said, give them a great advantage over the Bolsheviks, with whom the Allied Governments would not treat."[87] After the audience with Buchanan, Skobelev left for Mogilev where he was supposed to start implementing the part of the plan calling for the concentration of armed forces against the Bolsheviks. But, while Chaikovsky supported this plan with conviction, Skobelev had many doubts in his own mind.

In any case, the plan was rejected by the Socialist Revolutionary group headed by Chernov and by the majority of those gathered in Mogilev. There is not one eyewitness whose testimony describes the position taken by Chernov as other than "indefinite." Chernov did not take the position of the Committee of Salvation, nor did he reject it openly. For this reason he was able at one time to assume the role of "delegate" from the Committee of Salvation, while at other times he was definitely in opposition to the Committee. On the very day that Chaikovsky was holding talks with the ambassadors, Chernov, in a conversation by direct wire with a representative of the Central Committee of the Socialist Revolutionary party in Petrograd, defined his approach at the moment as follows: "Political isolation of the Bolsheviks and mobilization of our forces for a more painless liquidation of this adventure, and subsequently organization of a homogeneous democratic government without Bolsheviks. Disintegration of the latter is an accomplished fact."

Naturally these tendencies, mutually incapacitating one another, created a "confusion of debate" in Mogilev, to quote Stankevich, which was exacerbated by the presence of the leftist delegation from the Vikzhel. The delegation showed up on October 31 with a definite task — to push through the Vikzhel platform and to block the formation of a government in Mogilev.

Under the cross-fire effect of the various currents of thinking, the All-Army Committee, which was supporting the platform of the Committee of Salvation, changed its position. It is apparent from the telegrams dispatched to all the army organizations that the All-Army Committee adopted the Vikzhel viewpoint. In view of the fruitless talks at the Vikzhel conference, "chiefly due to the inflexible position adopted by the leaders of extreme Bolshevism, Lenin and Trotsky, who remained deaf to the general demands," the All-Army Committee proposed that the army in the field, represented by its front and army committees, "take upon itself the initiative of setting up a government" in accordance with the Vikzhel formula, "from the People's Socialists to the Bolsheviks," in order to save Russia from "internal disintegration." The All-Army Committee nominated the "leader of the Socialist Revolutionary Party, Victor Mikhailovich Chernov," for the post of prime minister.

Characteristic details about the course of the behind-the-scenes preliminary talks are given by Stankevich: "Chernov himself spoke in favor of this idea, in an externally evasive but essentially unambiguous way. (At a meeting of Mogilev Socialist Revolutionaries, Chernov said: 'If the party places this burden upon him he will submit.') Gots, a very close friend of Chernov, objected to this sharply, even bitterly and indignantly. He believed that the attempt was doomed to failure and would only compromise the party, which was to play a decisive role at the Constituent Assembly." In general, the majority of replies from the armies were in favor of such a decision. For example, the Special Army, demanding the immediate creation of a general socialist government, announced (of course the committee did the announcing) that it would accept Chernov's candidacy as the result of a decision of the parties and not as a new type of dictatorship leading to a new civil war.[88] But the situation changed as a consequence of an unfavorable response from Petrograd. The Menshevik newspaper published an article calling all the political proposals at General Headquarters an adventure. After this article the Mensheviks voiced a vigorous objection to the attempt to organize a government at General Headquarters, and took their leave. The Socialist Revolutionaries exerted pressure on their leader, who also hastened to repair to Petrograd, not even waiting for all replies from the army. The situation was described somewhat differently by Semenov, who had arrived at Mogilev: "In his first conversation with me, Gots, gesticulating despairingly, stated that the All-Army Committee was impotently marking time, that the committee had few forces at its disposal, and that obviously nothing would come of it."

On November 11 the All-Army Committee issued a declaration that stated that its initiative had encountered the resistance of the political parties and that therefore the committee refused to "set up a government immediately." Its future program of action had four points: (1) not to recognize the authority of the Council of People's Commissars; (2) to promote formation of a government composed of representatives of all parties from the People's Socialists to the Bolsheviks; (3) to preserve the neutrality of General Headquarters by force of arms and not to permit the arrival of Bolshevik troops at headquarters; and (4) to continue the ideological struggle with the Bolsheviks. The position of neutrality, called for by the third point of this program, was preserved by General Headquarters until its very end and the tragic death of General Dukhonin, who was killed by a Bolshevik mob on November 20.

THE "ZEMSKY SOBOR"

Ideological struggle with the Bolsheviks, to which the declaration by the All-Army Committee referred, signified the abandonment of any active opposition to the dictatorship of the extremists. In a conversation with Tseretelli and Zenzinov on the night of November 9-10 in Petrograd, Chernov, Gots, and Skobolev summed up the results of their sojourn in Mogilev: "There is no question that the nation will have to go through a state of disintegration until a counterbalance to the Bolshevik adventure is created among the groups that sober up." The task at hand for the revolutionary democracy was not to struggle against the Bolsheviks but rather to consolidate these forces for the future. This concept, carried to extremes, was developed most vividly by Tseretelli in an address delivered on November 10 before the newly convened "Zemsky sobor."*

This so-called Zemsky sobor was convened in Petrograd at the initiative of the City Duma on November 9 to try once again to organize a government. The intent was to mobilize a potential force which the activities of the revolutionary democracy had bypassed, namely, the network of the zemstvo (rural) and city self-governing bodies inherited from the pre-revolutionary period, which included representatives of non-socialist parties and persons without party affiliation. The attempt proved futile, because there were scarcely ten authorized representatives among those who came to Petrograd from other cities at the request of Mayor Shreider. The activities of the meeting boiled down to debate, and the passage of one resolution and one proclamation.

However, Tseretelli's addresss at the meeting was a sign of the times. Tseretelli shared the then almost universal assumption that Bolshevik authority was ephemeral. How can one combat "this gang of adventurers?"

*This designation was applied to the consultative assemblies of representatives from various parts of the country convened in sixteenth and seventeenth century Russia to discuss major political issues. Its application to this meeting of zemstvo and city self-government bodies is largely ironic. Eds.

"This," opined Tseretelli, "is the easiest of all tasks facing us. The very policies pursued by the usurpers will inevitably lead to the collapse of their power, since these men have been compelled by fate to take steps which will lead to their destruction . . . ." He concluded that it was possible to fight the Bolsheviks "only by relying on the conscience and consciousness of the democrats" – only "by bringing the democrats to their senses" was a favorable outcome possible. But this was a slow process.

Tseretelli's address could satisfy no one. "It was quite rightly pointed out," explained Tseretelli in reply to his opponents, "that my address contained no clear indication of a way out of our grave situation. I must confess that under the present conditions of absence of any authority I see *no way out* . . . . Never before has the ground under democracy been so shaky. One must confess that the rightist maximalist groups have more of a chance than the democrats. We must prevent a clash between maximalist groups, which would threaten the existence of the democracy." "If the democrats," concluded Tseretelli, "now fail to become master of the situation, we shall see the arrival of that new power from the right which will say, 'now it is my turn!' "

To one degree or another many representatives of the revolutionary democracy also had Tseretelli's psychology, and his fear of the "new power from the right." Of course these men were not capable of offering resistance to the Bolsheviks. Nor were they capable of concentrating the forces of society for a future struggle. One more slip of paper was left to history by the resolution of the Zemsky sobor appealing to the democracy to organize a "center" that could "act against the usurpers of power."

Tseretelli expressed his pessimistic views with even greater pointedness at sessions of the old VTsIK, which continued to convene secretly. On November 12 Tseretelli acknowledged that it was impossible to organize a new government – this would be an "adventure." There was only one way out, "participation in the Bolshevik government," but this would merely worsen the situation, since "all the democrats will be forced to share responsibility." At that particular time "the primary task of the democrats is to unite their forces, not to struggle against Bolshevism, which might alienate many extremely useful elements, but rather to consolidate our own ranks and to save the Revolution." Once again, Tseretelli believed that the revolution had to be saved from the bourgeoisie, not from the Bolsheviks. "The entire bourgeois Kadet party is united under the slogan of bloody reprisal against the Bolsheviks. There is no question in my mind but that liquidation of the Bolshevik uprising means mass executions of the proletarians, and, foreseeing this, we always feared a Bolshevik uprising." The minutes of the meeting recorded Tseretelli's ominous words: "The harm that [the Bolsheviks] presently bring is not as great as it will be in the future, when the retribution comes."[89] I call this phrase ominous because it was taken up by many of those who shared Tseretelli's views and led to a fatal thesis during the Civil War period: "Socialism will perish if the Bolsheviks are crushed by force."*

An almost identical position was taken at this time by *Delo Naroda,* the official organ of the Central Committee of the Socialist Revolutionary party. On November 4 the newspaper stated: "While the Bolsheviks are winning in the north, Kaledin is winning in the south. They are joining hands to destroy the Revolution. It is our task to strike at both sources of counter-revolution − against the Bolsheviks by force of organization, and against Kaledin by force of arms." Consequently the newspaper's statement, "We are against Civil War," must be taken in a very limited way − it only referred to armed conflict with the Bolsheviks.

Such a position was leading at best to the doctrine that the socialists should refrain from fighting the Bolsheviks in order to preserve the purity of their political garments for history. "Bolshevism, speaking objectively," alleged Abramovich in the party organ of the "Bund" (November 13), "is a class movement of politically immature and unenlightened laboring masses. Should we, the conscious social democratic and less numerous segment of the working class, join with the bourgeois and petit-bourgeois segment of the army and help crush the majority of the working class with fire and sword? . . . . What would the historian of the Russian Revolution have to say about that?" Then he quotes Dan: "The working class in retrospect will forgive the sins and crimes of the Bolsheviks, since they were with the masses. But it will not forgive us, although we would be certainly right in acting against these masses together with their class enemies."

UNDERGROUND GOVERNMENT

Hopes for a Constituent Assembly further decreased civil resistance, which in turn meant a de facto recognition of the Bolshevik victory. For the time being virtually nobody doubted that the victory was a temporary one. One should not attach too much importance to those literary forms in which appeals to the public were sometimes clothed. The Zemsky sobor inserted the following words in its proclamation: "Our blood-battered

*It should be noted that twelve years later, when he was in exile, Tseretelli recognized that the widely accepted notion that "the revolution knows no enemies from the left" was wrong. "Left extremism posed a much more real danger to democracy than the extremism of the right . . . . We did not foresee that the Bolsheviks themselves will assume the practical realization of the most horrible reaction." I.G. Tseretelli, *Vospominaniia,* vol. II (Mouton & Co., 1963), pp. 409-417. S.G.P.

homeland stands at the edge of doom, and if there is a small hope of saving Russia and its great people from foreign domination and ultimate internal disintegration, this hope lies with the Constituent Assembly." In actuality, contemporaries did not have this tragic sense, and the views of the initiator of the sobor, Shreider, seemed excessively "optimistic" to Buchanan. Vishniak, in his study of the Constituent Assembly, quotes a very indicative excerpt from an address by Merezhkovsky at a meeting of writers, in which he expressed the opinion of a rather extensive array of civic leaders: "The 'Sun over the Russian land' cannot be extinguished. When it rises, all spectres will disappear. Or perhaps the vampire will wish to extinguish the Sun? Well, let him try. One need not be a prophet to predict that Lenin will break his neck at the Constituent Assembly."

Only in the context of this passive expectation of the inevitable and the appeals "not to dissipate forces prior to the Constituent Assembly" can one understand the activities of the underground Provisional Government. Today one examines the published rough minutes of its secret sessions with a certain degree of perplexity. Only confidence that life would soon return to normal explains allocation of 10,000,000 rubles to the Special Conference on Fuels to make urgent payments "for food, clothing, and tools," a 7,500,000-ruble loan for procuring firewood for the municipal government, the allocation of 431,000 rubles to reorganize the railroad technical schools, and so on. They even discussed the possibility of allocating 4,800,000 rubles "to work oil shales near Petrograd." The fiscal operations of the underground government had to end when the State Bank ran out of cash following the Bolshevik requisition, reported by State Bank Chairman Friedman on November 14. The minutes of November 15 note that a "request by the Ministry of Agriculture for 4,500,000 rubles for a farm census" was rejected.

Demianov described the situation as follows: "The Bolshevik leaders were sitting in Smolny as in a sanctuary." The man in the street "did not acknowledge Bolshevism, but this was the only indication of his opposition." Could such a situation endure? The materials appended to the proceedings of the underground government include the text of a letter from Professor Kirsh, head of the Special Conference on Fuels, addressed to Prokopovich and dated November 8. Kirsh opposed continuation of the "strike of government agencies," a strike which was indirectly financed with appropriations from the shadow government. Kirsh said the strike was causing "definite harm to the country" – more "than the Bolsheviks" – and he accused the group "carrying out the duties of the Provisional Government" of "wishy-washy tactics." What did Kirsh propose? He proposed a "loud" declaration that the Provisional Government was "continuing its current activities divorced from any and all influence and intervention by the MRC, totally ignoring the latter," and that it would "immediately" stop functioning again "at the slightest interference by the MRC." "It seems to me that this is a very appropriate moment to announce and demonstrate our work and authority. For there is no longer anyone who can even assume command at Smolny Institute." Because of this the "members of the Provisional Government who are still free should declare that they feel obliged to continue running the country until the Constituent Assembly convenes."

The self-hypnosis reflected in the slogan "until the Constituent Assembly" paralyzed the will to fight of those "cabinet men" who dominated the underground government, and a like psychology afflicted those persons, who, we shall assume, were better suited for active struggle.

THE AGREEMENT BETWEEN THE BOLSHEVIKS
AND LEFT SOCIALIST REVOLUTIONARIES

Lenin described everything going on around him as "chatter and mush." This was not so bad. Indeed, what was falling apart was not so much Bolshevism as the anti-Bolshevik action directed by the revolutionary democracy. As a result of the unsuccessful Vikzhel talks where, as Hippius graphically expressed it in her journal, "the compromisers have swallowed the swill in vain," the Bolsheviks extended their social base and finally won over the Left Socialist Revolutionaries. This took place at the All-Russian Congress of Soviets of Peasant Deputies, which was held in Petrograd on November 10th. From that moment on the "Leninist Guard" was assured a "colossal majority" in the Constituent Assembly, Bukharin told the Central Committee.

I shall not go into detail about this interesting page in the history of the times; it lies outside the scope of this work. But a few features are needed as an epilogue. The Congress was dominated by the Left Socialist Revolutionaries. The faction of "rightists," led by Chernov, was unable to take a definite stand – three times it walked out of the Congress, only to return because it considered "strife" to be "criminal" at such a critical moment. Finally, Chernov and his 150 followers stayed out and formed a special all-Russian conference of peasant deputies. "In view of the extremely charged atmosphere," those remaining at the Congress proceeded first of all to discuss the matter of setting up a government. This question, discussed so many times *ad nauseam*, had actually lost its edge. It was now possible to come to an agreement only with the Bolsheviks, and Zinoviev, speaking for the VTsIK, greeted all comers with open arms. Having voted, as if to cleanse their consciences, for the formula "from the People's Socialists to the Bolsheviks," and stipulating that if disagreements occurred authority should reside in those backing the platform of the Second Congress of Soviets, the Left Socialist Revolutionaries gave up their policy of isolating Lenin and capitulated to the Bolsheviks. It was decided to merge the VTsIK and the Soviet of Peasant Deputies on a parity basis. Sverdlov came to the Congress and invited the delegates to go to Smolny. The address delivered by Sverdlov, who proclaimed the agreement to be "one of the eminent facts of the revolution," was cheered with cries such as "Hail democratic unity!" and "Hail the end to civil war!" Then the Congress, led by its elected chairman, Maria Spiridonova, headed toward Smolny with banners waving and was solemnly greeted at the entrance by the Red Guards. At a joint session Zinoviev announced: "Our slogan – all power to the workers, peasants, and soldiers – has been implemented in practice." The 14th was a red-letter day. Agreement was reached between those who continued to believe that the immediate implementation of socialism was the "inflamed chimera of dreamers and utopians," those who declared that the tactics of the Bolsheviks could be successful only among masses who had lost their senses, those who spoke against civil war, and those who preached civil war and were leading the country through it toward "socialism." "The Socialist Proletarian Revolution has begun," proclaimed Lenin three days later at the Peasant Congress, simultaneously declaring that "the Bolsheviks are making concessions" by adopting the Left Socialist Revolutionary land program, of which the Bolsheviks did not approve. The Bolsheviks and Left Socialist Revolutionaries also reached agreement on the make-up of the government. The party that had come to Smolny to share power with the insurgents decreed: "Under no circumstances shall Smolny be abandoned as long as it occupies the center of the revolution." And, at the congress of the Left Socialist Revolutionaries, voices already rang out proclaiming that the Constituent Assembly "will be a hindrance to us."

The Left Socialist Revolutionaries were followed by other participants in the Vikzhel meetings. On November 17 the Menshevik Internationalists rejected Martov's proposal that the faction not participate in the VTsIK until the Bolsheviks recognized the sovereign rights of the Constituent Assembly and abandoned the use of terrorist methods. Considering the tactic of boycott to be "misguided," they announced their willingness to participate in the Council of People's Commissars if invited to do so. The Vikzhel likewise sent representatives to the VTsIK.

Under the circumstances, it was hardly likely that anyone would be impressed by the resolution voted by the 150 splinter deputies from the Peasant Congress rehashing old stuff about homogeneous socialist rule. This stage had already been passed. Election by the Congress of a special commission "to organize a government" and Chernov's plea that the faction not insist on his candidacy for prime minister and not demand that the Bolsheviks be excluded from the government sounded like an anachronism.

BEFORE THE CONSTITUENT ASSEMBLY

The "Leninist Guard" also pondered over the dilemma created by the imminent convocation of the Constituent Assembly. According to

Trotsky, "during the first days, if not hours, following the revolution" Lenin brought up the question of the Constituent Assembly. Initially it seemed that the question was merely one of postponing the assembly, but the leader, constituting a minority of one, felt that life had already "bypassed this stage," that the assembly was "an old fairy-tale." Those around him feared to disappoint the masses, whose expectations the Bolsheviks themselves had aroused. "For a month and a half we worked and shouted to guarantee the holding of a Constituent Assembly," Bukharin reminded the Central Committee. Indeed the Bolshevik press systematically, day after day, drove home the claim that it was the "Mensheviks and S [ocialist] R [evolutionaries] who are helping the bourgeoisie to prevent the holding of a Constituent Assembly" (article by Stalin on October 5), and that for this purpose a "democratic cover in the form of a counterrevolutionary Pre-Parliament" had been created. When the Bolsheviks walked out of the Pre-Parliament they declared: "Hail the Constituent Assembly." The day after the revolt *Pravda* issued a declaration that stated: "Comrades, with your own blood you have guaranteed the on-schedule convening of the Master of Russia – the All-Russian Constituent Assembly." Sensing their isolation in the Smolny citadel, the new authorities were even inclined to engage in a flirtation with the Provisional Government's commission to convene the Constituent Assembly; Bonch-Bruevich "warmly" thanked its chairman, Nabokov, in the name of the Council of People's Commissars when Nabokov informed him that the commission had resolved to "renew its activities" and at the same time to "unconditionally ignore the Council of People's Commissars, not to recognize its legal authority, and to enter into no relations with it whatsoever." The Bolsheviks' attitude lulled the public to sleep. Even the Constitutional Democrats, who three weeks later were proclaimed enemies of the people, were able to organize election meetings freely. For a while Lenin indulged these "constitutional illusions," but in keeping with his usual methods he gradually "beat" into the heads of the members of his guard the idea of the "necessity of taking exceedingly severe measures to save the revolution." "Ten times a day," claims Trotsky, "he hammered away on the historical necessity of pitiless revolutionary terror," and Trotsky himself made statements to the same effect. The obedient guards of Leninism were easily persuaded, and the fate of the Constituent Assembly was predetermined. As early as November 8 Volodarsky predicted at a meeting of the Petrograd Committee that "perhaps we shall be forced to disperse the Constituent Assembly with bayonets." The masses must be told that "if we are not in the majority at the Constituent Assembly, the possibility of a third revolution will be on the agenda." "Would it then not be best not to hold the Constituent Assembly?" a local representative asked him; "the power is in our hands." "If Petrograd were all of Russia," replied Volodarsky, "then of course we could refrain from convening the Constituent Assembly."

On the 14th of November the first results of the elections to the Constituent Assembly became known. In Petrograd, the Bolsheviks received forty-five percent of the vote.* This fact staggered many. "It became obvious," writes Stankevich, "that the path of democracy, the majority of the votes of the formally expressed will of the nation, lay extremely close to the Bolsheviks." To attempt to oppose a party so influential among the masses "by force of arms . . . was an obvious absurdity." Similar sentiments were voiced at the party conferences of the Socialist Revolutionaries and the Mensheviks, which convened at the end of November in Petrograd.

The successes of the Bolsheviks at the polls in Petrograd and Moscow cannot be explained away merely by the masses' lack of political maturity, at which many representatives of the socialist democracy were inclined to point. Nor can it be explained by the fact that the masses are always more or less inclined to support those seeming to possess power at the moment. What message for the masses did the revolutionary democracy have, languishing as it was in a state of total disorder? "Deep breaches split our party into pieces. There is no unity of action, no unity of immediate objectives," acknowledged the Central Committee of the Socialist Revolutionary party in the middle of November, announcing the convening of its congress. At the opening session of the Menshevik party congress, Potresov stated: "Our party is presently going through a catastrophic state. It has become almost totally eliminated from the political arena." But this was not only due to the fact that the revolutionary democracy had not revealed its face to the masses and was paying for that. It was also due to the fact that it had a two-faced image. Some of the democratic socialists opposed the slogans of peace, land, and control of the factories by the workers, slogans that were understandable to the masses and were being implemented by the Bolshevik authorities. In place of these tangible things they offered the abstract hope that a Constituent Assembly would provide for the realization of essentially the same aspirations under a different management. At best this seemed to be merely a question of methods, about which the masses were quite indifferent. In addition, the workers had been told by the democratic socialists that liquidation of the Bolshevik uprising would be followed by "a bloody reckoning with the

*Due to conditions at the time, the votes for the Constituent Assembly — Russia's only free election based on universal suffrage and equal representation — were never fully tabulated (the election was held three weeks after the Bolshevik takeover). An authoritative estimate of the results has been made by Oliver Henry Radkey in his *The Election to the Russian Constituent Assembly of 1917* (Cambridge, Mass., 1950). They are based on complete returns from twenty-three electoral districts, and partial returns from thirty-seven districts; returns are missing from eight districts, and in twelve districts, mostly in Central Asia, no elections were held. The following summary table is calculated from Radkey's data. Eds.

RESULTS OF ELECTIONS TO THE CONSTITUENT ASSEMBLY NOV. 12, 1917

	Country as a Whole (60 electoral districts)		Army and Navy at the Front (6 districts)		Petrograd and Moscow (2 districts)	
Bolsheviks	9,844,000	23.6%	1,646,000	40.4%	790,000	46.3%
Socialist Revolutionaries	17,067,000[1]	40.9%	1,551,000	38.1%	215,000	12.6%
Mensheviks	1,238,000[2]	3.0%	134,000	3.3%	51,000	3.0%
Other Socialists	505,000[3]	1.2%	18,000	.4%	69,000	4.0%
Kadets	1,986,000	4.8%	65,000	1.6%	510,000	29.9%
Rightist groups	1,518,000[4]	3.6%	3,000	.1%	64,000	3.8%
Ukrainian parties	5,010,000[5]	12.0%	536,000	13.2%	4,000	.2%
Muslims & minor national groups	3,372,000[6]	8.1%	19,000	.4%	4,000	.2%
Unclassified	1,147,000	2.8%	102,000	2.5%	—	—
Totals	41,687,000	100.0%	4,074,000	100.0%	1,707,000	100.0%

Notes:
1. Includes joint lists with the Ukrainian Socialist Revolutionaries (1,219,000 votes)
2. Excludes an overlap with Socialist Revolutionaries in Olonets Province (127,000 votes)
3. Includes People's Socialists (322,000 votes)
4. Includes some 916,000 Cossack votes
5. Includes Ukrainian and Tatar joint lists (53,000 votes)
6. Includes "unclassified" group in Transcaucasia (751,000 votes)

working class." The Bolsheviks had only to add the warning: either us or the reckoning. Where would "instinct" lead the worker at the polls? Is it surprising that the votes went to the Bolsheviks?

At the beginning of the revolution the idea of a Constituent Assembly may have evoked in the masses, or rather in the intelligentsia, "a sacred tremble," but this fetish grew tarnished after nine months of waiting. There was hardly any chance of turning the masses against the soviets in the name of the Constituent Assembly. The leader of the Socialist Revolutionary party himself, Chernov, made a demagogic slip of the tongue when speaking at the Congress of Soviets of Peasant Deputies on May 5, he said, "the soviet — our socialist constituent assembly." The soviets had forced the Constituent Assembly out of the revolutionary ideology.

A graphic illustration of the above is given to us by the Socialist Revolutionary Sokolov in his description of the southwestern-front congress in Berdichev in the middle of November. Two-thirds of the congress delegates were members of the Socialist Revolutionary party. Avksentiev arrived on the second day of the congress. "All his attempts," relates Sokolov, "to explain the essence of the Bolshevik takeover and to demonstrate that it was directed primarily against the principle of popular rule and the Russian Constituent Assembly foundered on the stone wall of misunderstanding among the majority of those at the congress," who felt that since the Provisional Government was gone and the Constituent Assembly was not yet in session, it was logical to support the soviets. Only after great effort did Avksentiev succeed in explaining that "it is impossible to combine and merge the two slogans, 'all power to the soviets' and 'all power to the Constituent Assembly.'" Under these conditions it was not difficult for the Bolshevik Krylenko, who arrived shortly after Avksentiev, to win over the audience. He merely demanded confirmation of the slogan "all power to the soviets until the Constituent Assembly is convened." (According to the Bolshevik conception, the soviets were then to propose that the Constituent Assembly introduce the soviet system.) The non-party masses, not bound by discipline, supported the formula proposed by the Bolsheviks and spoke in favor of giving all power to the soviets, that is, for an essentially Bolshevik government. But during the balloting the overwhelming majority of this same body voted for the list of Socialist Revolutionary candidates.

The only logical way of countering the Bolshevik takeover successfully was to oppose it without compromise and to seek out the necessary coalition partners in the hidden political resources of the nation. Such an approach was rejected in principle by the majority of the revolutionary democracy, which insisted on liquidating the October revolt "without repression" and was only willing to allow "noncooperation" as a means of attaining this objective. Moods of resignation and compromise could not create enthusiasm for battle, and so all the efforts by the leaders of the revolutionary democracy to create an armed force to defend the Constituent Assembly and to appeal directly to the people were stillborn. At the party conference in Petrograd, Chernov said: "If anyone acts against the Constituent Assembly he will force us to remember the old methods of fighting against coercion, against those who impose their will on the people." The declaration was received with "loud applause," but it proved to be nothing but empty words.

The "Leninists" and "Trotskyites" were no longer to be intimidated by loud words. Sensing victory, they quite openly embarked on a course of repressions, as their leader prescribed. And in the Central Committee Bukharin candidly posed the question, "should or should not the Constituent Assembly be held?" – that Constituent Assembly through which "false friends of our people, traitors to the revolution and betrayers of the people's interest, former revolutionaries who have sold out to the American capitalists" (as the new supreme commander, Ensign Krylenko, declared in his proclamation of November 30 to all members of the revolutionary army and navy) were endeavoring to "throttle the government of workers and peasants. If the assembly is convened, the 'Kadets' must be eliminated and the Left be declared a 'revolutionary convention.' " The "line" about a convention of the Left was pushed by Trotsky. Lenin did not even speak during the debates of November 29. It was all too clear that the fate of the Constituent Assembly had already been settled.

On December 12 Lenin published his "Theses on the Constituent Assembly," in which he argued that "the Republic of Soviets is a higher form of democracy than a conventional bourgeois republic with a Constituent Assembly," and that the composition of members elected to the approaching Constituent Assembly did not correspond to the will of the electorate at the time, since during the election the overwhelming majority of the people were unable to grasp as yet the entire depth and significance of the October, soviet, proletarian-peasant revolution, which began after the presentation of lists of candidates to the Constituent Assembly. "The course of events and development of the class struggle have led to a situation where," continued Lenin, "the slogan 'all power to the Constituent Assembly,' failing to take into account the conquests of the worker-peasant revolution, failing to recognize soviet power . . . is in fact a slogan of the 'Kadets,' Kaledinists, and their accomplices. The entire nation is beginning to realize that this slogan in fact signifies a struggle to do away with soviet rule" – that is, to restore the "slave-owner's" rule. Lenin felt that the only chance for a painless resolution of the crisis was "exercise by the people, as soon and on as broad a basis as possible, of the right to reelect delegates to the Constituent Assembly, adherence by the Constituent Assembly to the law of the VTsIK concerning these reelections, and an unconditional recognition by the Constituent Assembly of soviet power" and its policies on peace, land, and worker control over industry. Other than under these conditions, states the last, the 19th, "thesis," "the Constituent Assembly crisis can be resolved only by revolutionary means – by means of the most vigorous, swift, firm and decisive revolutionary measures on the part of the Soviet Government."[90]

The "Leninist Guard" was also winning on the second line of battle. The Committee of Salvation was dying. The only means of struggle it had left was that of the political strike, which was losing its practical significance. Thus by the time the MRC decided to arrest the Committee of Salvation, the committee was no longer important. The underground Provisional Government also ended its days in almost total isolation.

The declaration made on November 15 by the People's Socialists and representatives of the Kadet party who attended an illegally convened meeting of the Moscow City Duma had a lonely tone: "The Duma should, in the name of the people of Moscow, address an urgent request to the Provisional Government to step forth, as the sole legal authority, to issue a categoric protest in the name of Russia against the treasonous policies of Lenin and Trotsky on the peace question, appealing to all organized forces of the nation to gather solidly around local agencies of self-government and committees of salvation to carry on the struggle against Bolshevism."

Instead of supporting this appeal, the Moscow City Duma belatedly discussed the question of organizing a homogeneous socialist government. Socialist Revolutionary Mayor Rudnev opposed "agreement with a band of adventurers" and doubted the feasibility of setting up any new government prior to the convocation of the Constituent Assembly. Much stronger doubts were echoed by Kadets Astrov and Novgorodtsev. Nevertheless, a Duma resolution was hastily adopted, under the threat of dispersion by a detachment of soldiers commanded by an MRC commissar, which appeared on the premises of Shaniavsky University, where the Duma session was being held with the participation of delegates from all of Moscow's democratic civic institutions. The resolution, which included a protest against the actions taken by the "irresponsible usurpers, against the arrest of members of the Provisional Government and the treasonous separate peace," appealed to the people to join ranks around the Constituent Assembly. "The Duma firmly believes," the resolution said, "that in spite of all coercive measures directed against the will of the electorate, the people will be able to give our country an intelligent and honest popular representation, and that the authoritative voice of the Constituent Assembly will soon ring out over exhausted Russia. But prior to the convening of the Constituent Assembly only a homogeneous . . . socialist government . . . could constitute that sole force capable of restoring order and calm to this country."[91]

The fragments of the Provisional Government received no real support in Moscow. "Strangely, as if from oblivion," to quote Rengarten's diary, rang out the national appeal of the Provisional Government which appeared on

November 17 in the newspapers. Designating November 28 as the day for convening the Constituent Assembly, the Provisional Government announced from its hiding place that "at the present time we are this country's sole legal authority" and that it was continuing its functions in order to prevent "insurgents from taking over the edifice of government." But this was not a call to battle. This was a plaintive cry about the absence of support, a self-justification of its inactivity. The Provisional Government had no desire to participate in setting up a new government "a few days before the Constituent Assembly." The declaration was truly a voice from the grave. It was only able to inspire a new "demonstration of impotence" at the Tauride Palace – in which, however, 10,000 persons participated, according to some eyewitnesses.*

The Bolsheviks ordered the arrest of those persons who had signed the declaration in the name of the Provisional Government and shut down the newspapers that had printed it. But placing no trust in the garrison, they ordered the troops "not to leave the barracks during the demonstrations." The safety of the Council of People's Commissars was secured by the Latvian Rifles.

On November 28, the mayor of Petrograd, Shreider, "following the instructions of the Provisional Government," did convene the "exalted Assembly" – that is a meeting of those delegates to the Constituent Assembly who responded to the appeal of the underground Provisional Government and were in the city of Petrograd by that time. Forty-three members were present. They acknowledged that there was no legal quorum and adjourned, having pronounced some eloquent phrases of protest against the felonious assault of the Bolsheviks. A message was also received from those members of the Provisional Government who were still in prison, transferring their authority to the Constituent Assembly and pleading for release.

Another colorful episode in the efforts to undermine the Bolshevik government through noncooperation was the plenary session of all the departments of the Governing Senate on November 28. The Senate, the highest legal and supervisory administrative agency of the Imperial government, survived the February revolution; it now called upon all the functionaries employed in government, municipal and zemstvo offices not to carry out the unlawful orders of the commissars at Smolny, who had seized power through criminal violence. This statement, formulated by the elderly

---

Izvestiia put the number of demonstrators at 1,000. Antonov-Ovseenko, who at that time was the military commander of the district, estimated that there were 5,000, a figure which, according to him, was greatly magnified in the imagination of the Bolshevik leadership. S.P.M.

senator Tagantsev, was duly printed in the traditional statute books, the "Collection of Laws and Regulations."

The plenary session of the Constituent Assembly did eventually convene on January 5, 1918. Despite a heavy Bolshevik vote in the capitals, only 161 of 520 delegates elected to the assembly were Bolsheviks; the preponderance of the rural vote gave the Socialist Revolutionaries an absolute majority of 267 delegates. Non-socialist parties received only meager representation. Chernov was elected chairman of the assembly, and Tseretelli gave a memorable speech.

Lenin listened to the proceedings from the balcony, and the aisles of the meeting hall in the Tauride Palace were filled with armed Bolshevik guards. The Bolshevik agenda for the meeting was defeated by 237 to 136 votes. The Bolshevik delegates withdrew, the Bolshevik-dominated VTsIK approved Lenin's decree dissolving the assembly, and on the night of January 6 the delegates were ordered by Bolshevik armed guards to leave the Tauride Palace.

THE CONQUEST OF THE COUNTRY

"To have an overwhelming superiority of forces at the decisive moment at the decisive point – this law of military success is also a law of political success," wrote Lenin after the upheaval. The Bolsheviks were victorious because they had a powerful backing in the capital cities. There is no question that capitals decide the political fate of nations to a considerable degree. The psychological importance of the capital, where the artery of government throbs and where the bulk of the nation's material and cultural resources is concentrated, is great indeed.

The environment in which the October events took place was not capable of producing a core around which a will to act against the Bolsheviks could begin to crystallize. The revolutionary democracy proved impotent, because for there to be a unity of objectives there must be a unity of will. This was clearly emphasized at the time by one of the People's Socialist leaders, Peshekhonov, in his article "The Struggle Against the Bolsheviks and Bolshevism," which was published on November 3 in *Narodnoe Slovo*. He summed up the still unfinished activities of the Committee of Salvation and testified to the inability of the two leading parties (the Mensheviks and the Socialist Revolutionaries) to act in concert at the decisive moment: they had become entangled in conflicting decisions. This inability to act had penetrated and infected the revolutionary democracy, rendering ineffective its attempts to unify around the Committee of Salvation. Peshekhonov appealed for the support of those *segments* of the parties which had not become contaminated with Bolshevism. (An organized attempt to do this was made only several months later – it was the so-called "Alliance for the

Rebirth of Russia.") Non-socialist groups were missing during those days from the political arena; we see almost none playing effective roles. The Constitutional Democratic party expressed the assurance in its declaration of November 10 that "men will be found who will help their country put a quick end to dangers and calamities such as she has never known." The declaration made an appeal "not to accept a situation that threatens Russia's very survival" and "to oppose implementation of the decrees on peace and land." This was one of those wordy resolutions that Nabokov treats so negatively in his memoirs because he fails to see any concrete plan of action in them.

Unexpectedly, it was Moscow – where Lenin proposed starting the insurrection against the Provisional Government because he thought it would succeed more easily there – that became the arena of the most serious resistance. On the evening of October 25, as news from Petrograd was reaching Moscow, the City Duma headed by Mayor Rudnev, a Socialist Revolutionary, formed its Committee of Public Security. The next morning, Red Guards sent by the local military revolutionary committee occupied the Kremlin but were quickly surrounded by cadet and Cossack patrols. Lengthy negotiations between the Committee of Public Security and the military revolutionary committee followed, and on October 28 the Bolsheviks in the Kremlin surrendered.

However, the vacillating commander of the Moscow garrison, Colonel Riabtsev, was not inclined to press the Committee of Public Safety's order that the military revolutionary committee be disbanded. And the socialist-dominated committee was not eager to organize armed units of its own to counter the Red Guards. Representatives of the Provisional Government from Petrograd preferred to remain in the background, and armed combat with Bolshevik troops, which erupted on October 28, was carried on for the most part spontaneously by volunteer detachments of military cadets, officers, and students. The great majority of the Moscow garrison, as was the case with other garrisons, remained neutral.

As further negotiations between the Committee of Public Safety and the military revolutionary committee dragged on (the Vikzhel was involved as a mediator), armed crowds of soldiers and workers, directed by Bolshevik committees from peripheral districts of the city, swelled. They acquired artillery and by the evening of November 2 had forced the defenders of the government to surrender. When the street fighting was over, the Bolsheviks buried 238 dead, and their adversaries 55.*

*A detailed description of the "Moscow week" is given in the original Russian edition of this book. It has been omitted from this translation. Eds.

In the provinces, the victory of the Bolsheviks was not accepted immediately or without protest. A totally false picture is given by Trotsky, who likened the echoes of the October coup d'état to those of the February Revolution, which had seized Russia "by telegraph." The fact is that the Bolshevik political telegraph operated rather slowly. The best refutation of Trotsky's claim is the list of the "most important cities where power is in the hands of the soviets" published in *Pravda* on November 11, that is two weeks after the coup. These "most important" cities included county seats in the Moscow region, such as Serpukhov, Podolsk, and Orekhovo-Zuevo; besides, the definition of what constituted soviet power was rather broad.* In reality, Kiev, Odessa, Rostov-on-the-Don and many other cities listed in *Pravda* were not yet ruled by soviets. It is true that "soviet rule" was formally proclaimed in Nizhni Novgorod on November 21, but only three days prior to that the All-Russian Postal-Telegraph Congress meeting in the city was officially greeted by the local commissar of the Provisional Government, while the Bolshevik representative was not allowed to appear. This is not to speak of far-off Siberia, the Cossack regions, and the Rumanian front, where "October" dragged on for several months, nor of the Ukraine, with its peculiar national conditions, where the Ukrainian Rada and the Bolsheviks in Kiev initially acted together against the government forces but where subsequently the Rada suppressed Bolshevik activities. Looking at the central areas alone one must inevitably acknowledge that "Red October" crawled comparatively slowly over the land, in spite of the efforts of the 644 commissars dispatched from Petrograd. In Ruza, near Moscow, the beginnings of soviet authority were not evident until a month later. Novgorod did not experience its "October" until December 3, and in Borovichi, in the Novgorod province, the local Bolshevik chroniclers admit that even as late as January 1918 one could not openly "call oneself a Bolshevik." The Bolshevik epic in Rybinsk was delayed until the arrival of a detachment of sailors. Along the Volga and in the Urals change began toward the end of December. The Peasants' Conference in Voronezh (only 24 out of the 489 deputies were Bolsheviks) was not dissolved until December 28. In Viatka, power was seized by the provincial zemstvo assembly, which appointed a special "supreme council" to govern. In the region of Vologda, the municipal government and zemstvo were still functioning in the summer of 1919.

Russia was far from being Bolshevik. The elections to the Constituent Assembly attest to this fact. In the country as a whole the victors were able to collect only one-fourth of the vote, despite the extremely favorable

*The public at that time tended to view soviet power as the power of freely elected Soviets, and did not necessarily identify it as yet with the dictatorship of the Bolshevik party. Eds.

conditions prevailing for the Bolsheviks and the considerable absenteeism. In some areas no more than thirty-five per cent of the electorate came to the polls. Thus events quickly belied Lenin's assertion, made by him in October, that "we are not Blanquists, not proponents of the seizure of power by a minority." Of course, Lenin still felt free to claim that the elections to the Constituent Assembly were at variance with the "people's will" – they were "the revolution's yesterday." No one any longer remembered the "leader's" solemn declaration at the Congress of Soviets that the Bolsheviks would submit to the will of the people even if the Socialist Revolutionaries received a majority of votes in the Constituent Assembly – now that they had the majority.

In order to complete the general picture of the process of the conquest of the country by the Bolsheviks, or their "triumphal march," to quote Lenin, one must perform a large, rather specialized, and painstaking job of studying local sources. Having the same social psychology as the capital cities, the provinces had to repeat in miniature, although in different forms and shapes, that which was taking place in Petrograd and Moscow – right up to the sometimes involuted verbosity. In Saratov, for example, a revolutionary committee was formed at the proposal of the Socialist Revolutionaries when news of the uprising arrived, not for the purpose of fighting the usurpers of authority, but in order to forestall the "inevitable rampage of reaction" after the defeat of the Bolsheviks. The executive committee of the Simferopol soviet, while holding the Bolshevik seizure of power to be an "insane and criminal venture," abstained from supporting the Provisional Government.

But things were quite different in the provincial city of Kaluga (about 100 miles south of Moscow). On October 26 the Municipal Duma, at a joint session with representatives of the political parties, soviets, trade unions, and military units, passed the following resolution: "The Assembly feels obliged to offer its solemn oath to the Provisional Government that the resources, lives, and property of the citizens of Kaluga are at the disposal of the Provisional Government." A temporary executive body composed of the commissar, the troop commander, the garrison commander, the municipal administration and representatives of professional and political organizations was organized to lend support to the government. Such unity was easy to achieve due to the specific situation in Kaluga on the days preceding October. The energetic government commissar, Galkin, dissolved the soviet and with the help of a small detachment of shock troops disarmed the Bolshevik elements in the garrison, which were hindering the dispatch of companies of reinforcements to the front. The Bolshevik press at the time devoted much space to the events in Kaluga and to the government's "reign of terror." Actually, the disarming took place without bloodshed. One Cossack was "slightly scratched" in the clash. Things were so well under control that Kaluga was able to preserve its own identity even after the fall of Moscow.

When Shakhovskoy and Kuskova went to Petrograd from Moscow to inform the underground Provisional Government of attitudes in the outlying districts, they delivered a suggestion from Kaluga that it be accepted as the seat of the Provisional Government.

On the 14th a semi-punitive and semi-investigatory "commission" composed of Vikzhel representatives went to Kaluga from Moscow. The commission preferred to follow the path of compromise. It reached an agreement with the "organ of provincial authority to save the revolution." It was decided that this body would be dissolved and that authority would be transferred to a special "Revolutionary-Socialist Committee" formed of representatives of all the socialist parties. The Bolsheviks immediately attempted to violate the agreement and formed their own military revolutionary committee without the participation of the Mensheviks and Socialist Revolutionaries. It proved powerless. The City Duma dispersed the military revolutionary committee with the aid of shock troops. The city continued to be administered by the formally dissolved "organ of provincial authority," and no one recognized orders coming from the Bolshevik military revolutionary committee. This situation continued for almost two weeks.

All told, the authority of the Provisional Government, in the person of its local agents, who were supported by the revolutionary democracy, lasted an entire month in Kaluga. Of course, isolated Kaluga, organizationally supported by no one, could not become the rallying point for all Russia. The Kaluga story is merely an episode, but the features characteristic of Kaluga can be seen in a number of provincial cities and indicate what might have happened in Russia.

If the persons active during the October events of 1917 had been able to peer into the future, perhaps their social psychology would have changed somewhat and the "ravings," as Plekhanov called the April Theses, of "a man gone mad" – as Trotsky characterized Lenin in April – could not possibly have influenced the rather passive masses.

Perhaps nobody has defined "Leninism" so aptly as that "finest Bolshevik," Trotsky (Lenin described him thus – according to Trotsky), when he attributed the following words to the "greatest man of our Revolutionary Era": "You blockheads! History is made in the trenches, where the soldier, plunged in the nightmare of the intoxication of war, skewers his officer with his bayonet and then flees to his native village, riding the coupling of a freight car, there to put his landlord's house to the torch. Does this barbarity not suit you? Cool your wrath, replies history. You are welcome to what we have. This is merely the conclusion of all that has gone before."

This political outlook characterizes not only "Leninism," but subsequent "Trotskyism" and "Stalinism" as well. This is the essence of the tactics that resulted in "Red October" and of the concept of "civil war on a world scale."

APPENDIX

THE PEASANT MOVEMENT IN 1917

Lenin believed that one of the reasons why his uprising would succeed was the increase in the number of peasant "rebellions." Opponents of his in the party, objecting to the self-delusion of their leader, claimed that "the peasant movement has barely started."

Who was right? Soviet historians have no doubt about the answer. "Red October" moved into the village with "dizzying swiftness," claims M. Martynov, commenting in *Krasnyi Arkhiv* on the documents of the Provisional Government's Chief Land Committee. In October the peasant movement had already escalated "to the stage of war," concludes I. A. Iakovlev in his preface to a collection of documents of the Provisional Government's Chief Administration of the Militia (published in 1927 in the series *Arkhiv Oktiabrskoi Revoliutsii*, with the title "The Peasant Movement in 1917"). And it may be that the greater part of émigré historical literature has drawn approximately the same conclusion, and that even the sharpened perception of contemporaries sometimes assesses the situation almost identically.

Of course, the scope of personal observation is always limited, and it is a risky matter on the basis of individual deductions to form a general conclusion. It is better to make use of that statistical material that is at our disposal. At the present time the only more or less complete statistics of agrarian disturbances during the days of the revolution are the data gathered by the Chief Administration of the Militia from private complaints reaching the central authorities or from weekly reports received from government agents about "important events" and local "law violations." Every month the Chief Administration drew up a summary of these reports under specific headings, supplementing them with newspaper accounts. As a result of this, extremely important historical material was collected.

Many years have passed since these materials were published, but unfortunately it seems that they have not been adequately analyzed. I shall attempt to give the reader at least a general idea of the conclusions one can draw from an examination of the information contained in the reports of the Chief Administration of the Militia. They differ from the conclusions of Soviet historians. The above-mentioned Iakovlev wrote in his preface: "The peasants made their choice in September and October. . . . The agrarian movement swelled to the level of a peasant war . . . . October alone accounted for 42.1% of all cases of riots and property destruction recorded since the February revolution . . . . The number of estates seized by the agrarian movement rose 30.2% in September over August, while in October the figure rose 43.2% over September."

We do not know what principle Iakovlev followed in making his calculation for October. The information bureau of the Chief Administration of the Militia in October was no longer able to collate its statistics. The last collations made by the bureau were for the period ending in September. It may be that the investigator came up with a 30 percent increase in peasant disturbances in September over August because he mechanically added some figures from various columns of the militia report. An increase can be deduced by such artificial means, but it is no big task to dissipate such fictions. Let us examine the content of these columns.

The data on the number and type of violations of the law recorded by the Chief Administration of the Militia covers such diverse items as counter-revolutionary acts or the prohibition of playing billiards, which was enacted illegally by the Oranienbaum Township Committee. It is obvious that statistics for such things should be ignored. We are left with four main categories: violations committed against landed property, pogroms and seizures of property, violations committed against trades and industry, and excesses committed by the military. It is also obvious that the latter two, although not entirely divorced from the village, cannot be of interest to us. What facts did the persons preparing the report place in the column headed pogroms and seizures? Acts of mob justice, riots, theft, and robbery. From these we should eliminate all violations of a type not directly connected with the land question: riots resulting from grain requisitioning, acts of violence committed against food boards, mob law in cases of horse theft, ordinary robbery and murder, and other such excesses. Let us especially note that the seizure and destruction of estates, as well as cases of arson, are entered in a special column and placed in the section devoted to violations committed against landed property. Now, if we take the report for September we are immediately struck by the lack of correspondence in every single province between the figures for "pogroms and seizures" and landed property offenses. The greatest number of "pogroms and seizures" were in the Moscow province – one hundred – but there were only three violations against landed property. In the Petrograd province there were eighty-two "pogroms and seizures" and only four landed property violations. That is, the capitals lead the list. They are followed by provinces containing a large city – such as Kharkov, forty-three and eighteen; Kherson, forty-two and eight; Iaroslavl, eleven and one. But even more significant is the fact that in the Riazan province, which had the second highest number of agrarian disturbances, including sixty-one landed-property violations, there were only eight "pogroms and seizures." Only in the Tambov province is there a certain, rather accidental, coincidence of figures — eighty-two and eighty-four.

What conclusions suggest themselves? That in characterizing agrarian disturbances one should eliminate from the statistics the entire group of offenses entered in the pogroms-and-seizure column although acts of physical violence are probably to be found in this group. Of course, statistics showing an increase in the number of such offenses give a picture of the anarchy spreading throughout the country (387 in July; 444 in August; 958 in September), but they do not give a picture of the peasant movement being heavily concentrated in provinces with a large urban population. In the overwhelming majority of cases the offenses were not connected with the peasant movement at all. The statistics of violations committed against landed property provide us with results that differ from the conclusions reached by Soviet historians. The agrarian movement reaches its high point in July — 1,122 landed property offenses; then it begins to drop — 691 in August, and 629 in September. These totals become even more significant if we examine the special column devoted to the seizure and destruction of estates: 236 in July; 180 in August; 112 in September (in the figure for September we have included cases of estate-burning, which by this time was itemized separately in the reports).

The literature on the subject gives various explanations for the decline in the peasant movement in August. Soviet sources mention the temporary influence of the government's punitive policy; émigré investigators point to a decline in the number of desertions from the front lines, the harvest season in farming, and so on. But would it not be more correct to stress the organizational activities of the land committees? (These committees were established by the Provisional Government at the local level to inventory landed property and to lay the groundwork for land reform.) It is true that their activities can be viewed as unsatisfactory. The land committees were not always the champions of the government. Sometimes not only the township but even the county committees were initiators of the peasant movement. But generally they undoubtedly acted as peacemakers. The materials gathered by the militia provide us with rather graphic illustrations. And it becomes to a certain degree understandable why from August on we see an increase in the number of cases of disorganized peasant disturbances, as opposed to those organized by local bodies such as the soviets. Perhaps some of the former should be credited to the Bolsheviks; the disturbances may be an indication of how successful the unbridled demagoguery of newly arrived "Baltic" and other agitators was with unstable rural elements. These elements were not only unstable but sometimes hungry as well. The data gathered in an official survey made of the food situation in various localities clearly establishes a direct link at times between disturbances and hunger, when the populace, after the total exhaustion of its own grain stocks, began consuming "substitutes" and looting public stores. "Hunger rebellions" should actually be listed separately among the overall statistics of agrarian offenses.

If we continue our analysis, limiting ourselves to the statistics dealing with the seizures and destruction of estates, we shall discover another characteristic phenomenon: "warfare" was not continuous. Each surge of violence was followed by an abatement. A wave of agitation would be followed by a period of calm. Here is the scale — cases of estates destroyed in the months of July, August, September in some of those provinces that investigators call centers of Bolshevik activity: Voronezh – 10, 9, 0; Tambov – 2, 8, 58; Orel – 11, 5, 4; Riazan – 8, 2, 32; Tula – 7, 4, 0; Penza – 18, 11, 3; Saratov – 13, 1, 5; Samara – 8, 16, 0; Simbirsk – 2, 2, 0; Kazan – 22, 1, 0. September shows a decisive decrease in the violence, with the exception of the provinces of Tambov and Riazan. A Tambov provincial commissar reported that a wave of disorders swept through fourteen townships of Kozlov county. "Fifty-four estates and separate farmsteads were struck, eighteen of them were completely or partially burned to the ground, others suffered damage and looting. About one-third of those hit were peasants, independent farmers, holders of consolidated plots, and small owners." Very revealing is the report made by a Socialist Revolutionary party representative named Sletova, which appeared in *Delo Naroda* on September 24. She stated that in Kozlov county one village sometimes fought another over the division of plunder or because one of them refused to attack a landowner's estate. The peasants of some villages begged the police for assistance. The second largest number of cases of property destruction during September occurred in Riazan province, where the food shortage was particularly acute. Almost all the farms and estates destroyed (thirty-two cases recorded) were in Ranenburg county, which adjoined Kozlov county. The official report notes that the estates in Ranenburg county were attacked chiefly by peasants from Kozlov county, plus strangers armed with pistols and explosives. Perhaps the Kozlov peasants included some peasants from hungry areas, who had gathered in Kozlov in large numbers, buying up grain and thus sending the "grain prices to fantastically high levels." According to the writer Nazhivin, the mob looting and destruction in Ranenburg county was under the guidance of an obviously deranged individual, the playwright Polevoi.

The grand total of landed property offenses during the seven revolutionary months from February to October 1, according to the figures contained in the reports, was 3,499. Of these, 767 are under the heading "seizures and destruction of estates."*

*The latter figure represents less than one percent of the landed estates in Russia at that time. Eds.

How complete are these figures? There can hardly be any doubt that even with a most careful collection of figures, the information division of the Chief Administration of the Militia could not record all the cases of "spontaneous clashes between tens of millions of peasants and tens of thousands of landowners." The compilers point out that in the (unpublished) summary report on "major offenses between 1 March and 1 October" there is an insufficiency of data. "The local authorities still fail to realize fully the necessity of the strictest fulfillment of requests made time and again by the Chief Administration for data shedding light on the most important local events." However, the reports also contained exaggerations. Isolated cases referred to in telegrams were sometimes characterized in the report as "offenses" occurring throughout the country. What is more important, most of the information originated with persons who had been the victims of violence and naturally tended to exaggerate and generalize. I shall cite merely one example, which occurred during the October events. On the 17th of October the All-Russian Union of Landowners sent a telegram to the prime minister stating: "Anarchy is on the increase in this province [Tula]. In Efremov county 10 to 20 estates a day are totally wrecked." A few days later the same group telegraphed: "More than 30 estates in this province have been wrecked." Nevertheless, whatever their shortcomings, the statistics of the Chief Administration do provide us with a source for determining the intensity of the agrarian movement during the months of the revolution.

How intense did the peasant movement become during the first three weeks of October? The militia reports do not go beyond September. It is an extremely risky matter to make independent computations without being acquainted with the methods used in obtaining the figures of the preceding months, particularly since the materials that the reports were based on were not printed in toto. The only communications included were those that referred to rural areas in one way or another. Under such conditions an independent computation can lead to quite arbitrary conclusions. But we do possess one rather objective indication, though of a formal nature — the number of reports received by the central agencies from local sources. It is quite natural that wherever the movement intensified, the number of notifications would increase. And we see that in many of those central provinces which were used by us above, about the same number of reports were received in October as in September: compare 8-10; 10-12; 8-8; 7-7; 7-6, etc. There was no unusual deviation. Agrarian disturbances held at approximately the same level. The number remained high in Riazan province: twenty-three cases were reported in September and twenty-four in October. Unrest continued in Ranenburg county and gradually embraced Skopin and Dankov counties. "Baltic agitators" appeared on the scene. (Were these the same strangers carrying "explosives" who were active in Kozlov county?)

Things quieted down in Tambov province, where the number of cases reported dropped to nine (compared with twenty in September) and the provincial commissar reported the following: "During the last two weeks there have been no disturbances of the peace in this province. Contributing to the prevention of agrarian riots are the regulations by the land board concerning registration of all private estates and the indication that they may be transferred to the land committees." But from Spassk county came a laconic report on the 14th that the "estates are being demolished." Tula province showed a sharp upward trend; there were nineteen cases reported, compared with nine in September. From neighboring Riazan province the disturbances spread to Efremov county.

Thus, we do have before us instances of the spread of peasant disturbances when the contagion of mass emotion swept from place to place. But we are still far from justified in characterizing the peasant movement as a "war." Local reports in October differ little in content from reports received during the preceding months, and at any rate they are not at all of such a "destructive" nature as is depicted in the subjective accounts of contemporaries and the "objective" conclusions of some investigators. Available materials give us no reason to assert that whereas before the Bolshevik uprising the agrarian movement was marked by acts of partial destruction, afterwards there were "acts of total destruction and house-burning." It would seem that the opposite was the case. There were some provinces in which there were no rural disturbances to speak of until November. It is possible that the decrease in the number of agrarian disturbances in some areas was due partially to the fact that the land had been taken over by the land committees. At any rate, in the month before the elections to the Constituent Assembly the Provisional Government was not being threatened by an agrarian revolution. There was no incipient "All-Russian Pugachev Rebellion" directed against the "Kerensky government," as Lenin claimed.*

*How exaggerated the assertions of Soviet historians are about the so-called peasant war in Russia in the fall of 1917 is convincingly shown by the collection of documents published in *Vtoroi Vserossiiskii S"ezd Sovetov Rabochikh I Soldatskikh Deputatov* [The second All-Russian Congress of the Soviets of Workers' and Soldiers' Deputies] (Moscow, 1957), pp. 228-371. The second chapter of this publication contains answers given by Bolshevik delegates at the Congress to a questionnaire, question 19 of which read: "Were there [in your region] any agrarian disturbances (*volneniia*); what influence does the local soviet exercise among the peasants, and what role did the soviet play in the agrarian movement (*dvizhenii*)?" Of the 139 Bolshevik delegates at the Congress who filled out the questionnaire, about 20 represented various military units and organizations out of touch

---

with the countryside and did not answer for that reason. About 50 more left question 19 unanswered, evidently because they had nothing to report on the subject. About 40 answered that there were no disturbances (*ne bylo*). Only about 30 delegates reported some agrarian disturbances, but the majority of the disturbances were characterized as "not serious" or "unimportant" and as having been settled by the intervention of the local soviet. Only the delegate from the Soviet of Soldiers' Deputies in Kiev reported that "the agrarian disturbances (*besporiadki*) are getting more intensive." But at the same time the delegate of the Kiev Soviet of Workers' Deputies had nothing to report about any agrarian disturbances, and the delegate of the regional soviet of the southwestern region (which included the province of Kiev) reported: "There were [some agrarian disturbances] in the region but they were soon terminated (*skoro likvidirovany*)." Thus none of the 120 Bolshevik delegates coming from various regions of Russia brought to Petrograd any information about the "peasant war" that, according to Lenin (and Soviet historians), was "raging" throughout Russia at the time. In October 1917 only 144 cases of serious agrarian disturbances (the seizure and destruction of landowners' countryseats) were registered in the whole country, according to A.V. Shestakov, *Ocherki po sel'skomu khoziaistvu i krest'ianskomu dvizheniiu v gody voiny, pered Oktiabrem 1917* [Essays on Agriculture and the Peasant Movement During the War and Before October 1917] (Leningrad, 1927), p. 141. S.G.P.

Reference Matter

CHRONOLOGY OF EVENTS

(Dates are according to the old style – thirteen days behind the Western calendar. Thus October 25 O.S. is November 7.)

Feb. 23-26 Strikes and street demonstrations in Petrograd.

Feb. 27 Petrograd garrison mutinies and refuses to fire on demonstrators. Collapse of the imperial government. Formation of the Temporary Committee of the State Duma "to restore order and establish relations with public institutions." Formation of the Petrograd Soviet of Workers' and Soldiers' Deputies.

Mar. 1 Soviet issues "Order Number One" to the Petrograd garrison, establishing a kind of self-government in military units.

Mar. 2 Provisional Government, headed by Prince Georgi Lvov, with P. Miliukov as Foreign Minister and A. Kerensky as Minister of Justice is formed.
Emperor Nicholas II abdicates.

Mar. 3 Grand Duke Michael refuses the throne.

Apr. 3 Lenin arrives in Petrograd from Switzerland, via Germany, Sweden, and Finland.

Apr. 4 Lenin announces his "April Theses" (published in *Pravda* Apr. 7).

Apr. 18 Miliukov's note to the Allies assuring them of continued Russian participation in war.

Apr. 20 Miliukov's note published. Anti-war demonstrations in Petrograd.

Apr. 24-29 Bolshevik party conference approves Lenin's program.

May 2 Miliukov resigns from government.

May 4 Trotsky arrives in Petrograd from the United States.

May 5 First coalition government, including representatives of the socialist parties, formed.

June 3-24 First All-Russian Congress of Soviets (dominated by the Mensheviks and Socialist Revolutionaries); Central Executive Committee of Soviets (VTsIK) formed.

June 18 Russian offensive in Galicia starts.

July 1-3 Agreement concerning the autonomy of the Ukraine reached. Kadet ministers resign from the government.

July 3-5 "July days": demonstrations and uprising in Petrograd under the slogan "All power to the Soviets."

July 4-7 Provisional Government takes steps to curtail Bolshevik activities: *Pravda* suppressed; several leaders arrested; Lenin goes into hiding.

July 6-11 German counteroffensive in Galicia; rout of the Russian army.

July 7-23 Prince Lvov resigns; Kerensky forms second coalition government.

July 18 General Kornilov appointed supreme commander.

July 26- Bolshevik party congress in Petrograd; "mezhraiontsy" (a group
Aug. 3 of Social Democratic "internationalists," including Trotsky) join
the Bolshevik party.

Aug. 12-15 "State Conference" in Moscow.

Aug. 18-21 Germans break through the Russian northern front and occupy
Riga; Petrograd menaced.

Aug. 25-30 The Kornilov movement. Formation of Bolshevik Red Guards in
response.

Aug. 30 Kornilov dismissed; Kerensky becomes supreme commander of
the armed forces.

Aug. 31 Bolshevik resolution on "proletarian and peasant power"
adopted by the Petrograd Soviet.

Sept. 1 Russia officially proclaimed a republic; Kerensky forms a "directory" of five ministers.

Sept. 9 Petrograd Soviet adopts a Bolshevik resolution demanding reelection of its presidium; presidium composed of Mensheviks
and Socialist Revolutionaries resigns.

Sept. 14-22 "Democratic Conference" in Petrograd. Decides (Sept. 21) to
establish the All-Russian Democratic Council, (later renamed the
Provisional Council of the Russian Republic) which becomes
known as the Pre-Parliament.

Sept. 25 Trotsky elected chairman of the Petrograd Soviet. Kerensky
forms a new coalition cabinet ("the third coalition").

Oct. 7 Pre-Parliament opens; Trotsky reads a declaration against the
"bourgeois counterrevolution" and the Bolsheviks walk out.

Oct. 9 Petrograd Soviet forms the "Revolutionary Defense Committee"
(ostensibly to protect Petrograd from the German danger).

Oct. 10-11 A meeting of the Bolshevik Central Committee, with Lenin
present, adopts a resolution for the preparation of an armed
uprising.

Oct. 12 Congress of Soviets of the Northern Region passes resolution
calling for the transfer of power to the soviets. Executive
Committee of the Petrograd Soviet renames the Revolutionary
Defense Committee the Military Revolutionary Committee
(MRC).

Oct. 16 Meeting of the Bolshevik Central Committee, with Lenin present, discusses the political situation and decides to intensify
preparations for an uprising, while representatives from local
organizations testify about the absence of enthusiasm for an
armed uprising among the Petrograd workers.

Oct. 21 A conference of representatives from Petrograd military units
pledges "full support" to the MRC.

Oct. 22 "Day of the Petrograd Soviet": demonstrations, meetings, and speeches on soviet power, without reference to an armed uprising. MRC calls upon the Petrograd military units not to obey orders of military authorities unless countersigned by MRC.

Oct. 23 MRC dispatches commissars to Petrograd military units.

Oct. 24 Kerensky decides to take legal action against MRC and orders suppression of the Bolshevik papers *Rabochii Put'* and *Soldat.*

MRC issues a call for battle readiness against "counter-revolution" and orders continued publication of the Bolshevik papers.

Kerensky proclaims Petrograd in a "state of insurrection" and convokes meeting of the Pre-Parliament, but fails to receive from it clear-cut support in the struggle against the Bolshevik insurrection.

Night of Forces of the MRC take over the telegraph, telephone, the
Oct. 24-25 railroad stations and several other government buildings.

Oct. 25 From the early morning and throughout the day, forces of the MRC, commanded by Podvoisky, surround the Winter Palace, where an all-day meeting of the Provisional Government is taking place. The defense consists of several hundred military cadets and the women's battalion, about 130 strong.

(10 A.M.) MRC issues proclamation declaring that the Provisional Government is overthrown and that political power is in the hands of the MRC, representing the Petrograd Soviet.

(About 11:30 A.M.) Kerensky leaves Petrograd by automobile for Pskov to get reliable troops from the front.

(Noon) Pre-Parliament convenes and is dispersed by Bolshevik forces.

(2:35 P.M. to after 6 P.M.) Provisional Government rejects several ultimatums to surrender. Lenin appears publicly before the Petrograd Soviet.

(Evening) After the arrival of a detachment of Baltic sailors and noisy but harmless salvos from the cruiser *Aurora* and the Peter and Paul Fortress, attacks on the Winter Palace intensify and last through midnight.

(10:45 P.M.) Second All-Russian Congress of Soviets opens.

Oct. 26 (2:10 A.M.) Bolsheviks invading the Winter Palace arrest members of the Provisional Government.

Committee for the Salvation of the Country and the Revolution organized at City Duma to oppose the Bolsheviks.

(About 3 to 5 A.M.) Second Congress of Soviets proclaims "soviet power" over Russia, confirms a new government of the Council of People's Commissars (*Sovnarkom*), headed by Lenin, and ratifies Lenin's decrees on land (abolishing the property rights of landlords) and on a "just democratic" peace.

Oct. 27 Don Cossacks under ataman Kaledin, and the Orenburg Cossacks under ataman Dutov, refuse to recognize the Bolshevik rule.

Kerensky and Cossacks commanded by General Krasnov reach Gatchina on their way to Petrograd. Committee for the Salvation plans an uprising in Petrograd.

Oct. 28 Cossacks under Kerensky and Krasnov reach Tsarskoe Selo.

Uprising against the Bolsheviks in Moscow begins.

Oct. 29 Uprising of military cadets against the Bolsheviks in Petrograd begins and is suppressed.

All-Russian Executive Committee of the Railroad Workers' Union (Vikzhel) convenes a conference of the socialist parties to negotiate a coalition government; the Bolshevik Central Committee agrees to participate.

Oct. 30 Battle of Pulkovo; Krasnov's Cossacks repulsed by the Bolsheviks.

Nov. 1 Truce agreement reached at Gatchina; Krasnov arrested, Kerensky goes into hiding; General Dukhonin assumes duties of supreme commander.

Nov. 2 Moscow uprising suppressed.

Bolshevik Central Committee, under Lenin's pressure, rejects a coalition with other socialist parties.

Nov. 3 *Sovnarkom* publishes a declaration promising to all peoples of the former Russian empire full equality and the right of self-determination, including separation from Russia.

Nov. 4 Several notable Bolsheviks resign from *Sovnarkom* and/or the Central Committee of the Bolshevik party in protest against one-party rule.

Nov. 7 *Sovnarkom* orders Dukhonin to cease military operations and to start peace negotiations; the general refuses.

Nov. 8 Appeal from *Sovnarkom* to Allied Powers for an armistice.

Nov. 9 Dukhonin dismissed as supreme commander and replaced by Ensign Krylenko, a Bolshevik.

Nov. 11 Ataman Kaledin forms an anti-Bolshevik military government in the Don Region.

Nov. 12 Elections to the Constituent Assembly; Socialist Revolutionaries in the lead with 41 percent of the vote, Bolsheviks follow with 24 percent.

Nov. 18 An announcement made that Left Socialist Revolutionaries will enter the cabinet.

Nov. 20 Bolsheviks take over General Headquarters; Dukhonin murdered.

Nov. 19-28 Founding congress of a separate Left Socialist Revolutionary party.

Nov. 22 Preliminary agreement for an armistice with the Central Powers signed in Brest-Litovsk (confirmed on December 2).

Nov. 28 *Sovnarkom* decree on the arrest and trial of Kadet party leaders as "enemies of the people".

Dec. 7 *Sovnarkom* decree establishing the "All-Russian Extraordinary Commission for struggle against counterrevolution and sabotage" (the notorious Cheka).

Dec. 13 *Pravda* publishes Lenin's "Theses on the Constituent Assembly" in which he states that the Constituent Assembly should not be allowed to function unless it recognizes soviet power.

Jan.5-6,1918 Constituent Assembly convenes and is disbanded.

NOTES

Melgunov did not provide references for the many quotations he used. The editor, therefore, traced the sources of the more important quotations, and in some cases included their later Soviet editions or English translations. These are likely to be much more accessible to the reader than some of the original sources, such as the daily press, which Melgunov relied upon. Complete bibliographic information about the sources can be found in the Bibliography.

CHAPTER 1: A SCHEDULED UPRISING

1 V.I. Lenin, Letter of August 30, 1917, in *Sochineniia,* 2nd ed., vol. 21 (Moscow, 1928), p. 119.
2 Lenin, Letter of September 13-14, *ibid.,* p. 199.
3 Lenin, Letter of September 29, *ibid.,* pp. 240-41.
4 Lenin, Letter of October 3-7, *ibid.,* pp. 293-94.
5 Lenin, Letter of October 7, *ibid.,* pp. 290-92.
6 K. Riabinskii, *Revoliutsiia 1917 goda. Khronika sobytii. Oktiabr'* (Moscow and Leningrad, 1926), pp. 242-43; also *Protokoly Tsentral'nogo Komiteta R.S.-D.R.P. (b.) Avgust 1917-Fevral' 1918* (Moscow, 1958), pp. 85-86. A translation appears in James Bunyan and H. H. Fisher, eds., *The Bolshevik Revolution 1917-1918: Documents and Materials* (Stanford, 1961), p. 58.
7 G. Zinoviev and L. Kamenev, "Zaiavlenie . . . k tekushchemu momentu," *Proletarskaia Revoliiutsiia* 69 (October 1927) 265-71; also *Protokoly . . . Avgust 1917-Fevral' 1918,* pp. 86-92. Trans. in Bunyan and Fisher, *op. cit.,* pp. 59-62.
8 Minutes of the Central Committee meeting of October 16 in "Protokoly Tsentral'nogo Komiteta . . . ," *Proletarskaia Revoliutsiia* 69 (October 1927) 276-85; also *Protokoly . . . Avgust 1917-Fevral' 1918,* pp. 93-104.
9 *Proletarskaia Revoliutsiia* 69, p. 286; also *Protokoly . . . Avgust 1917-Fevral' 1918,* p. 104. Trans. in Bunyan and Fisher, *op. cit.,* p. 76.

CHAPTER 2: THE DECEIVED

10 Resolution of the Petrograd Soviet of October 9 in Riabinskii, *op. cit.,* p. 238. Trans. in Bunyan and Fisher, *op. cit.,* p. 69.
11 Riabinskii, *op. cit.,* p. 88.
12 *Ibid.,* p. 250-51.
13 V.D. Nabokov, "Vremennoe Pravitel'stvo," *Arkhiv Russkoi Revoliutsii,* vol. 1 (Berlin, 1921), pp. 79-80.
14 Riabinskii, *op. cit.,* p. 80.

15 Sir George Buchanan, *My Mission to Russia and Other Diplomatic Memories,* vol. 2 (London, 1923), p. 201.

16 Nabokov, *op. cit.,* p. 36.

17 V.B. Stankevich, *Vospominaniia 1914-1919* (Berlin, 1920), p. 258.

18 *Arkhiv Russkoi Revoliutsii,* vol. 7 (Berlin, 1922), p. 281. The conversation in this source is erroneously dated the night of October 21-22; it actually took place on the night of October 23-24.

CHAPTER 3: ON THE EVE

19 L.D. Trotsky, *Istoriia russkoi revoliutsii. Tom 3, Oktiabr'skaia revoliutsiia* (Berlin, 1933), trans. *The History of the Russian Revolution,* vol. 3 (New York, 1933), p. 209.

20 Riabinskii, *op. cit.,* p. 226-27; also *Petrogradskii Voenno-Revoliutsionnyi komitet; dokumenty i materialy,* vol. 1 (Moscow, 1966), p. 83. Trans. in Bunyan and Fisher, *op. cit.,* p. 95.

21 Trotsky, *op. cit.,* p. 360.

22 Lenin, Letter of October 24, in *op. cit.,* pp. 362-63.

23 Riabinskii, *op. cit.,* p. 168; trans. in R.P. Browder and A.F. Kerensky, eds., *The Russian Provisional Government 1917,* vol. 3 (Stanford, 1961), pp. 1772-78.

24 Riabinskii, *op. cit.,* p. 268; trans. in Bunyan and Fisher, *op. cit.,* pp. 91-92.

25 F.I. Dan, "K istorii poslednikh dnei Vremennogo Pravitel'stva," *Letopis' revoliutsii,* vol. 1 (Berlin, 1923), pp. 161-78; excerpts trans. in Browder and Kerensky, *op. cit.,* pp. 1781-83.

26 A.F. Kerensky, *Izdaleka; sbornik statei* (Paris, 1922), p. 196.

27 Riabinskii, *op. cit.,* pp. 170-71.

28 Kerensky, *op. cit.,* pp. 198-99.

29 A.N. Grekov, "Soiuz kazach'ikh voisk v Petrograde v 1917 godu," *Donskaia Letopis',* vol. 2 (Vienna, 1923), pp. 273-74.

30 P.I. Palchinskii, "Poslednie chasy Vremennogo Pravitel'stva v 1917 g," *Krasnyi Arkhiv,* no. 56 (Moscow, 1933), pp. 136-37.

31 Kerensky, *op. cit.,* pp. 200-201.

32 *Ibid.,* pp. 204-205.

33 N. Avdeev, "Vokrug Gatchiny," *Krasnyi Arkhiv,* no. 9 (1925), pp. 179-80.

CHAPTER 4: THE 25TH OF OCTOBER

34 S.V. Militsyn, "Iz moei tetradi; poslednie dni Preobrazhenskogo polka," *Arkhiv Russkoi Revoliutsii,* vol. 2 (Berlin, 1921), p. 175.

35 Sergei Uralov, "Stranichka Oktiabria," *Proletarskaia Revoliutsiia,* no. 33 (1924), p. 277.

36 I.I. Rengarten, "Oktiabr'skaia revoliutsiia v Baltiiskom flote; iz dnevnika," *Krasnyi Arkhiv,* no. 25 (1927), p. 50.

37 S.A. Korenev, "Chrezvychainaia komissia po delam byvshikh ministrov," *Arkhiv Russkoi Revoliutsii,* vol. 7 (1922), p. 29.

38 V.A. Auerbakh, "Revoliutsionnoe obshchestvo po lichnym vospomina-niiam," *Arkhiv Russkoi Revoliutsii*, vol. 14 (1924), pp. 25-26.

39 Nabokov, *op. cit.*, pp. 86-87.

40 P. Maliantovich, "V Zimnem Dvortse 25-26 oktiabria 1917," *Byloe*, vol. 12, bk. 6 (Petrograd, 1918), pp. 111-41; also in S.P. Kniazev and A.P. Konstantinov, eds., *Oktiabr'skoe vooruzhonnoe vosstanie v Petrograde* (Leningrad, 1956), pp. 405-13.

41 The conversation between Dieterichs and Danilevich in "Stavka 25-26 oktiabria 1917," *Arkhiv Russkoi Revoliutsii*, vol. 7 (1922), p. 295.

42 Aleksandr Sinegub, "Zashchita Zimnego Dvortsa," *Arkhiv Russkoi Revoliutsii*, vol. 4 (1922), pp. 173-90.

43 A colorful, but rather fictional account of the "storm" of the Winter Palace is contained in N. Podvoiskii, "Voennaia organizatsiia Ts.K.R.S.-D.R.P.(b.) i voenno-revoliutsionnyi komitet v 1917 g.," *Krasnaia Letopis';* vol. 8 (Moscow, 1923) pp. 25-30.

44 Buchanan, *op. cit.*, vol. 2, p. 208.

CHAPTER 5: AT THE FRONT

45 Transcripts of the teletype talks between General Headquarters in Mogilev and the headquarters of the northern front in Pskov were published in the *Arkhiv Russkoi Revoliutsii*, vol. 7 (Berlin, 1922), pp. 281-320, and in *Krasnyi Arkhiv*, nos. 23 and 24 (Moscow, 1927). The former version consists of excerpts from teletype tapes prepared at General Headquarters; these were salvaged by the Volunteer Army in the Fall of 1919 after it occupied Kiev. This version includes conversations between Headquarters and Petrograd, the western front, and other points. The latter, Soviet, version is apparently based on teletype tapes found at the headquarters of the northern front. Hence the only communications of General Headquarters it contains are those with the northern front; moreover, two important communications from the northern front with General Headquarters and with the western front are inexplicably lacking. S.P.M.

46 Kerensky, *op. cit.*, pp. 206-7.

47 "Stavka 25-26 oktiabria 1917 g.," *Arkhiv Russkoi Revoliutsii*, vol. 7 (1922), pp. 298-99.

48 *Ibid.*, p. 301.

49 V.A. Cheremisov, "Pokhod Kerenskogo na Petrograd," *Golos Rossii* (Berlin, 1921).

50 P.N. Krasnov, "Na vnutrennem fronte," *Arkhiv Russkoi Revoliutsii*, vol. 1 (1921), pp. 152-78.

51 Stankevich, *op. cit.* pp. 268-69.

52 Aleksei Budberg, "Dnevnik," *Arkhiv Russkoi Revoliutsii*, vol. 12 (1923), pp. 197-255.

53 *Ibid.*, p. 233.

54 "Oktiabr' na fronte," *Krasnyi Arkhiv*, no. 23 (1927), p. 174. Trans. in Bunyan and Fisher, *op. cit.*, p. 164.

CHAPTER 6: AFTER THE COUP

55 Stankevich, *op. cit.*, p. 267.
56 "Protokoly Petrogradskogo Komiteta R.S. - D.R.P. (b) za 1917 god. Zasedanie P.K. 29 oktiabria; doklady s mest," *Krasnaia Letopis'*, vol. 6 (Moscow, 1923), pp. 395-97.
57 The minutes, probably somewhat abridged, of MRC negotiations with the Petrograd garrison representatives can be found in *Petrogradskii Voenno-Revoliutsionnyi komitet; dokumenty i materialy* (1966), vol. 1, pp. 421-23.
58 V.D. Bonch-Bruevich, "Strashnoe v revoliutsii," *Na boevykh postakh Fevral'skoi i Oktiabr'skoi revoliutsii* (Moscow, 1930), pp. 293-96.
59 S. An-skii, "Posle perevorota 25-go oktiabria 1917 g.," *Arkhiv Russkoi Revoliutsii*, vol. 8 (1923), pp. 44-45.
60 Stankevich, *op. cit.*, p. 272.
61 A.G. Shliapnikov, "Oktiabr'skii perevorot i Stavka," *Krasnyi Arkhiv*, no. 9 (1925), p. 161.
62 For a relatively factual account, see Vera Vladimirova, *God sluzhby "sotsialistov" kapitalistam* (Moscow, 1927), pp. 38-54.
63 Bunyan and Fisher, *op. cit.*, pp. 155-56, trans. from *Novaia Zhizn'*, no. 167, November 12, 1917, p. 2.

CHAPTER 7: BLOODY SUNDAY

64 Gots' speech at the Moscow trial of Socialist Revolutionaries in *Revoliutsionnaia Rossiia*, nos. 21-22 (Berlin, October-November 1922), pp. 7-12.
65 Dushkin's testimony in "Zagovor monarkhicheskoi organizatsii V.M. Purishkevicha," *Krasnyi Arkhiv*, no. 26 (1928), pp. 179-81.
66 Testimony of the cadet Duke Leikhtenbergsky, *ibid.*, pp. 176-78.

CHAPTER 8: THE "WHITE ADVENTURE"

67 "Oktiabr' na fronte," *Krasnyi Arkhiv*, no. 24 (1927) p. 79.
68 *Petrogradskii Voenno-Revoliutsionnyi komitet*, (Moscow, 1966), vol. 1, p. 358.
69 "Oktiabr' na fronte," *Krasnyi Arkhiv*, no. 24, p. 82.
70 P.N. Krasnov, "Na vnutrennem fronte," *op. cit.*, pp. 172-178; his report to Cheremisov in *Krasnyi Arkhiv*, no. 24, pp. 93-94.
71 The following are major sources on the situation in Gatchina from October 27 to November 1: Krasnov, *op. cit.*, pp. 145-78; Kerensky, *op. cit.*, pp. 212-25; Stankevich, *op. cit.*, pp. 267-83; W.S. Woytinsky, *Stormy Passage* (1961), pp. 369-89; V.A. Veiger-Redemeister, "S Kerenskim v Gatchine," *Proletarskaia Revoliutsiia*, vol. 21 (1923), pp. 76-95; Avdeev, *op. cit.*, pp. 171-94; G.P. Tschebotarioff, *Russia, My Native Land* (1964), pp. 107-38.
72 Avdeev, *op. cit.*, pp. 186-90; Woytinsky's telegram to Cheremisov of November 1 in "Oktiabr' na fronte," *op. cit.*, no. 24, p. 90; trans. in Browder and Kerensky, *op. cit.*, vol. 3, p. 1813.

73 "Oktiabr' na fronte," *op. cit.*, p. 91-92.
74 Bunyan and Fisher, *op. cit.*, p. 173, trans. from *Delo Naroda* no. 198, November 3, 1917.

CHAPTER 9: ON A NEW TRACK

75 On the position of the Vikzhel and its participation in the conference see Vera Vladimirova, *op. cit.*, pp. 38-54 and P. Vompe, *Dni oktiabr'skoi revoliutsii i zheleznodorozhniki* (Moscow, 1924). Excerpts from documents trans. in Bunyan and Fisher, *op. cit.*, pp. 155-60, 190-97, 207-9.
76 An-skii, *op. cit.*, p. 49.
77 *Protokoly . . . Avgust 1917-Fevral' 1918*, pp. 124-30.
78 "Oktiabr' na fronte," *op. cit.*, pp. 99-101.
79 *Ibid.*, pp. 106-7.
80 *Ibid.*, p. 78.

CHAPTER 10: WAGER ON DISINTEGRATION

81 I.N. Liubimov, *Revoliutsiia 1917 goda. Khronika Sobytii. Oktiabr'-dekabr'* (Moscow, 1930), p. 424.
82 G.A. Solomon, *Sredi krasnykh vozhdei* (Paris, 1930), p. 15.
83 Lenin, *Sochineniia*, 2nd ed., vol. 22, Appendix, pp. 551-52; also in *Protokoly . . . Avgust 1917-Fevral' 1918,* pp. 135-36. Trans. in Bunyan and Fisher, *op. cit.*, pp. 203-4.
84 Lenin, *ibid.*, p. 551; also in *Protokoly . . ., ibid*, p. 136. Trans. in Bunyan and Fisher, *ibid.*, pp. 202-3.
85 Text of Lozovskii's letter in Liubimov, *op. cit.*, pp. 424-25. Trans. in Bunyan and Fisher, *ibid.*, pp. 204-6.
86 Lenin, *op. cit.*, vol. 22, pp. 58-61.
87 Buchanan, *op. cit.*, vol. 2, pp. 220-21.
88 Stankevich, *op. cit.*, pp. 287-88.
89 "Protokoly zasedanii Ts.I.K̇. i biuro Ts.I.K.S.R. i S.D. l-go sozyva posle oktiabria," *Krasnyi Arkhiv*, no. 10 (1925), pp. 101-5.
90 Lenin, "Tezisy ob uchreditel'nom sobranii," *op. cit.*, vol. 22, pp. 131-34.
91 "Moskovskaia gorodskaia duma posle oktiabria," *Krasnyi Arkhiv*, no. 28 (1928), pp. 61-62.

BIBLIOGRAPHY

The extensive bibliography in the original Russian edition of the Bolshevik Seizure of Power *suffers from some formal defects, such as the omission of authors' initials and places of publication, and contains a few factual errors. In his book* The Fate of Emperor Nicholas II after his Abdication *(Paris, 1951), Melgunov recognized and explained some of these shortcomings: "The bibliography has some deficiencies. The author could not correct them, not having had all the sources at hand, since he was forced to sell out half his library during and after the German occupation of Paris." (p.415).*

The editor of the present edition has, thanks to the vast resources of the Yale University library, been able to check most items in Melgunov's bibliography against the sources, and he has been able to supply most of the missing data. Items that could not be verified are indicated by an asterisk *.

A supplementary bibliography, consisting of some pertinent works not listed by Melgunov or published after he completed his manuscript, has been added by the editor. Also included are items in Melgunov's bibliography that have been translated into English and some bibliographical works.

The resulting list of books and articles does not claim completeness, but it is hoped that it will be of help to readers and researchers. A listing of serials and periodicals is given separately.

The spelling of names follows that of the Library of Congress and other catalogues, rather than the one adopted for ease of English readability in the body of the text.

Akashev, K. "Kak ushla artilleriia iz Zimnego Dvortsa" (How the Artillery Left the Winter Palace). *Byloe*, no. 27-28, Leningrad, 1925, pp. 282-285.

*Aldanov, M.A. "Kartiny oktiabr'skoi revoliutsii. Den' perevorota" (Pictures of the October Revolution. The Day of the Coup d'Etat). *Poslednie Novosti*, Paris, Oct. 6, 1938.

Anet, Claude [Jean Schopfer]. *La révolution russe*. 4 vols. Paris, 1917-1919, Cit. Vol. II.

Anishev, Anatolii. *Ocherki istorii grazhdanskoi voiny 1917-1920 gg.* (Essays on the History of the Civil War, 1917-1920). Leningrad, 1925.

An--skii [Iu. K. Rapoport]. "Posle perevorota 25-go oktiabria 1917 goda" (After the Coup d'Etat of October 25th, 1917). *Arkhiv Russkoi Revoliutsii*, vol. 8, Berlin, 1923, pp. 43-55.

217

218   Bibliography

Antonov-Ovseenko, V.A. "Baltflot v dni kerenshchiny i krasnogo Oktiabria (vospominaniia)" (The Baltic Fleet in the Days of Kerensky's Government and of the Red October. Recollections). *Proletarskaia Revoliutsiia,* vol. 10, 1922, pp. 118-124.

——. *V semnadtsatom godu* (In 1917). Moscow, 1933.

——. *Zapiski o grazhdanskoi voine* (Notes about the Civil War). 4 vols. Moscow, 1924-1933. Cit. vol. I.

Argunov, A.A. "Bez svobody" (Without Freedom). *Na Chuzhoi Storone,* vol. 13, Prague, 1925, pp. 86-130.

Auerbakh, V.A. "Revoliutsionnoe obshchestvo po lichnym vospominaniiam" (Society in the Period of the Revolution, According to Personal Recollections). *Arkhiv Russkoi Revoliutsii,* vol. 14, Berlin, 1924, pp. 5-38.

Avdeev, N., ed. "Vokrug Gatchiny" (Around Gatchina. Testimonies of Ensign Knirsha and others). *Krasnyi Arkhiv,* no. 9, 1925, pp. 171-194.

*Avksent'ev, N.D. "Iz oktiabr'skikh vospominanii" (From My Recollections of October). *Dni,* Paris [no date].

Belogorskii, N. "V dni Kaledina" (In Kaledin's Days). *Beloe Delo,* vol. 4, Berlin, 1928, pp. 39-70.

"Biulleten'Ts. K. R.S.-D.R.P. (bol'shevikov)," no. 8, Nov. 7, 1917 (Bulletin of the Central Committee of the Russian Social-Democratic Workers' Party) (Bolsheviks). In *Proletarskaia Revoliutsiia,* vol. 4, 1922, pp. 289-291.

Blagonravov, G.I. "Oktiabr'skie dni v Petropavlovskoi kreposti" (The October Days in the Peter and Paul Fortress). *Proletarskaia Revoliutsiia,* vol. 4, 1922, pp. 24-52.

*——. "Zimnii vziat i nashi tam" (The Winter Palace is Taken and Our People are There). *Izvestiia,* 1922, no. 252.

Bol'sheviki v bor'be za Oktiabr' (The Bolsheviks in the October Struggle). Moscow, 1933.

Bonch-Bruevich, V.D. *Na boevykh postakh Fevral'skoi i Oktiabr'skoi revoliutsii* (On the Battle Lines of the February and October Revolutions). Moscow, 1930. 2nd ed., 1931.

*Breslav, B.A. "15 let nazad" (Fifteen Years Ago). *Katorga i Ssylka.* Moscow, vol. 96.

Bublikov, A.A. *Russkaia revoliutsiia. Vpechatleniia i mysli ochevidtsa i uchastnika* (The Russian Revolution. Impressions and Thoughts of an Eyewitness and Participant). New York, 1918.

Buchanan, Sir George. *Moia missiia v Rossii. Vospominaniia diplomata.* vol. II, Paris, 1924. (Russian translation of *My Mission to Russia and Other Diplomatic Memories.* 2 vols. London and New York, 1923.) Cit. vol. II.

Budberg, Baron Alexei. "Dnevnik 1917 goda" (Diary of 1917). *Arkhiv Russkoi Revoliutsii,* vol. 12, Berlin, 1923, pp. 197-290.

Buisson, Etienne. *Les Bolcheviki (1917-1919).* Faits—Documents—Commentaires. Paris, 1919.

Bunyan, James and Fisher, H.H., eds. *The Bolshevik Revolution 1917-1918.*

Documents and Materials. Stanford, Calif., 1934 (Hoover Library Publications, no. 3) [2nd printing 1961].

*Burtsev, V.L. "Moi otvet Kerenskomu" (My Answer to Kerensky). *Obshchee Delo*, Paris [no date].

——. *V bor'be bol'shevikami i nemtsami* (The Struggle Against the Bolsheviks and the Germans). 2 vols. Paris, 1919.

Chaadaeva, O.N. "Kak burzhuaziia gotovilas' k Oktiabriu" (How the Bourgeoisie Prepared for October). *Krasnyi Arkhiv*, no. 21, 1927, pp. 218-220.

*Chebyshev. "Blizkaia dal' " (The Nearby Remoteness). *Vozrozhdenie*, Paris, Dec. 8, 1928.

*Cheremisov, V.A. "Pokhod Kerenskago na Petrograd" (Kerensky's Campaign Against Petrograd). *Golos Rossii*, Berlin, 1921.

*Chernov, V.M. "Chernyi peredel v 1918 godu" (The Black Partition in 1918). *Zapiski izucheniia Rossii*, vol. II.

——. *Rozhdenie revoliutsonnoi Rossii* (Fevral'skaia Revoliutsiia) (The Birth of Revolutionary Russia; the February Revolution). Paris and New York, 1934.

*Dan, F.I. "K istorii poslednikh dnei Vremennogo Pravitel'stva" (On the History of the Last Days of the Provisional Government). *Letopis' Revoliutsii*, no. 1, 1923, Berlin, pp. 161-176.

——. *Dva goda skitanii* (1919-1921) (Two Years of Wandering). Berlin 1922.

Degtiarev, L.S. "Oktiabr' Rumynskogo fronta" (October on the Rumanian Front). *Krasnaia Letopis'*, no. 6, 1923, pp. 207-278.

Demianov, A.S. "Moia sluzhba pri Vremennom Pravitel'stve" (My Service under the Provisional Government). *Arkhiv Russkoi Revoliutsii*, vol. 4, 2nd ed. Berlin, 1922, pp. 55-120.

——. "Zapiski o podpol'nom Vremennom Pravitel'stve" (Notes on the Underground Provisional Government). *Arkhiv Russkoi Revoliutsii*, vol. 7, Berlin, 1922, pp. 34-52.

Denikin, A.I. *Ocherki russkoi smuty* (Essays on the Russian Turmoil). 5 vols. Paris, 1921-1926. Cit. vol. I-II.

Domergue, Gabriel. *La Russie Rouge.* Paris, 1918.

Doroshenko, D.I. "Voina i revoliutsiia na Ukraine" (The War and the Revolution in the Ukraine). *Istorik i Sovremennik*, vol. 5, Berlin, 1924, pp. 73-125.

Drezen, A.K., ed. "Baltflot v iiul'skie dni 1917 goda" (The Baltic Fleet in the July Days of 1917; documents with an introduction by A. Drezen). *Krasnyi Arkhiv*, no. 46, 1931, pp. 70-109.

Dybenko, P.E. *Miatezhniki* (The Rebels). Moscow, 1923.

Elov, B. "Rol' petrogradskogo garnizona v oktiabr'skie dni" (The Role of the Petrograd Garrison in the October Days). *Krasnaia Letopis'*, no. 6, 1923, pp. 98-134.

Fleer, M. "Vremennoe Pravitel'stvo posle Oktiabria" (The Provisional Government after October). *Krasnyi Arkhiv,* no. 6, 1924. pp. 195-221.

Flerovskii, I. "Kronstadt v Oktiabr'skoi revoliutsii. Vospominaniia" (Kronstadt in the October Revolution; Recollections). *Proletarskaia Revoliutsiia,* vol. 10, 1922, pp. 130-150.

Fokke, D.G. "Na stsene i za kulisami Brestskoi tragikomedii" (On the Stage and Behind the Scenes of the Brest Tragicomedy). *Arkhiv Russkoi Revoliutsii,* vol. 20, Berlin, 1930, pp. 5-207.

Francis, David R. *Russia from the American Embassy, April 1916-November 1918.* New York, 1921.

Gessen, I.V. *V dvukh vekakh. Zhiznennyi otchet* (In Two Centuries. Account of a Life). Berlin, 1937.

Gippius, Zinaida N. *Siniaia kniga; peterburgskii dnevnik 1914-1918* (The Blue Book, a Petrograd Diary, 1914-1918). Belgrade, 1929.

God russkoi revoliutsii (1917-1918); sbornik statei (The Year of the Russian Revolution, 1917-1918; A Collection of Essays). Moscow, "Zemlia i volia," 1918.

Golovin, N.N. *Rossiiskaia kontrrevoliutsiia v 1917-1918 godakh* (Russian Counterrevolution in 1917-1918). 5 parts. Paris, 1937.

Gotz, A.R. "Rech' na moskovskom protsesse S.-R." (Speech for the Defense at the Moscow Trial of the Socialist-Revolutionaries). *Revoliutsionnaia Rossiia,* no. 21-22, Berlin and Prague.

Grekov, A.N. "Soiuz kazach'ikh voisk v Petrograde v 1917 godu" (The Union of the Cossack Troops in Petrograd in 1917). *Donskaia Letopis',* vol. 2, Vienna, 1923, pp. 229-283.

Grenard, Fernand. *La Révolution russe.* Paris, 1933.

*Grigoriev, G. "Oktiabr'skaia revoliutsiia v Belorussii" (October Revolution in Byelorussia). *Izvestiia,* 1929, no. 212.

*I.V. "General Dukhonin v Stavke" (General N. Dukhonin at General Headquarters). *Golos Minuvshego,* Moscow, 1918, no. 1-3.

Iakovlev, Ia.A., ed. *Krest'ianskoe dvizhenie v 1917 godu* (Peasant Movement in 1917). Moscow and Leningrad, 1927.

Iaroslavskii, E. "Bol'sheviki v Oktiabre" (The Bolsheviks in October). *Proletarskaia Revoliutsiia,* vol. 69, 1927, pp. 26-90.

*Ignat'ev, A. "V noch' na 25 oktiabria 1917 goda. Iz vospominanii soldata" (In the Night of October 25th; Reminiscences of a Soldier). *Krasnaia Letopis',* no. 6, 1923, pp. 313-314.

Ignatiev, V.I. *Nekotorye fakty i itogi chetyrekh let grazhdanskoi voiny (1917-1921)* (Some Facts and Results of the Four Years of the Civil War in 1917-1921). Moscow, 1922.

Ivanovich, St. [Portugeis, S.O.] *A.N. Potresov, Opyt kul'turno-psikhologicheskogo portreta* (A.N. Potresov, An Attempt at a Cultural-Psychological Portrait). Paris, 1938.

Izgoev, A.S. "Piat' let v sovetskoi Rossii" (Five Years in Soviet Russia). *Arkhiv Russkoi Revoliutsii,* vol. 10, Berlin, 1923, pp. 5-55.

Kakurin, E.N., comp. *Razlozhenie armii v 1917 godu* (Demoralization of the Russian Army in 1917). Ed by M.N. Pokrovsky and Ia. A. Iakovlev. Moscow, 1925.

*Karinskii, N.S. "Kto osvobodil bol'shevikov pered oktiabr'skim perevorotom" (Who Released the Bolsehviks Before the October Coup d'Etat). *Zeleny Zhurnal*, no. 10, 1924.

Kelson, Zigfried. "Militsiia Fevral'skoi revoliutsii" (The Militia of the February Revolution). *Byloe*, no. 30, Leningrad, 1025, pp. 151-175.

Kerensky, A.F. *Delo Kornilova* (The Kornilov Affair). Moscow, "Zadruga," 1918.

——. *L'Experience Kerenski*. Paris, 1936.

——. *Izdaleka, Sbornik statei 1920-1921* (From Afar; Collected Essays of 1920-1921). Paris, 1922.

——. *La Révolution Russe*. Paris, 1928.

Klimushkin, P. "Agrarnoe dvizhenie v 1917 godu" (The Agrarian Movement in 1917). *Volia Rossii*, Prague, 1925, VI, pp. 74-83.

Kolbin, I.N. *Kronshtadt v 1917 godu* (Kronstadt in 1917). Moscow, 1932.

Korenev, S.A. "Chrezvychainaia Komissiia po delam o byvshikh ministrakh" (The Extraordinary Commission on the Case of the Former Ministers). *Arkhiv Russkoi Revoliutsii*, vol. 7, Berlin, 1922, pp. 14-33.

Krasnov, P.N. "Na vnutrennem fronte" (On the Home Front). *Arkhiv Russkoi Revoliutsii*, vol. 1, Berlin, 1921, pp. 97-190. [Also: Leningrad, 1925.]

Krest'ianskoe dvizhenie v 1917 godu (The Peasant Movement in 1917). Kotel'nikov, K.G. and Meller, V.L., comp. and eds. Moscow and Leningrad, 1927. (Tsentrarkhiv. Arkhiv Oktiabr'skoi revoliutsii. 1917 god v dokumentakh i materialakh.)

Krol', L.A. *Za tri goda; vospominaniia, vpechatleniia, vstrechi* (Three Years: Reminiscences, Impressions, Encounters). Vladivostok, 1921.

Krylenko, N.V. *Za piat' let (1918-1922 gg.); obvinitel'nye rechi* (Five Years [1918-1922]. A Prosecutor's Indictments). Moscow, 1923.

Kudelli, P.F., ed. *Leningradskie rabochie v bor'be za vlast' sovetov, 1917* (The Leningrad Workers in the Struggle for Soviet Power in 1917). Leningrad, 1924.

*Kul'man, N.K. "Nakanune 25 oktiabria" (On the Eve of October 25). *Obshchee Delo*, Paris, 1921, no. 355.

*Kuskova, E.D. "Belletristicheskii pamflet" (A Political Pamphlet in Fictional Form). *Golos Rossii*, Berlin, Sept. 4, 1922.

* ——. "Noch' " (Night). *Vlast' Naroda*, Moscow, Oct. 28, 1917.

* ——. "Pis'ma iz Berlina" (Letters from Berlin). *Poslednie Novosti*, Paris, 1923, May 29.

Kvasha, G.I. *Ocherki russkoi revoliutsii* (Essays on the Russian Revolution). New York, 1919.

Larsons, M. [Maurice Laserson]. *Na sovetskoi sluzhbe* (In the Service of the Soviets). Paris, 1930.

Lelevich, G. "Oktiabr' v belogvardeiskom opisanii" (October as Described by the Whiteguardists). *Proletarskaia Revoliutsiia*, vol. 21, 1923, pp. 31-78.

Lenin, V.I. *Sochineniia* (Works), 2nd ed., 30 vols. Moscow, 1926-1932. Cit. vols. 21 and 22.

——. "O nashei Revoliutsii" (About our Revolution). *Pravda*, 1923, no. 117 [Also in *Sochineniia*, 2nd ed., vol. 27, 1930, pp. 398-400].

Leninism i Trotskism. Moscow. "Moskovskii Rabochii," 1924.

Leninskii sbornik (Lenin Symposium). vol. 4, ed. by L.B. Kamenev. Leningrad, 1925.

Lidak, O.A., ed. *Partiia i oktiabr'skoe vosstanie v Petrograde* (The Party and the October Uprising in Petrograd). Leningrad, 1933.

Liubimov, I.N. *Revoliutsiia 1917 goda. Khronika sobytii. Oktiabr'-Dekabr'* (Revolution of 1917. Chronicle of Events. October-December). Moscow and Leningrad, 1930. [vol. 6 of *Revoliutsiia 1917 goda. Khronika sobytii.*]

Lozinskii, Z. "Vremennoe Pravitel'stvo v 'bor'be' s promyshlennoi razrukhoi" (The Provisional Government in the 'Struggle' against the Disintegration of Industry). *Proletarskaia Revoliutsiia*, vol. 69, 1927, pp. 138-165.

*Lukomsky, G. "Poslednii den' Kerenskogo" (The Last Day of Kerensky). *Novosti Zhizni*, Harbin, 1923.

Maliantovich, P.N. "V Zimnem Dvortse 25-26 oktiabria 1917 goda; iz vospominanii" (In the Winter Palace on October 25-26, 1917; Reminiscences). *Byloe*, vol. 12, no. 6, Petrograd, 1918, pp. 111-141 [Also in: *Oktiabr'skoe vooruzhennoe vosstanie v Petrograde, vospominaniia . . .* (The October Armed Uprising in Petrograd. Reminiscences . . .). Ed. by S.P. Kniazev and A.P. Konstantinov. Leningrad, 1956. Appendix, pp. 398-423.]

Martynov, M., ed. "Agrarnoe dvizhenie v 1917 godu po dokumentam glavnogo zemel'nogo komiteta" (The Agrarian Movement in 1917, according to the Documents of the Main Land Committee). *Krasnyi Arkhiv*, vol. 14, 1926, pp. 182-226.

Martynov, V. "Ot Fevralia k Oktiabriu; glava iz istorii Baltiiskogo sudostroitel'nogo zavoda" (From February to October; a Chapter from the History of the Baltic Ship-building Yard). *Krasnaia Letopis'*, vol. 58, 1934, pp. 57-78.

Melgunov, S.P. *Rossiiskaia kontr-revoliutsiia. Metody i vyvody Gen. Golovina* (The Russian Counter-revolution. Methods and Conclusions of Gen. Golovin). Paris, 1938.

* ——. "S kem on? Otvet g. Chernovu" (Whom is He With? An Answer to Mr. Chernov). *Poslednie Novosti*, Paris, January 28 and May 8, 1925.

Militsyn, S.V. "Iz moei tetradi. Poslednie dni Preobrazhenskogo polka" (From My Note-book. The Last Days of the Preobrazhensky Regiment). *Arkhiv Russkoi Revoliutsii*, vol. 2, Berlin, 1921, pp. 170-193.

Miliukov, P.N. *Istoriia vtoroi russkoi revoliutsii* (History of the Second Russian Revolution). vol. I, part 3: *Agoniia vlasti* (Agony of the Provisional Government). Sofia, 1924.

——. *Rossiia na perelome; bol'shevistskii period russkoi revoliutsii* (Russia at the Turning Point; the Bolshevik Period of the Russian Revolution). vol. I, Paris, 1927.

Miliutin, B., ed. "Nakanune oktiabr'skogo perevorota. Vopros o voine i mire. —Otchety o sekretnykh zasedaniiakh Vremennogo Soveta Rossiiskoi Respubliki" (On the Eve of the October coup d'état; the Question of War and Peace; Reports of Secret Sessions of the Provisional Council of the Russian Republic). *Byloe*, vol. 12, no. 6, June 1918, pp. 3-41.

Mints, I.I., ed. *Dokumenty velikoi proletarskoi revoliutsii* (Documents of the Great Proletarian Revolution). Moscow, 1938.

"Moskovskaia Gorodskaia Duma posle Oktiabria" (The Moscow City Council after October). With a Preface by M. Vladimirskii, edited and annotated by I. Tobolin. *Krasnyi Arkhiv*, 1928, no. 27, pp. 58-109; no. 28, pp. 59-106.

Mstislavskii [Maslovskii], S.D. *Piat' dnei; nachalo i konets Fevral'skoi revoliutsii* (Five Days; the Beginning and the End of the February Revolution). Berlin, 1922.

Nabokov, V.D. "Vremennoe Pravitel'stvo" (The Provisional Government). *Arkhiv Russkoi Revoliutsii*, vol. 1, Berlin, 1921, pp. 9-96.

"Nakanune peremiriia" (On the Eve of the Truce; Documents). *Krasnyi Arkhiv*, no. 23, 1927, pp. 195-249.

Nazhivin, I.F. *Nakanune* (On the Eve). 1923 [no place indicated].

*Nevskii, V.I. "Istoricheskoe zasedanie nakanune oktiabr'skogo vosstaniia" (A Historic Meeting on the Eve of the October Uprising). *Byloe*, vol. 12, June 1918.

* ——. "V oktiabre" (In October). *Katorga i Ssylka*, vol. 96 [Also in: *Oktiabr'skoe vooruzhennoe vosstanie v Petrograde. Vospominaniia aktivnykh uchastnikov revoliutsii*] (The October Armed Uprising in Petrograd; Recollections of Active Participants). Ed. by S.P. Kniazev and A.P. Konstantinov. Leningrad, 1956, pp. 140-161.

Nevskii, V.I., and Belov. "Na drugoi den' posle vosstaniia. Dokumenty . . ." (The Day After the Uprising. Documents . . .). *Krasnaia Letopis'*, vol. 6, 1923, pp. 309-315.

Niessel, Henry Albert. *Le triomphe des bolcheviks et la paix de Brest-Litovsk. Souvenirs, 1917-1918*. Paris, 1940.

Nikitin, B.V. *Rokovye gody* (The Fatal Years). Paris, 1937.

Nol'de, Baron B.E. "V.D. Nabokov v 1917 godu" (V.D. Nabokov in 1917). *Arkhiv Russkoi Revoliutsii*. vol. 7, Berlin, 1922, pp. 5-13.

Noulens, Joseph. *Mon ambassade en Russie Soviétique, 1917-1919*. Paris, 1933.

Oberuchev, K.M. *V dni revoliutsii* (In the Days of the Revolution). New York, 1919.

"Oktiabr' na fronte" (October at the Front). *Krasnyi Arkhiv*, 1927, no. 23, pp. 149-194; no. 24, pp. 71-107.

Oktiabr'skaia revoliutsiia pered sudom amerikanskikh senatorov. Ofitsial'nyi otchet "Overmanskoi komissii" Senata (October Revolution on Trial Before the American Senators: The Official Report of the "Overman Committee" of the Senate [1919]). Trans. by V. Vel'sky. Moscow and Leningrad, 1927.

"Oktiabr'skii perevorot (vospominaniia uchastnikov)" (The October Revolution; Reminiscences of Participants). *Proletarskaia Revoliutsiia*, vol. 10, 1922.

Oktiabr'skii perevorot. Fakty i dokumenty (The October Revolution. Facts and Documents). Compiled by A.A. Popov. Ed. by N.A. Rozhkov. Petrograd, 1918.

Oldenbourg, S.S. *Le coup d'état bolcheviste, 20 octobre – 3 decembre 1917, recueil des documents relatifs a la prise du pouvior par les bolchevistes* (The Bolshevik coup d'état, October 20-December 3, 1917; a Collection of Documents Concerning the Bolshevik Seizure of Power). Paris, 1929.

Palchinskii, P.I. "Poslednie chasy Vremennogo Pravitel'stva v 1917 g." (Last Hours of the Provisional Government in 1917; notes). *Krasnyi Arkhiv*, no. 56, 1933, pp. 196-198.

*Peshekhonov, A.V. "Bor'ba s bol'shevikami i bol'shevismom" (The Struggle Against the Bolsheviks and Bolshevism). *Narodnoe Slovo*, Petrograd, 1917, no. 124.

Piontkovskii, S.A. *Oktiabr'skaia revoliutsiia v Rossii; ee predposylki i khod* (The October Revolution in Russia; Its Background and Course). Moscow, 1923.

——. "Voenno-revoliutsionnyi komitet v oktiabr'skie dni" (The Military-Revolutionary Committee in the Days of October). *Proletarskaia Revoliutsiia*, vol. 69, 1927, pp. 110-137.

"Podgotovka k nastupleniiu na Petrograd" (Preparations for the Offensive Against Petrograd). *Krasnyi Arkhiv*, no. 24, 1927, pp. 201-108.

Podvoiskii, N.I. *Krasnaia gvardiia v oktiabr'skie dni* (The Red Guards in the Days of October). Moscow, 1927.

——. "Voennaia organizatsiia Ts. K.R.S.-D.R.P. (bol'shevikov) i Voenno-Revoliutsionnyi Komitet v 1917 g." (Military Organization of the Central Committee of the Russian Social-Democratic Labor Party [Bolsheviks] and the Military-Revolutionary Committee in 1917). *Krasnaia Letopis'*, 1923, no. 6, pp. 64-97; no. 8, pp. 7-43.

Pokrovsky, M.N. "Bol'sheviki i front v oktiabre-noiabre 1917 goda" ("The Bolsheviks and the Front in October-November, 1917). *Krasnaia Nov'*, Moscow-Leningrad, 1927, vol. 11 (November), pp. 157-170.

Polianskii, V. "Razgovor Lenina s Kronshtadtom po priamomu provodu" (Lenin's Conversation by Direct Wire with Kronstadt [in October 1917]). *Proletarskaia Revoliutsiia*, vol. 10, 1922, pp. 455-459.

Polovtsov, P.A. *Dni zatmeniia* (The Days of Eclipse). Paris, 1927.

*"Poslednii den' Pravitel'stvuiushchego Senata" (The Last Day of the Governing Senate). *Za Svobodu*, Warsaw, Sept. 28, 1927.

*Prokopovich, S.N. "Pis'mo v redaktsiiu" (Letter to the Editor). *Rul'*, Berlin, Aug. 18, 1922.

"Protokoly Peterburgskogo komiteta R.S.-D.R.P. (b) za 1917 god" (Minutes of the Petrograd Committee of the Russian Social-Democratic Labor Party [Bolsheviks] for 1917). *Krasnaia Letopis'* 1923, no. 6, pp. 373-432.

"Protokoly Tsentral'nogo Komiteta R.S.-D.R.P.(b), Sentriabr'-Oktiabr' 1917 goda" (Minutes of the Central Committee of the R.S.-D.L.P.[B]; September-October, 1917). *Proletarskaia Revoliutsiia*, vol. 69, 1927, pp. 246-298.

Protokoly Tsentral'nogo Komiteta R.S.-D.R.P.(b), avgust 1917-fevral' 1918 (Minutes of the Central Committee of the R.S.-D.L.P. [Bolsheviks], August 1917-February 1918). M.A. Savel'ev, ed., Moscow, 1929.

Protsess es-erov. Vypusk II. Rechi zashchitnikov i obviniaemykh. (The Trial of the Socialist Revolutionaries. Issue 2. Speeches for the Defense and Speeches of the Defendants). Moscow. 1922.

Rabinovich, S.E. *Bor'ba za armiiu v 1917 godu* (Struggle for the Army in 1917). Moscow, 1930.

Rafes, M.G. *Dva goda revoliutsii na Ukraine (evoliutsiia i raskol "Bunda")* (Two Years of Revolution in the Ukraine; Evolution and Split of the "Bund"). Moscow, 1920.

Rakh'ia, E. "Poslednee podpol'e Vladimira Il'icha" (Lenin's Last Underground Hideout). *Krasnaia Letopis'*, no. 58, 1934, pp. 79-90.

Rapoport, Iu.K. "Cherez 20 let" (After Twenty Years). *Novyi Grad*, vol. 13, Paris, 1938, pp. 127-239.

Raskol'nikov, F.F. *Kronshtadt i Piter v 1917 godu* (Kronstadt and Petrograd in 1917). Moscow, 1925.

——. "Oktiabr'skaia revoliutsiia" (The October Revolution). *Proletarskaia Revoliutsiia*, vol. 33, 1924, pp. 33-72.

Reed, John, *Desiat' dnei, kotorye potriasli mir* (Russian translation of: *Ten Days That Shook the World*). Moscow, 1918. (2nd ed., with Lenin's preface, Moscow, 1924.)

Rengarten, I.I. "Oktiabr'skaia revoliutsiia v Baltiiskom flote" (Iz dnevnika I.I. Rengartena) (The October Revolution in the Baltic Fleet; From the Diary of Captain I.I. Rengarten). *Krasnyi Arkhiv*, no. 25, 1927, pp. 34-95.

Riabinskii, K. *Revoliutsiia 1917 goda. Khronika sobytii. Oktiabr'* (The Revolution of 1917; Chronicle of Events. October). Moscow and Leningrad, 1926. (vol. 5 of *Revoliutsiia 1917 goda. Khronika sobytii.*)

*Rudnev, V.V. *Pri vechernikh ogniakh* (By the Evening Lights). 1928.

Sadoul, Jacques, *Notes sur la revolution Bolchevique, octobre 1917-janvier 1919*. Paris, 1919.

——. *Notes sur la revolution Bolchevique; quarante lettres de Jacques Sadoul*. Paris, 1922. [Many editions followed.]

Savinkov, B.V. *Bor'ba s bol'shevikami* (The Struggle Against the Bolsheviks). Warsaw, 1920.

* ——. "K vystupleniiu bol'shevikov" (Concerning the Bolsheviks' Action). *Russkiie Vedomosti*, Moscow, 1917, no. 255.

Semenov, G. (Vasiliev). *Voennaia i boevaia rabota partii Sotsialistov-Revoliutsionerov v 1917-1918 gg.* (Military and Fighting Activity of the Party of the Socialist Revolutionaries in 1917-1918). Berlin, 1922.

Shidlovskii, S.I. *Vospominaniia* (Reminiscences). Part 2. Berlin, 1923.

Shklovskii, V. *Revoliutsiia i front* (The Revolution and the Front). Petrograd, 1921.

Shliapnikov, A.G. "K Oktiabriu" (Toward October). *Proletarskaia Revoliutsiia*, vol. 10, 1922, pp. 3-42.

——. "Oktiabr'skii perevorot i Stavka" (The October Revolution and the General Headquarters). *Krasnyi Arkhiv*, 1925, no. 8, pp. 153-175; no. 9, pp. 156-170.

*Simanskii, P.N. "U sten Kremlia" (At the Kremlin's Walls). *Za Svobodu*, Warsaw, 1927, no. 256.

Sinegub, Alexander. "Zashchita Zimniago Dvortsa (25 Oktiabria-7 Noiabria 1917 g.)" (Defense of the Winter Palace, October 25-November 7, 1917). *Arkhiv Russkoi Revoliutsii*, vol. 4, 2nd ed., Berlin, 1922, pp. 121-197.

Smirnov, A.M. "Kratkie zametki iz zhizni samokatchikov 3-go batal'ona v oktiabr'kie dni 1917 goda" (Short Notes from the Life of the Third Cyclist Battalion in the October Days of 1917). *Krasnaia Letopis'*, no. 2-3, 1922, pp. 155-157.

*Smirnov, S. "Konets Vremennogo Pravitel'stva" (The End of the Provisional Government). *Rul'*, Berlin, Dec. 20, 1923.

Sokolov, Boris. "Zashchita Vserossiiskago Uchreditel'nago Sobraniia" (Defense of the All-Russian Constituent Assembly). *Arkhiv Russkoi Revoliutsii*, vol. 13, Berlin, 1924, pp. 5-70.

Sokolov, N.A. *Ubiistvo tsarskoi sem'i* (Murder of the Tsar's Family). Berlin, 1925.

Solomon, G.A. *Sredi krasnykh vozhdei; lichno perezhitoe i vidennoe na sovetskoi sluzhbe* (Among the Red Leaders; Personal Experiences and Observations in the Soviet Service). Paris, 1930.

Solov'ev, A. "Iunkerskoe vosstanie v Petrograde" (The Uprising of the Military Cadets in Petrograd). *Proletarskaia Revoliutsiia*, vol. 56, 1926, pp. 259-263.

Stankevich, V.B. *Vospominaniia 1914-1919 gg.* (Memoirs of 1914-1919). Berlin, 1920.

"Stavka 25-26 oktiabria 1917 goda" (General Headquarters on October 25-26, 1917). *Arkhiv Russkoi Revoliutsii*, vol. 7, Berlin, 1922, pp. 279-320.

*Struve, P.B. "Dukh belago dvizheniia" (Spirit of the White Movement). *Vozrozhdenie*, Paris, Nov. 16, 1930.

Sukhanov, N.N. *Zapiski o revoliutsii* (Notes on the Revolution). 7 vols. Berlin, 1922-1923.

Tobolin, Iv. "Zagovor monarkhicheskoi organizatsii V.M. Purishkevicha" (The Conspiracy of V.M. Purishkevich's Monarchist Organization). *Krasnyi Arkhiv*, no. 26, 1928, pp. 169-185.

Trotsky, L.D. *Istoriia russkoi revoliutsii* (History of the Russian Revolution). 3 vols. Berlin, 1931-1933. Cit. vol. 3: *Oktiabr'skaia revoliutsiia* (The October Revolution).

——. *Sochineniia (Works)*. vol. III, part 1-2. Moscow, 1925.

——. *Moia zhizn'. Opyt avtobiografii* (My Life; an Attempt at an Autobiography). Part 2. Berlin, 1930.

——. *O Lenine, materialy dlia biografii* (About Lenin; Materials for a Biography). Moscow, 1924.

Uralov, S. "Stranichka Oktiabria" (An October Page). *Proletarskaia Revoliutsiia*, vol. 33, 1924, pp. 274-279.

V dni velikoi proletarskoi revoliutsii. Epizody bor'by v Petrograde v 1917 godu (In the Days of the Great Proletarian Revolution. Episodes of Struggle in Petrograd in 1917). Moscow, 1937.

Veiger-Redemeister, V.A. "S Kerenskim v Gatchine" (In Gatchina with Kerensky). *Proletarskaia Revoliutsiia*, vol. 21, 1923, pp. 76-95.

Verkhovskii, A. I. *Rossiia na Golgofe* (Russia on Calvary). Petrograd, 1918.

Vertsinskii, E.A. *God revoliutsii* (A Year of Revolution). Tallinn, 1929.

*Vinaver, M.M. "V te dni" (In Those Days). *Poslednie Novosti*, Paris, no. 478.

*Vinberg, F.V. *V plenu u obez'ian* (In the Captivity of Apes). 1918.

Vishniak, M.V. *Vserossiiskoe Uchreditel'noe Sobranie* (The All-Russian Constituent Assembly). Paris, 1932.

Vladimirova, Vera. *God sluzhby "sotsialistov" kapitalistam. Ocherki po istorii kontr-revoliutsii v 1918 godu* (One Year of Service of the "Socialists" to the Capitalists. Essays on the History of the Counterrevolution in 1918). Moscow, 1927.

Vompe, P. *Dni oktiabr'skoi revoliutsii i zheleznodorozhniki* (The Days of the October Revolution and the Railroad Workers). Moscow, 1924.

Vrangel', Baron P.N. "Zapiski" (Memoirs). vol. 1-2. *Beloe Delo*, vol. 5-6, Berlin, 1928.

Vtoroi Vserossiiskii S'ezd Sovetov Rabochikh i Soldatskikh Deputatov (The Second All-Russian Congress of the Soviets of Workers' and Soldiers' Deputies). Edited by K.G. Kotel'nikov, M.N. Pokrovsky and Ia.A. Iakovlev. Moscow-Leningrad, 1928.

Vyrubova (Taneeva), Anna. *Stranitsy iz moei zhizni* (Pages from My Life). Berlin, 1923.

*Vyshgorodskii. "Poslednii prokuror Petrogradskoi sudebnoi palaty" (The Last State Attorney of the Petrograd Regional Court). *Segodnia*, Riga, March, 11, 1926.

Zenzinov, V.M. *Iz zhizni revoliutsionera* (From the Life of a Revolutionary). Paris, 1919.

*Zhdan-Pushkin. "24-25 oktiabria v Peterburge" (October 24-25 in Petrograd). *Vlast' Naroda*, Moscow, Oct. 28, 1917.

Zinov'ev, G.S. *Sochineniia. Tom VII. God Revoliutsii. Fevral' 1917 g.-fevral' 1918 g.* (Works. vol. 7. The Year of the Revolution. February 1917-February 1918). Leningrad, 1925.

SUPPLEMENTARY BIBLIOGRAPHY

Abramovitch, Raphael R. *The Soviet Revolution 1917-1939.* New York, 1962.

Anin, D. *Revoliutsiia 1917 goda glazami ee rukovoditelei* (The Revolution of 1917 through the Eyes of its Leaders). Roma, Edizioni Aurora, 1971.

Aronson, Gregory. *Rossiia v epokhu revoliutsii. Istoricheskie etiudy i memuary* (Russia in the Era of the Revolution. Historical Essays and Memoirs). New York, 1966.

Berezkin, A.V. *Oktiabr'skaia revoliutsiia i S.Sh.A., 1917-1922 gg.* (The October Revolution and the U.S.A., 1917-1922). Moscow, 1967.

Bol'shevistskie Voenno-Revoliutsionnye komitety (The Bolshevik Military-Revolutionary Committees. Documents). Moscow, 1958.

Browder, Robert P., and Kerensky, A.F., eds. *The Russian Provisional Government 1917: Selected Documents.* 3 vols. Stanford, Calif. 1961.

Buchanan, Sir George. *My Mission to Russia and Other Diplomatic Memories.* vol. II. London and New York, 1923.

Buchanan, Meriel. *The City of Trouble* [Petrograd during the War and Revolution]. New York, 1918.

Carmichael, Joel. *A Short History of the Russian Revolution.* New York, 1964.

Carr, Edward H. *A History of Soviet Russia. The Bolshevik Revolution 1917-1923.* 3 vols. New York, 1951-1953.

Chamberlin, William H. *The Russian Revolution 1917-1921.* 2 vols. New York, 1935. Reprinted: 1957. [Bibliography in vol. 2, pp. 505-523.]

Chernov, Victor M. *The Great Russian Revolution.* Trans. and abridged by Philip E. Mosely [from *Rozhdenie revoliutsionnoi Rossii*]. New Haven, Conn. 1936.

Daniels, Robert V. *Red October. The Bolshevik Revolution of 1917.* New York, 1967. (Includes an extensive bibliography.)

Daniels, Robert, ed. *A Documentary History of Communism.* New York, 1960.

Denikin, A.I. *The Russian Turmoil; Memoirs: Military, Social and Political* [abridged from *Ocherki russkoi smuty*]. London, 1922.

Deutscher, Isaac. *The Prophet Armed: Trotsky 1879-1921.* London, 1954.

Eremeev, K.S. "Osada Zimnego dvortsa" (Siege of the Winter Palace) in: *Petrograd v dni Velikogo Oktiabria* (Petrograd in the Days of the Great October), ed. by V.E. Mushtukov. Leningrad, 1967, pp. 381-401.

Erykalov, E.F. *Oktiabr'skoe vooruzhennoe vosstanie v Petrograde* (The October Armed Uprising in Petrograd). Leningrad, 1966.

Fainsod, Merle. *International Socialism and the World War.* Cambridge, Mass., 1935.

Fisher, Harold H. *The Communist Revolution. An Outline of Strategy and Tactics.* Stanford, Calif., 1955.

Gankin, Olga H. and Fisher, H.H., eds. *The Bolsheviks and the World War; the Origins of the Third International* [Documents]. Stanford, Calif., 1940.

Golder, Frank A., ed. *Documents of Russian History 1914-1917*. Trans. by E. Aronsberg. Gloucester, Mass., 1964 (Reprinted from the edition of 1927).

Gorodetskii, E.N. *Rozhdenie Sovetskogo gosudarstva, 1917-1918 gg.* (Origins of the Soviet State, 1917-1918). Moscow, 1965.

Gruber, Helmut. *International Communism in the Era of Lenin: A Documentary History*. Ithaca, N.Y., 1967.

Iakovlev, Ia. "Voprosy II Vserossiiskogo S"ezda Sovetov" (Questions concerning the Second All-Russian Congress of Soviets). *Proletarskaia Revoliutsiia*, vol. 71, 1927, pp. 53-91.

Katkov, George. *Russia 1917. The February Revolution*. New York, 1967.

Kennan, George F. *Soviet-American Relations, 1917-1920. vol. I. Russia Leaves the War. vol. II. Decision to Intervene*. Princeton, N.J., 1956-1958.

Kerensky, Alexander F. *The Catastrophe. Kerensky's Own Story of the Russian Revolution*. New York and London, 1927.

———. *The Crucifixion of Liberty*. Trans. by G. Kerensky. New York, 1934.

———. *Russia and History's Turning Point*. New York, 1965.

Khaustov, F. "V oktiabre" (In October). *Krasnaia Letopis'*, no. 53, 1933, pp. 188-195.

Knox, Sir Alfred. *With the Russian Army 1914-1917 (Being Chiefly Extracts from the Diary of a Military Attaché)*. 2 vols. London, 1921.

Kommunisticheskaia partiia Sovetskogo Soiuza v rezoliutsiiakh i resheniiakh s"ezdov, konferentsii i plenumov Ts.K. (The Communist Party of the Soviet Union in Resolutions and Decisions of its Congresses, Conferences and Plenums of the Central Committee). Part I, 1898-1924. 7th ed. Moscow, 1954.

Krasnaia Letopis' (Red Chronicles). *Iubileinyi sbornik k 15-letiiu Oktiabria* (A Symposium on the Occasion of the 15th Anniversary of October). *Krasnaia Letopis'*, no. 50-51, 1932.

Latsis (Sudrabs), M.Ia. *Chrezvychainaia Komissiia po bor'be s kontr-revoliutsiei* (The Extraordinary Commission for Struggle Against the Counterrevolution). Moscow, 1921.

———. *Dva goda bor'by na vnutrennem fronte. Obzor dvukhgodichnoi deiatel'nosti Chrezvychainoi Komissii po bor'be s kontr-revoliutsiei, spekuliatsiei i prestupleniiami po dolzhnosti* (Two Years of Struggle on the Home Front; Survey of Che-Ka Activities). Moscow, 1920.

Lenin, V.I. *Sochineniia* (Works). 2nd ed., 30 vols. Moscow, 1926-1932. The works of the first year of the Revolution are contained in vol. 20-22. The 2nd edition contains detailed annotations and many informative appendices which were "amended" or deleted in subsequent editions.

———. *Polnoe sobranie sochinenii* (Complete Collection of Works). 5th ed. 55 vols. Moscow, 1960-1968. vol. 31: March-April 1917; vol. 32: May-July 1917; vol. 34: July-October 24, 1917; vol. 35: October 25, 1917-March 1918.

———. *Collected Works*. Moscow: Foreign Languages Publishing House, 1960. vol. 24: April-June 1917; vol. 25: June-September 1917; vol. 26: September 1917-February 1918.

———. *Selected Works in Twelve Volumes.* Ed. by A. Fineberg. International Publishers: Moscow and New York, 1935. *Vol. VI: From the Bourgeois Revolution to the Proletarian Revolution (1917).*

———. *Selected Works in Three Volumes.* Moscow, 1960-1961. Works of 1917 are contained in the 2nd volume.

Lenin. The Man, the Theorist, the Leader. A Reappraisal. Ed. by Leonard Schapiro and Peter Reddaway. New York and London, 1967. (This book of essays is cited as a guide to the voluminous and very uneven literature about Lenin).

McNeal, Robert H., ed. *The Russian Revolution. Why Did the Bolsheviks Win?* New York, 1960. (A symposium of interpretations).

Melgunov, S.P. *Krasnyi terror v Rossii, 1918-1923 (The Red Terror in Russia).* Berlin, 1924.

———. *The Red Terror in Russia.* London and Toronto, 1925; reprinted 1926.

———. *Zolotoi nemetskii kliuch k bol'shevitskoi revoliutsii* (The German "Golden Key" to the Bolshevik Revolution). Paris, 1940.

Mints, I.I. *Istoriia velikogo oktiabria. Tom 2. Sverzhenie Vremennogo Pravitel'stva; ustanovlenie diktatury proletariata* (History of the Great October. Vol. 2. The Overthrow of the Provisional Government; The Establishment of the Dictatorship of the Proletariat). Moscow, 1968.

Mints, I.I., ed. *Lenin i oktiabr'skoe vooruzhennoe vosstanie v Petrograde. Materialy vsesiouznoi nauchnoi sessii 13-16 noiabria 1962 g. v Leningrade* (Lenin and the October Armed Uprising in Petrograd. Materials of the Soviet Historical Conference in Leningrad, November 13-16, 1962). Moscow, 1964.

Mohrenschildt, Dimitri von, ed. *The Russian Revolution of 1917. Contemporary Accounts.* New York, 1971.

Moorehead, Alan. *The Russian Revolution.* New York, 1958.

Muratov, Kh.I. *Revoliutsionnoe dvizhenie v russkoi armii v 1917 godu* (The Revolutionary Movement in the Russian Army in 1917). Moscow, 1958.

Nevskii, V.I. "Istoricheskoe zasedanie Peterburgskogo komiteta R.S.-D.R.P. (bol'shevikov) nakanune oktiabr'skogo vosstaniia" (Historical Meeting of the Petrograd Committee of the Russian Social-Democratic Labor Party [Bolsheviks] on the Eve of the October Uprising). *Krasnaia Letopis',* no. 2-3, 1922, pp. 316-332.

Nikitin, B.V. *The Fatal Years.* London, 1938.

Oktiabr' na fronte; vospominaniia (October on the Front; Reminiscences). Comp. and ed. by P.A. Golub. Moscow, 1967.

Oktiabr'skoe vooruzhennoe vosstanie v Petrograde. Dokumenty i materialy (The October Armed Uprising in Petrograd. Documents and Materials, Sept. 12-Nov. 1, 1917). Comp. by I.A. Bulygin et al. Ed. by G.N. Golikov et al. Moscow, 1957.

Oktiabr'skoe vooruzhennoe vosstanie. Semnadtsatyi god v Petrograde. Kniga I. Na putiakh k sotsialisticheskoi revoliutsii. Dvoevlastie. Kniga II. Vooruzhennoe vosstanie. Pobeda sotsialisticheskoi revoliutsii (The October Armed Uprising. 1917 in Petrograd. Book I. On the Road toward the

Socialist Revolution. Duality of Power; Book II. Armed Uprising. Victory of the Socialist Revolution). Ed. by A.L. Fraiman et al. Leningrad, 1967.

Oktiabr'skoe vooruzhennoe vosstanie v Petrograde; vospominaniia aktivnykh uchastnikov revoliutsii (The October Armed Uprising in Petrograd; Reminiscences of Active Participants in the Revolution). Comp. and ed. by S.P. Kniazev and A.P. Konstantinov. Leningrad, 1956.

Page, Stanley W. *Lenin and World Revolution.* New York, 1959.

Pethybridge, Roger, ed. *Witnesses to the Russian Revolution.* London, 1964.

Petrograd v dni velikogo Oktiabria. Vospominaniia uchastnikov revoliutsionnykh sobytii v Petrograde v 1917 godu. (Petrograd in the Days of the Great October. Reminiscences of Participants in the Revolutionary Events in Petrograd in 1917). Comp. by I.S. Sazonov and Iu.S. Kulishev. Ed. by B.E. Mushtukov. Leningrad, 1967.

Petrogradskii Voenno-Revoliutsionnyi komitet. Dokumenty i materialy v trekh tomakh. (The Petrograd Military Revolutionary Committee. Documents and Materials in Three Volumes: vol. I, Sept. 12-Nov. 2, 1917; vol. II, Nov. 3-14; vol. III, Nov. 15-Dec. 14, 1917). Ed. by D.A. Chugaev et al. Moscow, 1966-1967.

Pipes, Richard, ed. *Revolutionary Russia. The Conference on the Russian Revolution, April 1967.* Cambridge, Mass., 1968.

Plekhanov, G.V. *God na rodine. Polnoe sobranie statei i rechei 1917-1918 v dvukh tomakh* (One Year in the Homeland: A Full Collection of Articles and Speeches of 1917-1918, in Two Volumes). Paris, 1921.

Potekhin, M.N. *Pervyi Sovet proletarskoi diktatury* (The First [Petrograd] Soviet of the Proletarian Dictatorship). Leningrad, 1966. [Bibliography includes a list of pertinent materials and documents published since 1917, pp. 307-309.]

Proletarskaia Revoliutsiia, vol. 10, 1922: *Stat'i i vospominaniia* (Articles and Memoirs on the October Revolution).

Protokoly Tsentral'nogo Komiteta R.S.-D.R.P.(b). Avgust 1917-Fevral' 1918 (The Minutes of the Central Committee of the Russian Social-Democratic Labor Party [Bolsheviks], Aug. 1917- Feb. 1918). Moscow, 1958.

Pushkarev, S.G. "Oktiabr'skii perevorot 1917 goda bez legend" (The October Coup D'etat without Legends). *Novyi Zhurnal*, vol. 89, New York, 1967, pp. 146-169.

Radkey, Oliver H. *The Agrarian Foes of Bolshevism. Promise and Default of the Russian Socialist Revolutionaries February to October 1917.* New York, 1958.

———. *The Election to the Russian Constituent Assembly of 1917.* Cambridge, Mass., 1950.

———. *The Sickle Under the Hammer. The Russian Socialist Revolutionaries in the Early Months of Soviet Rule.* New York and London, 1963.

Reed, John. *Ten Days that Shook the World.* With a Foreword by V.I. Lenin. Notes by Bertram D. Wolfe. New York, 1960 (First published in 1919).

S"ezdy Sovetov R.S.F.S.R. Sbornik dokumentov 1917-1922 (The Congresses of the Soviets of the Russian Socialist Federative Soviet Republic; A Collection of Documents, 1917-1922). vol. I. Moscow, 1959.

Shestakov, A.V. *Ocherki po sel'skomu khoziaistvu i krest'ianskomu dvizheniiu v gody voiny i pered oktiabrem 1917 goda* (Essays on Agriculture and on the Peasant Movement During World War I and Before October 1917). Leningrad, 1927.

Shestov, N.S., et al., eds. *V bor'be za pobedu Oktiabria. Sbornik statei* (In the Struggle for the Victory of October: A Collection of Essays.) Moscow, 1957.

Sobolev, P.N., ed. *Istoriia velikoi Oktiabr'skoi sotsialisticheskoi Revoliutsii* (A History of the Great October Socialist Revolution). Moscow, 1967. 1st ed. 1962.

Sorokin, Pitirim. *Leaves from a Russian Diary.* New York, 1924.

Spreslis, A.I. *Latyshskie strelki na strazhe zavoevanii Oktiabria 1917-1918* (The Latvian Rifles Guarding the Achievements of October in 1917-1918). Riga, 1967.

Sukhanov, N.N. *The Russian Revolution 1917, a Personal Record.* Edited, abridged and translated by Joel Carmichael from *Zapiski o Revoliutsii.* London and New York, 1955.

Trotsky, L.D. *The History of the Russian Revolution. 3 vols. vol. III. The Triumph of the Soviets.* Translated from the Russian by Max Eastman. New York, 1932. Reprinted: Ann Arbor: U. of Michigan Press, 1957.

——. *The Russian Revolution; the Overthrow of Tsarism and the Triumph of the Soviets.* Selected and edited by F.W. Dupee from the *History of the Russian Revolution;* translated from the Russian by Max Eastman. Garden City, N.Y. 1959.

——. *My Life, an Attempt at an Autobiography.* New York, 1930. Reprinted: New York, 1970.

——. *Lenin.* New York, 1925. Reprinted: New York, 1970.

Tschebotarioff, Gregory P. *Russia, My Native Land.* New York and London, 1964.

Tseretelli, I.G. *Rechi* (Speeches) [March-September 1917]. With a preface by St. Ivanovich. Petrograd, 1917.

——. *Vospominaniia o Fevral'skoi Revoliutsii* (Memoirs on the February Revolution). 2 vols. Paris—La Haye: Mouton Co., 1963. Appendix. "Prichiny porazheniia demokrattii" (Causes of the Defeat of Democracy), vol. II, pp. 401-417.

Tyrkova-Williams, Ariadna. *From Liberty to Brest-Litovsk. The First Year of the Russian Revolution.* London, 1919.

Velikaia Oktiabr'skaia Sotsialisticheskaia Revoliutsiia. Dokumenty i materialy. Revoliutsionnoe dvizhenie v Rossii nakanune oktiabr'skogo vooruzhennogo vosstaniia (1-24 oktiabria 1917 g.). (The Great October Socialist Revolution. Documents and Materials. The Revolutionary Movement in Russia on the Eve of the October Armed Uprising). Ed. D.A. Chugaev et al. Moscow, 1962.

Velikaia Oktiabr'skaia Sotsialiticheskaia Revoliutsiia. Khronika sobytii. V chetyrekh tomakh (The Great October Socialist Revolution. The Chronicle of Events). Moscow, 1957-1961. vol. I. Feb. 27 - May 6, 1917. Ed. N. Golikov et al.; vol. II. May 7-July 25. Ed. P.N. Sobolev et al.; vol. III. July 26-Sept. 11. Ed. I.G. Dykov et al.; vol. IV. Sept. 12-Oct. 25. Ed. I.G. Dykov et al.

Velikii Oktiabr'. Letopis' vazhneishikh sobytii (The Great October. The Chronicle of the Most Important Events). Comp. by L.M. Gavrilov and V.V. Kutuzov. Ed. by S. Bubenshchikov. Moscow, 1967.

Velikii Oktiabr'. Sbornik dokumentov (The Great October. A collection of Documents) [February 27-November 5, 1917]. Ed. by L.S. Gaponenko. Moscow, 1961.

Vernadsky, George. *The Russian Revolution 1917-1931.* New York, 1932.

Vospominaniia [Memoirs on the October Revolution: three articles, 29 pieces of reminiscences, and two pieces of documentary material]. *Krasnaia Letopis'*, no. 6, 1923.

Vrangel, P.N., baron. *The Memoirs of General Wrangel, the Last Commander-in-Chief of the Russian National Army.* Trans. by Sophie Goulston. London, 1929.

——. *Always with Honor* (Memoirs of General Wrangel, translation of *Zapiski*). With a foreword by Herbert Hoover. New York, 1957.

Vtoroi Vserossiiskii S"ezd Sovetov rabochikh i soldatskikh deputatov. Sbornik dokumentov (The Second All-Russian Congress of the Workers' and Soldiers' Deputies [Oct. 25-26, 1917]; Collection of Documents). Comp. by P.I. Anisimova and L.I. Terent'eva. Ed. by A.F. Butenko and D.A. Chugaev. Moscow, 1957.

Vyrubova (Taneeva), Anna. *Memoirs of the Russian Court.* New York, 1923.

Warth, Robert D. *The Allies and the Russian Revolution. From the Fall of the Monarchy to the Peace of Brest-Litovsk.* Durham, N.C., 1954. (Includes an extensive bibliography.)

Woytinsky, W.S. *Stormy Passage: A Personal History Through Two Russian Revolutions to Democracy and Freedom, 1905-1960.* New York, 1961.

Wrangel, P.N. see Vrangel, P.N.

Zeman, Z.A.B., ed. *Germany and the Revolution in Russia 1915-1918. Documents from the Archives of the German Foreign Ministry.* London, 1958.

BIBLIOGRAPHIES

Bibliografiia russkoi revoliutsii i grazhdanskoi voiny (1917-1921). Russkii zagranichnyi istoricheskii arkhiv v Prage (Bibliography of the Russian Revolution and the Civil War, 1917-1921. Russian Historical Archives in Prague). Comp. by S.P. Postnikov, ed. Jan Slavik, Prague, 1938.

Daniels, Robert D. "Soviet Historians Prepare for the Fiftieth." *Slavic Review*, vol. XXVI, no. 1, 1967, pp. 113-118.

Danishevskii, S.L. *Opyt bibliografii Oktiabr'skoi revoliutsii* (Attempt at a Bibliography of the October Revolution). Ed. by S. Piontkovskii. Moscow and Leningrad, 1926.

Dobranitskii, M. *Sistematicheskii ukazatel' literatury po istorii Russkoi Revoliutsii* (A Systematic Guide to the Literature on the History of the Russian Revolution). Moscow, 1926.

Gorodetskii, E.N., ed. *Velikaia Oktiabr'skaia Sotsialisticheskaia Revoliutsiia. Bibliograficheskii ukzatel' dokumental'nykh publikatsii* (The Great October Socialist Revolution. A Bibliographic Guide to Documentary Publications). Moscow, 1961.

Grierson, Philip. *Books on Soviet Russia 1917-1942. A Bibliography and a Guide to Reading*. London, 1943.

Karpovich, Michael. "The Russian Revolution of 1917. Bibliographical Article." *The Journal of Modern History*, vol. II, no. 2, June 1930, pp. 258-280.

Krasnaia Letopis, no. 50-51, 1932, pp. 300-309: "Bibliografiia. Oktiabr'-skaia Revoliutsiia v Petrograde (Spisok osnovnoi literatury)" (October Revolution in Petrograd; a List of Basic Literature). Comp. by M.I. Akun and V.A. Petrov.

Krasnaia Letopis, no. 53, 1933, pp. 211-228: "Ukazatel statei po istorii partiinoi organizatsii i revoliutsionnogo dvizheniia na fabrikakh i zavodakh Leningrada, pomeshchennykh v 'Krasnoi Letopisi' s 1922 po 1933 god, NN 1-52" (List of Articles on the History of the [Bolshevik] Party Organizations and of the Revolutionary Movement in Petrograd Factories published in *Krasnaia Letopis* in 1922-1933). Comp. by E.I. Viguro and M.L. Lur'e.

McNeal, Robert H. "Soviet Historiography on the October Revolution. A Review of Forty Years." *The American Slavic and East European Review*, vol. XVII no. 3, 1958, pp. 269-281.

Mints, I.I., ed. *Zarubezhnaia literatura ob Oktiabr'skoi revoliutsii* (Foreign Literature on the October Revolution). Moscow, 1961.

Mohrenschildt, Dimitri von. "Dartmouth Collection of Historical Material on the Russian Revolution." *The Russian Review*, vol. 6, no. 1, Autumn 1946, pp. 105-112.

Pankratova, A.M., ed. *25 let velikoi Oktiabr'skoi Sotsialisticheskoi revoliutsii 1917-1942: ukazatel' literatury* (25 Years of the Great October Socialist Revolution: an Index to Literature). Moscow, 1942.

Proletarskaia Revoliutsiia. Sistematicheskii i alfavitnyi ukazatel' 1921-1929 gg. (*Proletarskaia Revoliutsiia.* A Systematic and Alphabetical Index for 1921-1929). Leningrad, 1930.

Proletarskaia Revoliutsiia, vol. 33, Oct. 1924: "Literatura ob Oktiabr'skoi revoliutsii" (Literature on the October Revolution), pp. 200-239; "Literatura po istorii Oktiabria i grazhdanskoi voiny" (Literature on the History of October and the Civil War), pp. 240-267.

Shchegoleva, B.I. and Troitskaia, E.E., eds. *K 40-letiiu velikoi Oktiabr'skoi sotsialisticheskoi revoliutsii: sbornik bibliograficheskikh i metodicheskikh materialov* (To the Fortieth Anniversary of the Great October Socialist Revolution; a Collection of Bibliographical and Methodological Materials). Moscow, 1957.

Vodolagin, V.M. *Oktiabr'skoe vooruzhennoe vosstanie v sovetskoi istoricheskoi literature* (The October Armed Uprising in the Soviet Historical Literature). Moscow, 1967.

Zverev, R.Ia. *Krasnyi Arkhiv. Istoricheskii zhurnal, 1922-1941. Annotirovannyi ukazatel' soderzhaniia* (*Krasnyi Arkhiv*, the Historical Journal, 1922-1941. An Annotated Index to its Contents). Moscow, 1960.

LIST OF SERIALS AND PERIODICALS

Serials and periodicals referred to in Melgunov's text and bibliography. Since many of the periodicals listed were not available to the editors, and catalogues and bibliographies are not always reliable or complete, the publication dates and volume indications might not always be accurate.

Arkhiv Russkoi Revoliutsii. (The Archives of the Russian Revolution). A collection of memoirs and documents, edited by I.V. Gessen. Berlin, 1921-1937, 22 volumes.

Beloe Delo (The White Cause). A series of monographs and memoirs devoted to the history of the Civil War. Berlin, 1926-1933, 7 volumes.

Belyi Arkhiv (The White Archives). A collection of memoirs and documents. Paris, 1926-1928, 3 volumes.

Byloe (The Past). A journal of the history of the revolutionary movement in Russia, founded by V.L. Burtsev in 1900 and published in London and Paris; published in St. Petersburg, 1906-1907; suppressed in 1907; resumed publication in Petrograd (Leningrad) 1917-1927; issued in 1933 in Paris.

Delo Naroda (The People's Cause). A daily newspaper of the Socialist Revolutionary party, an organ of the Petrograd Committee and the Central Committee of the Party. Petrograd, March 1917-1918. Later assumed various titles, such as *Delo Narodnoe, Delo Narodov, Dela Narodnye, Delo*. Finally suppressed in March, 1919.

Den' (Day). "An organ of Socialist thought" without party affiliation. Petrograd, 1913-1918. Suppressed by the Bolsheviks, but reappeared under various titles, such as *Noch', Polnoch', Novyi Den'*.

Dni (Days) A daily newspaper edited by A.F. Kerensky. Berlin, then Paris, 1922-1928. Later a weekly journal.

Donskaia Letopis' (The Don Chronicle). A collection of materials on Don Cossack history after 1917. Belgrade and Vienna, 1923-1924. 3 volumes.

Edinstvo (Unity). A daily published by the Social Democrat "defensist" Unity party and edited by G.V. Plekhanov. Petrograd, 1917. Suppressed by the Bolsheviks January, 1918.

Golos Minuvshego (The Voice of the Past). A journal devoted mainly to the history of revolutionary movements. Moscow, 1913-1923. Later published as *Golos Minuvshego na chuzhoi storone* (The Voice of the Past in a Foreign Land), a "journal of history and literary history," ed. by S.P.

Melgunov, V.A. Miakotin, T.I. Polner, Berlin and Prague, then Paris, 1922-1928.

Golos Naroda (The Voice of the People). An "Organ of Russian Socialist Thought." Prague, 1920.

Golos Rossii (The Voice of Russia). Berlin, 1919-1922, daily.

Golos Truda (The Voice of Labor). A weekly publication of the Union of Anarcho-Syndicalists. Petrograd, 1917.

Istorik i sovremennik (The Historian and the Contemporary). A series of literary and historical almanacs. Berlin, 1922-1924, 5 volumes.

Izvestiia Tsentral'nogo Ispolnitel'nogo Komiteta Sovetov Rabochikh i Soldatskikh Deputatov (News of the Central Executive Committee of the Soviets of Worker and Soldier Deputies). A daily newspaper of the VTsIK, first appeared on February 28 in Petrograd; on October 27, 1917 taken over by the Bolsheviks and became the central organ of the Soviet Government, with the title *Izvestiia*, and varying subtitles.

Izvestiia Vserossiiskogo Soveta Krest'ianskikh Deputatov (News of the All-Russian Soviet of Peasant Deputies). A daily edited by the right Socialist Revolutionaries. Petrograd, 1917.

Katorga i ssylka (Forced Labor and Exile). A journal published by the society of former political prisoners. Moscow, 1921-1935, 116 volumes.

Krasnaia Letopis' (The Red Chronicle). A bi-monthly journal devoted to the history of the revolution. Moscow and Petrograd (Leningrad), 1922-1936.

Krasnaia Nov' (The Red Virgin Soil). A literary, critical and political journal, organ of the Union of the Soviet Writers. Moscow, 1921-1942.

Krasnyi Arkhiv (The Red Archives). A historical journal. Moscow, 1922-1941. 106 volumes.

Letopis' revoliutsii (Chronicle of the Revolution). A historical journal. Berlin, 1923. 1 volume.

Molot (Hammer). A Bolshevik newspaper for sailors. 1917.

Narodnoe Slovo (The People's Word). Daily "Organ of the Central Committee of the People's Socialist Party." Petrograd, 1917-1918.

Novaia Rossiia (New Russia). Petrograd, 1917. Daily, closed by the Provisional Government on October 24, 1917 because of alleged rightist agitation.

Novaia Zhizn' (New Life). A daily newspaper of the Social Democrat Internationalists, founded by Maxim Gorky. Petrograd, 1917; Moscow, 1918.

Novoe Vremia (New Times). A widely circulated daily of varying (liberal to conservative) political persuasion; founded in St. Petersburg in 1865; from 1876 to 1917 edited and published by A.S. Suvorin. After the Bolshevik takeover continued as *Utro*.

Novosti Zhizni (News of Life). Newspaper, Harbin, 1922-1925.

Novyi Grad (The New City). A series of almanacs on religion, philosophy and social issues. Paris, 1931-1939, 14 volumes.

Novyi Luch' (New Ray). A Menshevik daily. Petrograd, December 1917-June 1918.

Obshchee Delo (The Common Cause). A daily edited by V.L. Burtsev. Petrograd, 1917; Paris, 1918-1930.

Petrogradskii Golos (The Voice of Petrograd). January-July 1918. Daily, a continuation of *Petrogradskii Listok* (1915-1917).

Petrogradskoe Ekho (The Echo of Petrograd). Daily, 1917-1918; appeared originally as *Ekho*.

Poslednie Novosti (The Latest News). A liberal daily, reflecting left-wing Kadet views, edited by P.N. Miliukov. Paris, 1920-1940.

Pravda (Truth). Bolshevik daily published in St. Petersburg with many interruptions from April 1912 to June 1914; resumed publication in March 1917 as organ of the Bolshevik party; officially outlawed after July; resumed publication after the October seizure of power; transferred to Moscow in March 1918 as the central organ of the Communist party.

Proletarskaia Revoliutsiia (The Proletarian Revolution). A monthly historical journal dedicated to the history of the Communist party and the Revolution of 1917. Moscow, 1921-1941. 132 volumes.

Prostaia Gazeta (The Simple Newspaper). A Socialist Revolutionary daily. Petrograd, 1917.

Rabochaia Gazeta (The Workers' Newspaper). A Menshevik daily. Petrograd, March-October 1917; appeared as *Luch* and under various other names until early 1918.

Rabochii i Soldat (The Worker and the Soldier). A Bolshevik daily. Petrograd, August-October 1917.

Rabochii Put' (The Workers' Road). A Bolshevik daily, and the central organ of the party, published in Petrograd September - October 1917, in place of *Rabochii*, which was suppressed by the Provisional Government. After the October takeover, superseded by *Pravda*.

Rech' (The Speech). Daily; the organ of the Central Committee of the Constitutional Democratic party, edited by I. Gessen and P. Miliukov. Petrograd, 1906-1917. Suppressed after the Bolshevik takeover, reappeared as *Nasha Rech, Svobodnaia Rech, Vek, Novaia Rech, Nash Vek;* finally suppressed late in 1918.

Revoliutsiia 1917 goda; khronika sobytii (Revolution of 1917; a chronicle of events). A series of monographs, Moscow and Petrograd (Leningrad) 1923-1926, previously listed in part under individual authors: vol. 1, January-April and vol. 2, April-May, N. Avdeev; vol. 3, June-July and vol. 4, August-September, Vera Vladimirova; vol. 5, October 1-26, K. Riabinskii; vol. 6, October 27-December, I.N. Liubimov.

Revoliutsionnaia Rossiia (Revolutionary Russia). Monthly, central organ of the Socialist Revolutionary party in exile. Iur'ev (Tartu) 1920-1921; Berlin, 1922-23; Prague, 1923-1931.

Rul' (The Rudder). A liberal daily, reflecting right-wing Kadet views, edited by I. Gessen. Berlin, 1920-1931.

Russkaia Mysl' (Russian Thought). St. Petersburg (Petrograd), 1880-1918. A monthly journal, predominantly literary, at first reflecting Slavophile and populist, then liberal and Kadet ideas.

Russkaia Volia (The Russian Will). A daily, founded by the last imperial minister of the interior, Protopopov. Petrograd, 1916-1917.

Russkiia Vedomosti (The Russian Newspaper). A daily liberal newspaper, edited by V.M. Sobolevsky, 1882-1912; in 1906-1918 organ of the right KD's. Moscow, 1863-1918.

Russkoe Slovo (The Russian Word). A daily newspaper of liberal tendencies. Moscow, 1894-1917. Reappeared for a time as *Novoe Slovo.*

Segodnia (Today). "An independent democratic newspaper." Daily, Riga, 1919-1940.

Soldat (The Soldier). A Bolshevik daily issued for soldiers, 1917.

Sotsial Demokrat (Social Democrat). A daily organ of the Moscow provincial bureau and the city committee of the Bolshevik party. Moscow, 1917-1918.

Sotsialisticheskii Vestnik (The Socialist Herald). Central organ of the Menshevik organization in exile. Bi-weekly, monthly and bi-monthly, successively. Berlin, then Paris, then New York, 1921-1963.

Svoboda Rossii (Russia's Freedom). A daily reflecting Kadet views. Moscow, 1917-1918.

Utro Rossii (The Morning of Russia). A non-partisan democratic daily, financed by the industrialist P. Riabushinsky. Moscow, 1907-1917; in 1917 appeared as *Zaria Rossii.*

Vecherniaia Zvezda (The Evening Star). A Social-Democratic daily. Petrograd, 1918.

Vlast' Naroda (The People's Power). "A democratic and socialist daily." Moscow, 1917-1918.

Volia Naroda (The People's Will). Daily newspaper of the right-wing Socialist Revolutionaries. Petrograd, April-November, 1917; subsequently reappeared as *Volia, Volia Narodnaia, Volia Vol'naia, Volia Strany,* until Februrary, 1918.

Volia Rossii (Russia's Will). A Socialist Revolutionary periodical. Prague, daily 1920-1921; monthly, 1922-1934; 13 volumes.

Vozrozhdenie (Renaissance). Nonpartisan literary and political periodical. Paris, daily 1925-1936; weekly 1936-1940; monthly 1949-.

Vpered (Forward). Organ of the Menshevik Organization Committee, Petrograd, 1917-1918.

Zaria Rossii (Russia's Dawn). Anti-Bolshevik daily, Moscow 1917-1918.

Za Svobodu (For Liberty). "A Russian democratic newspaper." Daily, Warsaw, 1919-1930.

Zelenyi Zhurnal (The Green Journal). Edited by Kamyshnikov. New York, 1924.

Zemlia i Volia (Land and Liberty). A popular daily issued by the Regional Committee of the Socialist Revolutionary party, Petrograd, 1917.

Zhivoe Slovo (The Living Word). Daily, Petrograd, 1916-1917. Closed by the Provisional Government on October 24, 1917 for alleged rightist agitation.

Znamia Truda (The Banner of Labor). A daily, published by the Regional Committee of the Socialist Revolutionary party. Petrograd, 1917.

INDEX OF PERSONS

The annotated index of persons presented below cannot claim full accuracy or completeness. While the principal actors in the drama are sufficiently well known, data on the supporting cast and the extras are often fragmentary and contradictory. Full names, positions and affiliations, and sometimes even initials are lacking in the sources, and on occasion the spelling varies: Anan'in or Ananiev, Sediakin, Sidiakin, or Sidiatkin, Vompe or Volpe. The last names in the index are spelled in the anglicized manner of the text, while the first names and patronymics appear in correct Russian transliteration.

Abbreviations Used in the Index of Persons—

CC: Central Committee (*Tsentral'nyi komitet*), the leading body of a political party.

Defensists: a group of Russian socialists (led by Plekhanov and Potresov) who blamed World War I on "German militarism" and considered national defense and a military victory to be the prerequisites for peace.

EC: Executive Committee (*Ispolnitel'nyi komitet*), the leading body of a Soviet or another elected organization.

GHQ: General Headquarters of the Russian armed forces, located in Mogilev (*Stavka*).

Internationalists: a group of Russian socialists (led by the Mensheviks Martov and Dan and the Socialist Revolutionary Chernov) who blamed World War I on the "international bourgeoisie" and demanded a "general democratic peace without victors and vanquished," advocated by the international congress of left-wing socialist parties in Zimmerwald, Switzerland.

KD: (colloquially, Kadet), member of the liberal Constitutional Democrat Party (*Konstitutsionno-Demokraticheskaia Partiia*), led by Miliukov, the most influential opposition party in the State Duma in 1906-07. In 1917 the Kadets participated in the Provisional Government, but were considered "counterrevolutionary" by Bolsheviks and left-wing socialists.

MRC: Military Revolutionary Committee (*Voenno-revoliutsionnyi komitet*). The Petrograd MRC was organized October 9, 1917 by the Executive Committee of the Petrograd Soviet as the "Revolutionary Committee for Defense" (ostensibly against the threatening German invasion), and renamed MRC three days later. Essentially an organ of the Bolshevik party, supported by left Socialist Revolutionaries, the MRC was the most active body of the new regime during the October seizure of power and for several weeks thereafter. It was disbanded on December 5, 1917. After October 25, local MRC's were also established in Moscow and several other cities to assist local Bolshevik takeovers.

239

NS: (*Narodnyi Sotsialist*), member of the People's Socialist Party, a group of moderate socialists, led by Chaikovsky, Melgunov, Miakotin, and Peshekhonov, who advocated the democratization of Russia's political structure and the "nationalization" of land, to be allocated only to those who tilled it.

SD: *(Sotsial-demokrat)*, member of the Russian Social Democratic Workers Party (*Rossiiskaia Sotsial-Demokraticheskaia Rabochaia Partiia*, or R.S.-D.R.P.). After its second congress in 1903, the party was divided into the *Bolshevik* (members of the majority) and *Menshevik* (members of the minority) factions; the former, headed by Lenin, emphasized the revolutionary aspects of Marxism, while the latter stressed its evolutionary aspects. After sharp conflicts during the first Russian Revolution the Leninists formally organized themselves as a separate party—R.S.-D.R.P. (Bolsheviks) in 1912. In World War I, the Russian Social Democrats were divided three ways: the Leninists wanted to "turn the imperialist war into a civil war," and believed the defeat of the Russian army to be in the best interest of the international proletarian revolution; the majority of the Menshevik leaders were internationalists (see above), while Plekhanov headed the defensist (see above) group.

Sovnarkom: (*Sovet Narodnykh Komissarov*), Council of People's Commissars, the executive branch of the "Soviet" Government, established on October 26, 1917 by the Second Congress of Soviets, and chaired by Lenin until his death.

SR: (*Sotsialist revoliutsioner*), member of the Socialist Revolutionary Party, which claimed to represent primarily the Russian peasantry and enjoyed, with its program of abolishing private property on land and the "socialization" of land in the interest of the toilers, great popularity in the countryside during the Revolution. The party was headed by Chernov, but in 1917 his leadership encountered opposition from the right (Avksentiev, Zenzinov), and from the left. In November the left SR's (led by Spiridonova, Kamkov, Natanson) broke off and formed a separate party; in December, three of its representatives briefly entered the *Sovnarkom*.

VTsIK: (*Vserossiiskii Tsentral'nyi Ispolnitel'nyi Komitet Sovetov Rabochikh i Soldatskikh Deputatov*), the All-Russian Central Executive Committee of the Soviets of Workers' and Soldiers' Deputies; established by the First All-Russian Congress of Workers' and Soldiers' Deputies in June 1917. Dominated by Socialist Revolutionaries and Mensheviks and presided over by the Menshevik Chkheidze, the VTsIK was an influential working-class organization with quasi-governmental functions that the Provisional Government had to reckon with.

Sverdlov, Iakov Mikhailovich: *Bolshevik, member CC and MRC; after Second Congress of Soviets, president of VTsIK*–16, 175, 184, 185
Sviatitsky, N.V.: *writer, SR, member of EC of Petrograd Soviet; in October 1917 deputy commissar of Provisional Government on Northern Front*–115

Tagantsev, Nikolai Stepanovich: *eminent jurist, professor of criminal law, senator*–193
Teodorovich, Ivan Adol'fovich: *Bolshevik, member CC, commissar for food in first* Sovnarkom–172
Tereshchenko, Mikhail Ivanovich: *large sugar manufacturer, president of Kiev regional War Industries Committee; in 1917 minister of finance March-May, minister of foreign affairs May-October*–xviii, xxi, 37, 48, 77, 90
Tizengauzen: *officer of Keksholm regiment; VTsIK commissar at Rumanian Front*–119
Tolstoy, Count Pavel Mikhailovich: *deputy chief of War Ministry political administration*–48, 68, 71, 99, 100, 124, 128, 166, 177
Tretiakov, Sergei Nikolaevich: *prominent Moscow industrialist, in September-October 1917 chairman of Economic Council*–37, 60
Trotsky (Bronstein), Lev Davidovich: *prominent political writer and SD leader; joined Bolsheviks in August 1917, elected member of CC; chairman of Petrograd Soviet in September-October, also member of MRC; jointly with Lenin leader of uprising; subsequently people's commissar for foreign affairs in first* Sovnarkom–xvii, xxi, xxii, 4, 5, 10-12, 17-22, 28, 32, 35, 36, 39-43, 49, 58, 62, 64, 81, 82, 84, 89, 90, 93, 94, 125-127, 129, 143, 148, 154, 157, 160-162, 170, 171, 175, 177, 179, 186, 190, 191, 195, 197
Trubetskoy, Prince Evgenii Nikolaevich: *philosopher, professor of Moscow University; prior to 1917, elected member of State Council, and leader of party of "Peaceful Reconstruction" (mid-way between KD and Octobrists)*–27
Tseretelli, Iraklii Georgievich: *Georgian and Russian SD, Menshevik leader; member of EC of Petrograd Soviet; leading member of VTsIK; minister of post and telegraph in May-June 1917; minister of interior in July*–xv, xviii, xxii, 25, 86, 128, 180-182, 193

Uralov (Kisliakov-Uralov), S.G.: *Bolshevik; member of Central Council of Factory Committees in Petrograd; MRC commissar at printing plant of* Russkaia Volia–65
Uritsky, Mikhail Solomonovich: *SD Menshevik, joined Bolsheviks in August 1917; member CC and MRC; in 1918, chairman of Petrograd* Cheka–4, 16

Valden (or Velden): *colonel, active in Bolshevik military operations on October 30-31*–147

254   Index of Persons

GENERAL INDEX

Agrarian disturbances, xxiii-xxiv, 198-204. *See also* Agrarian reform; Land, distribution of; Peasants

Agrarian reform, xvi. *See also* Agrarian disturbances; Land, distribution of; Peasants

All-Army Committee, 102, 112, 156, 159, 163-64, 168, 176-77, 179-80

Allied governments, xviii, 59, 166, 178

All-Russian Congress of Soviets of Peasants' Deputies, xix, 86, 136, 176, 184-85, 189

executive committee of, 20, 47, 58, 85, 86, 122

All-Russian Congress of Soviets of Workers' and Soldiers' Deputies, xviii-xix, 100, 172. *See also* VTsIK

Amur, 87

Armed (Bolshevik) uprising, 10, 11, 12, 16, 17, 18, 20, 28, 29, 30, 31, 33, 44

Aurora, 37, 41, 54, 62, 80, 83, 84, 85, 87, 90

Baltic fleet, 7, 9, 56, 65, 71, 113

Bolshevik Central Committee, 3-10, 12-16, 17, 19, 41, 93, 146, 157, 162, 169, 172, 174, 175, 184, 186, 190

Bolshevik Military Organization, xxi, 4, 6, 7, 13, 14, 34. *See also* Military Revolutionary Committee

Bolshevik Petrograd Committee, xvii, 6, 7, 12, 14, 125, 186

Bolsheviks

after armed conflict and before Constituent Assembly convened, 170-74, 184-91

during attack on Winter Palace, 62-68, 71, 75-84, 88-94

during battle of Pulkovo, 146-48

during battles at the front, 108-10, 113-118, 121

during "Bloody Sunday" uprising, 139-44

at Constituent Assembly, 192-93

during debate about armed uprising, 10-17, 18-24

military attitudes toward, 48-54, 56-58, 63-66, 98-103, 105-21, 126-27, 138-40, 143-44, 164-69

after MRC began operating openly, 33, 34-42, 53, 56

before October 1917, xv, xvii-xxiv, 3-9

other parties' attitudes toward, 20-24, 25-28, 43-48, 82-83, 86-87, 93-94, 122-25, 130-34, 135-36, 137-38, 148-51, 157-61, 172-85, 193-94

during peace talks at Gatchina, 153-55

Provisional Government's attitude toward, 28-33, 36-39, 43, 46-48, 55-58, 145, 153, 177-78, 183-84

strength in provinces, 194-97, 200

during Vikzhel conference, 157-63, 175-76

votes for, 26n, 187-88

Borovichi, 195